Mike Ashley was born in 1948 and has spent all his working life in Local Government. He has been writing since 1965 and has published over forty books and some five hundred articles and reviews, including many contributions to encyclopedias on fantasy and science fiction. He has published the definitive bibliography of Algernon Blackwood, on whose biography he is working, and has written a major survey of the early days of science fiction. He has edited the previous Arthurian anthologies, *The Pendragon Chronicles*, *The Camelot Chronicles* and *The Merlin Chronicles*, and has compiled *The Mammoth Book of Historical Whodunnits* and *The Mammoth Book of Historical Detectives*. He has also compiled two anthologies of classical stories, including *Classical Whodunnits* and is completing *The Mammoth Book of British Kings and Queens*.

THE CHRONICLES OF
THE HOLY GRAIL

The Chronicles of the

of the

Holy Grail

Edited by
Mike Ashley

RAVEN BOOKS
London

Robinson Publishing Ltd
7, Kensington Church Court
London W8 4SP

First published in the UK by Raven Books
an imprint of Robinson Publishing Ltd 1996

Collection, introduction and introductory material
copyright © Mike Ashley 1996

A copy of the British Library Cataloguing in Publication
Data for this title is available from the British Library

ISBN 1-85487-433-0

Printed and bound in the EC

10 9 8 7 6 5 4 3 2 1

CONTENTS

Copyright acknowledgements

The editor acknowledges the following authors and their representatives for granting the right to use the stories in this volume. He also acknowledges the source of all reprinted stories. Every effort has been made to identify the copyright holders. The editor would be pleased to hear from anyone if there has been an inadvertent infringement of copyright.

"The Figure in Darkness" © 1996 by Ken Alden. First publication, original to this anthology. Printed by permission of the author.

"Hunt of the Hart Royal" © 1996 by Cherith Baldry. First publication, original to this anthology. Printed by permission of the author.

"The Secret History" © 1996 by Peter T. Garratt. First publication, original to this anthology. Printed by permission of the author.

"The Last Rainbow" © 1978 by Parke Godwin. First published in *Fantastic Stories*, July 1978. Reprinted by permission of the author.

"The Story of Peredur" by Lady Charlotte Guest reprinted from *The Mabinogion*, London: Everyman's Library, J.M. Dent, 1906. This version originally published in 1849 under the title "Peredur, Son of Evrawc".

"The Treasures of Britain" © 1996 by Heather Rose Jones. First publication, original to this anthology. Printed by permission of the author.

"Galahad's Lady" and "An Idyll of the Grail" both © 1996 by Phyllis Ann Karr. First publication, original to this anthology. Printed by permission of the author.

"The Kingdoms of the Air" © 1988 by Tanith Lee. First published in *Weird Tales*, Summer 1988. Reprinted by permission of the author.

"Honour Before Glory" © 1996 by Steve Lockley. First publication, original to this anthology. Printed by permission of the author.

"The Great Return" © 1915 by Arthur Machen. First published in the *Evening News*, October 21–November 16, 1915. Reprinted from *Tales of Horror and the Supernatural* (London: Richards, 1949) by permission of A.M. Heath & Co. Ltd, on behalf of the author's estate.

"Reliquary" © 1996 by F. Gwynplaine MacIntyre. First publication, original to this anthology. Printed by permission of the author.

"Perronik the Fool" © 1924 by George Moore. First published by Boni & Liveright, New York. Reprinted by permission of Colin Smythe Ltd, on behalf of the author's estate.

"The Legend of Sir Dinar" © 1895 by Sir Arthur Quiller-Couch.

First published in *Wandering Heath* (London: Cassell). Reprinted by permission of G.F. Symondson, on behalf of the author's estate.

"Shrouded in Mist" © 1996 by Lawrence Schimel and Mark A. Garland. First publication, original to this anthology. Printed by permission of the authors.

"The Unwanted Grail" © 1996 by Darrell Schweitzer. First publication, original to this anthology. Printed by permission of the author.

"The Lost Romance" © 1996 by Brian Stableford. First publication, original to this anthology. Printed by permission of the author.

"The Castles of Testing" © 1996 by Keith Taylor. First publication, original to this anthology. Printed by permission of the author.

"Maidens of the Grael", "Launcelot's Grail" and "Epilogue" all © 1996 by Peter Valentine Timlett. First publication, original to this anthology. Printed by permission of the author.

"The Magic Bowl" © 1996 by Peter Tremayne. First publication, original to this anthology. Printed by permission of the author and the author's agent, A.M. Heath & Co. Ltd.

DRAMATIS PERSONAE
A guide to Arthurian characters

The following is a short guide to the main Arthurian characters you will encounter in this and the companion volumes. There are so many names in Arthurian lore that it's not always easy to know whether you've encountered someone of significance or not, and when those names can be subjected to so many alternative spellings, it can become very confusing. I hope the following helps. It does not include minor characters or those invented by the writers.

Aglaval/Aglovale. Knight of the Round Table and brother of Sir Percevale. He carries out King Arthur's wishes in the punishment of Guinevere and is killed by Lancelot.

Agravaine. Son of King Lot and Morgause of Orkney, and brother of Gawain, Gaheris and Gareth. He sided with Mordred in the plot to reveal the adultery between Lancelot and Guinevere.

Ambrosius Aurelianus, also known as **Emrys.** Historically "the Last of the Romans", he governed Britain in the last half of the fifth century and helped stem the tide of Saxon advance in the days immediately prior to Arthur. In Arthurian legend he is sometimes depicted as Arthur's uncle. It was during his reign that Merlin raised Stonehenge.

Amfortas, see **Fisher King.**

Angharad Law Eurawc, or **Angharad Golden-hand.** The lover of Peredur.

Arthur/Artorius/Artos. High King of Britain, son of Uther Pendragon and Igraine, raised as foster-son of Ector of the Forest Sauvage and foster-brother of Sir Kay. Founded the Fellowship of the Round Table, married Guinevere. By his half-sister Morgause he fathered Mordred who later waged war against him, resulting in the final battle at Camlann where both Arthur and Mordred fell.

Aurelianius, see **Ambrosius.**

Balin. A Northumbrian knight who was imprisoned by Arthur for killing the king's cousin. He also angered the king by beheading the Lady of the Lake. It was Balin who committed the Dolorous Stroke when he stabbed King Pellam with the Spear of Longinus and thus turned the country into a Waste Land.

Bedivere/Bedwyr. One of Arthur's earliest and most trusted knights who served as his aide. It was he who restored Excalibur to the Lady of the Lake at the time of Arthur's passing.

Blaise. A hermit monk to whom Merlin's mother went for her confession. He became Merlin's tutor.

Bors. Son and successor of King Bors of Gannes (or Gaul) and cousin to Sir Lancelot. He was one of the three successful knights in the search for the Holy Grail. Legend has it that Bors died on a crusade to the Holy Land.

Brân. A hero of Welsh legend, who lived at about the time of Christ. His story is recounted in the "Daughter of Llyr" episode of *The Mabinogion.* Brân led an expedition against the King of Ireland, in which Brân was mortally wounded. He ordered that his head be cut off and buried on the Hill of Ravens (Tower Hill in London – Brân means raven) as a protection against the future invasion of Britain. The legend still lives on, of course, in the belief that if the ravens ever leave the Tower of London, England will fall. Brân is recorded as the father of Caractacus, king of the Catuvellauni at the time of the Roman invasion in AD 43. Brân is also linked with Brons, the brother-in-law of Joseph of Arimathea, and is thus made one of the guardians of the Grail. He is also regarded as an ancestor of Arthur.

Cac/Cei, see **Kay.**

Caradog/Caradoc Vreichras, or Caradog Strong-arm. In Celtic legend the son of the wizard Eliavres and Ysaive, wife of Caradog of Nantes in Gaul. Caradog is sent a horn by King Mangoun of

Moraine which will betray the infidelity of the wife of any man who drinks from it. Caradog is regarded as the ancestor of the kings of Gwent. His wife was Tegeu Eurfon.

Cerdic. A Saxon invader who landed with his son Cynric near Southampton in AD 495. He is claimed by the annalists as the first king of Wessex, though little is known about him.

Constans. The elder brother (or in some stories father) of Ambrosius Aurelianus and Uther Pendragon, who was raised to the High Kingship of Britain by Vortigern only to be murdered.

Constantine. Arthur's cousin and son of Cador, King of Cornwall. A close and trusted knight, he became King Arthur's successor, after defeating the sons of Mordred. There was an historical king Constantine of Dumnonia (Devon) in the early sixth century, though he was a murderous, deceitful king.

Culhwch, see **Kilhugh.**

Cunobel/Cunobelinus/Cymbeline. King of the Catuvellauni and High King of the British, who ruled at the time of the Roman conquest in AD 43.

Drustan, see **Tristan.**

Dubric/Dubricius/Dyfrig. Celtic bishop of Caerleon (or Carlisle) who crowned Arthur. His life has been equated with that of Merlin.

Ector. Sir Ector was the foster-father of Arthur and the father of Sir Kay.

Elaine. There are three Elaines in the Arthurian cycle: **Elaine of Garlot,** the half-sister of King Arthur; **Elaine de Astolat,** a maiden who fell in love with Sir Lancelot and was called "The Lady of Shalott" by Tennyson; and **Elaine of Corbenic,** daughter of King Pelles or Pellam and, by Lancelot, the mother of Sir Galahad.

Emrys, see **Ambrosius Aurelianus.**

Etlym Gleddyv Coch, or Etlym of the Red Sword. Earl of Eastern Britain, who was a companion of Peredur's in his battle against the lake monster, the Addanc.

Ewaine, see **Owain.**

Fisher King. The Guardian of the Holy Grail in the Castle of Carbonek. There were a succession of Fisher Kings since the Grail was brought to Britain by Joseph of Arimathea. At the time of King Arthur the Fisher King was called Pellam, though some legends call him Amfortas.

Gaheris. Third son of King Lot and brother to Agravaine, Gareth and Gawain. Half-brother of Mordred.

Galahad/Gwalhwavad. Son of Sir Lancelot and Elaine of Corbenic and the purest of all the Knights of the Round Table. He was the only knight able to sit at the "Siege Perilous" of the Round Table.

Gareth. The youngest son of King Lot of Orkney and brother of Gawain, Gaheris and Agravaine. He first arrived anonymously at Camelot and was given the nickname "Beaumains" by Sir Kay, owing to his fine hands.

Gawain/Gwalchmai. The eldest son of King Lot of Orkney and brother of Gareth, Gaheris and Agravaine. He was one of the strongest knights of the Round Table. He features in the earliest legends of Arthur and appears in the Celtic texts as Gwalchmai, meaning the Hawk of May. He undertook the challenge of the Green Knight, Sir Bertilak.

Geraint. A king of Dumnonia (Cornwall and Devon) and the hero of the Welsh tale "Gereint and Enid". It may have been a dynastic name in Dumnonia, for there was a historical king Geraint who was killed in battle in AD 710.

Gildas. A British monk and contemporary of Arthur who wrote the *De Excidio et Conquestu Britanniae* in or around the year AD 547. The book was a diatribe against the existing kings of Britain whose morals and weaknesses were leading to the ruin and conquest of Britain by the Saxons. Later legends make him a cousin of Arthur, or related to Mordred by marriage, but Gildas makes no mention of this in his writings.

Gorlas/Gorlois/Gorlodubnus. Duke of Cornwall, husband of Igraine, and father of Morgan le Fay, Morgause and Elaine of Garlot.

Grainne see Igraine.

Guinevere/Gwenhwyvar/Gwynhwfar. Daughter of Leodegrance,

King of Cameliard, and wife of King Arthur. Her adultery with Sir Lancelot causes the downfall of the Fellowship of the Round Table. She was condemned to death by Arthur but rescued by Lancelot and ended her days in a nunnery.

Gwalhwavad, see Galahad.

Gwalchmai, see Gawain.

Gwenddolau. A British chieftain who died at the battle of Arfderydd in around AD 573. Merlin was believed to be his bard and adviser.

Gwenhwyvar/Gwynhwfar, see Guinevere.

Gwyn ap Nudd. A Welsh deity who seems originally to have been King of the Underworld. He is later seen as King of the Fairies. He is in perpetual battle against Gwythr for the hand of Creudylad, daughter of King Llud.

Howel. The son of Emyr Llydaw and Prince of Armorica (or Brittany). He was a great supporter of Arthur in his wars against Rome

Igraine/Igerna/Ygraine. Wife of Duke Gorlois of Cornwall and, by him, mother of Morgan le Fay, Morgause and Elaine. Seduced by Uther Pendragon and became mother of Arthur. Later married Uther.

Ironside. Also known as the Red Knight of the Red Lands. He was originally a bad knight who besieged the castle of the Lady Lyonesse until she was rescued by Gareth. He and Gareth later became close friends.

Iseult/Isolde/Isolt/Yseult/Ysolt. Wife of King Mark of Cornwall but lover of her husband's nephew, Tristan of Lyonesse. Not to be confused with **Iseult of Brittany,** whom Tristan married after his banishment from Cornwall.

Joseph/Yosep of Arimathea. A Jewish merchant and a member of the Sanhedrin. A supporter of Jesus, he arranged for the burial of Christ's body after the crucifixion. According to legend Joseph also acquired the chalice used by Jesus at the Last Supper and used this to catch Jesus's blood from the Cross. This became the Holy Grail that Joseph later brought to Britain in around AD 63, when he established the first British Christian church at Glastonbury.

Josue/Joshua. The nephew of Joseph of Arimathea and one of the Grail Keepers.

Kay/Kai/Cai/Cei/Caius. Son of Sir Ector and foster-brother of Arthur. He becomes the king's High Seneschal and is noted for his sour temperament. In the earliest legends Kay is an heroic knight, but in later versions he becomes Arthur's irascible steward.

Kilhugh/Culhwch. A cousin of Arthur who was under an obligation to marry Olwen. Olwen's father, the giant Yspadaddan (or Thornogre Thistlehair), would only grant her hand if Kilhugh could complete a set of impossible tasks. The full story is told in *The Mabinogion*.

Lamorack of Gaul. Son of King Pellinore and one of the strongest knights of the Round Table. He became the lover of Morgause after the death of King Lot and was killed by Gawain and his brothers.

Lancelot/Launcelot/Llancalot. Son of King Ban and greatest of the Knights of the Round Table. His castle was called the Joyous Gard. His love for Guinevere led to the downfall of the Fellowship of the Round Table. After the deaths of Arthur and Guinevere he became a hermit.

Leodegrance/Lodegreaunce. King of Cameliard and father of Guinevere.

Linet, see **Lunetta.**

Lot. King of Orkney who opposed Arthur for the crown of Britain. He was the husband of Arthur's half-sister Morgause and father of Gawain, Agravaine, Gaheris and Gareth. He was killed by King Pellinore and his sons.

Lunetta/Lynette/Linet/Lunet. Sister of Lady Lyonesse and Sir Gringamore of the Castle Perilous. She led Sir Gareth on his first quest. Although she later fell in love with Gareth she was given in marriage to his brother Gaheris. In Celtic myth she is the mistress of the Lady of the Fountain.

Margawse/Margause, see **Morgause.**

Mark/Marc. King of Cornwall and husband of Iseult.

Medraut, see **Mordred.**

Merlin/Merrillin/Merdyn/Myrddin. Magician and adviser of King Arthur. He was the offspring of a girl and a demon of the air and was raised in a nunnery. His prophecies began in the last days of King Vortigern. He later raised Stonehenge. He put a glamour on Igraine so that she mistook Uther Pendragon for her husband Gorlois. Merlin became guardian to the young Arthur and later contrived the episode of the sword in the stone so that Arthur was recognized as the future High King. He created the Round Table. He became enamoured of the enchantress Nimuë/Niniane/Viviane, who imprisoned him in a cave. Merlin was probably more a title or office than a personal name. See introduction for more details.

Mordred/Medraut/Modred/Modreuant. The incestuous child of Arthur and his half-sister Morgause. He later attempted to seduce Guinevere and claimed the throne of Britain. He met in mortal battle with Arthur at Camlann.

Morfudd. The twin sister of Owain and the lover of Arthur's knight Cynon.

Morgan le Fay/Morgana/Morgaine. Daughter of Gorlois and Igraine and half-sister of King Arthur. She was educated in the sorcerous arts and became Arthur's major enemy, forever seeking the downfall of the Round Table. By hiding the scabbard of Excalibur, which had previously protected Arthur, she rendered him mortal. She was the mother of Owain.

Morgause/Margause/Margawse. Daughter of Gorlois, sister of Morgan le Fay, wife of Lot of Orkney, and mother by him of Gawain, Agravaine, Gaheris and Gareth. She was also the mother of Mordred by Arthur, her half-brother.

Nascien. A hermit and priest, originally called Seraphe, who was the son-in-law of the pagan king Evelake. The two were baptized by Joseph of Arimathea and Nascien accompanied Joseph to Britain. He became a prophet of the Grail.

Nimuë/Niniane/Viviane. An enchantress who is perceived in a number of roles in the Arthurian legend. She is called the Lady of the Lake, the foster-mother of Lancelot, who gave Excalibur to Arthur. She also became the lover of Merlin whom she imprisoned in a cave. She is seen by some as a sister to Morgause and Morgan and thus equated with Elaine of Garlot.

Owain/Ewen/Uwaine/Yvain. In Celtic and Arthurian legend the son of Morgan le Fay and King Urien. Historically he was a king of Rheged (Cumbria and Galloway) at the end of the sixth century AD.

Parsival, see Percivale.

Pellam/Pelleas/Pelles. The King of the Grail Castle and possibly synonymous with the Fisher King. He was the grandfather of Sir Galahad and is sometimes named as the brother of King Pellinore. He was wounded by Sir Balin, and this became known as the Dolorous Stroke which caused Logres to become a Waste Land.

Pellinore. King of the Isles and one of the mightiest of the Knights of the Round Table who, in an early episode, overpowered Arthur and would have killed him had he not been enchanted by Merlin. He was involved in the search for the Questing Beast. He was the father of Sir Lamorack and, in some versions, also of Sir Percivale. In later legends he is treated as the brother of Pellam, the Fisher King. He killed King Lot and was, in turn, killed by Sir Gawain.

Percivale/Parsival/Parzival/Peredur. The knight most closely associated with the Quest for the Holy Grail. Early legends have him raised in the wilds of Wales, but others state he was the only surviving son of Evrawc, Earl of the North. There was a real Peredur, who was king of York between AD 560–580.

Peredur, see Percivale.

Peronnik. A foolish young man who became a fated knight. His adventures form part of the Breton strand of the Arthurian legends.

Red Knight, see Ironside.

Rhydderch. A historical king of Strathclyde who ruled AD 580–612. Rhydderch fought with Urien against the Saxons.

Tristan/Tristram/Drustan. Son of King Melodias of Lyonesse and nephew of King Mark of Cornwall, whose wife, Iseult, he fell in love with. Banished from Cornwall, he entered King Arthur's court as one of the mightiest knights, until forced to flee to Brittany, where he married another Iseult.

Uther Pendragon/Uverian. The brother of Ambrosius Aurelianus whom he succeeded as High King of Britain. He was the father of Arthur, by Igraine.

Vivian, see Nimuë/Niniane.

Vortigern. King of Britain whose reign preceded Ambrosius in the mid-fifth century. He invited Hengist to Britain to rid the land of Saxons, but Hengist in turn conquered Kent. Merlin first appears in Vortigern's reign.

Ygraine, see Igraine.

Yosep, see Joseph.

Yseult, see Iseult.

Yvain, see Owain.

INTRODUCTION
THE HOLY GRAIL

Mike Ashley

The Arthurian legends are bountiful in their variety with so much that has a clear life and identity of its own. Merlin, Lancelot, Guinevere, Excalibur – each have their own separate identity as well as being clearly part of the overall legend. But there is one legend associated with King Arthur that possibly has an even greater life of its own, and that is the legend of the Holy Grail.

How often have we used the phrase "Holy Grail" when we've felt we were after something unattainable, something that was just too perfect to achieve? To reach it would require insurmountable trials and hardship. That is exactly what the Quest for the Holy Grail was. It was the quest for ultimate perfection. Yet behind that simple statement there is so much more – so much that is not said but is only hinted at.

> *What was the Holy Grail?*
> *Where was it?*
> *Why did so many fail in the Quest?*
> *What was its secret?*
> *What became of it?*

Those are the questions that the authors in this anthology seek to answer, and in doing so they not only begin to unravel many of the mysteries of the Grail, but they also bring us a wonderful array of quests and adventures, perils and heroics. And they also challenge us.

For if we are to have any understanding of the Grail, and these stories and their history, then we have to understand a little more about ourselves and the world we live in. As you travel through this book you will undertake your own Quest, and only you are in control of that.

For those who want some help on the way, it's worth spending a little while just considering the nature of the Holy Grail and its background, which will help set these stories in context. It will also give me a chance to explain how the original history of the Holy Grail began and how it became related to the Arthurian legends.

So let's begin at the beginning.

The word "grail" is easily enough explained – it's probably the only easy thing to explain in this whole legend! It is a serving dish. The word comes from the Latin word *gradale*, which is the same root as our word "grade", and means something that is part of a series or sequence. This grail, or serving dish, was something that was brought to the dining table at certain stages during a meal. It came to be something of a special dish, containing rich meats or delicacies.

I'm sure we could start to find deep, philosophical meanings in even that simple origin, but let's move on. The first use of this word "grail", or in this case *graal* (being the Old French usage), in the Arthurian romances came from the writings of Chrétien de Troyes. Chrétien was the first great writer of Arthurian romances. He took the legend from the basic Celtic sources and developed the bulk of the Arthurian stories as we know them. It was he who introduced the character of Lancelot, and named Arthur's court at Camelot. We don't know much about Chrétien other than that he lived in the second half of the twelfth century and was the poet at the court of Countess Marie de Champagne, the daughter of the French king Louis VII. He wrote several Arthurian romances, but the one that concerns us most is *Le Conte de Graal*, composed during the 1180s and left unfinished at the time of Chrétien's death.

This is the story of the young Perceval, who had been raised in a sheltered existence by his mother who kept him ignorant of the world. One day Perceval encounters some knights and, despite his mother's advice, he leaves for Arthur's court. From there he embarks on his first adventure and encounters a strange castle where, while partaking of a meal, he is witness to an unusual procession, known as the Procession of the Grail. Perceval does not ask about the nature of the procession. He later learns that this omission has meant that the ailing Fisher King has not been cured.

Hang on . . . who's the Fisher King, and why was he ill?

Chrétien does not go into details on this. Indeed, although he sets Perceval off on a quest of expiation, the story remains unfinished. It is one of the great cliff-hangers of medieval literature, and set scores of other poets and writers off on their own quests to complete the story.

It is clear from the whole description that Chrétien was drawing upon some older legend with profoundly deeper meaning. In fact the basis of his story comes from a Celtic legend which surfaces elsewhere as the tale of "Peredur, Son of Evrawc" in *The Mabinogion*. This is a collection of Celtic tales and legends, some of which date back certainly to the years before the Norman Conquest, although none survive in writing earlier than the twelfth century. Their appearance in books is thus contemporaneous with Chrétien's stories. It is interesting that it was at the same time that both the Norman French court and Celtic scholars were bringing the Arthurian stories into the written form. How much of this was national pride and rivalry and how much of it was a serious attempt to explore the mysteries and realities of the past is difficult to say. Whatever the reason, the twelfth and thirteenth centuries saw a remarkable flowering of Arthurian literature which was to dominate the Anglo-Norman world for two centuries.

I have reprinted the Celtic "Story of Peredur" complete in this anthology, as it reflects somewhat closer to home the start of the Grail mystery. You will find in this story the description of the Grail procession and the challenge to Peredur as to why he had not questioned the nature of the procession and thus restored the Fisher King to health.

At this point a more distant story has started to emerge. In the shape of Peredur, or Perceval, we come to see that here is an innocent youth who realizes that he must understand the nature of the Grail (not acquire the Grail itself) in order to restore the Fisher King (who may signify the Land) to health. Evidently some time before this story happens the Land has been despoiled, and something must be done to restore it. Just what that is, is the crux of the Grail legend.

It is worth just mentioning in passing that there was a real Peredur. He was a Celtic ruler of York in the sixth century, living perhaps fifty years after the time of King Arthur. He was one of the strong kings of the North who fought at the Battle of Arthuret in *c.* AD 575, at Galloway just north of Hadrian's Wall. He and his allies were trying to save Britain from the invading Saxons and

Norsemen as well as the Picts and Irish. One could read into this a very real origin for the notion of the failing health of Britain, with the land being invaded and plundered from all directions in the centuries following the fall of Rome. Although it is Arthur who is remembered above all in legend as the man who held back the Saxon onslaught, he was not alone – clearly other legends stuck to other heroes, and with Peredur we may have a rather more mystical portrayal of a king who, despite valiant efforts, failed to restore the Realm.

The fascination with Chrétien's unfinished Grail story led to others seeking to complete it. The main scribe was another Frenchman, Robert de Boron, from Burgundy, who survived Chrétien by about twenty years. He wrote three long romances, *Le Roman de l'Estoire dour Graal, Merlin* and almost certainly *Perceval*. This last has been lost, but a prose reworking of it has survived.

It was Robert de Boron who gave us the background of the Grail. He made it the vessel from which Jesus drank at the Last Supper and which was used to represent the Chalice which symbolically held the blood of Christ. According to Robert, it was in this chalice that Joseph of Arimathea caught the blood of Christ from the Cross after Jesus was speared by the centurion Longinus. Thereafter Joseph brought the Grail safely to Britain, where it was protected by Joseph's descendants.

It is unlikely that Robert de Boron simply made this up. Like Chrétien, he would have been drawing from a rich vein of tradition, but by linking the Grail to Christianity he also transformed the Arthurian stories from pagan legend to something considerably more significant.

The idea of a cup, or, more appropriately, a horn or cauldron that was plentiful and could restore life (as Christianity would bring everlasting life to those who followed Christ) was something that existed in Celtic legend as the Cauldron of Plenty. It is also known as the Cornucopia, or Horn of Plenty from Greek legend. Early Celtic poems and tales such as "The Spoils of Annwfn", tell of the plunder by Arthur and his men of the land of Annwfn whereby they acquired what became known as the Treasures of Britain. This includes a magic cauldron which will not boil the food of a coward. In this anthology, Heather Rose Jones makes clever use of the legend and its links to the Grail in "The Treasures of Britain".

It is the Joseph of Arimathea connection, however, which adds special fascination to the legend. Peter Tremayne opens our collection with "The Magic Bowl", which tells of how the Grail came to Britain and what happened to it.

According to one legend, Joseph was sent to Britain in AD 63 as head of a delegation of disciples by the apostle Philip, then in Gaul. Joseph acquired land from a local king and established the first Christian church at Glastonbury. This particular legend was, perhaps not surprisingly, promoted by the Abbey of Glastonbury itself, almost certainly as part of its continuing propaganda in the twelfth and thirteenth centuries, when it sought to establish itself as both the resting place of Arthur and as the primacy of Christianity in Britain.

The legend states that Joseph then entrusted the Grail to someone who is named Brons or Brân, who may have been one of Joseph's companions, or possibly even his brother or brother-in-law. This man became the second Guardian of the Grail after Joseph. There are links here to Brân the Blessed, another great Celtic hero and protector of Britain. Brân was reputed to own a magic cauldron that could restore life. He was mortally wounded, and before his death he commanded that his head be buried at the White Mount, in what is now London, to serve as a talisman protecting the Land. This is reputedly now the site of the Tower of London.

Some legends nickname Brân the Fisher King, because he provided fish for Joseph. Other legends reserve the title Fisher King for later Guardians of the Grail, in particular one who is wounded in a joust and is thereafter unable to ride. He thus passes his time fishing. All these attempts to give a reason for the name are colourful but ineffective. There is a much stronger attribution linked directly to the Christian message. Christ called his disciples "fishers of men", and the early symbol of Christianity, prior to the use of the cross, was of a fish. The title Fisher King makes much more sense when linked to the Christian faith and seen as indicating the Head of that faith in Britain – in other words the King or Leader of the Fishers of Men.

The concept of a Fisher King separate and distinct from the Head of the Roman church in Britain, which was established by Augustine at Canterbury in AD 596, highlights yet more conflict. There was considerable opposition to Augustine from the Celtic church, already established in parts of Britain, and Augustine's efforts to establish his sovereignty over the native British at the Conference of Aust on the Severn in AD 603 was unsuccessful. In fact this rift was part of a much greater schism that had arisen as far back as the year AD 416. In that year the teachings of a British monk, Pelagius, were regarded as heresy. Pelagius challenged the beliefs of the Roman church, particularly on the grounds of free will and original sin, but he also maintained that the apostolic succession of the Roman church from St Peter was debatable. Although he did not directly confirm a British primacy, the implication is there. How much did Pelagius know about the story of Joseph of Arimathea, and about the origins of the Celtic church?

So here is more fragmentation of Britain in the years both before and after Arthur. Not only was Britain being conquered by Saxon and other invaders, but the Celtic church was under threat from Rome. We can add even more problems. There had been a total eclipse of the sun in AD 538, visible clearly from Britain, which would have been regarded as an omen and a portent. This was in or around the same year that saw the death of King Arthur at Camlann, and was followed by a devastating bubonic plague that decimated Europe in the mid-sixth century. The powerful Welsh king Maelgwyn died of it in AD 549. There was indeed considerable illness in the land, and the Fisher King was ailing. No wonder there was a yearning from the Celtic church to restore the King and help the Land.

Somewhere in all of this, however, greater mystical matters were being implied. Henry Lincoln and Michael Baigent caused quite a stir with their book *The Holy Blood and the Holy Grail* in 1983, when they suggested that the Grail was the true body of Christ. They maintained that He had survived the Cross and had been brought out of Palestine by Joseph, along with Mary Magdalene, whom Jesus later married. She bore Him a son. It was that bloodline that the Guardians of the Grail protected from that day to this. The authors maintain that Jesus's descendants became the Merovingian kings of France. These kings were contemporaries of Arthur, establishing a dynasty that ruled from around AD 460 to AD 751. If there is any truth in this, then it raises another fascinating line of enquiry.

The reason Augustine landed in Kent and was able to establish his church at Canterbury was because Kent was already converted to the Church of Rome. The Kentish king Ethelbert had a few years earlier married Bertha, the daughter of the Merovingian king Charibert. The marriage arrangement stipulated that Bertha be allowed to continue her faith, and she thus established a core of adherents to the Church of Rome amongst the English, who were still predominantly pagan. The bloodline of Christ would thus have continued through the sons of Ethelbert, although, ironically, Ethelbert's son and successor, Eadbald, remained a pagan. The strife that followed Ethelbert's death to establish Christianity amongst the English, and in opposition to the Celtic church, resulted in considerable conflict in the land. It is quite possible that if the legend of the Merovingian descent had leaked out, then rumours of the true Grail being with the Saxons and not the Celts would have caused considerable confusion and consternation amongst the followers of Christ. Who were they to follow? What was the answer? Indeed, what was the question?

Maybe here we have some hint of the problem that faced Peredur/Perceval. His failure to ask the right question and consider the nature of the Grail meant that the Land was not restored. We can start to see that what was facing the Grail Questers was the whole problem about who they should be following. Was the Church of Rome the real harbour of the Grail of Christ, or did it still rest firmly with the British, through the Fisher King?

Its links at this stage to the Arthurian legend are clearly tenuous, but because the strife in the Land, both temporally and spiritually, happened contemporaneously with the development of the Arthurian mythos, it is not surprising that the oral tradition that developed should start to make connections.

One of these connections is slightly bizarre, but under analysis may help our understanding a little further. In the Arthurian legend as consolidated by Thomas Malory in *Le Morte d'Arthur* we have the story of the Knight of the Two Swords, Sir Balin. His story, as retold by John Steinbeck, was reprinted in the first of these Arthurian volumes, *The Pendragon Chronicles*. Balin was something of a hothead, who killed almost anything that moved. He was a staunch supporter of Arthur, though he managed to incur Arthur's wrath by killing the Lady of the Lake in one of his wilder moments. Balin was always questing, and on one of his adventures he encounters an invisible knight, Sir Garlon. He kills Garlon, which angers Garlon's brother, King Pellam. Pellam and Balin now clash. In the battle Balin's sword is broken, and as he is chased around Pellam's castle he finds the Spear of Longinus on the walls and, wrenching it free, turns and stabs Pellam.

Pellam is known elsewhere as Pelleam or Pellehan, and is the Maimed King whose health must be restored. It can only be restored if his wounds are avenged. The Maimed King is sometimes treated as the Fisher King, or the Fisher King's brother. Either way, we realize that it was Balin's action, using the very spear that had maimed Jesus on the Cross, that has brought destruction to the Land. His action has been called the Dolorous Stroke. It was this destruction that Perceval could have reversed had he asked about the nature of the Grail procession, which meant he had to gain an understanding of how the Maimed King came to be injured and who it was he needed to avenge.

If we revert to our original concept of a Britain split between the Celtic church and the Church of Rome, then it becomes fairly evident that Perceval's question had to relate to identifying the nature of that division. Since it was a Roman spear that had injured the Maimed King (and had also maimed Christ) then by extension it was the Roman church that was the enemy and the Celtic church that had to be avenged. The Quest for the Holy Grail became a Quest to rescue the Celtic church and to prove its pre-eminence over the Roman church. It thus had to prove that the Celtic church's claim to its Christian origins was stronger than the claim of the Roman church. This conflict raged through Britain for three generations until it was resolved by King Oswy of Northumberland at the Synod of Whitby in AD 664, when he found in favour of the Roman church.

Little wonder, then, that at that stage the Celtic church resorted to establishing its tales and legends to perpetuate its own beliefs. The Waste Land of Britain that was drawn into the Arthurian legend was the strife between the two churches further aggravated by the continual encroachment on Celtic lands by the Saxons and Norsemen. By their Quest for perfection and ultimate redemption, the knights of King Arthur would establish the primacy of the Celtic church.

All of this, though, is just one interpretation of the Grail myth at a very superficial level. The Celtic church's Quest very rapidly became the quest of each individual to search in his heart for an understanding of the true religion and to follow that course. It was a difficult decision. Somewhere in the background, though, we can imagine that the successors of the Fisher King continued, maintaining their right to the primacy of the Christian church. Maybe in so doing they had some physical proof. Not just proof of the Grail itself, in physical form, but of other Treasures or Relics – in particular those portrayed in the story of Peredur. These are also known as the Four Hallows: the Sword which beheaded John the Baptist, the Platter on which the Baptist's head was carried, the Lance which speared Jesus's side at the crucifixion and the Cup or Chalice that held his blood. Were these treasures held somewhere in Britain, in the Grail Castle, defended by a succession of Protectors?

This would certainly account for the legend of the Grail acquiring more mystical and ritual aspects. Down through the centuries the legend, and its many contributory aspects, has become integrated with other beliefs and practices until it has become so overlaid with ritual that its innermost secrets are almost impossible to plumb. There are clearly much deeper mystical interpretations of the Grail that see it as a symbol of perfection which, once attained, allows the spirit to advance from this mortal plane of existence onto a greater spiritual plane. This shows that much earlier Gnostic beliefs have been added to the Grail legend – or, more likely, Christian beliefs were added to earlier Gnostic teachings. Either way you have a story which suggests that a true understanding of the nature of the Grail (i.e. a true understanding of the teachings of the Church) will result in an immortal or transcendent existence – the secret of eternal life. That is a quest that we all undertake throughout life. Arguably it is the search for the meaning of life itself. As such, the search for the Holy Grail is the ultimate quest to understand life and to ensure the salvation of our spirit to the next world or plane of existence.

By this token the Grail has no beginning and no end. It is a perpetual myth throughout the ages, which is why it has as much meaning today as it did a thousand years ago.

The contributors to this anthology have each sought to explore the Grail legend through the hearts and minds of many characters through history. The bulk of the anthology, not surprisingly, consists of many quests by the knights to seek that ultimate goal. Some succeed, some fail. In chronicling their quests authors Cherith Baldry, Keith Taylor, Phyllis Ann Karr, Lawrence Schimel, Ken Alden, Darrell Schweitzer, Tanith Lee, Peter Garratt, Steve Lockley and Peter Valentine Timlett explore many aspects of the Grail, and challenge us to consider its implications. *En route* we not only discover the Grail Castle, the Fisher King and the Meaning of Life, but we also bring into the legend other tales, including the Wandering Jew and what would later be called the Shroud of Turin.

And after the age of Arthur the Grail lives on. Its continued impact is explored through the centuries by F. Gwynplaine MacIntyre, George Moore, Parke Godwin, Brian Stableford (who makes the connection with another hero of legend) and Arthur Machen, who brings the Grail legend into the modern day.

So now it's your turn. The Grail Quest lies before you. Let us see what answers it provides.

Mike Ashley
February 1996

THE MAGIC BOWL

Peter Tremayne

Peter Tremayne is the alias of Celtic scholar and author Peter Berresford Ellis (b. 1943). Under his real name he has written several books which will also be of interest to the Arthurian reader, including A Dictionary of Celtic Mythology *(1992),* Celt and Saxon *(1993) and* The Druids *(1994). Under the Tremayne alias he has written over thirty books, including two collections of Irish horror and fantasy stories,* My Lady of Hy-Brasil *(1987) and* Aisling *(1992). Most recently he has found fame with the character of Sister Fidelma, a seventh-century advocate and investigator of the Irish Brehon Court, whose adventures have appeared in several short stories and the novels* Absolution by Murder *(1994),* Shroud for an Archbishop *(1995),* Suffer Little Children *(1995) and* The Subtle Serpent *(1996). Peter sets us on our quest for the Holy Grail by setting the scene and exploring how it came to Britain in the first place.*

Skentoleth, the scholar, stretched under the shade of the tall oak and smiled at the group of children who sat in a semicircle at his feet, eyes wide and faces enthralled. The old man nodded his head in emphasis.

"It is the truth that I speak," he averred, in his treble, sing-song voice. "As surely as I stand here beneath the sacred oak tree of Bíle, which was fertilized by the divine waters from heaven at the beginning of time."

One of the elder boys leant forward, eagerness showing on his face. It was Mapanden, the apprentice to Ferror the smith and chief among craftsmen of the tribe of Ruel, who dwelt by the great sea in the land of Kernow. Mapanden was fifteen years old, two years before the "age of choice", when he would arrive at manhood – the time he would become a craftsman himself.

"But where did this magic bowl originally come from, Skentoleth?" he demanded. "Who made it?"

"It was told by the ancient ones that the children of the Divine Dôn, our sublime Mother Goddess, had four great cities in the Otherworld, and the magic bowl was wrought in the one which was called Murias. It was an object of great wonder, for it had been created by the hand of the god of all arts and crafts, Lugus, and given to the Father of the Gods – whose name is . . . ?"

Skentoleth suddenly posed the question to the gathered children, for this was not merely a story-telling session but their lesson for the day. Each morning the children of the people of Ruel came to be taught by the ageing scholar under the shelter of the great oak at the edge of the village.

"He whose name is unspoken but whom we call 'the Good God'," replied Mapanden immediately, proud of his knowledge.

Skentoleth smiled approvingly.

"And when the time came for the children of Dôn to set forth to people the world with their seed, they took four great treasures from the cities of the otherworld. What did they take from Gorias?"

"The Terrible Spear of Lugus," cried a child in the back row.

"And from the city of Falias?"

"The Stone of Destiny, which has the power to recognize a just and righteous king," called another boy.

"And from Finias?" demanded Skentoleth.

"From Finias they brought with them the Invincible Sword of Power."

"And from Murias?" smiled the old scholar.

"The Magic Bowl!" cried Mapanden.

"Just so. It could quench the thirst of entire armies and no one went away from it parched; it could feed twice the number of tribes in the land and still feed more, and to imbibe from its rim would mean the sick and lame would be cured – even those who fell in battle could be returned to life in this world."

"But where is the Magic Bowl now, Skentoleth?" demanded Mapanden.

"Only the Good God knows that, for wars and conquests have caused it to be lost. Many warriors have set out in search of the Magic Bowl of Murias but none have found it."

Skentoleth looked up at the sky.

"And now, children, the sun nears its zenith. That is all for today."

"Can we talk more of the hunt for the Magic Bowl later?" demanded Mapanden as the children reluctantly climbed to their feet and began to disperse towards their respective homes.

Skentoleth looked in amusement at his eager pupil.

"I hope that you show as much eagerness in the work of Ferror's smithy-shop as you do in these tales, Mapanden?" the old man queried.

It was in the way of a rhetorical question, and before Mapanden could reply, Skentoleth waved his hand in dismissal and turned away.

Rodda, the wife of Ferror the craftsman, stood at the door of her husband's smithy and watched with a critical eye as he removed a small piece of bronze from the forge with a pair of tongs.

Ferror's muscles rolled, shiny with sweat, as he raised a hammer in his right hand while keeping the metal in its place on his anvil with the left. Thrice the blows resounded, metal against metal, each aimed with unerring accuracy, before he sighed and returned the bronze to the fierce heat of the furnace.

Rodda sniffed, as if in disapproval.

"The stranger said he would be back before the new moon, and that was three days ago," she remarked, her voice sounding querulous.

Ferror sighed and turned to glance at her across his broad shoulder. He was a big, well-muscled man in the prime of his life. His dark hair was flecked with grey and his light-coloured eyes shone with blues and greens, as if inhabited by the colours of the sea.

"Then something has delayed him," he replied gravely. "The stranger is a man to be trusted. He will return."

Rodda's jaw came up pugnaciously. She was an attractive, plump, middle-aged woman, but with unhappiness etched in her features. Her face bore lines of anxiety.

"He said he would return before the new moon," she repeated.

With a suppressed sigh, Ferror ceased pumping at the bellows and drew the copper-tin alloy on which he was working from the forge. He wiped his hands on his leather apron and came forward to take his wife's reluctant hands in his in a reassuring gesture.

"Why are you so worried?" he asked chidingly. "The stranger left me enough gold and silver for the materials."

"But he has not paid for the precious stones you have inlaid, and who bears that cost? And you have laboured on this task for a full month. If he does not return, who will pay for all the time spent? Times are hard enough these days."

"I will still have the cup to sell," said Ferror patiently.

"But who will buy it in these hard times?"

Ferror knew that work and money were scarce. Most craftsmen had turned their smithies to making weapons of war, for there were rumours that the empire of the Caesars of Rome was finally going to invade the "Island of the Mighty".

It had been nearly a hundred years since the legions of the first of those Caesars, one named Julius, had attempted to invade, and not once but twice had landed his mighty legions to fight against the tribes of the Cantii further up-country. Twice the Britons had pushed them back, and after the second time they had come no more.

Now, merchants trading up and down the coast, and between Britain and Gaul, bought rumours that the new Roman emperor, Gaius Caesar, was gathering another great army at the ports of Gaul, ready to invade once more.

There was little market for the work of a craftsman like Ferror in these days of war preparations, though Ferror's jewellery and silver and gold artefacts had once been sought by the powerful and wealthy.

His work graced the halls of Cunobel, High King of the tribes of southern Britain, and of Conaire Mór of Tara, as well as lesser kings and queens. Even merchants from Gaul and Iberia, from Massilia and Carthage had come to his forge. But all people wanted these days were weapons – better and bigger weapons of war than their neighbours. And, as great a craftsman as Ferror was, he refused to lend his hand to such instruments of death and destruction.

Ferror was of the Druid caste, a servant of the goddess Dôn, the Mother Goddess, whose divine waters had flowed from the heavens at the beginning of time and washed the sacred oak from which had sprung the children of Dôn. As a child, Ferror had sworn the sacred oath of his brotherhood, that life was sacrosanct and inviolable. Henceforth he had devoted his craftsmanship to create only objects of beauty and veneration.

But in these days work was scarce and times were lean. Even Ferror's wife had tried to persuade him that swords paid better than drinking-cups and jewellery for chieftains' wives. Yet Ferror had refused to break his sacred oath to Dôn, the Mother Goddess. Times had been precarious until the stranger had arrived.

Ferror was a metal-smith of the people of Ruel, who inhabited the extreme south-west of the "Island of the Mighty". His forge stood at the edge of the great forest at Cudden Point, overlooking the wide bay so much frequented by the ships of the merchants from the four corners of the world.

Last month a vessel with the bizarre sails and the outlandish lines of the eastern peoples had sailed into the bay, anchoring off the tiny island there. Ferror had often seen such ships arrive in the kingdom before. They were Phoenician traders, seeking tin and copper in return for wines from the east and other commodities. In good times Ferror had done a fair trade with them, but the rumours of war had cut down the number of traders now visiting the kingdom of Kernow.

Ferror had therefore been delighted when a tall, dark-skinned and elderly man had left the vessel and made his way to the forge. He had recognized the trader immediately as one who had frequented the coast a few years before, trading goods from the east for tin, copper and bronze. It had been many years since he had traded with this tall Phoenician named Yosep.

The trader had given Ferror a bag of gold and silver, asking him to use his best talent to create a precious metal setting into which a bowl of specific proportions would be placed. The metal would protect the bowl and also be part of it at the same time.

Yosep had given Ferror the bowl which, to Ferror's astonishment, was a thing of poor quality – a rough bowl of hardened clay, not even glazed pottery. He had demanded whether Yosep was joking, so reverently had he treated the object.

"It is a sacred object, Ferror," he had told the craftsman. "It is from this bowl that the Son of God drank."

"Then He must have been a poor god, indeed."

"Poor? That He was. He was born in earthly form as the son of a poor carpenter. This poor bowl reminds us that He made Himself humble among men in order to bring us the Word."

This was a tale Ferror could understand, for gods and goddesses moved in mysterious ways, with reasoning beyond the knowledge of mortals.

"So you would want this crude piece of clay enshrouded by

a work of ornate gold and silver?" And Ferror had agreed to undertake the work.

Yosep had further entreated him that no one should know of the work – not even Ferror's young apprentice. Ferror could hardly keep the work a secret from his wife, but he only worked on the bowl when Mapanden was away on errands or asleep, and thus he had completed the task without the young boy learning of it.

Yosep had told him that he wished to trade further up the coast, and had set sail the same day, promising to return. Because Yosep said he would return before the next new moon, Ferror had worked long hours, day and night, to ready the artefact, using the bowl which Yosep had given him as a pattern around which to create his work.

Ferror had created a beautiful chalice of gold and silver, inlaid with precious stones, which even the High King of the "Isle of the Mighty" would be proud to use at his heroes' feasts. And inside the chalice was set the crude clay bowl.

The sound of a horn woke Ferror from his reverie. He grinned triumphantly at his wife.

"That is the warning of a ship coming into the bay. What did I say? It will be the stranger returning for his bowl, just as he said he would."

Rodda was already making her way to the vantage point in front of the forge, which overlooked the sea and from where she could stare down into the bay.

She gave a disparaging exclamation.

"Not unless he has changed his ship, for it is a Roman one," she said drily. "Roman merchants!"

Ferror joined her and saw that his wife was right. A Roman ship was entering the bay below them. He could share his wife's disgust, for the Romans were not the best of traders – always trying to beat down the price and get a better bargain.

Ferror began to frown as he let his eyes run over the slim lines of the vessel.

The sleek cut of the ship was unlike any Roman merchantman that he had seen before, and he saw lines of oarsmen, who, as the crew furled the sails, took over, rowing the ship towards a safe anchorage in time to the monotonous beat of a drum.

"That is not a merchant ship. It is a ship of war," Ferror breathed softly.

The people of Ruel, in their village in the bay below, had already come to the same conclusion, for he could hear commands being shouted and some of the men running hither and thither in search of weapons.

"Can it be the Roman invasion?" gasped Rodda, fear now in her voice.

Ferror shook his head and placed a reassuring hand on her arm.

"One ship?" He smiled. "Besides, the Romans will not waste their time landing an army here. When and if their invasion comes, they will wish to land their forces up-country, against Cunobel, and defeat him. If Cunobel falls, then Britain will fall."

"Is it a raid, then?"

"No." Ferror shook his head again. "They would come in the darkness if they thought to raid our village. The ship below comes openly, without stealth."

Indeed, he could hear the thin squeal of a trumpet from the vessel, presumably announcing that it had no evil intentions. A number of figures were climbing down its sides into a small boat which was then rowed to the shore.

From their vantage point on the clifftop, Ferror and Rodda could see their chieftain, Ruel, marching down to the shore with his standard and bodyguard to meet the new arrivals.

"What does this mean?" whispered Rodda. "I do not like it."

Ferror shrugged and turned away, leading Rodda with him.

"It means," he said with a laugh, "that soon I shall starve, for surely it is long past midday and we have not eaten. Come, I have to finish off working that iron cauldron for Ruel while you must prepare our meal."

Rodda inclined her head in reluctant agreement. It was a short time later that Ferror heard the excited voice of his young apprentice, Mapanden, calling to him. He had been sent to Ferror at the age of seven to be educated and instructed in the craft of a smithy. He showed promise.

He could follow instructions and create superb workmanship if he was guided, but, Ferror found, he lacked an ability for conceptual thought. He could follow patterns, but could not create original work.

Well, there was no great crime in that – except Mapanden would always have to work under the instruction of a more creative craftsman. And, in truth, Ferror had grown fond of the boy, who represented the son that he and Rodda had never had.

Mapanden was shouting for him again.

Ferror could hear the boy's panting breath as he ran up the hill towards the forge.

He came out of the door, wiping his hands on his leather apron, and watched the boy approach with a grin.

"What ails you, boy?" he demanded.

Mapanden came running up, stopped, and was forced to wait a moment until he had recovered sufficient breath to speak.

"Roman warriors are coming this way. Ruel, the chieftain, is with them."

Ferror's eyes widened.

"Coming this way? Why?"

"To see you, master-smith," Mapanden gasped.

Before he could ask why, he saw a small group ascending the brow of the hill up to his forge. Indeed, walking side by side with Ruel, the chieftain, there strode a short, sallow-faced man, with a long red cloak and a golden helmet with a red plume. He wore armour under the cloak that, to Ferror's trained eye, looked well-made and expensively worked. He was clearly not just an ordinary warrior.

There were two more men clad in the outlandish fashion of the Roman stranger. One, in plain leather harness, carried a short spear and long shield, while the other was a thickset man with a fair skin and blond hair. He seemed of some rank, but clearly not as exalted as the man who stood by the chieftain. Several of Ruel's warriors brought up the rear of this curious party.

"The blessings of Dôn on you, Ferror!" called Ruel, coming forward and formally saluting the smith.

"And of Dôn's children on you, Ruel," replied Ferror solemnly, but his eyes had met the dark, inquisitive gaze of the stranger. He was aware that Rodda, alerted by the sounds of the arrival, had come to stand behind him.

"I bring a Roman stranger who wishes to speak with you," Ruel went on.

Ferror shrugged indifferently.

"Why would he wish to?"

He saw that the thickset blond-haired man was leaning forward to the tall Roman and whispering in his ear, clearly translating what was being said.

"The Roman has asked if an eastern ship put in here about a month ago. I told him one had. He seeks news of a tall, elderly trader named Yosep. I told him that Yosep the trader is known along this coast and came ashore last month to trade with you."

Ferror smiled faintly.

"That is certainly no secret."

The fair-haired man now took a pace forward and spoke in the rolling accent of Gaul.

"If I may speak directly?" He made his opening as an apology to Ruel. "Allow me, Ferror, to introduce the Tribune Servius Galba of the Imperial Army of Rome."

The Roman chieftain stiffened in acknowledgment of the mention of his name.

"I do not understand what you wish of me," Ferror said.

The Gaul – for although the fair-haired man wore the uniform of Rome, it was apparent that he was of that land – smiled reassuringly.

At the time when the Romans had tried to invade Britain they had conquered the tribes of Gaul, and now many Gauls served the Romans. It was often hard to differentiate between some Gauls and Romans, and Ferror could not help but feel some antagonism towards a man who had chosen to serve the conquerors of his people.

"We merely wish to find this man from the east. The trader named Yosep."

"Then I cannot help you. He came here, as you have already been told, a month ago. He stayed not even a day at anchor down there in the bay and then moved on." The Gaul bit his lip in annoyance at Ferror's response, but relayed this information in the tongue of the Roman. The stocky Roman frowned, clearly sharing the Gaul's irritation, and spoke rapidly.

"The Tribune Galba asks why this Yosep should come to see you," said the Gaul.

Ferror smiled disarmingly.

"Many people come to see me and many ask me to work for them."

Ruel, the chieftain, was grinning broadly.

"Ferror is well known in many lands for his exquisite craftsmanship, Gaul. He works in metals and precious stones."

"So the trader came with work for you?" pressed the Gaul eagerly.

"Why else would he approach me?" Ferror demanded.

"What work?" The Gaul almost broke the laws of hospitality by snapping his question abruptly.

Ferror decided to ignore him. "Again, no secret in that. He asked me to make a vessel – a drinking-bowl for him."

The news was at once relayed to the Roman. His face registered disappointment.

"And he has not been back since?"

"No."

"He has not returned to collect this bowl which you have made?"

"No."

"When do you expect him to return?"

Ferror frowned at the urgency of the question.

"I do not know," Ferror said, lying for the first time. "Why are you so keen to find him?" He asked the question looking directly at the Roman tribune. There was something about the cold, dark eyes of the man that he distrusted. They burned with some hidden, curious menace.

"The man is from one of our eastern provinces. A place where there is much rebellion. He is, as you know, a trader, and one involved with a band of rebels from a place called Nazareth. They are criminals and troublemakers trying to stir up insurrection against the lawful rule of the emperor. Their leader was executed a few years ago but they persist, and have even claimed that their leader has risen from the dead and still leads their rebellion."

Ferror was unresponsive.

"It is possible," he conceded. "In our land we believe that when a soul dies in this world it is reborn in the Otherworld. When it dies in that world, it is reborn in this world. Sometimes a great soul can exist in both worlds. Under the blessings of the Mother Goddess, Dôn, a great soul never dies."

The Roman's face broke into a sneer when this was translated. He spoke long and hurriedly.

"My officer is well aware of the beliefs of you Britons," said the Gaul. "Are you saying that you believe in this rebel, whose followers claim him to be an immortal?"

"What manner of name is given to him?" demanded Ruel, interrupting, interested in the exchange.

"They call him the anointed of their god – the Messiah, in their own tongue, and Christos in the tongue of the Greeks, many of whom now also begin to spread his rebellion."

Ruel shook his head ruefully.

"I have heard nothing of such a person, have you, Ferror? But, then, why should we be concerned with what gods and men do in faraway lands?"

"My officer says that the smith here speaks very much like a follower of this Messiah."

Ruel suddenly chuckled.

"Tell your officer that Ferror the smith is of our Druid caste. All *religieux* are alike, whichever part of the world they inhabit. They are all full of mysticism and allegory. Take no offence by it."

The Roman officer scowled when this was translated.

"We know all about Druids," he replied curtly, through the Gaul. "It is well known that the Britons have sent Druids to Gaul to foment unrest and rebellion. Perhaps this smith is one of them?"

Ruel scowled for the first time.

"We have granted you the hospitality of our shores, Roman, and replied to your questions courteously. It is not our custom to insult our guests, and neither do we expect our guests to insult us."

The Gaul, who understood the customs of the Britons, stirred uneasily, and the Roman had to press him for a translation, which he gave albeit unwillingly. The Roman's scowl deepened and he replied with thinly veiled anger.

"This Yosep is an evil plotter who would dare overthrow the rule of Rome and even displace the worship of the divine Caesar," interpreted the Gaul rapidly as the Tribune spoke.

"That means little to us. We worship our own gods in this land, Roman," replied Ruel, annoyance having displaced his tolerant look. He clearly felt that he had allowed the Roman enough courtesy. "It is clear that this trader Yosep, from . . .?"

"From Arimathea," supplied the Gaul.

"It is clear that he is not here."

"Why would he ask this smith to make him a drinking vessel?" the Roman demanded through the translation of the Gaul. "Did he leave any object, any artefact with the smith?"

"The answer to your first question is surely one that only Yosep can answer," replied Ferror coldly. "As for your second question, all I can say is that Yosep asked me to make a bowl."

Rodda, standing behind Ferror, gasped at the way her husband had sidestepped the question. The Roman officer was quick to notice the involuntary action.

Ferror's face was stony. He was determined not to relay any further information to this enemy of the Phoenician trader.

The tall Roman gazed at Ferror grimly for a moment, and then he inclined his head sharply and turned on his heel.

"The Tribune thanks you for your help," the Gaul said hurriedly, clearly trying to make up some dignified parting remark, and turned quickly away after him.

Ruel glanced apologetically at Ferror and gave an eloquent shrug. "I have heard that these Romans have little in the way of manners," he observed. "In a way, I would welcome their attempt to invade here, and then we can show them that their arrogance is ill-founded."

He turned and left with his men.

Rodda moved forward anxiously to her husband's side.

"The stranger must have committed terrible deeds to be chased across the world by the Romans. Do you think he stole something of great value?"

Ferror watched the departing group and shook his head. "Perhaps he stole the Romans' sense of pride?" he commented drily.

"The Roman said he was a criminal, a rebel. Maybe the Roman wanted that clay cup which he left you?"

"Yosep is a kind man. A man of peace and spirituality. I know he is a good man. As for the bowl being something of value to that high and mighty Roman . . . well, you saw yourselves that it is only a baked clay bowl, and a poorly made one at that. It is not worthwhile sailing across the world to retrieve it."

Mapanden was still standing with them.

"I have never seen Romans before, Ferror," he commented. "Is it true that they mean to conquer us?"

Ferror chuckled dismissively and reached out a hand to pat the boy's shoulder.

"No man can be truly conquered, Mapanden, while he remains free in his mind and spirit. Remember that. Now get into the forge and bring the fire back to a good heat. I still have Ruel's cauldron to finish."

When the boy had left, Ferror turned to Rodda, his face suddenly set in serious lines.

"Perhaps it was lucky that the boy was away when Yosep came here. The less he knows about the bowl, the better. It seems, from what the Roman said, that they will not let the matter rest."

Rodda was perplexed.

"Do you think some danger threatens from the Romans, Ferror?" she demanded.

Ferror shrugged.

"There is something about the Romans that I distrust. I feel some threatening evil in their presence."

*   *   *

Mapanden halted abruptly and a cry of astonishment was forced from his throat, being lost immediately against the hissing and crack of the incoming tide against the shore.

He had been walking the long, sandy curves of the seashore, as he did most mornings just after dawn, looking for any flotsam that might be washed up, when he'd seen what appeared to be a bundle of clothes moving in the shallows, pushed here and there by the powerful wavelets. He had walked forward with curiosity and then realized that it was the body of a man.

Only when he drew nearer did he realize that the man was still alive. Although Mapanden was only a boy, he was a strong youth, and he managed to pull the body up the shore beyond the eager clutches of the sea. He could see the man was a stranger; tall, dark-looking with curious clothing that reminded the boy of the saturnine eastern traders who sometimes traded along the coast.

The man, whose breath was rasping a little, coughed, spewed up seawater, and, panting, opened his eyes. For a while he simply stared at the boy, and then managed to grunted something in a foreign tongue.

Mapanden frowned and replied in his own language, "I do not understand."

"What is this place?" repeated the stranger in the same language, the words curiously accented.

"You are on the shore of Kernow."

The man slowly sat up. There was a bloody gash across his brow.

"Am I anywhere near the land of the people of Ruel, near Cudden Point?"

Surprised that a foreigner should know the name of the place where he lived, the boy pointed to the brooding headland along the shoreline.

"That is Cudden Point."

"God is good! There is no other God but God!" cried the stranger, as if invigorated by the news.

The boy stared in surprise, for everyone knew that there were many gods and goddesses and that Dôn was the Mother of them all. Why would the stranger declaim that there was no other God but God, and which god did he mean? Perhaps he was rambling.

"Who are you?" he demanded. "How did you get washed ashore here? Were you shipwrecked?"

The stranger frowned, trying to follow Mapanden's rapidity of speech.

"Shipwreck? Yes, yes. My vessel was sunk by a Roman warship just before dawn. The Romans came out of the darkness and attacked us. All are lost. My crew, all lost. I was lucky. I found a spar and clung onto it until the tide carried me to the shore. God is good!"

"Indeed, Manawydan, the god of the seas, took you in his arms," agreed the boy solemnly. "But how do you know of Cudden Point?"

"I have traded many times along this coast," the stranger replied. "I was here a month ago. Do you know Ferror the craftsman?"

Mapanden's eyes widened.

"He is my master. I am apprentice at his forge."

"Then God is good indeed! I commissioned him to do some work for me. I must see him. That was why I was returning here."

He suddenly started to cough again. Mapanden saw that there was blood dribbling from his mouth and realized that the stranger was in a poor condition. He needed warmth, and something to put vigour in him. The boy looked round the empty stretch of shore.

"There is a cave in the cliffs along here," he told the stranger. "It will give you some warmth while I run to Ferror and get his help. If I support you, can you walk a while?"

The stranger nodded slowly.

"I can try, boy. I will try."

They moved slowly, painfully slowly, across the sands. It took a good half an hour for the boy to bring the stranger to the small cave when it would normally have taken him only a few minutes to traverse the distance. The cave was small, but at least provided a dry shelter out of the blustery coastal winds.

The man was shivering in his sodden clothes. Mapanden looked round for something to build a fire with but there was no dry kindle nor, indeed, any other suitable wood. He hesitated, glancing down at the stranger, who was clearly weakened from his efforts.

"I will go for Ferror. I will try not to be long."

The stranger grasped at arm of the boy in spite of his exhausted state.

"Warn Ferror against the Romans. If they know I have left anything with him then they will attempt to destroy it."

The boy frowned.

"But a Roman ship landed in the bay yesterday, and their chieftain came to see Ferror."

"Do they know I left . . . left a bowl with him?" The stranger's eyes widened in alarm.

The boy shrugged,

"I don't know that. The Romans did ask Ferror if you had left anything with him but he did not reply."

The stranger sighed with relief.

"Tell Ferror that they think they have destroyed me and sunk my ship. If they learn about the bowl then they will come ashore and destroy him. He is in mortal danger. Hurry and tell him. My name is Yosep."

The urgency of the stranger's voice galvanized Mapanden into action, and he set off running along the seashore, scrambling up the cliff path which wound up towards the distant headland.

He was still a long way off when he saw the plume of smoke rising from Cudden Point. At first he thought it was the smoke of the fire from Ferror's forge, but then he realized it was too thick, too strong.

A fear began to rise within him. He quickened his pace.

By the time he reached the headland people from the village of Ruel were running hither and thither with pails of water, and the buildings of Ferror's forge were all ablaze.

It was Ruel himself who caught Mapanden as the young boy ran forward.

The chieftain's face was set grimly.

"Go no further, lad," he said flatly. "Ferror and Rodda are dead."

The boy stared at him in disbelief.

The chieftain put a burly arm around the boy's shoulders.

"A bad thing, is this," he said. His voice seemed unemotional, but it was clear that anger lurked in his soul.

"What happened?" mumbled Mapanden. "Who would do such a thing? Ferror and Rodda harmed no one."

"It was the Romans who were here yesterday. Their ship must have been anchored under the headland. Some of their warriors climbed up, slaughtered Ferror and Rodda and set fire to the forge. They appeared to be looking for something, for they wrecked all the buildings in a search before they fired the place . . . Some of the villagers heard the sounds of the attack and saw the Roman devils heading back to their ship, which even now stands out to sea."

He waved his hand towards the horizon and Mapanden could make out a tiny sail, far out to sea.

The boy's jaw clamped tight as he sought to control the emotions that welled within him.

"Do you know what they were looking for?"

Ruel spread his hands expressively.

"Who knows? Yesterday they asked Ferror if a trader named Yosep had left anything with him. Do you know anything of that?"

"I was not here when the trader came," the boy replied truthfully.

"That is so," agreed Ruel. "Well, what is certain is that the Romans have broken the laws of hospitality. A strange people, these Romans. We have heard enough tales from Gaul, where our cousins have long been under their heel. Well, we shall know how to treat them in future.

"I have posted look-outs along the coast so that they will not surprise us again and I have sent word of this terrible deed to Conan the king. If the Romans want war, then they shall have war."

The boy looked with dry-eyed sadness at the now smouldering buildings of the forge. There were signs of destruction everywhere. The iron cauldron which he knew Ferror had been working on for Ruel had been dented and twisted out of shape by the ferocity of the heat. Blankets covered the bodies of Ferror and Ruel where they lay.

It was the sight of them that reminded the boy of his duty to the stranger.

He glanced around, realizing that perhaps it would be unwise to let Ruel and the others know of the stranger's presence at this time. He would keep it to himself until the stranger was well enough to advise him.

But the stranger stood in immediate need of dry clothing and food. He waited until Ruel had turned back to the forge and the attention of the others was concentrated on extinguishing the remaining fires and then he turned, making his way quickly down to the village.

Ferror's house had been destroyed, and so had the room in which Mapanden used to sleep. He felt he had little choice to make other than to borrow what he needed from one of the village houses. All the villagers were at Ferror's forge, so he would be able to help himself to what was wanted without any unnecessary questions.

He found a blanket and some bread and cheese and some goat's milk in Ruel's empty house. He had no compunction at helping himself. As chieftain, Ruel did not lack in anything, and he could well spare the items Mapanden took.

There was a bundle of dry kindle-sticks ready by the oven and near at hand some flints; he took these also. There was also a flagon of strong mead standing cooling in the shade. He hesitated before adding this to his prizes and then made off, as fast as he could, back along the beach to the cave.

The stranger was in a bad way now. The boy lit a small fire at the cave entrance, hoping that the smoke would not be seen from the headland and attract attention. Then he undressed the stranger, taking the damp, clammy clothes from him, and wrapped him in a blanket, forcing some of the strong mead between his lips.

The stranger grunted in appreciation, his eyes still closed while he lay shivering in the warmth of the blanket.

"I am not long for this world, boy," he said abruptly. "Where is Ferror?"

Mapanden bit his lip and then decided there was no other path save that of truth.

"He is dead. Both he and his wife Rodda are slaughtered. The Romans came and killed them even while we were on the beach."

The stranger closed his eyes and let out a small cry of pain and despair.

"I have brought this misfortune upon the innocent! God forgive me!"

Mapanden did not know what to say, so he remained quiet.

"Did they get the bowl?" The stranger opened his eyes and made his demand suddenly.

Mapanden frowned, wondering if fever had set in.

"The bowl," repeated Yosep. "I gave Ferror a bowl to enhance in precious metals. Did the Romans take it?"

Mapanden remembered that the stranger had talked of a bowl before.

"I do not know. I do not think so, as I do not recall ever seeing a cup of that value in the forge. But then . . . then Ferror did have a hiding place for goods of value. If the Romans did not look there, then it will still be there."

"Then go and fetch it, boy. Fetch it quickly."

There was such urgency in the man's voice that Mapanden rose immediately.

"No, wait!" A skeletal hand clung onto his arm.

Mapanden paused, and looked down at the stranger in confusion.

"I am not well, boy. I do not have long for this world. I am sure of it. Let me tell you what this bowl means, then you will know why you must find it and protect it.

"In my land, which lies far to the east, the Son of God came to live among us. He took human shape but was betrayed by those He trusted and executed."

Mapanden had no problems with this, for his own people told many stories of gods and goddesses in mortal shape who were betrayed and killed. And he knew that the gods and goddesses could change shape at will.

Hadn't the son of the god of physicians been killed while in mortal form? There were many such stories of gods and goddesses slain because they had taken on all the vulnerability of the form they represented. Well, gods and goddesses had no business changing their shape if they feared to be killed.

Silently the boy offered the stranger another drink of mead. The stranger swallowed and coughed, and then cleared his throat to continue his story.

"Being the Son of God, He knew what would happen – knew that He would be betrayed and killed. So He gathered His followers around for one last supper before He was betrayed and taken to be executed by the Romans. He drank wine from a bowl and then gave it to each of His disciples to drink after Him. It came to pass that He was betrayed that very night and taken the next morning. He was mocked by disbelievers and executed. But He rose from the dead and ascended into heaven –"

"Heaven?" interrupted Mapanden.

"You call it the Otherworld, the land of the ever-young," Yosep explained wearily. "His followers now must preach His word and convert all to His path."

"Was he a good god or an evil god?" demanded Mapanden.

"His way is Truth, Peace and Fellowship!" exclaimed Yosep. "I was a rich trader in my land, a member of the Sanhedrin, the religious council of my faith. I heard His word and followed. Indeed, it was in my house that the last fateful meal was taken. I saved the bowl from which He and the others drank and brought it with me."

Mapanden's eyes had brightened. "Such a bowl would have great magic, being touched by the lips of a god's son."

"The Son of God," corrected the stranger wearily. "My fellow members of the Sanhedrin, Caiaphas the High Priest and the Romans who rule my unfortunate land, discovered I had this cup. They were scared, for the rumours of Our Lord's resurrection were running though the land and already many were being converted to the path of Our Saviour.

"They knew that I was one of the brethren; knew, also, that I held a sacred relic of Our Lord, and so I had to flee. My enemies feared the sacred power of this relic would cause many to rise and follow the Messiah."

"Messiah?" Mapanden frowned as he recalled the foreign name uttered by the Roman.

"He who is the anointed of God," explained the stranger.

"But which god?" insisted Mapanden.

"There is no god but Yah, the nameless one."

"The nameless one? Ah, do you mean the Good God?" Mapanden began to feel an excitement as, for the first time, he saw a logic to what the stranger was saying.

The stranger strained to catch his words.

"God is good!" he acknowledged. "The bowl touched His Son's lips and so is blessed. The bowl will feed the starving, restore those who thirst, heal the sick and resurrect the dead."

The boy's eyes widened and now he smiled broadly.

"Now I understand. You speak of the Magic Bowl of Murias! The magic bowl of the Good God!"

The stranger frowned, not able to understand the boy's excited tones. His knowledge of the language was not so perfect as to catch all the inflections.

"It is God's cup," he replied. "God is good. There is no God before God!"

The boy gazed down at the stranger, a little in awe. "Why did you bring it here, bring it to this land?"

"I told you – I was a trader, boy. I used to come to this coast trading for tin and copper. I thought that I might be able to hide here, beyond the boundaries of the great empire of Roman which scourges the world. I thought I could keep the relic safe here until Rome and the Sanhedrin ceased to search for me. I did not know how determined the Romans were – that they would send a warship after me, even to the edge of the world."

"Why did you give this sacred relic to Ferror?" pressed Mapanden.

The stranger heaved a sigh.

"Your people are famed for your skill in metalwork, and from my past trading I knew that Ferror's work was famous along the coast. I thought that Ferror could enhance the bowl so that people in time to come would realize that the lips of the Son of God had touched and blessed it."

He reached forward and seized the boy, sudden anxiety in

his eyes. "Are you sure that the Romans did not destroy it?"

"All I know is that Ferror had a secret hiding place for his most precious work. It was behind his forge in a hidden cave. I am sure that he would have hidden it there."

"You must go there, boy. Bring me the cup. For even the sight of it will give me strength."

Mapanden began to rise to his feet, but the hand held him down.

"If my fate should be otherwise, boy, and you find the cup, remember all I have told you of it."

Mapanden nodded emphatically.

"I will remember. I swear it."

"It is a Magic Bowl, touched by the lips of the Son of God. It is a symbol of Liberty and Peace for the whole world, boy . . . the hope of the world."

Mapanden rose. "I will go and get it now. The Romans are gone."

"You are a good boy," sighed the stranger. "What is your name?"

"Mapanden."

The old man smiled.

"Does that name have a meaning?"

"Yes. It means 'Son of Man'."

Yosep started up, his eyes full of incredulous hope, but Mapanden had already turned and hurried away. Yosep slumped back against the cave wall with a smile of contentment wreathing his face.

"God is good," he muttered, before he closed his eyes in weariness.

When Mapanden returned to Cudden Point the villagers had dispersed back to their homes. The sea's long, dim level was devoid of ships. Only the smouldering blackened ruins of Ferror's forge bore silent testimony to the coming of the Romans. The bodies of Ferror and Rodda had been removed and their rebirth in the Otherworld would be celebrated for the next night and day before they were interred in the burial ground beyond the village.

Mapanden walked warily around the ruins of Ferror's forge to make sure that he was quite alone. Then he moved quickly to the outcrop of rocks behind what had been the forge buildings. There was a small, hidden cave there in which, he knew, Ferror had used to store his precious materials out of harm's way.

No one had known of the hiding place except Ferror and Rodda. Mapanden had only chanced upon it when he had come from the forge one evening to find Ferror hiding some gold upon which he was working. Ferror had not noticed him and Mapanden had not made himself known.

Now, on hands and knees, Mapanden squeezed between the stones under the overhanging outcrop and into the small aperture. There were several lumps of metal there which Mapanden knew to be silver. The tin and copper, used for smelting into bronze, were stored by the forge, for they were not as precious as gold or silver. There was also a small wooden box.

Mapanden opened it and found it filled with coins – coins from many of the tribes of Britain and of Gaul, and coins of Rome and other places of which he had no knowledge.

He looked further around in the gloom and saw a sack. He drew it forth and peered inside.

Mapanden had seen many beautiful artefacts but the bowl inside the sack surpassed all others. It was more than a simple bowl. It was exquisite. And it was clearly the bowl that the stranger sought. Any son of a god would be proud to drink from such a vessel. It seemed untouched.

Perhaps Ferror had not begun to work on it, for he could see no sign of the magnificent cup being enhanced at all. One curious thing which he did notice was that the interior of the bowl was a rough old piece of cracked clay pottery – a baked clay cup around which the bowl was made. He wondered what it signified. Perhaps the stranger had the answer.

He thrust it back into the sack and left everything else where it was.

Later he would return and tell Ruel of this place, for all in it now belonged to the tribe of Ruel.

He slung the sack over his shoulder and hurried back towards the cave. In his anxiety to scramble up to the cave-mouth he momentarily lost his footing – and his hold on the sack. It fell from his hands and crashed against the rocks.

Mapanden was so worried lest he had ruined the beautiful work that he ignored the pain of his scraped shins and scurried down to retrieve the sack. He peered inside. The brilliant gold and silver metalwork was not even dented. The jewels sparkled all in their allotted places. He renewed his climb. This time, however, he kept a more careful hold on the sack.

"I have it –" he began as he reached the entrance of the small cave.

The stranger was laying crumpled up on his side.

"I have brought the Magic Bowl!" he called.

The man did not move.

Mapanden set down the sack and reached forward, rolling the stranger over on his back.

The eyes were wide and glazed, staring unseeingly upward. The face was already waxy pale.

Mapanden reached for a pulse in the side of the man's neck, the way Rodda had often shown him. He could not find it. The stranger was dead. Mapenden prayed that he would have a good rebirth in the Otherworld.

Then he recalled his promise.

He turned to the sack and drew forth the gold and silver bowl, noticing again with wonder the precious stones set in patterns around it. It was an exquisite piece of workmanship – no wonder that he could not find anything Ferror had added to it. It was beyond any superlatives that he could find.

He paused and noticed that some dust was scratching against the surface of the bowl. He examined it carefully. Dropping the bowl had doubtless cracked the baked clay inset, and pieces were crumbling and falling out.

Mapanden bit his lip, wondering.

It was then that the explanation came to him. The maker of the bowl had used the rough clay design as a pattern base around which to model the bowl. How often had Ferror provided him with such a pattern and exhorted him to follow it? It was obvious that the stranger had given the bowl to Ferror and asked him to remove the baked clay pattern without damage to the bowl. Well, Mapanden was craftsman enough to complete that task.

He took a sharp instrument from his bag, dug the remains of the dry, baked clay out of the bowl and let the pieces scatter on the floor of the cave. Then he took out a cloth and industriously polished the interior of the bowl.

So this was the vessel that the god's son had drunk from. This was the Magic Bowl of Murias which the son of Dôn, Mother of all the gods, had brought from the Otherworld. He held it out at arm's length with pride.

Mapanden realized that he had found a purpose in life which

eased the suffering and pain of the loss of his master Ferror and Ferror's wife, Rodda. He, Mapanden, had been chosen by the gods as Keeper of the Magic Bowl. He would pass on its secret and its story to his descendants, so that when their time came they, too, could be Keepers, and they, in turn, would pass on the story.

Now he must hide it in a safe place. If ever the Romans or any other strangers came to the Island of the Mighty, the people of Dôn would find in the Magic Bowl of Murias a symbol to sustain them in the conflict. He, Mapanden, and his descendants, would recite the story of the Magic Bowl and hand down the tradition. He felt a welling pride. With reverence, he replaced the Magic Bowl in the sack.

Then he turned from the cave and the pale body of the dead stranger, crushing the broken pieces of the crumbled baked clay bowl underfoot.

MAIDENS OF THE GRAEL

Peter Valentine Timlett

Peter Valentine Timlett (b. 1933) is the author of the Seedbearers trilogy, The Seedbearers *(1974),* The Power of the Serpent *(1976) and* The Twilight of the Serpent *(1977), plus a handful of short horror stories. Timlett is a student of the occult and has made a special study of the Holy Grail, and his knowledge emerges in two stories included in this anthology, as well as in a longer, as yet unpublished novel about Merlin. In this story he shows how the cult of the Grail developed.*

With the tiny metal tongs the boy picked up the selected fragment, coated one edge with the merest wisp of fish-glue, then, holding his right wrist with his left hand to hold it steady, he delicately placed the fragment into its allotted place and lightly pressed it home.

Gwythyas, the Guardian, stood watching him. "It fits?" he said.

The boy breathed lightly. "Yes."

The bench on which the boy worked was strewn with hundreds upon hundreds of fragments of pottery, all pieces of the one cup, each one laid in position with meticulous care by the boy. For week upon week the Guardian had watched him arrange and rearrange the pieces. "How long did it take you to select that one piece for that position?"

The boy shrugged. "Since de-Súl."

Gwythyas did a quick calculation. Four days – for one piece.

But, as the boy had said, as the work progressed there would be fewer and fewer pieces left to select and thus matters would proceed more quickly. There was now no doubt that the work would be completed by Imbolc, as the Master had hoped.

"You have done well, Benesek," he said, and because he was an honest man he added, "I had grave doubts when the Master selected you for this task, but I was wrong." He remembered how the smashed bowl had been found in a cave by the seashore far to the south-west in the land of the Dumnonii, and how its provenance had been discovered. The Venerable High Master himself, Gwyryoneth, had let it be known that the work of restoration was a task of the highest importance. "If the work is ended as well as it has begun, Benesek," he went on kindly, "then I for one will urge that you be appointed as Menystror – Cupbearer."

The boy looked up at him, his eyes suddenly swimming. "Th-thank you," he stammered, his head awhirl. As Menystror it would be his task at the quarterly rituals, in the presence of the assembled senior degree, including the Venerable High Master himself, to bring the chalice containing the Perpetual Light into the lodge and place it upon the altar. "Thank you."

Gwythyas nodded and turned away. Benesek. A strange boy. Ungifted in many ways, slow of mind, clumsy, and yet in matters of delicate handcraft he was a master. Even the *benengwyk*, the woman of the woods, on one of her rare visits had told the tale of how she had seen Benesek repair the broken wing of a raven, a feat that she would not have believed possible for anyone not of her craft.

He walked out of the craft-hut and stood for a moment in the sunshine. The breeze was quite strong today and he felt his white robe flatten against his body. It was one full moon beyond Samhain and soon would come the shortest day of the year, the nadir. Already there was early-morning frost on the ground and the first patches of ice on the sea-marshes and lakes.

To his left were the stables of the great draught horses, and beyond them the ironsmith's forge. Two of the *mebyon-goves*, the apprentice-smiths, were unloading iron ingots from a cart, and a third was leading one of the great animals into the forge itself. Down the slope on the banks of the stream were the fuller-sheds, where the rough cloth from the weavers was thickened and shrunk, and to his right were a multitude of craft-huts: the weavers and tanners, the robemakers and carpenters, the masons and lanternmakers, and myriad other trades and crafts.

And there on the far side were the great kitchens and refectories, girt about by long storehouses and tithe-barns, where the villagers brought one-tenth of their produce as offering to the gods and those who served them. In return the locals received the benefit of the healer-priests, both for themselves and their animals, and shared in the knowledge of when to sow and when to reap – for the Druid priesthood could read the stars, foretell the weather and commune with the gods themselves.

But there, dwarfing the storehouses and craft-huts, was the great round stone-built Druid college of Glaston, known and honoured by all the tribes from the Dumnonii in the west to the Cantiaci in the east, aye, and across the narrow sea to Gaul and beyond to Egypt and to Rome.

Beyond the college stood Glaston itself, the Green Hill, measured as being three hundred and thirty-eight common cubits high, steep-sided on all sides, dominating the landscape, and on its flat-topped summit was a circle of great stones, at the centre of which stood a tall, thin stone known locally as the Dew-bys, the Finger of God. On the flank of the green hill, nestling close into it, rose the dreaming green slopes of Chalcelle, the lesser hill, at whose feet sprang the ancient holy well that drew its sacred water from deep within the earth

The trackway led from the great gates of Glaston College up the slope to the holy well of Chalcelle and then wound round and round Glaston itself, three times, rising higher and higher, and came out at the summit. Four times a year, at Lammas, Samhain, Imbolc and Beltaine, the Druid priests and priestesses, followed by the villagers from far around and visiting bards, would wind their way up the trackway in procession, singing the ancient chants, and there on the summit, at the Dew-bys itself, they would perform the ancient rituals to renew the contacts between outer and inner.

Gwythyas lifted his head to stare up at the summit, remembering, and then became aware that someone stood before him. "Yes?" he said, and saw that it was a young blue-robed seer.

"Gwyrdôn, the Master, requests your presence, Guardian," she said gravely. "He is in the library."

She was a slim girl, scarcely beyond childhood, and her blue robe stirred prettily in the fresh breeze. "I will come at once," he said.

*   *   *

The forest grew down to the river's edge, often dipping its branches into the cold, clear water. Morenarth lay on her front on the bank and slowly, slowly dipped her right hand into the water and then held it still. A standing stone, broken in two halves, had lain half-submerged at the river's edge for untold centuries, and had created a pool of still water, safe from the central current. The big fish liked to lie when the sky was overcast. The trout was barely two hands' length beneath the surface.

"Go on," whispered Glanna, "or you'll miss him."

"Shhhhhh." Slowly, so very slowly, so that no ripple would reach the fish, her hand crept lower and lower, and then, when her arm was in the water almost to her shoulder, she gently turned her hand under the fish.

"Let him go," whispered Tregereth. "He is of the children of Dôn, as are we."

Morenarth grunted, and in a sudden lunge she scooped the fish out of the water. High in the air it flew, its scales gleaming, and then it flopped onto the grass, panting for its life. Glanna laughed with delight and clapped her hands, but Tregereth ran to the fish and picked it up, cradling it in her arms. "May I put it back?" she begged, her eyes pleading.

Morenarth looked at her and her heart stirred. She remembered that time after a moonlit forest ritual at the great oak, when Tregereth had said, "Whenever a creature dies something in me dies as well." She ate no meat, no fish, no fowl, no eggs. She was thin and pale, her skin almost translucent, but Morenarth looked on her with love and sometimes wished that she could be more like her.

She shrugged. "If you wish," she said, and watched her slide the fish back into the river, where with one flick of its tail it vanished into the river's deeps. "A fisherman would die hungry," she said to Glanna, "if he took Tregereth to wife." But she said it kindly, her eyes warm with fondness.

Tregereth shivered and pulled her cloak around her shoulders. "It's cold."

Clouds were coming in from the east and already the sun was hidden.

Gwyryoneth, the Venerable High Master, was an old, old man, and the light of his eyes was beginning to dim. He could feel his inner self beginning to prepare to withdraw from the earth plane. He would climb the tor one last time at Imbolc, for the rite of

Washing the Earth's Face, but then it would be fitting for him to go. Troubled times were coming, and Druidry would need a stronger and younger man.

Gwyrdôn, the Master, was a man in the full strength of his middle years, a tall, broad man with heavy shoulders. The features of his face were strong, and he had a shaggy mane of fair hair, with great, beetling eyebrows over a strong hooked nose. Gwyryoneth chuckled to himself. The man looked more like a warrior than a priest, but he was a good man, a strong man – and above all he was the finest healer that Gwyryoneth had ever known, and there would be a need for healers.

They sat in the scryers' chamber watching Barenwyn at the seers' highly polished metal mirror. The Mistress was even older than himself – old beyond counting. She had been a priestess since fifteen, of the Silurian tribe beyond the Usk. If the High Master was the head of the Order, then the Mistress was its heart. A venerable woman, already a legend in her own lifetime, a living perfection, she was revered by the bards, who sang of her with love throughout the land as though she were a goddess.

Her old head was bent over the mirror, her eyes unfocused, but presently she looked up and sighed. Gwyryoneth waited a few moments for her to return fully, and then said softly, "What did you see, Barenwyn?"

A great shuddering sigh escaped her as she adjusted to the physical world. "I saw three of our own priestesses on the riverbank. Glanna, Morenarth and Tregereth. They caught a fish but returned it unharmed to the water."

"A fish?" said Gwyrdôn. Both men waited, but the Mistress was now deep in thought, her mind far away.

"What meaning can you give to what you saw?" asked Gwyryoneth quietly.

She sighed. "I do not know. I have had strange visions of late, whose meanings are hidden from me." Then she shook her head and spoke more briskly. "But it is often the way, as you know. The meaning will come in time; it always does."

Gwyryoneth nodded, and turned to Gwyrdôn. "So, the restoration of the Cup goes well. You chose wisely when you chose the boy."

"He has done well. The Cup will certainly be ready for Imbolc."

The High Master sighed. "These are strange times – a common bowl of baked clay, a cup. Did you discover the word for 'cup' in the carpenter's own language?"

"Not as yet," said Gwyrdôn. "In Frankish or Gaulish it is probably '*graal*', or '*grael*'. Early Latin, so the scholar-priests tell me, has it as '*gradalis*', a dish, and Latin also has '*gradale*', a step, a rung, a rising in stages – though steps to what, I cannot say."

"To Dôn," said Barenwyn suddenly. "Steps to the throne of God." She clenched her fists and struck the table excitedly. "Yes, yes, *now* I understand – in part at least." Her face was like old parchment, her hair thin and straggly, but her eyes shone brightly. "The strange visions were visions of differing futures, only one of which will occur. In one of them I saw a great chalice from which came the force of the living god, and that vessel was called the grail, the Holy Grail."

Gwyrdôn made as if to speak, but Barenwyn waved him silent. "But in this vision Druidry was no more. Glaston was destroyed, its stone blocks used for a different faith, the Dew-bys tumbled from the tor. I saw great champions in shining armour searching for this Grail."

She paused, and her eyes were focused on scenes and forms that were not yet formed. "But I saw the servants of the Grail, young maidens pure and brave – the Grail Maidens. They were servants of Dôn, even as our maidens are servants." She turned to them, her eyes suddenly refocused. "We are being told what we must do. If the Holy Grail is to be a great symbol in the future it will be because we are preserving the *graal* today. If the Grail Maidens of the future are to exist, then we must begin the tradition today."

"The three priestesses by the river?" said Gwyryoneth.

"Yes."

"And the fish?"

She shook her head. "I do not know, but of the rest I am sure. The magic cauldron will have found a new form, from which new life will still spring, and Peredur will live again in a different name. Dôn, the mother of the gods, and Bel of the fires have decreed that this shall be so. Agrona and Camulos, the gods of war and slaughter, stand guard to aid us, as will Cernunnos of the bulls and stags."

Gwyryoneth could feel the tiredness of old age deep within his bones. "There is much death in your visions, Barenwyn, as indeed there is in mine. I too have seen that the day will come when Druidry is no more, but we will go not gently into the Otherworld. Death and great slaughter I see."

"If that is so," said Gwyrdôn, "then we will go in honour. Remember the three pillars of our faith – to worship

God, to be just to all men and to die for your country or your faith."

"All men must die," said Barenwyn, "as must all maids, but we will be reborn in the Otherworld as we have always been before. Meanwhile we need a new rite, a new initiation to begin the tradition of the maids."

"And you are determined on the three you saw in your vision?" said Gwyrdôn.

"It is the gods who chose, not I."

"But Glanna? She is barely beyond childhood."

"Were I to choose, I could choose no better. Glanna, because she is pure of heart and mind. Tregereth because her heart knows mercy and compassion beyond any normal measure."

"And Morenarth? Wilful, headstrong. How many times have you disciplined her yourself?"

Barenwyn chuckled. "More than I care to remember," she admitted. "But she has strength and courage – qualities that will be much needed."

Gwyryoneth waved them both silent. "The inner has spoken on this matter. Let it be so."

The two senior bards crossed the courtyard of Glaston College and entered a side door into a small antechamber and then into the *lyverva* itself, where the High Master waited for them. They had seen the great library before, many times, but always with a sense of awe.

The chamber was lined with oak shelves from flagstoned floor to ceiling on all four walls, and every shelf was crammed to overflowing with rods upon rods of manuscripts – thousands of them. Some written in the lifetime of those present, and some so ancient that they seemed but the stuff of legend, written in an ink composed of lampblack and gum.

There were Greek manuscripts, Phoenician and Etruscan scripts, Lycian and Phrygian, Cretan pictographs, Gaulish and Germanic manuscripts written in Latin, and others in languages long dead to common usage. There were scrolls of parchment of sheep or goatskin, Egyptian papyri made of reeds that once swayed in hot winds along the Nile, baked clay tablets, and some from across the western sea written in old Goidelic script on bark and thin wands of hazel or aspen.

But there were no Druid manuscripts, beyond a few common records of trade items, for it was forbidden to make a record of

Druid knowledge. What could be written in one language could be understood by all. Let knowledge be handed down from mouth to ear. Let the secret rituals be held only in the memory of priests and priestesses, and let other knowledge – the history of the tribes, the knowledge of journeys to other lands, knowledge of the stars in their courses, knowledge of the healing arts – let all of this be held in the memories of bards, to be recited or sung as required.

The study-tables, with their raised borders for holding open the manuscripts, took up most of the space; their ink-horns had been gathered together and lay on a side-table. One of the tables had been pulled forward and Gwyryoneth sat at the head. The two bards made obeisance to him.

"I see by your faces that you bear grave news," he said. "Please, be seated." And the two bards, young men who had been born when Gwyryoneth was already old, sat and poured out their tale.

When they had finished he sent them with a novitiate to the Mistress of the Blue, who would see to their welfare. He then sent for Barenwyn, Gwyrdôn and Furneth, the librarian. Furneth was a grim, dour man, more at home with his beloved scripts than in communion with his fellow priests, but as Archivist he needed to be kept informed on non-ritual matters.

"Evil times have come to our land," sighed Gwyryoneth when they were seated. "Courage and sacrifice will be required before the new candle can be lit from the stub of the old."

"What is the news?" said Furneth sharply.

Gwyryoneth smiled grimly. Furneth was ever a man to cut to the quick of any matter. "The Romans, as we know, have been moving westwards along the south coast. Thirty battles they have fought and won against the Cantiaci, the Regnenses, the Belgae and other lesser tribes, and over twenty hill-forts have been taken and destroyed. Now they are virtually at our doorstep. The bards tell me that two days ago they took Maidun and massacred almost every man, woman and child in it."

Furneth's face went grey. Maidun was the main fortress of the Durotriges, situated to the south of Glaston – a massive set of earthworks that were held to be impregnable. "Maidun!" he whispered. "By all the gods, there were seven ramparts, each higher than the other – it reached over seventy cubits high." He shook his head in bewilderment. "What about the chieftains? Were they not there?"

"Yes," said Gwyryoneth heavily. The warriors of all the tribes of the Durotriges were gathered at Maidun to stand against the Romans – and all were slain."

"*All* of them?" Furneth could not conceive of such a thing. All his life the bards had sung of the great earthworks at Maidun, the most formidable in the land. "How was such a thing possible?"

"They have machines that fire arrows," said Gwyrdôn quietly. "*Ballistae*, they call them, and *catapultae* that throw rocks."

"They took Maidun in one day," said Gwyryoneth. "They drove back the defenders by *ballista* fire, burned down the gates, stormed the ramparts and massacred everyone they could find. People were struck in the back as they tried to run; women had their hands tied behind their backs and were then clubbed to death."

"They will live again," said Barenwyn gently.

Furneth glanced at her briefly before turning again to the High Master. "Did each Druid stand with his chieftain?" he said.

"Aye, and all perished along with the others." He sighed and clasped his hands in front of him. "After the massacre the bards sat amongst their campfires, as they have often done," he said slowly. "They sang tales of the heroes of old, which the Romans seemed to like. And afterwards, when the fires were heaped high against the cold, and the wine was strong within them, the bards picked up information that was useful to the chieftains. Their army, apparently, is the Roman Second Legion – Legio II Augusta, they call it in their tongue, under the command of a man called Vespasian – Titus Flavius Sabinus Vespasianus."

Gwyrdôn heard an odd note in Gwyryoneth's voice. There was something else, something that would affect themselves. "The Romans are coming here?" he guessed.

"No. The legion left Maidun in a hurry and is moving westwards towards the Exe." He looked round the table. "No, what concerns us is that a small detachment of cavalry – a *vexillum*, they call it – has been sent ahead of the main legion with orders to search in the land of the Dumnonii, down past Legis Tor and Duloe to the far south-west."

Furneth tried to visualize the parchment map of the lands to the west. "Searching for what?"

"A cup – a jewelled chalice forged by a Celtic smith in a coastal village," he said quietly. "A chalice to hold a certain piece of pottery – a crude vessel once owned by a lowly carpenter in a far land – a bowl – a cup – a *grael*."

*　　*　　*

The Centurion sat his horse comfortably and picked his way along the gloom of the forest trail, his men strung out in line behind him. He glanced at the sky through the bare winter trees. It was leaden in colour, overcast, and the sharp wind came keening through the bare treetops. It was bitterly cold but the worst of the winter was over. If his reckoning was correct it lacked but a few days to the ides of Februarius. In Rome they would be holding the public purification feasts, but his mother would remain in the house and grieve for his father, who had died a bloody death in the bitter forests of Germany.

When the son had followed the father into Legio II Augusta she had been troubled, but had put a brave face on it. "Be strong, my son," she had said. "For the honour of Rome and our family."

So Marcus Cornelius Quintilianus had gone to war, and his ferocity in battle had quickly gained him the *vitis* – the vine-branch staff of the centurion's rank. And now this, an independent command, a *vexillum* of his own – though not much of one, with just thirty men mounted on thirty of the finest horses the legion could provide.

"Ride hard and fast," the Tribune had said. "News of Maidun will not travel faster than you. Find that cup. And remember, Centurion," he had added, "this is by imperial command from Rome. Come back without it and Vespasian will feed you to the wild boars."

A cup, a common bowl of baked clay – perhaps it was true what was said in the market-place, that Cl-Cl-Claudius was feeble-minded. Marcus sighed. But if the Emperor wanted that particular bowl then he, M. Cornelius Quintilianus, would get it for him if he had to spit every barbarian in Britannia.

But the village in the far south-west to where the cup had been traced lay abandoned. Its huts were derelict and even the old forge had been thrown down. The smith was dead these many a year, and his wife with him. There had been an apprentice, but he had gone to seek his fortune in the lands to the north. A cup? Yes, there had been talk of a cup in that village, but that was all it had been – just talk.

The search had been fruitless. It was not that the natives had been hostile, at least not at first, nor deliberately concealing information. Their language was similar to that of Gaul, and surprisingly refined, and some of their travelling bards could speak a little Latin. It was simply that they did not understand, or perhaps could scarce believe, that they were looking for one particular bowl. They had been offered dozens of bowls, hundreds, but when asked whether *this* was the bowl from *that* particular cliff-top village they could only shrug.

They were wary, of course. They had seen Romans before, those that had been coming here for a century or more to trade for tin, fine metalwork or packs of trained hunting dogs, but they had not seen Roman cavalry – not this far west. But then news of Maidun began to filter through and their bearing changed to fear and hatred. They had visited dozens of villages and questioned hundreds of natives but to little avail, though there were always rumours to spur them on, suggestions, possibilities.

Now they were headed north, and soon he would have to make a decision – whether to rejoin the legion empty-handed and risk being thrown to the boars, or take back any old baked clay bowl and pretend that it was the one that Rome sought. Either way was fraught with danger for a mere Centurion with no powerful connections.

Young Flavius spurred his horse alongside. "Who is that?" he said, pointing ahead to where the trees opened up to reveal a small clearing where a cloaked woman with a basket was plucking small plants from the undergrowth. No horse stood near, no hut was visible, no dogs, but she bore herself calmly as they rode into the clearing and surrounded her. The crude cloak that she wore flung around her shoulders was mute evidence that she was no high-born lady, but by her bearing she was clearly no peasant either.

"Are you a priestess?" Marcus said gruffly, on impulse, and young Flavius translated it.

"I am," she said coolly. Her voice was as honey, deep and rich. She was tall, very tall, and her hair was a deep orange-red, like living flame, and her eyes were as green as emeralds.

"Ask her if she's Druid."

The woman shook her head and spoke volubly.

"No, apparently not," said Flavius, "though she does not wish them ill. She is of the woods, and these," he added, waving his hand to indicate the enormous trees of the deep, dark forest, "are her gods." Marcus remembered the woman waving her arm. "She warns us to tread gently."

"Does she indeed? Tell her that her blood will soak the roots of her gods if she does not speak more prudently. No, tell her we will take our pleasure of her, all thirty of us. Tell her that."

Flavius translated, and a sudden fear stabbed through him as the woman flung back her head and laughed in such eerie tones that the hairs on his neck stood on end.

"Tell your captain," she said tauntingly, "that if he enters me he enters into a living death, the never-ceasing horrors of the half-life. Tell him that for him there is no warmth or comfort in my embrace, only a living agony and a fear so sharp that it shall pierce his very spirit. Tell him!"

Several of the men gasped when Flavius translated, but M. Cornelius Quintilianus merely smiled. Now that he had had a few moments to study her he could see that she was no longer young, indeed, there were deep lines on her face, and beneath her cloak he could see that her breasts hung low. "She is probably right," he said. "As it would be with any hag." He stroked his horse's neck to soothe her restlessness. "Ask her the usual questions – about the cup."

Flavius spoke at length and the woman answered briefly as each question was put. Then Flavius sighed and turned to report, "Same answers as we always get, and yet . . ."

"And yet? Go on."

Flavius shook his head. "She knows something about it that she is not revealing. But," he added quickly, "force will not get it from her. She has no fear of us – none whatsoever. She knows that she is safe from us – not believes, but *knows* she is safe."

"Hey!" said the woman suddenly, and Flavius turned to her. "Your captain is too young in spirit to understand these things. He does not believe; I can see it from his face." She came towards him and stood before him, legs apart and arms akimbo. "But you, young in years but older than your captain in matters of the inner, you know the truth of what I say."

Flavius looked into her eyes and shivered. "Yes," he said, "I do. But it is only a little thing we ask of you. We seek a certain cup, that is all."

She looked at him thoughtfully. "Big enough for it to be an imperial command. Big enough for your Commander to send your captain scouring the land for it."

"You are well informed," Flavius grunted.

"Knowledge is always available for those with ears to hear," she said cryptically. "As I said, I bear Druidry no ill will, but there are strange signs on the inner which do not augur well for the future of this land, or of the Elder Faith."

"What signs?" said Flavius quickly.

"A new rite to be installed at Glaston at Imbolc – a *grael* – three chosen to serve, the Maidens of the Grael. All this I hear, though I do not know its import."

"Imbolc?"

"One of the four great rites of the year. Imbolc is due again in two days' time. I hear that a *grael* is to be placed upon the high altar."

"And after that," said Flavius softly, "there will be a great procession up to the stone circle on the summit."

Her eyes narrowed dangerously. "For a Roman you too are well informed."

"Perhaps I have ears to hear."

"And perhaps tongues can wag as well as ears can flap," she said drily. "Well, no matter. It is no secret."

"But will this *grael* be carried in the procession, do you think?"

She shook her head. "Perhaps, but I doubt it. Washing the Earth's Face is a different rite."

"So the *grael* will be unguarded."

"No, the three will stand before it, and behind them stands the inner. I tell you this, Roman, because *if* that is the cup you seek then it is now beyond your reach, and perhaps you will now abandon your search and return whence you came." She glanced up at the Centurion. "And perhaps your captain will now serve the wild boars."

Flavius's face drained of all colour. "How did you know of that?" he whispered.

"What is it?" said the Centurion sharply. He had been growing more and more impatient during the exchange, cursing the fact that he could not speak the barbarian tongue. Flavius told him all that the priestess had said, except about the boars. "And do you believe her, about the cup being at Glaston?"

"Yes, but whether it is the one we seek I do not know, and neither does she."

Marcus sighed. "Well, we have no other choice. Two days, you say?"

"To Imbolc, yes." Flavius looked down at the woman. She was still standing there, arms akimbo, utterly unafraid.

The Centurion said nothing for some time. Then he said briefly, "Kill her," and turned his horse away.

"Kill her?" Flavius was shocked. "Why? She helped us."

The Centurion's voice was cold and sharp like ice. "She knows where we're going, and why. Kill her."

The woman said something, and Flavius replied in the barbarians' tongue. Then the woman said something again, and the tone of her voice was taunting.

Marcus reined his horse. "What did she say?"

Flavius did not want to reply, but he had come to know the Centurion very well. He knew what would happen. He could see the final scene as though it had already occurred. "She said . . ." he replied slowly, "she said let your captain kill me himself – if he can."

Marcus smiled as he looked back at the woman, but there was no warmth in his smile. She stood there in the snow, her eyes full of fire, challenging him, believing that her calling would protect her. He turned his horse and walked it back to her, and reined it in when it was almost touching her. He then drew his sword and raised his arm aloft.

He looked down at her and saw that she was still unafraid, utterly confident that he would stay his hand at the last moment, supremely confident of her own power. These damned barbarians, uncouth savages, uncivilized primitives – it was such as these that had killed his father and many another good Roman.

His sword flashed down and the blade buried itself in her neck. Her blood sprayed the icy air, and for one moment her body remained upright, her green eyes registering an intense shock – and then the eyes glazed and she fell back in the snow, the red blood staining the white. And M. Cornelius Quintilianus turned his horse away.

Flavius looked down at the body and his heart surged in sympathy for her. The others cantered past him and followed the Centurion out of the clearing. Flavius sighed and turned his horse aside to follow them. A few minutes ago they had not even known that she existed, and now she was dead – and they didn't even know her name.

The antechamber to the Hall of Ritual was quiet. The darkness of late afternoon was illumined by a single tall candle that burned upon the low table. Three priestesses sat in three oaken chairs, their hands folded in their laps, deep in meditation, preparing themselves for the ritual to come. Their robes were silver to represent the light of the gods, and their headdresses were gold to symbolize the sun. They had not understood all that Barenwyn had said, except that they were to serve the inner *grael* of which the physical cup that Benesek had completed was a symbol.

Today was the rite of Imbolc, but before the procession to the tor began Benesek, as Menystror, would carry the Perpetual Light into the Hall of Ritual and place it upon the altar, as the Cupbearer did at all rituals.

But then would come the new rite. The Guardian would summon the priestesses to the Hall. They were to rise and follow him. Morenarth was to carry the jewelled chalice containing the restored clay bowl and at the appropriate moment she was to place it on the altar in front of the Perpetual Light and thus link the two ritually.

Glanna and Tregereth sat with eyes closed, preparing themselves, but Morenarth sat watching Benesek. The boy had been so proud to be appointed Menystror, and so nervous. He had never served in any ritual office before, and it was now his task to light the wick in the glass bowl to symbolize the Perpetual Light, and to carry that bowl into the Hall of Ritual in the presence of the assembled degrees and place it upon the altar.

She could see that his hands were trembling slightly as he lit the wick from the fire in the iron basket. He then opened the door to the ritual chamber and picked up the glass bowl. Morenarth saw him take a deep breath and then move slowly and evenly into the lodge, as he had been taught. Through the open door Morenarth could see the circle of the assembled degrees – the white-robed seniors, the green Ovates behind them, and the blue robes of the Bardic degree at the rear. Gwyryoneth sat at the eastern portal, Barenwyn in the south, and Gwyrdôn in the west with the Sword of Power across his lap.

At the door to the chamber stood Gwythyas the Guardian, his hand resting upon the hilt of the symbolic dagger at his belt. The priestesses were singing a low chant so ancient that none knew its origin. Their voices were soft, the chant hauntingly beautiful. Morenarth felt her spirit soar with joy to become as one with the gods.

She saw Benesek reach the centre and place the Perpetual Light reverently upon the altar. She then saw him bow to the east and withdraw to take his seat near the chamber door. For a moment all was still. Only the soft chanting was heard; all eyes were upon the flickering light upon the altar. Then she saw Gwyryoneth rise and approach the altar. He reached for the bowl and raised the Perpetual Light high into the air.

"Let all here assembled," he cried in a powerful voice, "enflame this symbol within your hearts." And the chanting rose to a paean of love and power. Then the High Master returned to the east.

The Guardian then turned and faced the antechamber. "Let the Priestesses of the Grael draw near," he cried.

Morenarth rose, and could sense Glanna and Tregereth rising with her. Morenarth picked up the jewelled chalice containing the restored Cup and moved forward into the lodge, Glanna and Tregereth on either side. The Guardian closed the great door and then turned to face the Magus.

"Who comes?" said Gwyryoneth in the east.

"Three who bear the symbol of the Grael," said the Guardian.

"By what need do these come among us?"

The Guardian drew himself up and replied in a strong and powerful voice, "By the need to link inner and outer, to link the past with the present and with that which is to be."

"What is the symbol of that Office?"

Morenarth moved forward past the Guardian and stopped at the circle of the Lodge. She could feel the forces within her welling up, using her as a channel. "The Cup," she cried in ringing tones, holding it high so that all should see, "that in *yesu* shall be known as the Grael."

"Who serves this Grael?"

Glanna and Tregereth came to stand on either side of Morenarth. "We serve the Grael," cried Glanna in her young voice. "That it shall remain pure and unsullied in our keeping."

"With mercy and compassion shall we serve the Grael," cried Tregereth.

"With strength and courage shall we guard it from harm," said Morenarth firmly.

There was a deep silence as the low chanting died away. The Perpetual Light flickered upon the altar, and in Morenarth's hands the jewelled chalice containing the Cup glittered with reflected light. The smoke from aromatic gums wafted through the Lodge, bringing the scents of olibanum and galbanum and kypphi from the far lands across the sea.

Then the Magus rose in the east and held wide his arms. "Worthily answered, Maidens of the Grael. Let that Cup be placed upon the altar to indicate that the powers of your Office are now functioning in the Lodge."

And the three moved forward and Morenarth placed the chalice on the altar, and the chanting rose again to a paean of joy.

"Let now the rite of Imbolc begin," cried the Magus, and he moved deosil around the circle. But it was seen that the Messenger, a priestess of the outer court, rose to circumambulate with him,

Gwyryoneth leaning heavily upon her. As he moved past the south Barenwyn rose and followed him, then Gwyrdôn from the west. Three times the senior officers circled the Lodge, and then Gwythyas the Guardian flung wide the door and the Officers left the Lodge, with the Guardian following them. Then the whole Lodge rose and joined the procession, the chant rising powerfully – save the new Maidens, who were to remain in the Lodge with the Grael.

As the process left the antechamber and moved into the courtyard young blue-robed novitiates of the Bardic order rushed forward with cloaks of fur. The stars shone in a clear night but snow lay on the ground and the evening breeze was bitterly cold. More bards rushed to the great gates and swung them open, and beyond the villagers and craftsmen waited, myriad lanterns winking in the darkness.

A shout rose as the procession emerged, and Gwyryoneth, High Master of all Druidry, led the way along the ancient trackway up Chalcelle and thence to Glaston itself. The chanting rose, the lanterns danced and the stars shone brilliantly. Three times the trackway wound around ancient Glaston, and then, on the summit, with priesthood and people gathered around, Gwyryoneth flung wide his arms before the Dew-bys and began the rite of Washing the Earth's Face, as every High Master had done before him since Druidry had begun.

It was early evening on the day of Imbolc. The Centurion had stayed all afternoon in a copse of trees an hour's ride from Glaston, waiting for the cover of darkness. They knew from a peasant they had captured that morning that the procession did not begin until nightfall and that everyone in the village would take part. "You can see the lights of the lanterns winding up the hill from across the lake and as far as the great forest," he had said enthusiastically. "It is a wonderful sight." But he too had been shocked when the sword bit into his neck.

And now they waited.

Soon Flavius pointed across the lake to where the flickering lights had begun to appear on the side of the Green Hill. The Centurion nodded and waved the men forward and out onto the track that would lead them to Glaston itself.

The procession had left and the three remained in the Lodge. It was their task to rise on the inner and establish the link between the newly installed Grael on the altar and the final rite at the summit of the tor at the Dew-bys itself. By powerful names they had conjured the forces, their priestess powers backed by the powers of all Druidry, and soon the mist could be seen upon the altar, growing more evident, thickening, swirling around the chalice that held the Cup.

Morenarth guarded the western gate, Glanna the south, and Tregereth stood in the north to represent the Earth-mind itself. The vapour roiled and swirled upon the altar and the three could see deep within it a shape begin to form; tenuous, without detail, it had the hint of a human form, a suggestion of eyes, a strange air of other times and other places not of this world. But above all it held an emanation of great power.

"Who art thou?" cried Morenarth in bold and ringing tones. "Who dares intrude upon these sacred rites?"

The voice, when it came, carried the imprint of great age, of antiquity, and yet strangely also the feeling of the burst of new life. "I am a priest after the Order of Melchizadek. I am he who will in centuries to come, long after your earthly bodies have mouldered in your graves, walk once more upon the earth of thy land to bring to pass that which must be. Great events wait upon the Lords of Time, yet it will be as naught if thou fail of your task. That which has been placed in thy weak hands shall in that far off time be claimed by a son of the Dragon, and all glory shall result therefrom."

"You speak of the Cup that the stranger placed in our hands for a reason we know not. Nor did he, save that we are compelled beyond our understanding."

"Guard it well, Maidens, for there will come those with swords to wrest it from thee."

They glanced at each other, and Morenarth pulled her robe more closely around her body, as though to shield it from the menace foretold. "And whence shall these robbers come?"

"From across the sea. Even now they march upon thy land with bloody feet. Soon they will pound upon the very door of thy Lodge."

Outside the air remained bitterly cold, but the wind had dropped to nothing. The stars shone brilliantly in the black night, and on the summit of the Green Hill the lanterns flickered as the rite of Imbolc was performed as it had been for uncounted generations.

At the base of the tor the gates of Glaston College stood ajar, and in the antechamber to the Hall of Ritual Gwythyas stood before the door, feet astride, his hand upon the knife at his waist, the symbol of his Office. Nearby a young bard newly brought to Glaston, a boy of seven years, waited patiently to carry any messages that might be needed, or to ring the great bronze bell that warned of danger.

Suddenly, from the courtyard, there came the sound of a horse snuffling, and the clip of its hooves upon the stone. The bard looked at the Guardian. Gwythyas frowned. The only horses in the village were the wagoner's great draught horses, and they were in their stables. He had seen them there himself, just before he had come to robe for the ritual. A latecomer? Unlikely – particularly on horseback. The sound came again, but this time from more than one horse – two, perhaps, maybe three, perhaps more. Difficult to tell.

"Stand by the side door," he whispered to the boy. "If aught untoward happens then run like the wind and sound the alarm." He glanced behind him and hesitated. It was no small matter to interrupt a ritual. He had never known such a thing. Even on the night of the Great Storm, the year after his initiation, with the foundations of Glaston trembling to their very roots, even then the ritual being performed had calmly continued to its proper conclusion. But that had been an act of nature – this was something quite different. And as Guardian it was his responsibility.

He took a deep breath and opened the lodge door. The three priestesses were still in their positions around the altar. At the sound of his entry Morenarth turned.

"Who comes?" she said calmly.

"I am Gwythyas, Guardian of the Lodge," he said ritually. "By the powers of my Office I command thee to close the Lodge and make all secure."

Morenarth bowed to him, though her mind was awhirl. "It shall be as you command."

Gwythyas left the Lodge and closed the door behind him. "Be alert," he said to the bard, and strode quickly to the outer door and eased it open a fraction.

Two Roman officers sat their horses in the middle of the courtyard. Near them two riderless horses were tethered to a post, and beyond the great gates he could see several dozen mounted Romans waiting. Even as he took all this in two soldiers came out of the library.

"Just full of parchments," said one of them. "Hundreds of them – but no sign of any Druids."

"Search that room there," said one of the officers, and pointed straight at him.

Gwythyas eased the door closed. "Go!" he whispered fiercely to the bard, and the youngster slipped through the side door just as the main doors were flung open. Gwythyas turned to face the intruders. "Stop!" he cried. "Thou hast no dominion here!"

The men hesitated and glanced back at their officers. Marcus and Flavius urged their horses forward. "And who are you?" the Centurion growled, and Flavius translated.

"I am Gwythyas, Guardian of the Lodge," he proclaimed, but his heart had begun to pound in his chest.

"Are you, now?" said Marcus, when that had been translated. "Flavius, tell him who we are and what –" But at that moment there came the deep tones of a bell – a huge bell, by the sound of it. "Stop that!" he snapped, and two soldiers raced outside. "So, sending a warning, are we?" he said coldly.

Flavius translated, and added, "If you wish to live, Druid, then I suggest you tell us where the cup is, and quickly."

"What cup is that?" said Gwythyas, but his voice betrayed him.

"You know which cup. Believe me, Druid, the Centurion will snuff out your life without a moment's thought. Now, where is it?"

The sounds of the bell ceased.

Gwythyas drew himself up. "You shall not have it," he cried. "It is now under our protection."

"So," said Marcus with grim satisfaction when that had been translated, "it *is* here. Search that room beyond."

Flavius moved as if to push past the Druid, but the man pulled a knife. Instantly, with an instinct born of years of training and bloody warfare, Flavius thrust upwards with his short sword straight into the man's heart. As the body toppled he pulled clear his sword and then reached for the man's knife. He straightened and carried it to the fire-basket, to see it more clearly, then turned back to the Centurion.

"It is a sham knife – a toy – a ceremonial knife, no more." The dead man lay on his back, his eyes staring. "I do not understand these Druids. Why would a man give his life for a baked clay bowl?"

"For the same reason the Emperor wants it," growled the Centurion, dismounting. "Whatever that is. Go and see what's happening outside."

Flavius left and Marcus walked to the door that the man had been trying to guard.

Inside the Lodge, Morenarth took her ear from the door and ran to the altar. She took the chalice containing the Grael and handed it to Tregereth. "Leave by the rear door. Hide the chalice where none may find it."

"But where . . . ? What . . . ?"

"Quickly, now. Go. Hide the Grael. Glanna and I will try to delay them here. You heard the bell. Even now the villagers will be racing down the hill to our rescue. Go! Go!"

Tregereth hurried away and slipped through the small door at the far end of the Lodge, and Morenarth turned to Glanna. "We must delay them as much as we can – cost what it may."

Glanna looked at her and her eyes were moist. Morenarth's heart ached for her. She was so young, so pure in heart. She put her hand on the younger girl's arm. "We shall be born again, Glanna, together in the Otherworld."

Glanna flung her arms around her. "Oh, yes, yes."

But then came a furious thudding on the Lodge door, and Morenarth gently put her by and reached for the glass bowl containing the Perpetual Light. "Open the door," she said calmly, "and then follow me – and if I fall, take the Light and bear it bravely."

Glanna ran to the door and grasped the handle. Morenarth raised the Light high and walked towards her. As she did so Glanna flung the door open and then moved to walk behind Morenarth in a procession of two.

The Centurion barred their way, sword in hand. He stared at the priestesses, and for a brief moment lust flared in his loins. But then he saw the bowl and the Light. "Give me that," he said roughly. Only the gods knew what reward Vespasian would give him for this. "Give it to me."

But Morenarth continued to walk forward, slowly, ritually, the Light held high, Glanna following behind her. Morenarth began the beautiful and very ancient chant that preceded the Rite of Love, which was always sung by the massed ranks of priestesses as the fires of Bel were being lit.

It was hauntingly lovely, and for a moment the Roman fell back. But then he recovered and stepped forward again. "Stop!" he cried, but Morenarth stared into his eyes, and for the first time in his life M. Cornelius Quintilianus felt fear in his heart.

He took a pace back, and then another as the priestess bore

down on him. Her eyes glittered strangely. It was no woman that stared at him from those strange eyes; it was Circe herself – the evil one, the witch-goddess.

"Back!" he cried, but still she came on. "Back, back!" And the Centurion raised his sword. Larger grew her eyes, glittering pools of fire in which he could see himself reflected. "Back, back!" he cried again, but the eyes grew and the power from them streamed into his soul.

In one savage burst of fury, to break himself free of the Druid spell, the Centurion brought his sword down with all his might and buried the blade in her neck.

The blood spurted high as he tugged the sword clear, and then, unbelievably, the priestess smiled at him and came on. Again he raised his sword and again he buried it in her neck. And again the blood spurted across her robe and ran down her body. The priestess smiled again and turned to her companion. "Take thou this Light, Maiden of the Grael," she said softly. "And let none take it from thee."

The other bowed, and with steady hands, so young, so tender, took the bowl. As she did so her friend sank to her knees, her eyes glazing over with death. Then the second priestess came on, bearing the bowl, singing that same sweet chant, though now there was sadness in it, grief and pain.

"Stop!" he cried, but she too came on. Again he backed away, and there came into his mind a red mist of shame and guilt. Again he raised his sword, and this time thrust it point-first into her young breast.

So slight was her maiden's body, so slender, that the sword pierced her completely. Slowly she sank to her knees, still bearing the Light, and unbelievably she smiled up at him. "This is not the cup you seek," she said gently.

He tried to free the sword but it would not move, and he could not bring himself to thrust his boot to her chest to lever it free. He let go and stepped back, and still she knelt there, the flame of the wick burning steadily.

Then a figure appeared in the Lodge doorway, and another young priestess entered. Slowly she walked forward and bent over her friend. Gently she took the Light from her, and as she did so the body fell sideways and the eyes closed.

Tregereth raised the bowl and looked at the Roman. "This is not the cup you seek," she said. "See, it is a glass bowl with a simple wick." And she turned and bore it away, back towards the altar.

"Where is the Cup then?" he bellowed. "Where is the Cup?"

Tregereth reverently placed the Light upon the altar and turned to face him. "It is beyond your reach, Roman. I have hidden it where you would not find it if you searched for a thousand years."

The main door crashed back and Flavius raced into the ante-chamber. "Hurry – the whole damn village is pouring down towards us. There are hundreds of them, hundreds and –" He stopped short as he took in the scene. "By all the powers, Marcus," he whispered, "what have you done?"

"They knew where the Cup is," the Centurion shouted, "but they would not tell me!" He stamped his boot on Glanna's chest and heaved his sword free. "But she knows – that one! She's hidden it!"

Flavius grabbed him. "Come away, Marcus! Haven't you done enough?"

The Centurion pulled himself free savagely. "I will have it, I tell you! I will have it!"

Tregereth walked softly to where Morenarth lay and gently placed her hand on her brow. "Wait for me," she said softly.

"Where is it?" shouted Marcus in a frenzy, his mouth foaming.

Flavius grabbed him again. "Come away, Marcus, or we are all dead! We few cannot stand against that horde. Come away – forget the cursed cup!"

Tregereth walked over to where Glanna's body lay. "Dear Glanna," she whispered, "you wait for me too. I am coming now. I am coming." And she turned to face the demented Roman.

The Centurion wrenched himself free, raced over to her and seized her by the throat. "Where is the cup, you bitch-maiden? Where is it?"

The red, bloated face of the Roman was so close she could feel his foul breath on her. His fingers dug into her throat cruelly, but Tregereth smiled. "You will never know, Roman," she whispered hoarsely. "You will never know."

In the frenzy of the moment the Centurion snatched a long, thin-bladed knife from his belt and thrust it upwards with all the force he could muster, so that the blade plunged into her chest and pierced her heart.

"You will never know . . ."

The Roman let out a cry of bestial rage and flung the body aside. And then, and only then, could Flavius lead him away.

*   *   *

The young bard who had sounded the alarm now crept out of hiding, his face full of tears – of grief, of pain and of shame that he had been able to do naught but watch the tragedy unfold.

But there was awe in his heart as well, and pride. He crept to Glanna and with his new blue robe began to wipe the blood from her face, and he cried and cried until he thought his heart would break.

And there they found him and heard his tale, and when he had done the healer-priests bore him sobbing away.

Gwyryoneth and Barenwyn remained in the antechamber, their hearts aching with grief. Gwyrdôn came in to report that the Romans had ridden away in time.

Gwyryoneth sighed. "They will be required to pay their debt to the life-force in due time." He looked down at the four bodies. "Great honour came to Druidry today," he said softly.

"But where is the Cup?" said Gwyrdôn. "And where the chalice?"

"It is hidden from our eyes too," said Barenwyn quietly. "Do not ask me how I know, for I would be unable to tell you." She looked up at them both. "Oh, we will hunt for it; our bards will scour the whole of Glaston for it. But it will not be found. The inner have concealed it, using Tregereth as their instrument – hidden it until a son of the Dragon shall find it, long after we are dead."

Gwyryoneth walked slowly and painfully to the altar and lifted the Perpetual Light high in the air. "To the Grail Maidens of the far future!" he cried. "Here has begun thy tale; begun with great courage and sacrifice. Do so thou likewise when thy time comes!"

THE STORY OF PEREDUR

Lady Charlotte Guest

Charlotte Guest (1812–1895), the daughter of the Earl of Lindsey, began a translation of the Welsh texts of The Mabinogion *in her early twenties, publishing the first of her translations in 1838, and the complete text in three volumes in 1849. During this time she became fascinated with the connections between the Celtic tales and the French Arthurian romances, and her extensive researches resulted in an abundance of notes attached to the final edition. These are not only a fascinating read but became a premier source for Arthurian research. The publication of* The Mabinogion *was a spur to the revival of interest in Arthurian legend, and in part inspired Tennyson's twelve-poem work* Idylls of the King, *which began to appear in 1859. With this story we have moved into the known Arthurian world, though one drawn from Celtic sources rather than the romanticized French adaptations. The story is that of Peredur, the son of Evrawc, and with it we encounter the Grail Castle and first discover the mysteries of the Grail Procession. I published Roger Lancelyn Green's more abbreviated version of this story in* The Pendragon Chronicles, *but here it is presented in its full power and glory.*

Earl Evrawc owned the Earldom of the North. And he had seven sons. And Evrawc maintained himself not so much by his own possessions as by attending tournaments, and wars, and combats. And, as it often befalls those who join in encounters and wars, he was slain, and six of his sons likewise. Now the name of his seventh son was Peredur, and he was the youngest of them. And he was not of an age to go to wars and encounters, otherwise he might have been slain as well as his father and brothers. His mother was a scheming and thoughtful woman, and she was very solicitous concerning this her only son and his possessions. So she took counsel with herself to leave the inhabited country, and to flee to the deserts and unfrequented wildernesses. And she permitted none to bear her company thither but women and boys, and spiritless men, who were both unaccustomed and unequal to war and fighting. And none dared to bring either horses or arms where her son was, lest he should set his mind upon them. And the youth went daily to divert himself in the forest, by flinging sticks and staves. And one day he saw his mother's flock of goats, and near the goats two hinds were standing. And he marvelled greatly that these two should be without horns, while the others had them. And he thought they had long run wild, and on that account they had lost their horns. And by activity and swiftness of foot, he drove the hinds and the goats together into the house which there was for the goats at the extremity of the forest. Then Peredur returned to his mother. "Ah, mother," said he, "a marvellous thing have I seen in the wood; two of thy goats have run wild, and lost their horns, through their having been so long missing in the wood. And no man had ever more trouble than I had to drive them in." Then they all arose and went to see. And when they beheld the hinds they were greatly astonished.

And one day they saw three knights coming along the horse-road on the borders of the forest. And the three knights were Gwalchmai the son of Gwyar, and Geneir Gwystyl, and Owain the son of Urien. And Owain kept on the track of the knight who had divided the apples in Arthur's Court, whom they were in pursuit of.

"Mother," said Peredur, "what are those yonder?"

"They are angels, my son," said she.

"By my faith," said Peredur, "I will go and become an angel with them." And Peredur went to the road, and met them.

"Tell me, good soul," said Owain, "sawest thou a knight pass this way, either to-day or yesterday?"

"I know not," answered he, "what a knight is."

"Such an one as I am," said Owain.

"If thou wilt tell me what I ask thee, I will tell thee that which thou askest me."

"Gladly will I do so," replied Owain.

"What is this?" demanded Peredur, concerning the saddle.

"It is a saddle," said Owain.

Then he asked about all the accoutrements which he saw upon the men, and the horses, and the arms, and what they were for, and how they were used. And Owain shewed him all these things fully, and told him what use was made of them. "Go forward," said Peredur, "for I saw such an one as thou inquirest for, and I will follow thee."

Then Peredur returned to his mother and her company, and he said to her, "Mother, those were not angels, but honourable knights." Then his mother swooned away. And Peredur went to the place where they kept the horses that carried firewood, and that brought meat and drink from the inhabited country to the desert. And he took a bony piebald horse, which seemed to him the strongest of them. And he pressed a pack into the form of a saddle, and with twisted twigs he imitated the trappings which he had seen upon the horses. And when Peredur came again to his mother, the Countess had recovered from her swoon. "My son," said she, "desirest thou to ride forth?" "Yes, with thy leave," said he. "Wait, then, that I may counsel thee before thou goest." "Willingly," he answered; "speak quickly." "Go forward, then," she said, "to the Court of Arthur, where there are the best, and the boldest, and the most bountiful of men. And wherever thou seest a church, repeat there thy Paternoster unto it. And if thou see meat and drink, and have need of them, and none have the kindness or the courtesy to give them to thee, take them thyself. If thou hear an outcry, proceed towards it, especially if it be the outcry of a woman. If thou see a fair jewel, possess thyself of it, and give it to another, for thus thou shalt obtain praise. If thou see a fair woman, pay thy court to her, whether she will or no; for thus thou wilt render thyself a better and more esteemed man than thou wast before."

After this discourse, Peredur mounted the horse, and taking a handful of sharp-pointed forks in his hand, he rode forth. And he journeyed two days and two nights in the woody wildernesses, and in desert places, without food and without drink. And then he came to a vast wild wood, and far within the wood he saw a fair even glade, and in the glade he saw a tent, and the tent seeming to him to be a church, he repeated his Paternoster to it. And he went towards it, and the door of the tent was open. And a golden chair was near the door. And on the chair sat a lovely auburn-haired maiden, with a golden frontlet on her forehead,

and sparkling stones in the frontlet, and with a large gold ring
on her hand. And Peredur dismounted, and entered the tent. And
the maiden was glad at his coming, and bade him welcome. At the
entrance of the tent he saw food, and two flasks full of wine, and
two loaves of fine wheaten flour, and collops of the flesh of the
wild boar. "My mother told me," said Peredur, "wheresoever I
saw meat and drink, to take it," "Take the meat and welcome,
chieftain," said she. So Peredur took half of the meat and of the
liquor himself, and left the rest to the maiden. And when Peredur
had finished eating, he bent upon his knee before the maiden. "My
mother," said he, "told me, wheresoever I saw a fair jewel, to take
it." "Do so, my soul," said she. So Peredur took the ring. And he
mounted his horse, and proceeded on his journey.

After this, behold the knight came to whom the tent belonged;
and he was the Lord of the Glade. And he saw the track of the
horse, and he said to the maiden, "Tell me who has been here since
I departed." "A man," said she, "of wonderful demeanour." And
she described to him what Peredur's appearance and conduct had
been. "Tell me," said he, "did he offer thee any wrong?" "No,"
answered the maiden, "by my faith, he harmed me not." "By my
faith, I do not believe thee; and until I can meet with him, and
revenge the insult he has done me, and wreak my vengeance upon
him, thou shalt not remain two nights in the same house." And
the knight arose, and set forth to seek Peredur.

Meanwhile Peredur journeyed on towards Arthur's Court. And
before he reached it, another knight had been there, who gave a ring
of thick gold at the door of the gate for holding his horse, and went
into the Hall where Arthur and his household, and Gwenhwyvar
and her maidens, were assembled. And the page of the chamber
was serving Gwenhwyvar with a golden goblet. Then the knight
dashed the liquor that was therein upon her face, and upon her
stomacher, and gave her a violent blow on the face, and said,
"If any have the boldness to dispute this goblet with me, and
to revenge the insult to Gwenhwyvar, let him follow me to the
meadow, and there I will await him." So the knight took his horse,
and rode to the meadow. And all the household hung down their
heads, lest any of them should be requested to go and avenge the
insult to Gwenhwyvar. For it seemed to them, that no one would
have ventured on so daring an outrage, unless he possessed such
powers, through magic or charms, that none could be able to take
vengeance upon him. Then, behold, Peredur entered the Hall, upon
the bony piebald horse, with the uncouth trappings upon it; and in

this way he traversed the whole length of the Hall. In the centre of the Hall stood Kai. "Tell me, tall man," said Peredur, "is that Arthur yonder?" "What wouldest thou with Arthur?" asked Kai. "My mother told me to go to Arthur, and receive the honour of knighthood." "By my faith," said he, "thou art all too meanly equipped with horse and with arms." Thereupon he was perceived by all the household, and they threw sticks at him. Then, behold, a dwarf came forward. He had already been a year at Arthur's Court, both he and a female dwarf. They had craved harbourage of Arthur, and had obtained it; and during the whole year, neither of them had spoken a single word to any one. When the dwarf beheld Peredur, "Haha!" said he, "the welcome of Heaven be unto thee, goodly Peredur, son of Evrawc, the chief of warriors, and flower of knighthood." "Truly," said Kai, "thou art ill-taught to remain a year mute at Arthur's Court, with choice of society; and now, before the face of Arthur and all his household, to call out, and declare such a man as this the chief of warriors, and the flower of knighthood." And he gave him such a box on the ear that he fell senseless to the ground. Then exclaimed the female dwarf, "Haha! goodly Peredur, son of Evrawc; the welcome of Heaven be unto thee, flower of knights, and light of chivalry." "Of a truth, maiden," said Kai, "thou art ill-bred to remain mute for a year at the Court of Arthur, and then to speak as thou dost of such a man as this." And Kai kicked her with his foot, so that she fell to the ground senseless. "Tall man," said Peredur, "shew me which is Arthur." "Hold thy peace," said Kai, "and go after the knight who went hence to the meadow, and take from him the goblet, and overthrow him, and possess thyself of his horse and arms, and then thou shalt receive the order of knighthood." "I will do so, tall man," said Peredur. So he turned his horse's head towards the meadow. And when he came there, the knight was riding up and down, proud of his strength, and valour, and noble mien. "Tell me," said the knight, "didst thou see any one coming after me from the Court?" "The tall man that was there," said he, "desired me to come, and overthrow thee, and to take from thee the goblet, and thy horse and thy armour for myself." "Silence!" said the knight; "go back to the Court, and tell Arthur, from me, either to come himself, or to send some other to fight with me; and unless he do so quickly, I will not wait for him." "By my faith," said Peredur, "choose thou whether it shall be willingly or unwillingly, but I will have the horse, and the arms, and the goblet." And upon this the knight ran at him furiously, and struck him a violent blow with the shaft of his spear, between the neck and the shoulder. "Haha! lad," said Peredur, "my mother's servants were not used to play with me in this wise; therefore, thus will I play with thee." And thereupon he struck him with a sharp-pointed fork, and it hit him in the eye, and came out at the back of his neck, so that he instantly fell down lifeless.

"Verily," said Owain the son of Urien to Kai, "thou wert ill-advised, when thou didst send that madman after the knight. For one of two things must befall him. He must either be overthrown, or slain. If he is overthrown by the knight, he will be counted by him to be an honourable person of the Court, and an eternal disgrace will it be to Arthur and his warriors. And if he is slain, the disgrace will be the same, and moreover, his sin will be upon him; therefore will I go to see what has befallen him." So Owain went to the meadow, and he found Peredur dragging the man about. "What art thou doing thus?" said Owain. "This iron coat," said Peredur, "will never come from off him; not by my efforts, at any rate." And Owain unfastened his armour and his clothes. "Here, my good soul," said he, "is a horse and armour better than thine. Take them joyfully, and come with me to Arthur, to receive the order of knighthood, for thou dost merit it." "May I never shew my face again if I go," said Peredur; "but take thou the goblet to Gwenhwyvar, and tell Arthur, that wherever I am, I will be his vassal, and will do him what profit and service I am able. And say that I will not come to his Court until I have encountered the tall man that is there, to revenge the injury he did to the dwarf and dwarfess." And Owain went back to the Court, and related all these things to Arthur and Gwenhwyvar, and to all the household.

And Peredur rode forward. And as he proceeded, behold a knight met him. "Whence comest thou?" said the knight. "I come from Arthur's Court," said Peredur. "Art thou one of his men?" asked he. "Yes, by my faith," he answered. "A good service, truly, is that of Arthur." "Wherefore sayest thou so?" said Peredur. "I will tell thee," said he; "I have always been Arthur's enemy, and all such of his men as I have ever encountered I have slain." And without further parlance they fought, and it was not long before Peredur brought him to the ground, over his horse's crupper. Then the knight besought his mercy. "Mercy thou shalt have," said Peredur, "if thou wilt make oath to me, that thou wilt go to Arthur's Court, and tell him that it was I that overthrew thee, for the honour of his service; and say, that I will never come to the Court until I have avenged the insult offered to the dwarf and dwarfess." The knight pledged him his faith of this, and proceeded to the Court of Arthur, and said as he had promised, and conveyed the threat to Kai.

And Peredur rode forward. And within that week he encountered sixteen knights, and overthrew them all shamefully. And they all went to Arthur's Court, taking with them the same message which the first knight had conveyed from Peredur, and the same threat which he had sent to Kai. And thereupon Kai was reproved by Arthur; and Kai was greatly grieved thereat.

And Peredur rode forward. And he came to a vast and desert wood, on the confines of which was a lake. And on the other side was a fair castle. And on the border of the lake he saw a venerable, hoary-headed man, sitting upon a velvet cushion, and having a garment of velvet upon him. And his attendants were fishing in the lake. When the hoary-headed man beheld Peredur approaching, he arose and went towards the castle. And the old man was lame. Peredur rode to the palace, and the door was open, and he entered the hall. And there was the hoary-headed man sitting on a cushion, and a large blazing fire burning before him. And the household and the company arose to meet Peredur, and disarrayed him. And the man asked the youth to sit on the cushion; and they sat down, and conversed together. When it was time, the tables were laid, and they went to meat. And when they had finished their meal, the man inquired of Peredur if he knew well how to fight with the sword. "I know not," said Peredur, "but were I to be taught, doubtless I should." "Whoever can play well with the cudgel and shield, will also be able to fight with a sword." And the man had two sons; the one had yellow hair, and the other auburn. "Arise, youths," said he, "and play with the cudgel and the shield." And so did they. "Tell me, my soul," said the man, "which of the youths thinkest thou plays best." "I think," said Peredur, "that the yellow-haired youth could draw blood from the other, if he chose." "Arise thou, my life, and take the cudgel and the shield from the hand of the youth with the auburn hair, and draw blood from the yellow-haired youth if thou canst." So Peredur arose, and went to play with the yellow-haired youth; and he lifted up his arm, and struck him such a mighty blow, that his brow fell over his eye, and the blood flowed forth. "Ah, my life," said the man, "come now, and sit down, for thou wilt become the best fighter with the sword of any in this island; and I am thy uncle, thy mother's brother. And with me shalt thou remain a space, in order to learn the manners and customs of different countries, and courtesy, and gentleness, and noble bearing. Leave, then, the habits and the discourse of thy mother, and I will be thy teacher; and I will raise thee to the rank of knight from this time forward. And thus do thou. If thou seest aught to cause thee wonder, ask not the meaning of it; if no one has the courtesy to inform thee, the reproach will not fall upon thee, but upon me that am thy teacher." And they had abundance of honour and service. And when it was time they went to sleep. At the break of day, Peredur arose, and took his horse, and with his uncle's permission he rode forth. And he came to a vast desert wood, and at the further end of the wood was a meadow, and on the other side of the meadow he saw a large castle. And thitherward Peredur bent his way, and he found the gate open, and he proceeded to the hall. And he beheld a stately hoary-headed man sitting on one side of the hall, and many pages around him, who arose to receive and to honour Peredur. And they placed him by the side of the owner of the palace. Then they discoursed together; and when it was time to eat, they caused Peredur to sit beside the nobleman during the repast. And when they had eaten and drunk as much as they desired, the nobleman asked Peredur whether he could fight with a sword? "Were I to receive instruction," said Peredur, "I think I could." Now, there was on the floor of the hall a huge staple, as large as a warrior could grasp. "Take yonder sword," said the man to Peredur, "and strike the iron staple." So Peredur arose and struck the staple, so that he cut it in two; and the sword broke into two parts also. "Place the two parts together, and reunite them," and Peredur placed them together, and they became entire as they were before. And a second time he struck upon the staple, so that both it and the sword broke in two, and as before they reunited. And the third time he gave a like blow, and placed the broken parts together, and neither the staple nor the sword would unite as before. "Youth," said the nobleman, "come now, and sit down, and my blessing be upon thee. Thou fightest best with the sword of any man in the kingdom. Thou hast arrived at two-thirds of thy strength, and the other third thou hast not yet obtained; and when thou attainest to thy full power, none will be able to contend with thee. I am thy uncle, thy mother's brother, and I am brother to the man in whose house thou wast last night." Then Peredur and his uncle discoursed together, and he beheld two youths enter the hall, and proceed up to the chamber, bearing a spear of mighty size, with three streams of blood flowing from the point to the ground. And when all the company saw this, they began wailing and lamenting. But for all that, the man did not break off his discourse with Peredur. And as he did not tell Peredur the measuring or what he saw, he forbore to ask him concerning it. And when the clamour had a little subsided, behold two maidens entered, with a large salver between them, in which was a man's head, surrounded by a profusion of blood. And thereupon the company of the court made so great an outcry, that it was irksome to be in the same hall with them. But at length they were silent. And when time was that they should sleep, Peredur was brought into a fair chamber.

And the next day, with his uncle's permission, he rode forth. And he came to a wood, and far within the wood he heard a loud cry, and he saw a beautiful woman with auburn hair, and a horse with a saddle upon it, standing near her, and a corpse by her side. And as she strove to place the corpse upon the horse, it fell to the ground, and thereupon she made a great lamentation. "Tell me, sister," said Peredur, "wherefore art thou bewailing?" "Oh! accursed Peredur, little pity has my ill-fortune ever met with from thee." "Wherefore," said Peredur, "am I accursed?" "Because thou wast the cause of thy mother's death; for when thou didst ride forth against her will, anguish seized upon her heart, so that she died; and therefore art thou accursed. And the dwarf and the dwarfess that thou sawest at Arthur's Court were the dwarfs of thy father and mother; and I am thy foster-sister, and this was my wedded husband, and he was slain by the knight that is in the glade in the wood; and do not thou go near him, lest thou shouldest be slain by him likewise." "My sister, thou dost reproach me wrongfully; through my having so long remained amongst you, I shall scarcely vanquish him; and had I continued longer, it would, indeed, be difficult for me to succeed. Cease, therefore, thy lamenting, for it is of no avail, and I will bury the body, and then I will go in quest of the knight, and see if I can do vengeance upon him." And when he had buried the body, they went to the place where the knight was, and found him riding proudly along the glade; and he inquired of Peredur whence he came. "I come from Arthur's Court." "And art thou one of Arthur's men?" "Yes, by my faith." "A profitable alliance, truly, is that of Arthur." And without further parlance, they encountered one another, and immediately Peredur overthrew the knight, and he besought mercy of Peredur. "Mercy shalt thou have," said he, "upon these terms, that thou take this woman in marriage, and do her all the honour and reverence in thy power, seeing thou hast, without cause, slain her wedded husband; and that thou go to Arthur's Court, and shew him that it was I that overthrew thee, to do him honour and service; and that thou tell

him that I will never come to his Court again until I have met
with the tall man that is there, to take vengeance upon him for
his insult to the dwarf and dwarfess." And he took the knight's
assurance, that he would perform all this. Then the knight provided
the lady with a horse and garments that were suitable for her, and
took her with him to Arthur's Court. And he told Arthur all that
had occurred, and gave the defiance to Kai. And Arthur and all
his household reproved Kai, for having driven such a youth as
Peredur from his Court.

Said Owain the son of Urien, "This youth will never come into
the Court until Kai has gone forth from it." "By my faith," said
Arthur, "I will search all the deserts in the Island of Britain, until
I find Peredur, and then let him and his adversary do their utmost
to each other."

Then Peredur rode forward. And he came to a desert wood,
where he saw not the track either of men or animals, and where
there was nothing but bushes and weeds. And at the upper end of
the wood he saw a vast castle, wherein were many strong towers;
and when he came near the gate, he found the weeds taller than he
had seen them elsewhere. And he struck the gate with the shaft of
his lance, and thereupon behold a lean, auburn-haired youth came
to an opening in the battlements. "Choose thou, chieftain," said
he, "whether shall I open the gate unto thee, or shall I announce
unto those that are chief, that thou art at the gateway?" "Say
that I am here," said Peredur, "and if it is desired that I should
enter, I will go in." And the youth came back, and opened the
gate for Peredur. And when he went into the hall, he beheld
eighteen youths, lean and red-headed, of the same height, and
of the same aspect, and of the same dress, and of the same age
as the one who had opened the gate for him. And they were well
skilled in courtesy and in service. And they disarrayed him. Then
they sat down to discourse. Thereupon, behold five maidens came
from the chamber into the hall. And Peredur was certain that he
had never seen another of so fair an aspect as the chief of the
maidens. And she had an old garment of satin upon her, which
had once been handsome, but was then so tattered, that her skin
could be seen through it. And whiter was her skin than the bloom
of crystal, and her hair and her two eyebrows were blacker than
jet, and on her cheeks were two red spots, redder than whatever
is reddest. And the maiden welcomed Peredur, and put her arms
about his neck, and made him sit down beside her. Not long after
this he saw two nuns enter, and a flask full of wine was borne by

one, and six loaves of white bread by the other. "Lady," said they, "Heaven is witness, that there is not so much of food and liquor as this left in yonder Convent this night." Then they went to meat, and Peredur observed that the maiden wished to give more of the food and of the liquor to him than to any of the others. "My sister," said Peredur, "I will share out the food and the liquor." "Not so, my soul," said she. "By my faith but I will." So Peredur took the bread, and he gave an equal portion of it to each alike, as well as a cup full of the liquor. And when it was time for them to sleep, a chamber was prepared for Peredur, and he went to rest.

"Behold, sister," said the youths to the fairest and most exalted of the maidens, "we have counsel for thee." "What may it be?" she inquired. "Go to the youth that is in the upper chamber, and offer to become his wife, or the lady of his love, if it seem well to him." "That were indeed unfitting," said she. "Hitherto I have not been the lady-love of any knight, and to make him such an offer before I am wooed by him, that, truly, can I not do." "By our confession to Heaven, unless thou actest thus, we will leave thee here to thy enemies, to do as they will with thee." And through fear of this, the maiden went forth; and shedding tears, she proceeded to the chamber. And with the noise of the door opening, Peredur awoke; and the maiden was weeping and lamenting. "Tell me, my sister," said Peredur, "wherefore dost thou weep?" "I will tell thee, lord," said she. "My father possessed these dominions as their chief, and this palace was his, and with it he held the best earldom in the kingdom; then the son of another earl sought me of my father, and I was not willing to be given unto him, and my father would not give me against my will, either to him or any earl in the world. And my father had no child except myself. And after my father's death, these dominions came into my own hands, and then was I less willing to accept him than before. So he made war upon me, and conquered all my possessions, except this one house. And through the valour of the men whom thou hast seen, who are my foster-brothers, and the strength of the house, it can never be taken while food and drink remain. And now our provisions are exhausted; but, as thou hast seen, we have been fed by the nuns, to whom the country is free. And at length they also are without supply of food or liquor. And at no later date than tomorrow, the earl will come against this place with all his forces; and if I fall into his power, my fate will be no better than to be given over to the grooms of his horses. Therefore, lord, I am come to offer to place myself in thy hands, that thou mayest succour me, either by taking me hence, or by defending me here, whichever may seem best unto thee." "Go, my sister," said he, "and sleep; nor will I depart from thee until I do that which thou requirest, or prove whether I can assist thee or not." The maiden went again to rest; and the next morning she came to Peredur, and saluted him. "Heaven prosper thee, my soul, and what tidings dost thou bring?" "None other, than that the earl and all his forces have alighted at the gate, and I never beheld any place so covered with tents, and thronged with knights challenging others to the combat." "Truly," said Peredur, "let my horse be made ready." So his horse was accoutred, and he arose and sallied forth to the meadow. And there was a knight riding proudly along the meadow, having raised the signal for battle. And they encountered, and Peredur threw the knight over his horse's crupper to the ground. And at the close of the day, one of the chief knights came to fight with him, and he overthrew him also, so that he besought his mercy. "Who art thou?" said Peredur. "Verily," said he, "I am Master of the Household to the earl." "And how much of the countess's possessions is there in thy power?" "The third part, verily," answered he. "Then," said Peredur, "restore to her the third of her possessions in full, and all the profit thou hast made by them, and bring meat and drink for a hundred men, with their horses and arms, to her court this night. And thou shalt remain her captive, unless she wish to take thy life." And this he did forthwith. And that night the maiden was right joyful, and they fared plenteously.

And the next day Peredur rode forth to the meadow; and that day he vanquished a multitude of the host. And at the close of the day, there came a proud and stately knight, and Peredur overthrew him, and he besought his mercy. "Who art thou?" said Peredur. "I am Steward of the Palace," said he. "And how much of the maiden's possessions are under thy control?" "One-third part," answered he. "Verily," said Peredur, "thou shalt fully restore to the maiden her possessions, and, moreover, thou shalt give her meat and drink for two hundred men, and their horses and their arms. And for thyself, thou shalt be her captive." And immediately it was so done.

And the third day Peredur rode forth to the meadow; and he vanquished more that day than on either of the preceding. And at the close of the day, an earl came to encounter him, and he overthrew him, and he besought his mercy. "Who art thou?" said Peredur. "I am the earl," said he. "I will not conceal it from thee." "Verily," said Peredur, "thou shalt restore the whole of the maiden's earldom, and shalt give her thine own earldom in addition thereto, and meat and drink for three hundred men, and their horses and arms, and thou thyself shalt remain in her power." And thus it was fulfilled. And Peredur tarried three weeks in the country, causing tribute and obedience to be paid to the maiden, and the government to be placed in her hands. "With thy leave," said Peredur, "I will go hence." "Verily, my brother, desirest thou this?" "Yes, by my faith; and had it not been for love of thee, I should not have been here thus long." "My soul," said she, "who art thou?" "I am Peredur the son of Evrawc from the North; and if ever thou art in trouble or in danger, acquaint me therewith, and if I can, I will protect thee."

So Peredur rode forth. And far thence there met him a lady, mounted on a horse that was lean, and covered with sweat; and she saluted the youth. "Whence comest thou, my sister?" Then she told him the cause of her journey. Now she was the wife of the Lord of the Glade. "Behold," said he, "I am the knight through whom thou art in trouble, and he shall repent it, who has treated thee thus." Thereupon, behold a knight rode up, and he inquired of Peredur, if he had seen a knight such as he was seeking. "Hold thy peace," said Peredur, "I am he whom thou seekest; and by my faith, thou deservest ill of thy household for thy treatment of the maiden, for she is innocent concerning me." So they encountered, and they were not long in combat ere Peredur overthrew the knight, and he besought his mercy. "Mercy thou shalt have," said Peredur, "so thou wilt return by the way thou camest, and declare that thou holdest the maiden innocent, and so that thou wilt acknowledge unto her the reverse thou hast sustained at my hands." And the knight plighted him his faith thereto.

Then Peredur rode forward. And above him he beheld a castle, and thitherward he went. And he struck upon the gate with his lance, and then, behold, a comely auburn-haired youth opened the gate, and he had the stature of a warrior, and the years of a boy. And when Peredur came into the hall, there was a tall and stately lady sitting in a chair, and many handmaidens around her; and the lady rejoiced at his coming. And when it was time, they went to meat. And after their repast was finished, "It were well for thee, chieftain," said she, "to go elsewhere to sleep." "Wherefore can I not sleep here?" said Peredur. "Nine sorceresses are here, my soul, of the sorceresses of Gloucester, and their father and their mother are with them; and unless we can make our escape before daybreak, we shall be slain; and already they have conquered and

laid waste all the country, except this one dwelling." "Behold,"
said Peredur, "I will remain here to-night, and if you are in
trouble, I will do you what service I can; but harm shall you
not receive from me." So they went to rest. And with the break
of day, Peredur heard a dreadful outcry. And he hastily arose, and
went forth in his vest and his doublet, with his sword about his
neck, and he saw a sorceress overtake one of the watch, who cried
out violently. Peredur attacked the sorceress, and struck her upon
the head with his sword, so that he flattened her helmet and her
head-piece like a dish upon her head. "Thy mercy, goodly Peredur,
son of Evrawc, and the mercy of Heaven." "How knowest thou,
hag, that I am Peredur?" "By destiny, and the foreknowledge that
I should suffer harm from thee. And thou shalt take a horse and
armour of me; and with me thou shalt go to learn chivalry and the
use of thy arms." Said Peredur, "Thou shalt have mercy, if thou
pledge thy faith thou wilt never more injure the dominions of the
Countess." And Peredur took surety of this, and with permission
of the Countess, he set forth with the sorceress to the palace of
the sorceresses. And there he remained for three weeks, and then
he made choice of a horse and arms, and went his way.

And in the evening he entered a valley, and at the head of the
valley he came to a hermit's cell, and the hermit welcomed him
gladly, and there he spent the night. And in the morning he arose,
and when he went forth, behold a shower of snow had fallen the
night before, and a hawk had killed a wild fowl in front of the
cell. And the noise of the horse scared the hawk away, and a
raven alighted upon the bird. And Peredur stood, and compared
the blackness of the raven and the whiteness of the snow, and the
redness of the blood, to the hair of the lady that best he loved,
which was blacker than jet, and to her skin which was whiter than
the snow, and to the two red spots upon her cheeks, which were
redder than the blood upon the snow appeared to be.

Now Arthur and his household were in search of Peredur. "Know
ye," said Arthur, "who is the knight with the long spear that stands
by the brook up yonder?" "Lord," said one of them, "I will go and
learn who he is." So the youth came to the place where Peredur
was, and asked him what he did thus, and who he was. And from
the intensity with which he thought upon the lady whom best he
loved, he gave him no answer. Then the youth thrust at Peredur
with his lance, and Peredur turned upon him, and struck him over
his horse's crupper to the ground. And after this, four-and-twenty
youths came to him, and he did not answer one more than another,

but gave the same reception to all, bringing them with one single thrust to the ground. And then came Kai, and spoke to Peredur rudely and angrily; and Peredur took him with his lance under the jaw, and cast him from him with a thrust, so that he broke his arm and his shoulder-blade, and he rode over him one-and-twenty times. And while he lay thus, stunned with the violence of the pain that he had suffered, his horse returned back at a wild and prancing pace. And when the household saw the horse come back without his rider, they rode forth in haste to the place where the encounter had been. And when they first came there, they thought that Kai was slain; but they found that if he had a skilful physician, he yet might live. And Peredur moved not from his meditation, on seeing the concourse that was around Kai. And Kai was brought to Arthur's tent, and Arthur caused skilful physicians to come to him. And Arthur was grieved that Kai had met with this reverse, for he loved him greatly.

"Then," said Gwalchmai, "it is not fitting that any should disturb an honourable knight from his thought unadvisedly; for either he is pondering some damage that he has sustained, or he is thinking of the lady whom best he loves. And through such ill-advised proceeding, perchance this misadventure has befallen him who last met with him. And if it seem well to thee, lord, I will go and see if this knight hath changed from his thought; and if he has, I will ask him courteously to come and visit thee." Then Kai was wroth, and he spoke angry and spiteful words. "Gwalchmai," said he, "I know that thou wilt bring him because he is fatigued. Little praise and honour, nevertheless, wilt thou have from vanquishing a weary knight, who is tired with fighting. Yet thus hast thou gained the advantage over many. And while thy speech and thy soft words last, a coat of thin linen were armour sufficient for thee, and thou wilt not need to break either lance or sword in fighting with the knight in the state he is in." Then said Gwalchmai to Kai, "Thou mightest use more pleasant words, wert thou so minded: and it behoves thee not upon me to wreak thy wrath and thy displeasure. Methinks I shall bring the knight hither with me without breaking either my arm or my shoulder." Then said Arthur to Gwalchmai, "Thou speakest like a wise and prudent man; go, and take enough of armour about thee, and choose thy horse." And Gwalchmai accoutred himself, and rode forward hastily to the place where Peredur was.

And Peredur was resting on the shaft of his spear, pondering the same thought, and Gwalchmai came to him without any signs of hostility, and said to him, "If I thought that it would be as agreeable to thee as it would be to me, I would converse with thee. I have also a message from Arthur unto thee, to pray thee to come and visit him. And two men have been before on this errand." "That is true," said Peredur, "and uncourteously they came. They attacked me, and I was annoyed thereat, for it was not pleasing to me to be drawn from the thought that I was in, for I was thinking of the lady whom best I love, and thus was she brought to my mind: – I was looking upon the snow, and upon the raven, and upon the drops of the blood of the bird that the hawk had killed upon the snow. And I bethought me that her whiteness was like that of the snow, and that the blackness of her hair and her eyebrows like that of the raven, and that the two red spots upon her cheeks were like the two drops of blood." Said Gwalchmai, "This was not an ungentle thought, and I should marvel if it were pleasant to thee to be drawn from it." "Tell me," said Peredur, "is Kai in Arthur's Court?" "He is," said he, "and behold he is the knight that fought with thee last; and it would have been better for him had he not come, for his arm and his shoulder-blade were broken with the fall which he had from thy spear." "Verily," said Peredur, "I am not sorry to have thus begun to avenge the insult to the dwarf and dwarfess." Then Gwalchmai marvelled to hear him speak of the dwarf and the dwarfess; and he approached him, and threw his arms around his neck, and asked him what was his name. "Peredur the son of Evrawc am I called," said he; "and thou, Who art thou?" "I am called Gwalchmai," he replied. "I am right glad to meet with thee," said Peredur, "for in every country where I have been I have heard of thy fame for prowess and uprightness, and I solicit thy fellowship." "Thou shalt have it, by my faith, and grant me thine," said he. "Gladly will I do so," answered Peredur.

So they rode forth together joyfully towards the place where Arthur was, and when Kai saw them coming, he said, "I knew that Gwalchmai needed not to fight the knight. And it is no wonder that he should gain fame; more can he do by his fair words than I by the strength of my arm." And Peredur went with Gwalchmai to his tent, and they took off their armour. And Peredur put on garments like those that Gwalchmai wore, and they went together unto Arthur, and saluted him. "Behold, lord," said Gwalchmai, "him whom thou hast sought so long." "Welcome unto thee, chieftain," said Arthur. "With me thou shalt remain; and had I known thy valour had been such, thou shouldst not have left me as thou didst; nevertheless, this was predicted of thee by the dwarf and the dwarfess, whom Kai ill-treated and whom thou hast avenged." And hereupon, behold there came the Queen and her handmaidens, and Peredur saluted them. And they were rejoiced to see him, and bade him welcome. And Arthur did him great honour and respect, and they returned towards Caerlleon.

And the first night Peredur came to Caerlleon to Arthur's Court, and as he walked in the city after his repast, behold, there met him Angharad Law Eurawc. "By my faith, sister," said Peredur, "thou art a beauteous and lovely maiden; and, were it pleasing to thee, I could love thee above all women." "I pledge my faith," said she, "that I do not love thee, nor will I ever do so." "I also pledge my faith," said Peredur, "that I will never speak a word to any Christian again, until thou come to love me above all men."

The next day Peredur went forth by the high road, along a mountain-ridge, and he saw a valley of a circular form, the confines of which were rocky and wooded. And the flat part of the valley was in meadows, and there were fields betwixt the meadows and the wood. And in the bosom of the wood he saw large black houses of uncouth workmanship. And he dismounted, and led his horse towards the wood. And a little way within the wood he saw a rocky ledge, along which the road lay. And upon the ledge was a lion bound by a chain, and sleeping. And beneath the lion he saw a deep pit of immense size, full of the bones of men and animals. And Peredur drew his sword and struck the lion, so that he fell into the mouth of the pit and hung there by the chain; and with a second blow he struck the chain and broke it, and the lion fell into the pit; and Peredur led his horse over the rocky ledge, until he came into the valley. And in the centre of the valley he saw a fair castle, and he went towards it. And in the meadow by the castle he beheld a huge grey man sitting, who was larger than any man he had ever before seen. And two young pages were shooting the hilts of their daggers, of the bone of the sea-horse. And one of the pages had red hair, and the other auburn. And they went before him to the place where the grey man was, and Peredur saluted him. And the grey man said, "Disgrace to the beard of my porter." Then Peredur understood that the porter was the lion. – And the grey man and the pages went together into the castle, and Peredur accompanied them; and he found it a fair and noble place. And they proceeded to the hall, and the tables were already laid, and upon them was abundance of food and liquor. And thereupon he saw an aged woman and a young woman come from the chamber; and they were the most stately women he had ever seen. Then they washed and went to meat, and the grey man sat in the upper seat at the head of the table, and the aged woman next to him. And Peredur and the maiden were placed together, and the two young pages served them. And the maiden gazed sorrowfully upon Peredur, and Peredur asked the maiden wherefore she was sad. "For thee, my soul; for, from when I first beheld thee, I have loved thee above all men. And it pains me to know that so gentle a youth as thou should have such a doom as awaits thee to-morrow. Sawest thou the numerous black houses in the bosom of the wood? All these belong to the vassals of the grey man yonder, who is my father. And they are all giants. And to-morrow they will rise up against thee, and will slay thee. And the Round Valley is this valley called." "Listen, fair maiden, wilt thou contrive that my horse and arms be in the same lodging with me to-night?" "Gladly will I cause it so to be, by Heaven, if I can."

And when it was time for them to sleep rather than to carouse, they went to rest. And the maiden caused Peredur's horse and arms to be in the same lodging with him. And the next morning Peredur heard a great tumult of men and horses around the castle. And Peredur arose, and armed himself and his horse, and went to the meadow. Then the aged woman and the maiden came to the grey man: "Lord," said they, "take the word of the youth, that he will never disclose what he has seen in this place, and we will be his sureties that he keep it." "I will not do so, by my faith," said the grey man. So Peredur fought with the host, and towards evening he had slain the one-third of them without receiving any hurt himself. Then said the aged woman, "Behold, many of thy host have been slain by the youth; do thou, therefore, grant him mercy." "I will not grant it, by my faith," said he. And the aged woman and the fair maiden were upon the battlements of the castle, looking forth. And at that juncture, Peredur encountered the yellow-haired youth and slew him. "Lord," said the maiden, "grant the young man mercy." "That will I not do, by Heaven," he replied; and thereupon Peredur attacked the auburn-haired youth, and slew him likewise. "It were better that thou hadst accorded mercy to the youth before he had slain thy two sons; for now scarcely wilt thou thyself escape from him." "Go, maiden and beseech the youth to grant mercy unto us, for we yield ourselves into his hands." So the maiden came to the place where Peredur was, and besought mercy for her father, and for all such of his vassals as had escaped alive. "Thou shalt have it, on condition that thy father and all that are under him go and render homage to Arthur, and tell him that it was his vassal Peredur that did him this service." "This will we do willingly, by Heaven." "And you shall also receive baptism; and I will send to Arthur and beseech him to bestow this valley upon thee and upon thy heirs after thee for ever." Then they went in, and the grey man and the tall woman saluted Peredur. And the grey man said unto him, "Since I have possessed this valley I have not seen any Christian depart with his life, save thyself. And we will go to do homage to Arthur, and to embrace the faith and be baptized." Then said Peredur, "To Heaven I render thanks that I have not broken my vow to the lady that best I love, which was, that I would not speak one word unto any Christian."

That night they tarried there. And the next day, in the morning, the grey man, with his company, set forth to Arthur's Court; and they did homage unto Arthur, and he caused them to be baptized. And the grey man told Arthur that it was Peredur that had vanquished them. And Arthur gave the valley to the grey man and his company, to hold it of him as Peredur had besought. And with Arthur's permission, the grey man went back to the Round Valley.

Peredur rode forward next day, and he traversed a vast tract of desert, in which no dwellings were. And at length he came to a habitation, mean and small. And there he heard that there was a serpent that lay upon a gold ring, and suffered none to inhabit the country for seven miles around. And Peredur came to the place where he heard the serpent was. And angrily, furiously, and desperately fought he with the serpent; and at last he killed it, and took away the ring. And thus he was for a long time without speaking a word to any Christian. And therefrom he lost his colour and his aspect, through extreme longing after the Court of Arthur, and the society of the lady whom best he loved, and of his companions. Then he proceeded forward to Arthur's Court, and on the road there met him Arthur's household going on a particular errand, with Kai at their head. And Peredur knew them all, but none of the household recognized him. "Whence comest thou, chieftain?" said Kai. And this he asked him twice and three times, and he answered him not. And Kai thrust him through the thigh with his lance. And lest he should be compelled to speak, and to break his vow, he went on without stopping. "Then," said Gwalchmai, "I declare to Heaven, Kai, that thou hast acted ill in committing such an outrage on a youth like this, who cannot speak." And Gwalchmai returned back to Arthur's Court. "Lady," said he to Gwenhwyvar, "seest thou how wicked an outrage Kai has committed upon this youth who cannot speak; for Heaven's sake, and for mine, cause him to have medical care before I come back, and I will repay thee the charge."

And before the men returned from their errand, a knight came to the meadow beside Arthur's Palace, to dare some one to the encounter. And his challenge was accepted; and Peredur fought with him, and overthrew him. And for a week he overthrew one knight every day.

And one day, Arthur and his household were going to Church, and they beheld a knight who had raised the signal for combat. "Verily," said Arthur, "by the valour of men, I will not go hence until I have my horse and my arms to overthrow yonder boor." Then went the attendants to fetch Arthur's horse and arms. And Peredur met the attendants as they were going back, and he took the horse and arms from them, and proceeded to the meadow; and all those who saw him arise and go to do battle with the knight, went upon the tops of the houses, and the mounds, and the high places, to behold the combat. And Peredur beckoned with his hand to the knight to commence the fight. And the knight thrust at him, but he was not thereby moved from where he stood. And Peredur spurred his horse, and ran at him wrathfully, furiously, fiercely, desperately, and with mighty rage, and he gave him a thrust, deadly-wounding, severe, furious, adroit, and strong, under his jaw, and raised him out of his saddle, and cast him a long way from him. And Peredur went back, and left the horse and the arms with the attendant as before, and he went on foot to the Palace.

Then Peredur went by the name of the Dumb Youth. And behold, Angharad Law Eurawc met him. "I declare to Heaven, chieftain," said she, "woful is it that thou canst not speak; for couldst thou speak, I would love thee best of all men; and by my faith, although thou canst not, I do love thee above all." "Heaven reward thee, my sister," said Peredur, "by my faith I also do love thee." Thereupon it was known that he was Peredur. And then he held fellowship with Gwalchmai, and Owain the son of Urien, and all the household, and he remained in Arthur's Court.

Arthur was in Caerlleon upon Usk; and he went to hunt, and Peredur went with him. And Peredur let loose his dog upon a hart, and the dog killed the hart in a desert place. And a short space from him he saw signs of a dwelling, and towards the dwelling he went, and he beheld a hall, and at the door of the hall he found bald swarthy youths playing at chess. And when he entered, he beheld three maidens sitting on a bench, and they were all clothed alike, as became persons of high rank. And he came, and sat by them upon the bench; and one of the maidens looked steadfastly upon Peredur, and wept. And Peredur asked her wherefore she was weeping. "Through grief, that I should see so fair a youth as thou art, slain." "Who will slay me?" inquired Peredur. "If thou art so daring as to remain here to-night, I will tell thee." "How great soever my danger may be from remaining here, I will listen unto thee." "This Palace is owned by him who is my father," said the maiden, "and he slays every one who comes hither without his leave." "What sort of a man is thy father, that he is able to slay every one thus?" "A man who does violence and wrong unto his neighbours, and who renders justice unto none." And hereupon he saw the youths arise and clear the chessmen from the board. And he heard a great tumult; and after the tumult there came in a huge black one-eyed man, and the maidens arose to meet him. And they disarrayed him, and he went and sat down; and after he had rested and pondered awhile, he looked at Peredur, and asked who the knight was. "Lord," said one of the maidens, "he is the fairest and gentlest youth that ever thou didst see. And for the sake of Heaven, and of thine own dignity, have patience with him." "For thy sake I will have patience, and I will grant him his life this night." Then Peredur came towards them to the fire, and partook of food and liquor, and entered into discourse with the ladies. And being elated with the liquor, he said to the black man, "It is a marvel to me, so mighty as thou sayest thou art, who could have put out thine eye." "It is one of my habits," said the black man, "that whosoever puts to me the question which thou hast asked, shall not escape with his life, either as a free gift or for a price." "Lord," said the maiden, "whatsoever he may say to thee in jest, and through the excitement of liquor, make good that which thou saidst and didst promise me just now." "I will do so, gladly, for thy sake," said he. "Willingly will I grant him his life this night." And that night thus they remained.

And the next day the black man got up, and put on his armour, and said to Peredur, "Arise, man, and suffer death." And Peredur said unto him, "Do one of two things, black man; if thou wilt fight with me, either throw off thy own armour, or give arms to me, that I may encounter thee." "Ha, man," said he, "couldst thou fight, if thou hadst arms? Take, then, what arms thou dost choose." And thereupon the maiden came to Peredur with such arms as pleased him; and he fought with the black man, and forced him to crave his mercy. "Black man, thou shalt gave mercy, provided thou tell me who thou art, and who put out thine eye." "Lord, I will tell thee; I lost it in fighting with the Black Serpent of the Carn. There is a mound, which is called the Mound of Mourning; and on the mound there is a carn, and in the carn there is a serpent, and on the tail of the serpent there is a stone, and the virtues of the stone are such, that whosoever should hold it in one hand, in the other he will have as much gold as he may desire. And in fighting with this serpent was it that I lost my eye. And the Black Oppressor am I called. And for this reason I am called the Black Oppressor, that there is not a single man around me whom I have not oppressed, and justice have I done upon none." "Tell me," said Peredur, "how far is it hence?" "The same day that thou settest forth, thou wilt come to the Palace of the Sons of the King of the Tortures." "Wherefore are they called thus?" "The Addanc of the Lake slays them once every day. When thou goest thence, thou wilt come to the Court of the Countess of the Achievements." "What achievements are there?" asked Peredur. "Three hundred men there are in her household, and unto every stranger that comes to the Court, the achievements of her household are related. And this is the manner of it, – the three hundred men of the household sit next unto the Lady; and that not through disrespect unto the guests, but that they may relate the achievements of the household. And the day that thou goest thence, thou wilt reach the Mound of Mourning, and round about the mound there are the owners of three hundred tents guarding the serpent." "Since thou hast, indeed, been an oppressor so long," said Peredur, "I will cause that thou continue so no longer." So he slew him.

Then the maiden spoke, and began to converse with him. "If thou wast poor when thou camest here, henceforth thou wilt be rich through the treasure of the black man whom thou hast slain. Thou seest the many lovely maidens that there are in this Court; thou shalt have her whom thou best likest for the lady of thy love." "Lady, I came not hither from my country to woo; but match yourselves as it liketh you with the comely youths I see here; and none of your goods do I desire, for I need them not." Then Peredur rode forward, and he came to the Palace of the Sons of the King of the Tortures; and when he entered the Palace, he saw none but women; and they rose up, and were joyful at his coming; and as they began to discourse with him, he beheld a charger arrive, with a saddle upon it, and a corpse in the saddle. And one of the women arose, and took the corpse from the saddle, and anointed it in a vessel of warm water, which was below the door, and placed precious balsam upon it; and the man rose up alive, and came to the place where Peredur was, and greeted him, and was joyful to see him. And two other men came in upon their saddles, and the maiden treated these two in the same manner as she had done the first. Then Peredur asked the chieftain wherefore it was thus. And they told him, that there was an Addanc in a cave, which slew them once every day. And thus they remained that night.

And next morning the youths arose to sally forth, and Peredur besought them, for the sake of the ladies of their love, to permit him to go with them; but they refused him, saying, "If thou shouldst be slain there, thou hast none to bring thee back to life again." And they rode forward, and Peredur followed after them; and, after they had disappeared out of his sight, he came to a mound, whereon sat the fairest lady he had ever beheld. "I know thy quest," said she; "thou art going to encounter the Addanc, and he will slay thee, and that not by courage, but by craft. He has a cave, and at the entrance of the cave there is a stone pillar, and he sees every one that enters, and none see him; and from behind the pillar he slays every one with a poisonous dart. And if thou wouldst pledge me thy faith to love me above all women, I would give thee a stone, by which thou shouldst see him when thou goest in, and he should not see thee." "I will, by my troth," said Peredur, "for when first I beheld thee I loved thee; and where shall I seek thee?" "When thou seekest me, seek towards India." And the maiden vanished, after placing the stone in Peredur's hand.

And he came towards a valley, through which ran a river; and the borders of the valley were wooded, and on each side of the river were level meadows. And on one side of the river he saw a flock of white sheep, and on the other a flock of black sheep. And whenever one of the white sheep bleated, one of the black sheep would cross over and become white; and when one of the black sheep bleated, one of the white sheep would cross over and become black. And he saw a tall tree by the side of the river, one half of which was in flames from the root to the top, and the other half was green and in full leaf. And nigh thereto he saw a youth sitting upon a mound, and two greyhounds, white-breasted and spotted, in leashes, lying by his side. And certain was he that he had never seen a youth of so royal a bearing as he. And in the wood opposite he heard hounds raising a herd of deer. And

Peredur saluted the youth, and the youth greeted him in return. And there were three roads leading from the mound; two of them were wide roads, and the third was more narrow. And Peredur inquired where the three roads went. "One of them goes to my palace," said the youth; "and one of two things I counsel thee to do; either to proceed to my palace, which is before thee, and where thou wilt find my wife, or else to remain here to see the hounds chasing the roused deer from the wood to the plain. And thou shalt see the best greyhounds thou didst ever behold, and the boldest in the chase, kill them by the water beside us; and when it is time to go to meat, my page will come with my horse to meet me, and thou shalt rest in my palace to-night." "Heaven reward thee; but I cannot tarry, for onward must I go." "The other road leads to the town, which is near here, and wherein food and liquor may be bought; and the road which is narrower than the others goes towards the cave of the Addanc." "With thy permission, young man, I will go that way."

And Peredur went towards the cave. And he took the stone in his left hand, and his lance in his right. And as he went in he perceived the Addanc, and he pierced him through with his lance, and cut off his head. And as he came from the cave, behold the three companions were at the entrance; and they saluted Peredur, and told him that there was a prediction that he should slay that monster. And Peredur gave the head to the young men, and they offered him in marriage whichever of the three sisters he might choose, and half their kingdom with her. "I came not hither to woo," said Peredur, "but if peradventure I took a wife, I should prefer your sister to all others." And Peredur rode forward, and he heard a noise behind him. And he looked back, and saw a man upon a red horse, with red armour upon him; and the man rode up by his side, and saluted him, and wished him the favour of Heaven and of man. And Peredur greeted the youth kindly. "Lord, I come to make a request unto thee." "What wouldest thou?" "That thou shouldest take me as thine attendant." "Whom then should I take as my attendant, if I did so?" "I will not conceal from thee what kindred I am of. Etlym Gleddyv Coch am I called, an Earl from the East Country." "I marvel that thou shouldest offer to become attendant to a man whose possessions are no greater than thine own; for I have but an earldom like thyself. But since thou desirest to be my attendant, I will take thee joyfully."

And they went forward to the Court of the Countess, and all they of the Court were glad at their coming; and they were told it was not through disrespect they were placed below the household, but that such was the usage of the Court. For, whoever should overthrow the three hundred men of her household, would sit next the Countess, and she would love him above all men. And Peredur having overthrown the three hundred men of her household, sat down beside her, and the Countess said, "I thank Heaven that I have a youth so fair and so valiant as thou, since I have not obtained the man whom best I love." "Who is he whom best thou lovest?" "By my faith, Etlym Gleddyv Coch is the man whom I love best, and I have never seen him." "Of a truth, Etlym is my companion; and behold here he is, and for his sake did I come to joust with thy household. And he could have done so better than I, had it pleased him. And I do give thee unto him." "Heaven reward thee, fair youth, and I will take the man whom I love above all others." And the Countess became Etlym's bride from that moment.

And the next day Peredur set forth towards the Mound of Mourning. "By thy hand, lord, but I will go with thee," said Etlym. Then they went forwards till they came in sight of the mound and the tents. "Go unto yonder men," said Peredur to Etlym, "and desire them to come and do me homage." So Etlym went unto them, and said unto them thus, – "Come and do homage to my lord." "Who is thy lord?" said they. "Peredur with the long lance is my lord," said Etlym. "Were it permitted to slay a messenger, thou shouldest not go back to thy lord alive, for making unto Kings, and Earls, and Barons so arrogant a demand as to go and do him homage." Peredur desired him to go back to them, and to give them their choice, either to do him homage, or to do battle with him. And they chose rather to do battle. And that day Peredur overthrew the owners of a hundred tents; and the next day he overthrew the owners of a hundred more; and the third day the remaining hundred took counsel to do homage to Peredur. And Peredur inquired of them, wherefore they were there. And they told him they were guarding the serpent until he should die. "For then should we fight for the stone among ourselves, and whoever should be conqueror among us would have the stone." "Await here," said Peredur, "and I will go to encounter the serpent." "Not so, lord," said they; "we will go altogether to encounter the serpent." "Verily," said Peredur, "that will I not permit; for if the serpent be slain, I shall derive no more fame therefrom than one of you." Then he went to the place where the serpent was, and slew it, and came back to them, and said, "Reckon up what you have spent since you have been here, and I will repay you to the full." And he paid to each what he said was his claim. And he required of them only that they should acknowledge themselves his vassals. And he said to Etlym, "Go back unto her whom thou lovest best, and I will go forwards, and I will reward thee for having been my attendant." And he gave Etlym the stone. "Heaven repay thee and prosper thee," said Etlym.

And Peredur rode thence, and he came to the fairest valley he had ever seen, through which ran a river; and there he beheld many tents of various colours. And he marvelled still more at the number or water-mills and of wind-mills that he saw. And there rode up with him a tall auburn-haired man, in a workman's garb, and Peredur inquired of him who he was. "I am the chief miller," said he, "of all the mills yonder." "Wilt thou give me lodging?" said Peredur. "I will, gladly," he answered. And Peredur came to the miller's house, and the miller had a fair and pleasant dwelling. And Peredur asked money as a loan from the miller, that he might buy meat and liquor for himself and for the household, and he promised that he would pay him again ere he went thence. And he inquired of the miller, wherefore such a multitude was there assembled. Said the miller to Peredur, "One thing is certain: either thou art a man from afar, or thou art beside thyself. The Empress of Cristinobyl the Great is here; and she will have no one but the man who is most valiant; for riches does she not require. And it was impossible to bring food for so many thousands as are here, therefore were all these mills constructed." And that night they took their rest.

And the next day Peredur arose, and he equipped himself and his horse for the tournament. And among the other tents he beheld one, which was the fairest he had ever seen. And he saw a beauteous maiden leaning her head out of a window of the tent, and he had never seen a maiden more lovely than she. And upon her was a garment of satin. And he gazed fixedly on the maiden, and began to love her greatly. And he remained there, gazing upon the maiden from morning until mid-day, and from mid-day until evening; and then the tournament was ended and he went to his lodging and drew off his armour. Then he asked money of the miller as a loan, and the miller's wife was wroth with Peredur; nevertheless, the miller lent him the money. And the next day he did in like manner as he had done the day before. And at night he came to his lodging, and took money as a loan from the miller. And the third day, as he was in the same place, gazing upon the maiden, he felt a hard blow between the neck and the shoulder, from the edge of an axe. And when he looked behind him, he saw that it was the miller; and the miller said to him, "Do one of two things: either turn thy head from hence, or go to the tournament." And Peredur smiled on the miller, and went to the tournament; and all that encountered him that day he overthrew. And as many as he vanquished he sent as a gift to the Empress, and their horses and arms he sent as a gift to the wife of the miller, in payment of the borrowed money. Peredur attended the tournament until all were overthrown, and he sent all the men to the prison of the Empress, and the horses and arms to the wife of the miller, in payment of the borrowed money. And the Empress sent to the Knight of the Mill, to ask him to come and visit her. And Peredur went not for the first nor for the second message. And the third time she sent a hundred knights to bring him against his will, and they went to him and told him their mission from the Empress. And Peredur fought well with them, and caused them to be bound like stags, and thrown into the mill-dyke. And the Empress sought advice of a wise man who was in her counsel; and he said to her, "With thy permission, I will go to him myself." So he came to Peredur, and saluted him, and besought him, for the sake of the lady of his love, to come and visit the Empress. And they went, together with the miller. And Peredur went and sat down in the outer chamber of the tent, and she came and placed herself by his side. And there was but little discourse between them. And Peredur took his leave, and went to his lodging.

And the next day he came to visit her, and when he came into the tent there was no one chamber less decorated than the others. And they knew not where he would sit. And Peredur went and sat beside the Empress, and discoursed with her courteously. And while they were thus, they beheld a black man enter with a goblet full of wine in his hand. And he dropped upon his knee before the Empress, and besought her to give it to no one who would not fight with him for it. And she looked upon Peredur. "Lady," said he, "bestow on me the goblet." And Peredur drank the wine, and gave the goblet to the miller's wife. And while they were thus, behold there entered a black man of larger stature than the other, with a wild beast's claw in his hand, wrought into the form of a goblet and filled with wine. And he presented it to the Empress, and besought her to give it to no one but the man who would fight with him. "Lady," said Peredur, "bestow it on me." And she gave it to him. And Peredur drank the wine, and sent the goblet to the wife of the miller. And while they were thus, behold a rough-looking, crisp-haired man,

taller than either of the others, came in with a bowl in his hand
full of wine; and he bent upon his knee, and gave it into the hands
of the Empress, and he besought her to give it to none but him who
would fight with him for it; and she gave it to Peredur, and he sent it
to the miller's wife. And that night Peredur returned to his lodging;
and the next day he accoutred himself and his horse, and went to
the meadow and slew the three men. Then Peredur proceeded to
the tent, and the Empress said to him, "Goodly Peredur, remember
the faith thou didst pledge me when I gave thee the stone, and thou
didst kill the Addanc." "Lady," answered he, "thou sayest truth,
I do remember it." And Peredur was entertained by the Empress
fourteen years, as the story relates.

Arthur was at Caerlleon upon Usk, his principal palace; and in the
centre of the floor of the hall were four men sitting on a carpet of
velvet, Owain the son of Urien, and Gwalchmai the son of Gwyar,
and Howel the son of Emyr Llydaw, and Peredur of the long lance.
And thereupon they saw a black curly-headed maiden enter, riding
upon a yellow mule, with jagged thongs in her hand to urge it on;
and having a rough and hideous aspect. Blacker were her face and
her two hands than the blackest iron covered with pitch; and her
hue was not more frightful than her form. High cheeks had she,
and a face lengthened downwards, and a short nose with distended
nostrils. And one eye was of a piercing mottled grey, and the other
was as black as jet, deep-sunk in her head. And her teeth were long
and yellow, more yellow were they than the flower of the broom.
And her stomach rose from the breast-bone, higher than her chin.
And her back was in the shape of a crook, and her legs were large
and bony. And her figure was very thin and spare, except her feet
and her legs, which were of huge size. And she greeted Arthur and
all his household except Peredur. And to Peredur she spoke harsh
and angry words. "Peredur, I greet thee not, seeing that thou dost
not merit it. Blind was fate in giving thee fame and favour. When
thou wast in the Court of the Lame King, and didst see there the
youth bearing the streaming spear, from the points of which were
drops of blood flowing in streams, even to the hand of the youth,
and many other wonders likewise, thou didst not inquire their
meaning nor their cause. Hadst thou done so, the King would have
been restored to health, and his dominions to peace. Whereas from
henceforth, he will have to endure battles and conflicts, and his
knights will perish, and wives will be widowed, and maidens will
be left portionless, and all this is because of thee." Then said she

unto Arthur, "May it please thee, lord, my dwelling is far hence, in the stately castle of which thou hast heard, and therein are five hundred and sixty-six knights of the order of Chivalry, and the lady whom best he loves with each; and whoever would acquire fame in arms, and encounters, and conflicts, he will gain it there, if he deserve it. And whoso would reach the summit of fame and of honour, I know where he may find it. There is a castle on a lofty mountain, and there is a maiden therein, and she is detained a prisoner there, and whoever shall set her free will attain the summit of the fame of the world." And thereupon she rode away.

Said Gwalchmai, "By my faith, I will not rest tranquilly until I have proved if I can release the maiden." And many of Arthur's household joined themselves with him. Then, likewise, said Peredur, "By my faith, I will not rest tranquilly until I know the story and the meaning of the lance whereof the black maiden spoke." And while they were equipping themselves, behold a knight came to the gate. And he had the size and the strength of a warrior, and was equipped with arms and habiliments. And he went forward, and saluted Arthur and all his household, except Gwalchmai. And the knight had upon his shoulder a shield, ingrained with gold, with a fesse of azure blue upon it, and his whole armour was of the same hue. And he said to Gwalchmai, "Thou didst slay my lord by thy treachery and deceit, and that will I prove upon thee." Then Gwalchmai rose up. "Behold," said he, "here is my gage against thee, to maintain, either in this place or wherever else thou wilt, that I am not a traitor or deceiver." "Before the King whom I obey, will I that my encounter with thee take place," said the knight. "Willingly," said Gwalchmai; "go forward, and I will follow thee." So the knight went forth, and Gwalchmai accoutred himself, and there was offered unto him abundance of armour, but he would take none but his own. And when Gwalchmai and Peredur were equipped, they set forth to follow him, by reason of their fellowship and of the great friendship that was between them. And they did not go after him in company together, but each went his own way.

At the dawn of day Gwalchmai came to a valley, and in the valley he saw a fortress, and within the fortress a vast palace and lofty towers around it. And he beheld a knight coming out to hunt from the other side, mounted on a spirited black snorting palfrey, that advanced at a prancing pace, proudly stepping, and nimbly bounding, and sure of foot; and this was the man to whom the palace belonged. And Gwalchmai saluted him. "Heaven prosper thee, chieftain," said he, "and whence comest thou?" "I come," answered Gwalchmai, "from the Court of Arthur." "And art thou Arthur's vassal?" "Yes, by my faith," said Gwalchmai. "I will give thee good counsel," said the knight. "I see that thou art tired and weary; go unto my palace, if it may please thee, and tarry there to-night." "Willingly, lord," said he, "and Heaven reward thee." "Take this ring as a token to the porter, and go forward to yonder tower, and therein thou wilt find my sister." And Gwalchmai went to the gate, and showed the ring, and proceeded to the tower. And on entering he beheld a large blazing fire, burning without smoke and with a bright and lofty flame, and a beauteous and stately maiden was sitting on a chair by the fire. And the maiden was glad at his coming, and welcomed him, and advanced to meet him. And he went and sat beside the maiden, and they took their repast. And when their repast was over, they discoursed pleasantly together. And while they were thus, behold there entered a venerable hoary-headed man. "Ah! base girl," said he, "if thou didst think it was right for thee to entertain and to sit by yonder man, thou wouldest not do so." And he withdrew his head, and went forth. "Ah! chieftain," said the maiden, "if thou wilt do as I counsel thee, thou wilt shut the door, lest the man should have a plot against thee." Upon that Gwalchmai arose, and when he came near unto the door, the man, with sixty others, fully armed, were ascending the tower. And Gwalchmai defended the door with a chessboard, that none might enter until the man should return from the chase. And thereupon, behold the Earl arrived. "What is all this?" asked he. "It is a sad thing," said the hoary-headed man; "the young girl yonder has been sitting and eating with him who slew your father. He is Gwalchmai, the son of Gwyar." "Hold thy peace, then," said the Earl, "I will go in." And the Earl was joyful concerning Gwalchmai. "Ha! chieftain," said he, "it was wrong of thee to come to my court, when thou knewest that thou didst slay my father; and though we cannot avenge him, Heaven will avenge him upon thee." "My soul," said Gwalchmai, "thus it is: I came not here either to acknowledge or to deny having slain thy father; but I am on a message from Arthur, and therefore do I crave the space of a year until I shall return from my embassy, and then, upon my faith, I will come back unto this palace, and do one of two things, either acknowledge it, or deny it." And the time was granted him willingly; and he remained there that night. And the next morning he rode forth. And the story relates nothing further of Gwalchmai respecting this adventure.

And Peredur rode forward. And he wandered over the whole island, seeking tidings of the black maiden, and he could meet with none. And he came to an unknown land, in the centre of a valley, watered by a river. And as he traversed the valley he beheld a horseman coming towards him, and wearing the garments of a priest; and he besought his blessing. "Wretched man," said he, "thou meritest no blessing, and thou wouldest not be profited by one, seeing that thou art clad in armour on such a day as this." "And what day is to-day?" said Peredur. "To-day is Good Friday," he answered. "Chide me not that I knew not this, seeing that it is a year to-day since I journeyed forth from my country." Then he dismounted, and led his horse in his hand. And he had not proceeded far along the high road before he came to a cross road, and the cross road traversed a wood. And on the other side of the wood he saw an unfortified castle, which appeared to be inhabited. And at the gate of the castle there met him the priest whom he had seen before, and he asked his blessing. "The blessing of Heaven be unto thee," said he, "it is more fitting to travel in thy present guise than as thou wast erewhile; and this night thou shalt tarry with me." So he remained there that night.

And the next day Peredur sought to go forth. "To-day may no one journey. Thou shalt remain with me to-day and to-morrow, and the day following, and I will direct thee as best I may to the place which thou art seeking." And the fourth day Peredur sought to go forth, and he entreated the priest to tell him how he should find the Castle of Wonders. "What I know thereof I will tell thee," he replied. "Go over yonder mountain, and on the other side of the mountain thou wilt come to a river, and in the valley wherein the river runs is a King's palace, wherein the King sojourned during Easter. And if thou mayest have tidings anywhere of the Castle of Wonders, thou wilt have them there."

Then Peredur rode forward. And he came to the valley in which was the river, and there met him a number of men going to hunt, and in the midst of them was a man of exalted rank, and Peredur saluted him. "Choose, chieftain," said the man, "whether thou wilt go with me to the chase, or wilt proceed to my palace, and I will dispatch one of my household to commend thee to my daughter, who is there, and who will entertain thee with food and liquor until I return from hunting; and whatever may be thine errand, such as I can obtain for thee thou shalt gladly have." And the King sent a little yellow page with him as an attendant; and when they came to the palace the lady had arisen, and was about to wash before meat. Peredur went forward, and she saluted him joyfully, and placed him by her side. And they took their repast. And whatsoever Peredur said unto her, she laughed loudly, so that all in the palace could hear. Then spoke the yellow page to the lady. "By my faith," said he, "this youth is already thy husband; or if he be not, thy mind and thy thoughts are set upon him." And the little yellow page went unto the King, and told him that it seemed to him that the youth whom he had met with was his daughter's husband, or if he were not so already that he would shortly become so unless he were cautious. "What is thy counsel in this matter, youth?" said the King. "My counsel is," he replied, "that thou set strong men upon him, to seize him, until thou hast ascertained the truth respecting this." So he set strong men upon Peredur, who seized him and cast him into prison. And the maiden went before her father, and asked him wherefore he had caused the youth from Arthur's Court to be imprisoned. "In truth," he answered, "he shall not be free to-night, nor to-morrow, nor the day following, and he shall not come from where he is." She replied not to what the King had said, but she went to the youth. "Is it unpleasant to thee to be here?" said she. "I should not care if I were not," he replied. "Thy couch and thy treatment shall be in no wise inferior to that of the King himself, and thou shalt have the best entertainment that the palace affords. And if it were more pleasing to thee that my couch should be here, that I might discourse with thee, it should be so, cheerfully." "This can I not refuse," said Peredur. And he remained in prison that night. And the maiden provided all that she had promised him.

And the next day Peredur heard a tumult in the town. "Tell me, fair maiden, what is that tumult?" said Peredur. "All the King's hosts and his forces have come to the town to-day." "And what seek they here?" he inquired. "There is an Earl near this place who possesses two Earldoms, and is as powerful as a King; and an engagement will take place between them to-day." "I beseech thee," said Peredur, "to cause a horse and arms to be brought, that I may view the encounter, and I promise to come back to my prison again." "Gladly," said she, "will I provide thee with horse and arms." So she gave him a horse and arms, and a bright scarlet robe of honour over his armour, and a yellow shield upon his shoulder. And he went to the combat; and as many of the Earl's men as encountered him that day he overthrew; and he returned to his prison. And the maiden asked tidings of Peredur, and he answered her not a word. And she went and asked tidings of her father, and inquired who had acquitted himself best of the household. And he said that he knew not, but that it was a man with a scarlet robe of honour over his armour, and a yellow shield upon his shoulder. Then she smiled, and returned to where Peredur was, and did him great honour that night. And for three days did Peredur slay the Earl's men; and before any one could know who he was, he returned to his prison. And the fourth day Peredur slew the Earl himself. And the maiden went unto her father, and inquired of him the news. "I have good news for thee," said the King; "the Earl is slain, and I am the owner of his two Earldoms." "Knowest thou, lord, who slew him?" "I do not know," said the King. "It was the knight with the scarlet robe of honour and the yellow shield." "Lord," said she, "I know who that is." "By Heaven!" he exclaimed, "who is he?" "Lord," she replied, "he is the knight whom thou hast imprisoned." Then he went unto Peredur, and saluted him, and told him that he would reward the service he had done him, in any way he might desire. And when they went to meat, Peredur was placed beside the King, and the maiden on the other side of Peredur. "I will give thee," said the King, "my daughter in marriage, and half my kingdom with her, and the two Earldoms as a gift." "Heaven reward thee, lord," said Peredur, "but I came not here to woo." "What seekest thou then, chieftain?" "I am seeking tidings of the Castle of Wonders." "Thy enterprise is greater, chieftain, than thou wilt wish to pursue," said the maiden, "nevertheless, tidings shalt thou have of the Castle, and thou shalt have a guide through my father's dominions, and a sufficiency of provisions for thy journey, for thou art, O chieftain, the man whom best I love." Then she said to him, "Go over yonder mountain, and thou wilt find a lake, and in the middle of the lake there is a Castle, and that is the Castle that is called the Castle of Wonders; and we know not what wonders are therein, but thus is it called."

And Peredur proceeded towards the Castle, and the gate of the Castle was open. And when he came to the hall, the door was open, and he entered. And he beheld a chessboard in the hall, and the chessmen were playing against each other, by themselves. And the side that he favoured lost the game, and thereupon the others set up a shout, as though they had been living men. And Peredur was wroth, and took the chessmen in his lap, and cast the chessboard into the lake. And when he had done thus, behold the black maiden came in, and she said to him, "The welcome of Heaven be not unto thee. Thou hadst rather do evil than good." "What complaint hast thou against me, maiden?" said Peredur. "That thou hast

occasioned unto the Empress the loss of her chessboard, which
she would not have lost for all her empire. And the way in which
thou mayest recover the chessboard is, to repair to the Castle of
Ysbidinongyl, where is a black man, who lays waste the dominions
of the Empress; and if thou canst slay him, thou wilt recover the
chessboard. But if thou goest there, thou wilt not return alive."
"Wilt thou direct me thither?" said Peredur. "I will show thee the
way," she replied. So he went to the Castle of Ysbidinongyl, and
he fought with the black man. And the black man besought mercy
of Peredur. "Mercy will I grant thee," said he, "on condition that
thou cause the chessboard to be restored to the place where it was
when I entered the hall." Then the maiden came to him, and said,
"The malediction of Heaven attend thee for thy work, since thou
hast left that monster alive, who lays waste all the possessions of
the Empress." "I granted him his life," said Peredur, "that he might
cause the chessboard to be restored." "The chessboard is not in the
place where thou didst find it; go back, therefore, and slay him,"
answered she. So Peredur went back, and slew the black man. And
when he returned to the palace, he found the black maiden there.
"Ah! maiden," said Peredur, "where is the Empress?" "I declare
to Heaven that thou wilt not see her now, unless thou dost slay
the monster that is in yonder forest." "What monster is there?"
"It is a stag that is as swift as the swiftest bird; and he has one
horn in his forehead, as long as the shaft of a spear, and as sharp
as whatever is sharpest. And he destroys the branches of the best
trees in the forest, and he kills every animal that he meets with
therein; and those that he doth not slay perish of hunger. And
what is worse than that, he comes every night, and drinks up the
fish-pond, and leaves the fishes exposed, so that for the most part
they die before the water returns again." "Maiden," said Peredur,
"wilt thou come and show me this animal?" "Not so," said the
maiden, "for he has not permitted any mortal to enter the forest
for above a twelvemonth. Behold, here is a little dog belonging to
the Empress, which will rouse the stag, and will chase him towards
thee, and the stag will attack thee." Then the little dog went as a
guide to Peredur, and roused the stag, and brought him towards
the place where Peredur was. And the stag attacked Peredur, and
he let him pass by him, and as he did so, he smote off his head with
his sword. And while he was looking at the head of the stag,
he saw a lady on horseback coming towards him. And she took
the little dog in the lappet of her cap, and the head and the body
of the stag lay before her. And around the stag's neck was a golden

collar. "Ha! chieftain," said she, "uncourteously hast thou acted in slaying the fairest jewel that was in my dominions." "I was entreated so to do; and is there any way by which I can obtain thy friendship?" "There is," she replied. "Go thou forward unto yonder mountain, and there thou wilt find a grove; and in the grove there is a cromlech; do thou there challenge a man three times to fight, and thou shalt have my friendship."

So Peredur proceeded onward, and came to the side of the grove, and challenged any man to fight. And a black man arose from beneath the cromlech, mounted upon a bony horse, and both he and his horse were clad in huge rusty armour. And they fought. And as often as Peredur cast the black man to the earth, he would jump again into his saddle. And Peredur dismounted, and drew his sword; and thereupon the black man disappeared with Peredur's horse and his own, so that he could not gain sight of him a second time. And Peredur went along the mountain, and on the other side of the mountain he beheld a castle in the valley, wherein was a river. And he went to the castle; and as he entered it, he saw a hall, and the door of the hall was open, and he went in. And there he saw a lame grey-headed man sitting on one side of the hall, with Gwalchmai beside him. And Peredur beheld his horse, which the black man had taken, in the same stall with that of Gwalchmai. And they were glad concerning Peredur. And he went and seated himself on the other side of the hoary-headed man. Then, behold a yellow-haired youth came, and bent upon the knee before Peredur, and besought his friendship. "Lord," said the youth, "it was I that came in the form of the black maiden to Arthur's Court, and when thou didst throw down the chessboard, and when thou didst slay the black man of Ysbidinongyl, and when thou didst slay the stag, and when thou didst go to fight the black man of the cromlech. And I came with the bloody head in the salver, and with the lance that streamed with blood from the point to the hand, all along the shaft; and the head was thy cousin's, and he was killed by the sorceresses of Gloucester, who also lamed thine uncle; and I am thy cousin. And there is a prediction that thou art to avenge these things." Then Peredur and Gwalchmai took counsel, and sent to Arthur and his household, to beseech them to come against the sorceresses. And they began to fight with them; and one of the sorceresses slew one of Arthur's men before Peredur's face, and Peredur bade her forbear. And the sorceress slew a man before Peredur's face a second time, and a second time he forbad her. And the third time the sorceress slew a man before the face of Peredur;

and then Peredur drew his sword, and smote the sorceress on the helmet; and all her head-armour was split in two parts. And she set up a cry, and desired the other sorceresses to flee, and told them that this was Peredur, the man who had learnt Chivalry with them, and by whom they were destined to be slain. Then Arthur and his household fell upon the sorceresses, and slew the sorceresses of Gloucester every one. And thus is it related concerning the Castle of Wonders.

HUNT OF THE HART ROYAL

Cherith Baldry

*Cherith Baldry (b. 1947), a former teacher and librarian, has begun
to establish herself as a writer of children's books with her Saga of
the Six Worlds, a series set on a distant binary star system whose
settlers have long since forgotten about Earth. The series so far has
included* The Book and the Phoenix *(1989; published in America
as* A Rush of Golden Wings*),* Hostage of the Sea *(1990; published
in America as* Rite of Brotherhood*),* The Carpenter's Apprentice
(1992) and Storm Wind *(1994). She has long had a fascination
with the Arthurian world, and has a special interest in Sir Kay.
The following story, involving Sir Kay and Sir Gareth, explores
an incident which presages the start of the Grail Quest.*

"Look!" said Gareth of Orkney.

Sir Kay, riding just ahead of him, reined in. Their path wound
along the side of a hill, and across the valley the forest reached
towards them like the fingers of a spread hand. Camelot was an
airy silhouette on the horizon.

Gareth pointed. Along the edge of the forest was a glitter of
movement: horses, with riders gaily dressed, some followers on
foot, and hunting dogs. As Kay and Gareth watched they heard
a horn, faint and clear, and within minutes the whole troop had
disappeared among the trees.

"King Arthur hunts the white stag," Kay said.

His tone was indifferent, and he urged his horse forward

again. Gareth followed, pressing up as closely as he could on the narrow path.

"A white stag!" he said, marvelling. "Sir, is there really such a thing?"

"Oh, yes. I've seen one myself. And I've no wish to see this one." Now he sounded irritable. "Do you know the custom of the hunt?"

"No," Gareth said.

"The knight who kills the white stag," Kay instructed him, glancing over his shoulder with a sardonic look, "has the honour of kissing the most beautiful lady in the Court."

Gareth shrugged; he could think of prizes more exciting. "I suppose –" he began.

Kay paused again at a turn of the path.

"You don't see the point, lad, do you? What red-blooded knight doesn't think his own lady is most beautiful, and wouldn't challenge anyone who says different? Last time I thought we'd have a massacre on our hands."

Gareth began to understand.

"Why does Arthur do it, then?"

Kay's brows went up, disdain in his hawk's face.

"Custom. To entertain his guests. Honour." He reached out, soothing his black, Morial, as the horse grew restive. Now he was Kay at his most sarcastic. "If we hear tell of something wonderful, what else should we do but kill it?"

He moved on. Behind him, Gareth, half smiling, thought that even his back view looked disgusted, from crisp black curls to polished riding boots. Impossible to imagine Sir Kay contending for the prize of a kiss.

Kay and Gareth had left Camelot at dawn to visit nearby farms, paying for provisions supplied for the recent Easter Court and giving orders for the approaching Court at Pentecost. Gareth had assumed that Kay had undertaken this errand himself, instead of sending one of his staff, to avoid the exasperating influx of noble visitors. Now he guessed that Kay might also have wanted to avoid the hunt.

At each of the farms on their route Kay would have long and complicated discussions with the farmer, involving money and tallysticks. Afterwards would come a stroll around outside, to look at pigs or chickens or fields of green corn.

Kay listened more than he talked, seeming consumingly inter-ested in the ingredients of a horse drench or why certain hens were failing to lay. Not until Gareth saw him crouched in a cow byre, encouraging a calf to drink from a bucket, with the little creature determined to suck down his fingers along with the milk, did he realize that Kay was not pretending interest at all. Strangely, he belonged here in a way that he did not belong at Camelot.

Once they were on their way again, Kay said, abrupt and self-conscious, "I was brought up to this. My father's tenants. But for Arthur, I might have spent my whole life watching wool grow on sheep." As Gareth considered this new idea – for he could scarcely imagine Kay separated from the office of High Seneschal – Kay added, "I could milk a cow before I learned to use a sword." He released a spurt of laughter touched with bitterness. "There are those who would say I should have stuck to milking."

All day they rode in a wide circle, with Camelot at its centre, so that when they left the last farm they were still less than an hour's ride from home. The sun was sinking, their shadows growing long.

"The quickest road goes through the forest," Kay said, gesturing. His mouth quirked. "You might even see your stag."

Gareth felt anticipation quicken. A white stag; might it still be concealed among the brakes and thickets, or would the hunt have found it and pulled it down? He swallowed uncomfortably; he would rather not see that.

In the forest, all was quiet. The sunlight was reddening, the shadows of the trees lying across their path. There was no disturbance of the track or the undergrowth to show the hunt had ever been this way. Very faintly, Gareth could hear running water.

As they went on the sound grew louder; the path was descending and growing damp. Concentrating on his horse's footing, Gareth was not aware that Kay had reined in until he came up beside him and Kay's hand went out to his bridle.

"Listen."

Now that the horses were standing, Gareth could hear splashing from the water he still could not see, as if something large was wallowing around. From the distance came the call of a hunting-horn.

Kay dismounted, looped Morial's reins over a low branch and strode into the long grasses beside the track, vanishing as he skirted a hazel brake.

Hurrying after him, Gareth started to call out – and bit off the words as he caught up.

The stream ran in a deep cleft, the banks undercut. Kay knelt on the edge. Directly beneath him was the stag. It stood shoulder-deep in water, its forelegs pawing at the bank, which crumbled away as it tried to lever itself upwards. The head was lifted, close enough for Gareth, crouching at Kay's side, to have reached out and touched it, until the animal fell back in a surge of water.

When Kay had told him about the white stag, Gareth had not fully understood the wonder of it. The hide was the same pure silver as the water that bubbled around it; wet, it had the sheen of silk. The antlers were frozen light. Gareth wanted to hide his eyes, and yet he could not stop looking.

Kay breathed out. "It's wounded."

As the stag struggled upwards again Gareth saw the gashes along its flank – ugly, gaping mouths where blood flowed, mingling with the stream. An arrow was deep in its neck; its mouth was flecked with bloodstained foam. Once again it fell back, and this time the current carried it off its feet and threw it up against the bank further downstream.

Gareth heard the horn call again, and the distant yelping of a hound. He understood what had happened. The stag had taken to the water to break the scent; the huntsmen had lost it, but it was too badly wounded to escape. It would die – and not easily – from drowning or loss of blood.

Uncertainly Gareth glanced at Kay, wondering if there was anything they could do. Kay was looking white and sick. Still with his eyes fixed on the struggling animal, he unfastened his cloak and let it fall. Then he drew his dagger, the only weapon he was wearing.

"Sir, you can't!" Gareth exclaimed. "Wait for the hunt."

"The hunt, lad?" Kay's voice was scathing. "I might wait all night." Without hesitating, he swung himself over the edge of the bank.

Gareth watched, agonized. The water ran deep enough to drown in, let alone the danger of being injured by the thrashing hooves or the antlers.

Kay slithered down the bank into the water and let the current take him. The stag was pawing at the bank again, but already Gareth could see that it was weaker. Kay was driven against its flank, a dark, drenched shape against the glimmering silver. He reached for the shoulder and drew himself upwards. The stag turned its head and looked at him.

Briefly, Kay froze. Then he poised his hand, gripping the dagger, hesitated once more, and plunged the blade into the vein at the base of the stag's neck. Blood gushed out, over the stag's chest, over Kay's hand, to be lost in the swirling water.

The light in the antlers died; they were only horn, the colour of rancid fat. The gleaming hide grew dingy. The body slipped down the bank, only the head and one shoulder exposed, all the marvel of it dissolving away. It was nothing more than a dead animal.

Kay's grip slackened on the hilt of the dagger. He slid back, leaving the weapon buried in the stag's neck, and water closed over his head.

Terrified, Gareth scrambled along the bank, ready to go in after him, when he saw Kay's head break surface.

"Kay!" he cried.

Kay heard him, but he looked dazed, as if he had forgotten what to do. Gareth lay flat and reached an arm down to him, but the bank was too high. Clumsy in his haste, he tore off the belt of his tunic and let it hang down. Kay managed to clutch it. Gareth drew him in under the bank until he could stand, and then caught his wrists and hauled him out. He was dazed still, shuddering, and collapsed on the edge of the overhang. Gareth took him by the shoulders and dragged him to safety.

He did not realize until then that the hunt had drawn closer. The horn again; the baying of hounds; the crashing of horses in the undergrowth. Gareth looked up, over Kay's huddled body, and saw the riders pushing through the trees into the open space on the far bank. Arthur was the foremost of them.

The king dismounted and strode to the edge of the stream. For a moment he stood still, looking down at the dead stag. "Kay!" he said.

Kay raised his head.

"Kay, if you wished to win the prize, it would have become you better to have joined the hunt. There is no honour in stealing another man's kill."

Kay flinched at the tone, but said nothing.

"Follow us back to Court," Arthur ordered.

Unsteadily, Kay rose to his feet. His voice rasped in his throat. "My lord, I –" He broke off. His head went up, inflexible pride meeting Arthur's hostility. Mouth tightening, he turned and stumbled back towards the horses.

Gareth stared across the stream at the huntsmen, at the horses milling around in the confined space, the bright clothes of their riders breaking up the greens of the forest. Kay refused to defend himself.

Gareth wanted to do it for him, to explain that Kay had killed the stag out of mercy, not to steal the prize, but he knew Arthur would not listen. Here Gareth was no more than a kitchen boy, Kay's servant – too insignificant to speak to kings. He caught up Kay's discarded cloak and followed him.

There was light still in the sky when the company reached Camelot. Kay and Gareth rode through the gates of the citadel last of all. Inside, among the horses and huntsmen, Arthur was waiting. He stood alone, a little space around him.

"Kay," he said.

His voice was quiet, but it carried. Kay approached and dismounted, but remained clinging to his bridle. Gareth suspected that that was all that kept him on his feet.

"Kay," King Arthur said, "don't fail to be at supper tonight. We're all eager to see you claim the prize for your kill."

In the crowd, someone laughed.

Kay drew in a gasping breath, said, "But I –" and stopped.

He faced Arthur. His black hair was plastered to his head, streaked against a face white as bone. His clothes were sodden from the stream. He was still refusing to justify himself.

"As you will, my lord," he said.

Arthur contemplated him. There was something between the two men, fierce as swords. The king could not allay it. Without another word, he turned and went inside.

At once the knights began to press around Kay.

"Give the kiss to my lady, Kay," one said. "Or meet me in combat tomorrow."

"Kiss my lady, Kay, or feel my sword."

"Give it to my lady."

"No, to mine."

At last Gareth understood. Kay had no lady of his own, no reason to choose any of the Court ladies over another. But whoever he chose the other knights would challenge him, to defend their lady's beauty or simply to win an easy victory. Kay was no fighter, and his sharp tongue had made him unpopular. Plenty of men would be glad to see him humiliated.

Kay's only choices were to decline the prize and be branded a coward, or fight combat after combat until he was seriously wounded or killed. Now he stood silent, mouth set, eyes parrying the mocking threats. Gareth's heart twisted in pity.

As the crowd thinned out another figure approached Kay, tall, dark, grave-faced: Lancelot.

"Kay," he said. Kay's head snapped round to face him. "Kay," Lancelot went on, "give the kiss to the queen. If anyone dares challenge, I will answer. It is my right; I am Queen's Champion."

It was a way out. But almost before Lancelot had finished Kay was replying, a cutting edge to his words. "Does your sword grow rusty, Sir Lancelot? Or have you not honour enough? Would it please you if they said Kay cowered behind your shield? No. I fight my own battles."

Before Kay's quivering fury Lancelot inclined his head, and moved away, his gravity undisturbed.

Gareth saw Kay's taut defiance begin to relax, only to gather again as another man came up – Gareth's own brother, Sir Gawain.

Gareth drew closer, listening eagerly, irrationally beginning to hope. Gawain was smiling faintly, and held out a hand. But Kay ignored it.

"I'm sorry, Kay," Gawain said. "I know you never meant this. Listen – do as Lancelot says, and give the kiss to the queen. There'll be challenges, but we'll meet them together – you and I, Lancelot, Gaheris – and I'll find some others. We'll fight a mêlée. We'll do it to entertain the guests."

Gareth was grinning delightedly at Gawain's solution, until he saw Kay shake his head. He was not hostile, as he had been to Lancelot, and Gareth thought that Gawain's courtesy had almost broken him, but he was still refusing.

"I cannot, Sir Gawain," he said. "I must face it alone. There are those who will brand me coward, who would not dare say such a thing of Gawain of Orkney. But I thank you."

Gawain hesitated, and then touched his arm. "Tell me if you change your mind," he said, and was gone.

Kay stood with his face turned away into Morial's neck. He was shivering in the evening chill. Gareth was afraid that he was weeping. He took a tentative step forward.

"They rejoice to see me shamed," Kay choked out. "Even the king."

"Not Gawain," Gareth said instantly.

"No, not Gawain." The words were sighed out.

Kay's shoulders drooped. Gareth went to him, wanting to get

him inside before he collapsed in front of the grooms. He needed a bath and a change of clothes; even then he would not be fit to face the ordeal in the great hall.

Before he could touch him, Kay straightened. There were no tears on his face, but he had a wild, desperate look that terrified Gareth.

"I'll not endure it," he said. "Everyone spits on my name. Arthur scorns my service. I'll go, and end it."

As he spoke he mounted again, and gathered Morial's reins.

"No!" Gareth cried, appalled. "Sir, they'll call you coward. You won't be able to come back! Sir, listen to me – go and talk to Gawain –"

He was speaking to empty air. Kay was already thrusting Morial through the gate.

Gareth flung himself into the saddle and followed.

He tracked Kay through the city by the sharp sound of Morial's hooves on the cobbles. Kay was unaware of him, but at the city gate he had to wait for the guards to open it, and Gareth managed to come up with him.

"Sir, don't –" he gasped out.

"Go away!" Kay snapped, and urged Morial out into the gathering darkness.

Ignoring his order, Gareth still followed, but once through the gate Kay's horse leapt forward, arrow-swift. Despairingly, Gareth spurred his own horse into a gallop, but he knew that this stocky chestnut had no hope of catching Morial.

Kay was returning the way they had come. The road crossed the valley, breasted the hill beyond, and followed the edge of the forest. In the last dim streaks of daylight Gareth lost sight of Kay. He wondered whether to go back, find Gawain, beg him for help, but by then Kay could be miles away – lost.

At length the road turned under the trees. Gareth had to check his horse but he began to hope again, for he knew that Kay would do the same. He would never risk laming Morial by a wild gallop in darkness.

Soon Gareth began to hear sounds in front of him. He pressed forward as fast as he dared until he came out into a long forest ride, sloping down towards the stream. Not far ahead, he could see Kay.

"Sir!" he called. "Wait for me!"

Kay halted, and pulled Morial round. As Gareth approached he said roughly, "I told you to go away."

"I can't leave you, sir," Gareth said. "What will you do alone? You're not even armed. You –"

Kay interrupted him. "Go back. You can't help me."

"Come with me, then," Gareth urged. "You're High Seneschal, sir, you can't throw it all away. Talk to Gawain and –"

At first he thought Kay was wavering, but the mention of Gawain had been a mistake. Kay's hands clenched on the reins.

"No," he said.

"Then I'm coming with you," Gareth said.

Kay stared at him.

"Don't be a fool, boy," he said. "Your life is there. They'll make you Knight at Pentecost. You'll belong."

"I'm not going back," Gareth said steadily. He dared reach out and take hold of Morial's bridle. "Not without you."

He was not sure himself why he offered the sacrifice. Most of the knights probably thought that he hated Kay – and with good reason, when Kay had put him to work in the kitchens. Gareth was not used to analysing himself, but he knew that hatred was the last thing he felt. And somehow, without having the words to express it, he knew that Camelot would not be Camelot if it had no place for a man such as Kay.

If Gareth had wanted to explain himself there was no time. Kay wrenched the bridle out of his grasp. The wild look was back in his eyes. "In God's name, leave me alone!" he cried.

Before Gareth could answer, another voice rang out like the note of a bell.

"Sir Kay."

Kay's head whipped round. A few yards further down the ride was a bridge across the stream, not far from where Kay had killed the stag. On this bridge stood a lady.

Afterwards, Gareth would find it hard to describe her. She was not young, nor beautiful. Her hair was dark, and her eyes, and she wore a blue mantle. Her face held such deep serenity that he thought he might drown in it.

With a dazed look, Kay walked Morial towards the bridge. There he dismounted, and went down on one knee. "Lady," he said. "What do you want with me?"

"I need a knight's service," she replied.

A shaken laugh escaped Kay. He gestured down the road. "There lies Camelot, lady," he said, "where the best knights in the world will vie to serve you. You have no need of Kay."

The lady's eyes remained gravely on him. "Sir Kay, this task is yours," she said.

She drew a cup from the folds of her mantle, and held it out to him. It was a plain chalice – made of pewter, Gareth guessed, or possibly silver. If he had seen it on a table in the great hall he would have passed it without a second glance, but here it seemed to gather to itself all the light that remained as the forest drew towards the dark.

"Fill this cup from the source of the stream," the lady said, "and bring it here to me. Do this, and I will tell you how to fulfil the custom of the hunt at Arthur's feast tonight."

Terror clawed at Gareth. Who was the lady? How could she know Kay's desperate need – unless through sorcery, or something deeper than sorcery? All his instincts told him to turn and flee, but instead he dismounted and came to stand beside Kay.

Kay was looking up at the lady, with swift hope lighting his face.

"I will try," he said, and took the cup from her. Briefly he looked startled, as if it was heavier than he had expected.

"You answer well," she said, "for the task is not as simple as it seems."

"May I help him?" Gareth asked.

Kay, still kneeling, gave him a fierce look, but the lady smiled.

"You may go with him," she said, "for your heart is faithful and brave. But the task is Kay's alone, if he wishes to win the reward. Meet me here, Sir Kay, when it is done."

Kay rose, and bowed.

Somehow, without Gareth's seeing exactly how, the lady withdrew into the shadows.

Kay stood gazing down into the cup, and without being told Gareth unsaddled Morial so that the horse could graze.

When he began to do the same with his chestnut, Kay said, "I don't need a nursemaid, boy."

But he made no protest when Gareth followed him along the bank of the stream.

Soon they passed the place where the stag had died. Gareth could still see how the horses had trampled the grass, and the scars on the bank where the stag had struggled, but of the body there was no sign.

Gareth could not remember seeing the huntsmen carrying in their kill, but he was worrying about something more practical – how long it would take to reach the source of the stream. Even if the lady told Kay how to answer the challenge, it would be useless if Kay was late returning. By now the light was all but gone; they groped forward with only the sound of the stream as a guide.

Then Gareth began to make out Kay's dark form ahead of him, outlined in faint silvery light. It was like moonlight. But moonrise was hours away. Only gradually, as the light strengthened, did Gareth realize that it came from the cup.

Radiance struck outwards from it, frosting the grass and brambles that overhung the path. It caught the branches of the trees above, so that they looked like the vaulting of some great cathedral. Kay and Gareth were walking up an aisle flanked by living columns, where light drizzled down like rain. The cup itself had grown too dazzling for Gareth to look at, and he half believed that it must sear the flesh from Kay's hands.

Kay moved like a man in a dream.

At last they came to a wall of tumbled rock, where the stream poured out above their heads. Kay halted and looked up.

The light blanched his features, cruelly revealing the lines of strain. He was near exhaustion. But after a second's pause, without a word or even a glance at Gareth, he reached out to grip the rock and began to climb.

Gareth watched anxiously. One-handed, carrying the cup, Kay was slow and clumsy. If he fell, he might injure himself, and injury meant failure and self-imposed exile.

He reached the source at last, and leant over precariously, clutching a spur of rock, to fill the cup. As the stream splashed into it the water itself received the radiance, and fell like molten silver from a crucible, veining the rock beneath until the pool at its foot brimmed with incandescent light.

Kay drew back, and began to edge his way down. He slid the last foot or two to the ground, staggering and barely saving the cup. Light splashed over Gareth's hands as he steadied Kay by the shoulders. Kay shrank into himself, as if he still could not admit that Gareth was there.

The brilliance of the falls died behind them as they returned, until their way was lit only by the cup between Kay's hands. Gareth became aware of tiny flickering movements at the edge of his sight, but when he jerked his head round there was nothing. He felt uneasily that he preferred not to see what had been there.

At the same time he began to sense an oppressive weight overhead, as if the sky had suddenly clamped down at the level of the trees. The air seemed taut as a bowstring; it was hard to breathe. The forest was silent, except for their footsteps, yet the silence itself howled a malediction. Darkness pressed in on the fragile sphere of light shed by the cup, as if it could burst it like a bubble.

Kay was glancing swiftly from side to side, and up at the canopy, now drowned in darkness. Gareth heard his breathing grow harsh and shallow. He carried the cup as if its weight was almost too great to bear. At last he stumbled to a stop, and stood shivering.

Gareth knew that he himself had been only lightly brushed by the edge of the mystical pattern that was playing itself out in the forest. Kay was enmeshed more deeply in the heart of it, and the assault they endured now was hurled more savagely against him.

Daringly, Gareth slid an arm round him. "Sir?" he said.

Gasping for breath, Kay leant back against his shoulder. "Go – if you can," he said. "Take the cup."

"But it's your task, sir. The lady said so."

"You must do it. I can't. I am not – worthy."

He was trying to give the cup to Gareth. Light spattered out of it. In another minute he would drop it; unprotected, the dark would crush them. With his free hand Gareth steadied the cup, but he would not take it. He tightened his hold on Kay and urged him gently forward, half supporting him, so that all Kay had to do was keep the cup from spilling.

After a few paces like this Kay shook his head as if to clear it, and drew himself erect. The look he gave Gareth – mingled shame and gratitude, and a kind of derisive resolve – almost made Gareth weep.

Now Kay went on more firmly; it did not seem long before they came to the bridge where the lady waited.

"Welcome," she said.

As she spoke the tightness in the air was scattered. The unheard voices sank into true silence. The huge, imminent presence overhead lifted and was gone. Gareth felt that he could raise his head, and he drew a clean breath that became a gasp of astonishment.

Beyond the lady, twilight still glimmered along the ride, as if no time had passed since the three of them had first stood there.

Kay walked forward, holding out the cup, bearing it easily now. "I have what you asked for, lady," he said.

The lady smiled and took it from him. "You have done well, sir," she said. "And now come with me and see a wonder."

She led them along the opposite bank of the stream until they came to a clearing. Gareth was not surprised to see the stag there, lying dead among the creeping foliage of the forest floor.

The lady held the cup over the stag's head and tilted it. Liquid light poured out, and splashed between the antlers. Beneath it the velvet brow glimmered silver; trickles of silver began to creep down the muzzle, the neck, along the curve of the antlers. The trickles grew, spread, ran one into another, until a tide of silver was sweeping across the body – until it shone as Gareth had first seen it.

Only scars seamed the side where the wounds had gaped. The flank rose and fell gently in a regular rhythm. The eyes opened.

An anguished cry, stifled almost at once, was torn from Kay.

The stag raised one foreleg, then the other, and surged to its feet. The antlers laced the forest darkness like the ripple of moonlight on water.

The watchers stood in the circle of quiet radiance.

"What was dead lives," the lady said. "What was lost is restored. All pain is healed." She smiled at Kay. "And now, sir, your reward."

She drew close to Kay and spoke softly to him. Gareth could not hear the words, but he could see the change in Kay – the sudden light springing into his face, the indrawn breath that became a spasm of shocked laughter.

Then as he gazed into the lady's face all laughter dissolved in awe, and he fell to his knees. The lady raised the cup, and reached out her other hand to him in a sign of blessing.

On their return to Camelot Kay went to bathe and change, while Gareth was caught up in the final turmoil of preparing for the feast. When he went up to serve in the great hall he looked vainly for Kay. The first course was on the table before the Seneschal made his entrance.

It was an entrance.

Sir Kay was an austere man, but tonight he was dressed magnificently in a blue velvet robe, the high collar stiff with silver thread. He stalked down the length of the hall, dragging silence after him, and stood before Arthur with his head high.

Gareth edged closer.

"My lord," Kay said, "I am here as you commanded, to take the prize for the kill."

By now Arthur's anger had ebbed; he was looking uneasy. "Are you sure, Kay?" he asked. "Do you want more time to think?"

It was an overture of friendship, perhaps an offer of help, but Kay rejected it with all the arrogance of an untamed hawk.

"I have made my choice, my lord."

He was quite white, except for a hectic flush on his cheekbones. Gareth had seen him like this before – so tense you could have strung a bow with him. There was nothing Gareth could do except pray that no one would goad him into losing that precarious self-control.

Kay turned his back on the dais and faced the company in the body of the hall: the knights and their ladies, the guests for the Easter Court, the squires, pages and servants.

"I have made my choice," he repeated. "A choice that no one in this hall will quarrel with."

His confidence held them silent for a brief moment, until someone called out, "*I* claim quarrel, Kay, unless you choose my lady!"

Clamour erupted; some of the knights leapt to their feet. To Gareth's relief Kay held himself aloof, showing nothing but faint disdain. He spoke to Arthur.

"With your leave, my lord . . . ?"

Arthur nodded.

Kay beckoned to Gareth. "Boy, bring me the king's shield from the wall."

With an effort, Gareth stopped himself from gawking and went to do Kay's bidding. Arthur's shield hung behind his seat, at the back of the dais, with the shields of his knights alongside it.

As Gareth stretched to lift it down he began to understand. A tight knot of excitement grew in his stomach.

He carried the shield to where Kay was waiting. By this time Arthur had imposed silence again.

"The hall is filled with fair ladies," Kay said. "So beautiful that I should not presume to judge. Yet there is another more beautiful still, and she must be my choice."

He stepped forward and touched his lips to the icon of the Mother of God that Arthur bore on his shield.

The hall had been quiet before; now it was as if all sound had been wiped away with a sponge. Kay moved away from the shield and looked around. A gleam of triumph shone in his eyes.

"Do I hear a challenge?" he asked.

There was no reply.

Kay turned to the king with a faintly enquiring look. Arthur smiled, half reluctantly.

"No challenge, Kay," he said. He waved a hand at Gareth. "Put it away, boy."

As Gareth returned the shield to its place a babble broke out; he heard Bedivere saying, "Was that blasphemous, or just damn clever?"

Gareth smiled to himself, but the smile faded as he turned back and saw Kay bowing to the king as if he meant to leave.

"Don't go, Kay," the king said. "Take your place with us."

Kay drew himself up. His air of triumph had gone, leaving only that indomitable pride.

No! Gareth willed him. What was the good of pride, if all it led to was cold and loneliness and a bitter brooding? Kay had borne the cup; he had endured all the force of that evil assault; he had seen the wonder of the stag. None of these others, not even King Arthur himself, could understand that, but they could not be blamed for it. The last pain would not be truly healed unless Kay could dare to be reconciled.

There was an empty place at the high table, close to Arthur. Gawain, seated beside it, made a tiny gesture of invitation.

Kay raised a hand to his throat, as if he could not breathe. He made no move, but when Gawain rose and guided him to the seat he did not resist. He sat with eyes cast down, then Arthur leant across the table towards him, speaking earnestly.

Gareth let out a long sigh of relief, and went to fetch a jug to pour wine for his lord.

THE CASTLES OF TESTING

Keith Taylor

And so it begins. With this story we begin the first of the Grail Quests. The first to avow his allegiance to the Quest was Sir Gawain, and to a man all the other knights made their pledges. This story follows the adventures of Gawain's brother, Sir Gareth. Keith Taylor (b. 1946) is an Australian fantasy writer who is also an expert on Celtic history. He is best known for the Bard series of novels, set at the time of the fall of the Roman Empire. The series runs Bard *(1981),* The First Longship *(1989),* The Wild Sea *(1986), Ravens' Gathering *(1987) and* Felimid's Homecoming *(1991). He has written another series set in the turbulent days of ancient Ireland and dealing in particular with the enmity between two warring tribes, the Danans and the Friths. The series began with* The Sorcerers' Sacred Isle *(1989), but of special relevance to this anthology is the second book,* The Cauldron of Plenty *(1989).*

I

Gareth of Orkney walked from the Great Hall of Camelot, dazed, fervent, hardly aware of any earthly thing. The radiance that throbbed from the vision they had all seen still dazzled his sight. Intense and pure, it had surged in zones from the object that floated above their upturned, amazed faces, and traversed the Great Hall from end to end before disappearing. It had been draped in fine cloth whose folds had never stirred as it moved through the air.

Who could say what it had been? The king's awed declaration
that they had seen the Holy Grail was most likely correct. Gareth
was certain only that he had looked upon something other-worldly
– greatly, passionately to be desired.

He would seek it.

All the knights felt the same. Gareth's own brother had been first
to vow that he would ride in Quest of the object. "I shall search for
it a year and a day," he had said, "if it is to be found."

Gareth supposed he should be making preparations if he wanted
to leave on the morrow. Horses, weapons, armour and provisions
– and, more than all, a proper leavetaking from Leontyne.

But Gareth felt he sorely needed advice. Spirit aflame, thoughts
in a jumble, he walked after the man who had been his friend and
mentor from the day he came to Arthur's Court.

The tall figure of Lancelot in his flame-coloured jupon was
easy to follow. He never once looked back. Unlike the others,
he seemed to suffer no turmoil of mind and to know precisely
where he was going.

A woman waited for him in a window alcove. Gareth recognized
her at once. The heavy yellow hair, full figure and clear-cut beauty
had no equal in Arthur's court. Even Gareth's own wife Leontyne
was not as lovely. And that was saying a good deal.

"Lancelot," she said, and her tone was bitter.

"My lady." He took a swift step forward, then stopped dead
at the look she gave him.

"Arthur was grieved, wasn't he? When the knights all said they
would imitate Gawain, he wept. He said Gawain had taken all his
knights from him to follow a hard Quest from which many cannot
return, and had scattered the fellowship of the Round Table! He
was right. And he said that you above all others he would not
lose. But you will go."

"I must."

"You above all others *I* would not lose," Guinevere said.

Gareth had never seen a queen's heart breaking. He saw it now.
Neither of the two had noticed him, and he longed to turn and
go before they did, for clearly this meeting was private. But if he
hurried he might draw their attention.

"It may be best if you do!" Lancelot looked out of the
window, gripping the stone ledge, his arms rigidly straight. The
flame-coloured jupon stretched across the leopard's muscles of his
back. "You think I wish to go seeking the Grail?"

No turmoil of mind? Gareth saw he had been mistaken there.

"Of course. Do not lie to me. Didn't you say it to Arthur? We all heard you." She flung Lancelot's own words into his face. "'This Quest will be a great honour, and since a knight must die some time, how better can he die than in Quest of the Holy Grail?'"

"How better, indeed?" Lancelot asked. "*Madame*, the Grail cannot have appeared among us for nothing. It was a miracle; it is as though we have been summoned to seek it, and to strive with all our souls to be worthy." Irony entered his voice. "There are souls at the Round Table that could stand a certain amount of bettering. Mine among them."

"They could be bettered in Camelot as well as by chasing a vision to the ends of the earth. At least as well."

"Perhaps. But after what they have seen this day the knights will not stay."

"The knights are needed here!" Guinevere said hotly. "What about the oppressed, the weak, those threatened by bandits, monsters and evil neighbours? They make their appeals at this Court, knowing that here, unique of all the places on earth, they can find a champion. Not now! They will find the Round Table empty, their hope gone."

"Knights on a Quest can challenge evil men where they find them, *madame*," Lancelot said reasonably, but his tone, raw and tense as his posture, was greatly at odds with his words. "Alas, they will find them throughout the realm."

"But you have no need to go." Guinevere's voice trembled. "Lancelot, you are the Queen's Champion of England. What if I command you as queen to stay?"

"You must not! It's because I am your champion that I must leave, Guinevere. Say I remain here in Camelot. With you, as I swear is my heart's wish. Say that Lancelot du Lac does not ride in Quest of the Grail. Do you think there will be anybody who does not guess why?"

"Oh . . ." The word was a gasp of pain. At last the queen said, "Is that so significant, after all? There has been wicked gossip before. Perhaps this will inspire a whole new round of it – but Lancelot, what are whispers?"

"My lady," Lancelot said though clenched teeth, "they will do more than whisper. They will make it a bawdy joke. I'll have to fight twenty, no doubt slay some. Arthur has loved and trusted us too well to suspect, but even he may realize."

The word chilled Gareth to the bone. *Realize*. That was a word men only used of things that were true.

"Do not go."

"God's light, Guinevere! I'm called the best knight in the realm, but this is a vain Quest for me. I'd never achieve the Grail with sin in my heart that's dearer to me than all the virtues." Leopard-swift, he approached her and gripped her white shoulders. "I ride to keep safe your repute and perhaps your life. No other reason. I would there might be."

"No other reason?" Guinevere spat. "When your bastard came to the Court only today, and sits in the Siege Perilous, sent here by his mother and knighted by you? I think indeed you do not ride to find the Grail! Indeed there's another reason. The Lady Elaine still lives. By all accounts she is still beautiful after sixteen years."

There was no doubt left. Gareth knew the words and tone of a jealous woman. He'd been married to Leontyne, with all her fire of pride and passion, for four years now. They had had their share of scenes like this.

He turned to go. Too abruptly! He stumbled at the top step.

"Who's there?" Lancelot snapped.

The Orkney prince regained his footing and stared through a private darkness at his mentor, the man he revered as he never had his father.

"Gareth. I had wished to speak with you."

"Gareth?" Lancelot spoke the name with relief. There were so many other men it might have been — jealous enemies or scandal-mongers — and then he looked into Gareth's face and wondered if he would not have preferred that after all.

He tried to carry it off. "Well, my friend, was it nothing that could not wait? I hadn't a thought save that of asking my Lady Guinevere's leave to ride on the Quest. As her officer, I will need it."

"As her champion," Gareth said levelly. "It happens I was so close on your heels I heard it *all*."

He stressed the "all".

Guinevere felt a pang. Gareth would not betray them; there was no man less like a tale-bearer. And for that matter he had witnessed nothing that could be taken as firm evidence of guilt. Still, the disillusion in his face was hurtful to see. He was young, despite his prowess and worship, so young yet.

Would he be more mature if he could take adultery and treason with a laugh?

Lancelot's eyes glittered. He said fiercely, "And have you turned spy?"

Gareth whitened, but not from fear. "I came like an eager fool to ask if you might wish me to ride on the Quest at your side. Not now. You assume the Quest for appearances' sake! I don't know which way you will travel, but I shall be bound fast in the other direction."

He waited a moment, giving Lancelot a chance to reply. For a moment there was menace and anger in the other knight's face.

Although bigger and considerably younger than he, Gareth knew he would have small chance if challenged to battle. Lancelot had beaten bigger men beyond counting. Then he bent his dark head in shame.

Gareth regretted his words. He wanted to reach out his hand and tell his mentor that he was grieved to have spoken so. If he did that, it might be well between them again . . . or more probably he would sound like a whining puppy.

The words stuck in his throat and the moment was gone.

Guinevere came forward. She looked at Gareth in a way that scorned his condemnation and all the world's. She took Lancelot's hand.

"Leave us," she commanded.

Gareth could do nothing but bow and depart. Outraged honour came a sad second best to outraged love. But still the daylight seemed tarnished, and the glory of Arthur's Court seemed tarnished by what he had discovered.

He returned to the hall. Except for the brooding figure of the king, only two men remained there.

One was the tall, strong youth sitting in the Siege Perilous, the Seat of Danger, face upraised as though he still saw the shining vision of the Grail. Lancelot's son. He had all his father's superb grace and lightness of movement, and their faces were alike too, though the youth's held a tranquil, other-worldly longing. None of the father's reckless, quicksilver passions there.

He would never be found to do anything so human as to stumble on a stair – or sin with a woman. And the certain, wholly confident way he had walked to the dreadful Siege Perilous to seat himself there, never hesitating, had jarred on Gareth. He reckoned he would find it hard work learning to like the stranger. What was his name? Oh, yes . . . Galahad.

The other man present did not sit in a place of honour, or even at the Round Table itself. He sat in shadows, at one of the long tables against the wall. Even so, Gareth knew him at once. He knew him well.

"Sir Ironside," he said.

The notorious Red Knight turned his head. Eight years younger than Lancelot, he had long indulged his furious passions to such excess that his craggy face looked a complete decade older. Yet the man's uncommon strength had survived his vices. Stormy, bitter vitality blazed from him, and power to command.

Despite his great size, Gareth still looked too fresh-faced and pleasant to have conquered such a seasoned villain. But he had. He'd also won worship by overthrowing the Red Knight's brothers – as bad as he, as devoted to pillage and bloodshed – and slaying the eldest. Not that Ironside bore the Orkney prince a grudge on that account.

He looked more pensive now than Gareth had ever seen him.

"Hah, Sir Gareth," he said. "This has been a White Sunday of wonders, even for the king's Court! First that stranger boy sits in the Siege Perilous and survives it. Now the Grail appears. It was that; it had to be. I never saw such holy light revealed to my eyes before."

"Nor I." Gareth indicated the place on the bench beside Sir Ironside. "I would sit with you, by your leave."

"And welcome." Oddly, the Red Knight had more liking for the young man who had vanquished him than for most other knights of the Round Table. "I'm astonished, though. I'd have thought you would be eager to prepare and go like the rest."

"I was," Gareth said heavily. Sir Ironside glanced at him closely. "I *am*. I haven't so much as given thought to the direction, but that may not even matter. Surely the Grail is a thing of the spirit and can appear anywhere?"

The Red Knight nodded. "It makes sense to me."

He had no doubt that there was more to Gareth's change of mind than that. He observed what went on around him.

Lancelot, Gareth's ideal, had left the hall swiftly, and Gareth had followed. Not long after Gareth had returned, far slower and more troubled than when he had gone, and if a man were prepared to doubt the queen's virtue he might surmise a reason. Ironside had heard the gossip too. He tended to believe it.

He waited, all these things shut firmly behind his teeth.

"And do you go?" Gareth asked.

"What?" Ironside glared and half started up. "Is that a bad joke? Me seek the Grail? You did conquer me once, but if you insult me, Gareth, you will have it to do again, I promise you."

"Sit," Gareth bade him. "I don't fear your anger, but I should fear to joke about the Grail. You were allowed to see it, with all the rest of the fellowship. Why shouldn't you seek it?"

"You know why. Only a knight perfect in faith and pure in spirit can find the Grail. Ask your lady if she thinks I'm such a one."

Gareth knew indeed. He had rescued the Lady Leontyne from the Red Knight's besieging forces, and had spared his life on the condition that he renounce his bloody, evil ways.

Ironside was trying. He had entered Arthur's service and sought a place at the Round Table for two years, doing a number of great deeds in that time, and, what was even more remarkable in a man of his nature, had waited in patience.

Then his inner devil had broken loose. Sir Ironside's mistress had stabbed him with a dagger during a raging quarrel and he had killed her with his hands.

"You won pardon from the king."

"Yes," Ironside said with bleak amusement. "He commanded me a task that was all but certain death. At that price I kept my head. What of it? Slaying an ogre does not make a man worthy to achieve the Grail."

"We're none of us worthy," Gareth argued. "They say a man can clean his soul. Five years ago you were regarded in your parts as that ogre was in Lyonesse, with loathing and hatred. Today you're the hero who delivered them from a monster, and they are making songs about the Red Knight that will be sung for a hundred years. It isn't a matter of prowess only. Five years ago you would not have troubled to help them. You'd have gone somewhere else and turned to brigandage again."

"I'm growing more virtuous?" The Red Knight reached for the wine flagon. "Loathing and hatred are a good part of what makes the world turn, youngster. My brothers and I were weaned on it."

"I and mine were not quite fed on sweetness entire. Have you looked at Agravaine and Mordred?"

It was sharper bitterness than the Red Knight would have expected from Gareth. It was also very true. Satan would witness that any son of King Lot by Queen Morgause, even the most innocent, must know something about disgust and hatred. Perhaps that even explained Gareth's kindness to his former enemy, despite the Red Knight's grisly misdeeds, a certain fellow feeling . . .

Sir Ironside drank, deeply and quickly, to drown all such speculations. They were unmanly and a waste of time.

"I have looked," he said. "So. What am I likely to gain on the Grail Quest more than they would?"

"Even looking for purity and grace may lift a man's soul closer to it," Gareth answered. "And when he encounters earthly dangers, it's good to have a strong comrade. Will you ride with me?"

"Gladly," Ironside said. He clasped Gareth's big hand.

Well, thought the Red Knight. Maybe you are right and the Quest will uplift me. But I wish I might hear what your wife says when you tell her. You, riding after the Holy Grail, companioned by her old enemy who once besieged her in her own castle until you rescued her!

II

Being caught in cold grey rain with no shelter in sight makes tempers grow short. Sir Ironside's had never been long, and even Gareth's sweet nature had human limits. Blinking water out of his eyes, he groused again about something that had sat ill with him since their travels began.

"It were better to have ridden as a nameless knight. Let any see that shield or horse of yours, and we will have to fight them. The least they will do is bar their doors."

"Spine of God!" Ironside snarled. "Not that again, I pray you! I'll never hide my name or station! I've said nothing against those namby-pamby folded hands you use for a bearing. Don't wherrit at me concerning mine."

"It isn't shame or fear I advise," Gareth snapped back. "Your arms are a provocation to attack on sight, as well you know. It accords ill with our Quest."

He eyed his companion's red shield with its five red roundels on a silver pale. Even without the strange flame-coloured horse he rode, that blazon was enough to identify him from end to end of Britain.

Gareth had enemies too. During this Quest he did not wish to fight for worship or glory, or in any cause but defence of the weak, so he had left his Orkney blazon behind.

He wore a shirt of simple grey mail and his shield was purple, with a bearing of two white hands folded in prayer. Like the Red Knight, he carried full mail and helm on a following packhorse, but even among that gear there was nothing to show his name or princely rank.

"Cursed rain!" Ironside said, glaring into the thick, endless curtains of it. "Why did we have to ride north, tell me that? The place to look for the Grail is at Glastonbury, surely, down in the Summer Country. That is where it used to be kept."

"Yes. It used to be. Joseph of Arimathea brought it to Britain, with the Spear that pierced Our Lord, and so founded the Abbey. His descendants were abbots there for generations."

"I know the tale," Ironside said impatiently. "Who does not? Then one abbot looked with lust on a young pilgrim woman. He would have ravished her near the altar with the holy relics." He grinned savagely. "A rogue after my own heart! But the Spear flew of itself and pierced him through. More honour than he deserved, eh? Then Spear and Grail together both vanished away. The descendants of Joseph have never been abbots since. The line is dead."

"Then you know why we haven't looked for it in the Summer Country. We have been over that a score of times now."

"And I mean to make it twenty-one! We have nothing better to do. Certes, yes, the Grail and Spear are now in some enchanted castle that appears and vanishes like a wine vision. Why shouldn't it appear near Glastonbury? That is enchanted country, a place of visions and other-worldly matters. It ever has been. And that's where most of the knights have gone."

Gareth's long patience broke. "Rumours of strange enchanted castles come thickest from this north country. It's been so for a hundred years. If we find nothing, well, we can always return to the Summer Country. We've found adventures on this road, haven't we? You complain like a kitchen-maid."

Sir Ironside sneered. "You'd know about kitchen-maids. You worked among them long enough, to the disgrace of your lineage. Let us have the truth out to air! You wouldn't take the way to Glastonbury because it turned your pure stomach to think of meeting Lancelot there. What happened between you and he on White Sunday? Or could I guess?"

Between his teeth, Gareth said, "We're questing for a holy thing, the most holy of all that is in the world. Let us not quarrel."

"Bah! Not quarrel, you say, now that I've cut too near the bone. Perhaps we ought to quarrel! I've always thought you beat me more by fortune than by might and prowess, Gareth. How do you fight in adversity, when the ground is a mire and you can hardly see? I fight damned well."

"Listen!"

"Listen, the devil's cloven hoofs!"

"Sir Ironside, stint your noise and listen!" Gareth ordered. "Not to me. To *that*."

Distantly, through the sound of the drumming rain, came a different noise, like that of some vast millstone at work. It crept into Gareth's and Ironside's bones. Sitting on their tough, high-cantled saddles, with the rain drenching their woollen cloaks and dripping down their necks, they listened.

The direction from which it came was hard to judge. Gareth pointed to the north-east at last, and Ironside did not object. They trotted their chargers that way. The patient packhorses followed.

They came to a wide vale. Lightning showed its general shape even through the rain, so that the knights discerned rocky heights on either side. The stream running through it had brimmed its banks and flooded the valley.

Something stood in the middle of the waters, something square and buttressed, with a tall, square-battlemented tower at each corner, strong as bedrock despite its old-fashioned form. The stream divided to flow around it in a yellow-brown torrent. Lightning branched again, showing every detail from the stones in the towers – sharp and unworn, as though the masons had cut them yesterday – to the yeasty foam on the water.

"This isn't canny," Ironside shouted. "Who ever built a castle in the bottom of a valley instead of on a height?"

A bridge crossed the stream three-quarters of the way. It did not appear to have broken, or been undermined by the swollen stream; it stopped, straight and clean, as though it had been built no further than that.

Then, in stunned amazement, the knights saw why. The castle began turning. The entire massive structure revolved on its foundations before their eyes. This was the impossible huge motion that had made the millwheel racket.

They looked wildly at each other. Each saw mirrored in the other man's face his own urge to spur away from the spot as fast as he could, or cast himself into the torrent – for a sight such as that could collapse the mind into madness.

Gareth gripped the Red Knight's arm and pointed. He could not speak, not that he would have been heard.

The castle's front wall had come into view, pierced by a black arched gateway, wide open – and built outward from the gateway protruded the missing end of the bridge. Briefly, the two pieces opposed each other as the castle turned, while lightning showed a gap of two or three feet between them. Then the gateway passed from sight. One of the square corner towers came into view instead.

In the next moment the lightning ceased, and the castle halted its revolving also. Gareth saw a faint, wondrous light shine around its towers and battlements. He crossed himself.

"Ironside!" he shouted. Now that the miraculous castle was still and the thunder silent, he could make himself heard. "See! That's like the light of the Grail! Softer, dimmer, but on my knightly word it's the same!"

"You're right!" Sir Ironside roared. "By the Nails! We've come to the Grail Castle!" With an exuberant bellow, he slapped Gareth on the back. A weaker man would have toppled from his horse. "I eat my words! Your judgement was right!"

"God's been good," Gareth said. His soul filled with wonder. He was looking at a miracle by any sane man's standard. Somewhere in that castle, on the far side of the rushing, deadly water, lay the object of their quest – the Grail, symbol and vessel of redemption, imbued with the light that dispersed all blindness.

"How are we to get in there?" Even Ironside felt awe. Nevertheless, he looked at the revolving castle with the eyes of a man who had lived by plunder and pillage – as a professional problem of entry, to get at the treasures within. A lifetime's habits died hard.

"With courage and faith," Gareth answered. "When the castle turns, the gateway will come round opposite the bridge, as it did before. Then a bold man can spur his horse across and leap in at the right moment."

"Bold man or crazed fool? Spur across that wet slippery bridge? Blind in the rain? And leap that gap?"

"It's not wide."

True, it was not wide. They would have to make the leap while the castle revolved, though, and if they missed they would shatter their bones against the wall, then be ground under the churning foundations.

Ironside felt his stomach clench at the vision. And maybe it would be judgement on him for the various men he had treated to the rack, the boot and the ladder in order to find their treasures.

Gareth said earnestly, "We can't hold back. God has allowed us to come here even though we aren't worthy. The Grail must be within. If we shrink, I believe we'll never come so close to it again. I would rather die."

From most men, a speech such as that would have moved the Red Knight to his wolf's laughter. Gareth was different. He meant it. He also meant that "us" and "we".

Ironside glowered at the castle's looming walls. They were beginning to move again. Time to decide . . . Ah, hell burn it! Such respect as he commanded at Arthur's Court was based on the fact that no truthful man could call him coward. He laughed.

"Turn the packhorses loose! I'll follow where you lead. First man to leap has the best chance, and I won't crowd too close on your heels."

Gareth spurred his horse onto the bridge, fixing his gaze on the gateway alone. The stones rang. The bridge passed under him. His grey charger leaped, landed, and carried him through the gateway in one rush of motion. Gareth rode halfway across the courtyard to give the Red Knight room, then turned with a triumphant curvet.

Horse and man were blurred shapes as they made the leap. For them it lay at an angle, across a widening gap.

Their landing was awkward. Gareth was racing for the gateway again while they were still in mid-leap, for he saw their danger of falling.

He met them face to face on the stub of the bridge. Shoving his feet deep into the stirrups, he seized the bridle of Ironside's horse and cried a command to his own. Forefeet braced, it leaned backwards. Gareth hauled with all the strength of his big young body. A stirrup-leather burst from the strain.

The red charger's back hooves caught at the rim of the bridge. Men and horses clattered into the courtyard together. The red charger fell to its knees. Sir Ironside fell with it, cursing ferociously, and took some time to struggle clear. Then he gripped Gareth's hand.

"That was well done. I won't forget it."

He felt his warhorse's legs for damage.

"No bones gone," he said at last. "I cannot say yet about the tendons or hooves, but it seems he can walk to the stables. Surely this castle has some?"

"Stables?" Gareth looked at him in disbelief. "Man, somewhere in this castle the *Holy Grail* is to be found, and you talk of stables!"

"You may well believe I talk of stables." Ironside took his horse's bridle. "This destrier is one that I raised from a colt. He's been a truer comrade than my own brothers, and saved my life in a dozen frays and ambuscades. I like him better than I like most men."

Gareth was persuaded, at least to the extent of searching for stables, and when they found that the castle had them, with hay and oats in good measure and all else necessary, he owned that Ironside had been right.

"You are the sounder preacher, after all," he said. "Belike you will end your life as a bishop."

They crossed the courtyard towards the inner keep. At the entrance to the castle's Great Hall they met the first living creature they had found within – if he were not a spirit. It was a man in pristine white monk's robe and scapular, his face concealed within a deep cowl.

Gareth's skin prickled, and even Ironside's throat turned dry.

"Welcome, Sir Gareth, Prince of Orkney," he said. "Welcome, Sir Ironside of the Red Laundes."

"Who are you, holy sir?" Gareth asked bluntly.

"I am the Seneschal of this castle. Its lord is known as Le Roi Pêcheur."

"The Fisher King?" Gareth frowned in puzzlement. "I've never heard of him. Unless you mean the One who made His followers fishers of men?"

"No. They are not the same."

"I never heard of him either," Ironside said suspiciously.

"He is the Guardian of the Holy Grail. Yet he suffers a wound that cannot heal in this life. His kingdom is barren and blighted."

"Where is his kingdom?" Gareth asked.

"Sir knight, from that question I pray you to hold me excused. I may not tell you. Nor is it likely that you will see him."

"We came searching for that which he guards."

"Yes. Only those who seek the Grail can find this castle at all. Few can enter it."

"And what is its name?" Gareth asked.

"The Four-Cornered Castle, or the Turning Fortress. In the language that was spoken in Britain before the Romans, it is called Caer Pedryvan."

The Seneschal bowed, and led them to a chamber where all they needed lay prepared. He moved before them with a soundless gliding motion, like that in dreams.

Splashing in deep Roman baths, they were attended – most dreamlike, again – by unseen beings, who oiled, massaged, scraped and towelled them. Each man was dressed in tunic and hose afterwards – red for Ironside, gold, azure and white for Gareth. Then they were conducted to a hall where spiced meat, fruit and wine were brought by the same unseen hands.

They devoured course after course with famished appetites, in spite of the strange surroundings. The wine proved strong. It warmed the last lingering chill of the rainstorm from their flesh. The Seneschal did not appear again.

"The wine's agreeable," Ironside said contentedly. "If we were not on a holy Quest, the cellars of this castle might repay a visit."

Gareth thought sadly, but with a certain insidious smugness, that Lancelot would not even find the castle. Not now. After pledging his word to serve Arthur faithfully, he had presumed to love Guinevere. That oath was resoundingly broken. Why, Lancelot himself knew it.

And now Gareth, who had served humbly in the kitchens of Arthur's court for a year before receiving his knighthood, sat in the hall of the awesome Grail Castle, where no man who was perjured might enter.

What did the priests say? He who would be greatest among you, let him first be the least? Something like that. And Gareth had followed that counsel while still young and untried. Perhaps he would after all be the man who achieved the Quest.

Titling the flagon again, he said, "It's in my mind that we ought to find the chapel, Sir Ironside, and keep vigil there till dawn instead of sleeping. It's fitter preparation for seeking the Grail."

"Well thought of," Sir Ironside agreed, draining his own cup. He added caustically, "If a bit late."

The radiance in the hall had grown dimmer. There were shadows, high in its vaulted ceiling and piled deep in corners, that Gareth did not remember seeing when they had entered. In the doorway he brushed through a clinging cobweb that had certainly not been there before. It was odd.

"Gareth, is it my fancy, or does this enchanted light fade?" asked Ironside.

"It fades." Gareth was already reduced to feeling his way along the wall. "It does fade. There are cobwebs and dust now! I feel them thickening. Something's amiss."

Ironside stumbled. He voiced a raw oath which for him, nevertheless, was excessively mild. "Let's find torches! I'm not for blundering about in a place we don't know. Besides, the chapel may open off the courtyard."

They missed their way twice. Ironside lost his temper and roared for the Seneschal, even threatening to take off his head if he did not appear. Nothing answered except echoes. They seemed to distort, turning into the whimpers and groans of men who had died in his dungeon, the sobs of women he had ravished, the final shriek of his mistress. Cold sweat broke out on his skin and his ire died. He did not raise his voice again.

At last they stumbled into the courtyard, breaking through a vast grey curtain of spiderwebs to reach it. The rain had stopped. Moonlight shone through the ragged clouds, falling on wet pavestones that had become cracked and crooked.

"More enchantment." The Red Knight's voice was thick. "Listen! Our horses do not like it either."

Gareth said angrily, "This began when you talked of slaying the Seneschal! I will not give up. If I can find the chapel, all may be well yet."

He did not truly believe it. However, he made a flambeau and got it burning. The immense cobwebs across the entrance to the keep hissed and shrivelled as he swung the brand against them. Inside, every passage or door he entered led to blank walls, and when he came upon a stair he was stopped halfway, at the mouth of a black shaft too wide for leaping.

Frustrated, he turned to descend. The castle revolved again, with its vast millwheel noise, and stones fell with a lost, hollow booming. Gareth feared the whole stair would collapse before he reached the bottom again.

That was enough; he fled. There was no difficulty at all in finding his way out. The flambeau showed mildew scabbing the walls, wetness seeping from cracks. The message could not be mistaken.

Appalled, Gareth thought, It started so well. Why has it all gone wrong?

The fortress had stopped turning, with the bridge in its right position. Also, the rainstorm was over, and to leap the slight gap was child's play for horsemen like Gareth and Ironside.

The bitterness of failure sat with them in their saddles.

Ashamed, angry, smarting, they sought shelter beneath the rocky
heights. When they looked back, the Turning Fortress had gone.
Nothing remained but an immense muddy hole, stirred and swirled,
with floodwater pouring into it.

III

"Nae better are you than a heathen savage," Gareth said in fury.
"Talking o' horses and stables in the Grail Castle itsel', wanting
tae raid the wine cellars, and syne the threat you uttered against
its Senseschal! That caused us tae fail. I will never achieve the
Quest now."

The accents of his boyhood among Orkney fishers and crofters
came back to his lips when he was impassioned or anxious. His
wife liked it. The Red Knight was not his wife and did not like
it in the least.

"The fault's none of mine," he said shortly. "And mind your
tongue with me. Any more insults, boy, and this heathen savage
will yank it out with his fingers."

Gareth looked back at the Red Knight, his own anger waxing.
"I am a prince of Orkney, and the one wha' conquered you
and a' your brothers. I am not boy tae you or any man!"
Unless he's Lancelot. "As for ripping oot tongues, suppose
you try."

Bending forward from the waist, he thrust his arms and
head into the mail shirt he had doffed the night before, and
began the shrugging, wriggling contortions that were needed to
make it slide past his hips. The invisible servitors of the castle
had placed it with their chargers in the stable. They had not
cleaned it. The mail was still clogged with mire and beginning
to rust.

Ironside's fierce, ravaged face twisted with a rage so strong
it seemed scarcely human. "You say? Come on, then. Let's
settle this matter. With swords and shields, like knights, *boy*.
I'll take your pert tongue, as I said. And your head with
it!"

Gareth welcomed the other's challenge. Wretched with shame
and loss, seething with ire, he reckoned a fight to be the perfect
release. "We shall see who loses his head. Go, find a place where
it suits you to die, since you will have it. I'll finish arming and join
you directly!"

"That's good hearing!" Ironside roared. "Be quick or I'll come and fetch you."

Gareth strapped and buckled his leather harness over the mail shirt. Picking up his shield, on which the device of the praying hands was now obscured by mud, he grabbed his sword. Then he went to join the other man. Ironside waited on a comparatively level bit of the valley-side, still rough with rocks and tussocks, and drenched deep.

Knights of such strength and experience did not rush on each other blindly, like wild bulls. Ironside circled and struck, laying on his blows with care while getting the feel of the ground. His fury did not lessen while he played his waiting game. His eyes glared redly, the veins rose on his neck, and blood burst out of his nose with the force of his wrath.

"Christ," he snarled. "This time I'll kill you, Orkneyman."

They struck harder and faster, their feet sweeping the grass aside, stamping into the earth as they withstood the shocks of each other's blows. Gareth feinted at the Red Knight's head, and then smote downward at his knees with the lower edge of his shield.

Bones would have broken if the blow had struck home. It did not. The Red Knight sprang aside with a barked laugh. In his next breath he spoke a foul curse against Gareth, his brothers, his parents and the whole Orkney realm. Thereafter he saved his breath for fighting. He drove Gareth back several paces with the force and skill of his attack.

Then Gareth stood fast and fought back. He was nine years younger and somewhat bigger even than the Red Knight. Their swords rang together and boomed on the shields. Gareth cut down with a terrible stroke that sheared away a wedge-shaped piece of his foe's crimson shield. He charged against him.

The two shields crashed; the two swords rang. Locking their shields together, edge under edge, each knight tried to lever the other's shield aside in order to thrust at his body, until their feet turned all the ground to sliding mud beneath them.

They battled for more than an hour. Now they panted, bled, and moved clumsily. Their swords were beaten almost edgeless. Twice Gareth thought better of the combat, and called on the Red Knight to halt and make peace, but Ironside would not. His rage was like some devil's frenzy that tripled his strength.

Gareth's pride did not allow him to offer peace a third time. Staring into the other's distorted face, he felt his own rage rise to a fearful height.

"Will you have it so?" he choked. "Be damned to you, then! Hell gapes for you – you red swine!"

Swiftly, he cut at his adversary's side with a terrible stroke of his blade, but the Red Knight caught it on his much-battered shield, even though he stumbled. Then Gareth launched a great blow with his own shield at Ironside's hip. Yet he aimed the blow in pretence, great as it was.

In the next heartbeat he struck again, slashing for the temple. In desperation the Red Knight threw up his sword to parry, so that they clashed together. They would have been driven into his brain together by the might of the blow, except that Gareth's sword, blunted and deeply notched, broke apart a foot from the crossguard. Twenty-one glinting inches of steel flew down the hillside.

With a huge shout, Gareth drove at Ironside behind his shield. He knocked his foe flat. Gareth's big foot came down on his sword arm, pinning it to the muddy ground. With the other he kicked the crimson shield away. He shortened his arm to drive the jagged stub of his sword through Ironside's face.

The Red Knight twisted, swinging his great legs through half a circle, and kicked Gareth's feet from under him in the instant of his supposed victory. Gareth fell heavily upon a nearby rock. Pain lanced through his back. Strength went out of his sword-arm. In a moment, the tables had been turned for a second time. The Red Knight loomed above him, face bloody and fearful, with eyes like a beast's.

So, Gareth thought, this is the end.

A miracle occurred. In the moment of the kill, the Red Knight's face changed. Even while bringing his sword down to split Gareth to the spine he swung it aside and spent its force on the empty air. He stumbled on his own feet from the misplaced force of the stroke. It was comical to see.

Gareth, delivered from death by these antics, did not laugh at them; he lay amazed.

Ironside glared down at him. In a rasping, effortful voice, he raved, "Give thanks that you spared my life once! Give thanks that you saved me on the bridge! Any other man, *any other man*, I would have cut in pieces – *even the king*! But now the Quest is yours, and you may have it! Find any companion you like, Gareth of Orkney. You will find me no more. And Arthur will get my service no more."

Snarling, cursing, he swung astride his charger and rode off in search of the packhorse which carried his armour.

Gareth stared after him. In part he felt glad to be rid of the man. He felt more than glad to be still in one piece. Ironside could be a difficult companion. Maybe the Quest for the Grail could only be conducted alone with one's spirit and God.

No. That was self-righteous vapouring. If he wanted to think about God, let him think that God had intervened in this fight by breaking his sword and then letting Ironside bring him down. Without divine intervention, that would scarcely have happened.

Gareth had been a newly made knight of eighteen when he had overcome the Red Knight's brothers one after the other, and then, on the plain before Leontyne's besieged castle, the Red Knight himself. He was older now, stronger, more practised and skilled and confident. He should have been able to do it again.

The battle had gone against him for a reason.

But why? It hadn't been his fault!

Gareth gave it up. He felt too weary and his back hurt too much. He had better find a friendly dwelling and have it seen to.

Setting his teeth, he rose and whistled to his warhorse, who waited so patiently on his master's folly.

He travelled by highways and byways throughout the autumn. He found few adventures, and those hardly worth the telling.

As often as he asked about wonders and enchanted castles, he asked for news of a harsh-faced knight of great prowess, but the man seemed to have vanished. Nor was there mention of a flame-coloured horse or the blazon – gules and a pale argent with five roundels gules.

Gareth had abundant time to think about the reason for his defeat. "Not his fault" was a boy's cry. He'd provoked Sir Ironside's anger, knowing the man could never govern his fury when aroused, that it became a blood-madness like that of the ancient berserks. He'd started the fight. Also, despite the holy Quest on which they'd been engaged, when Gareth had had Sir Ironside at his mercy he'd never thought of showing any. He'd been about to kill. It had been Ironside, even in the grip of his legendary fury, who had refrained.

No wonder God had rewarded Gareth with defeat.

He rode far. He heard not a word and saw not a sign of the Grail. All Hallow's Eve came and went. Winter began.

In the end, disconsolate, he came into the region of the Scottish border. Though a northerner himself, he knew it was

not safe. Broken men abounded, and even the lords were
desperate.

The custom of the land was blood feud. Its laws were those of
hot trod and red hand. Honest wives were known to set a dish
of spurs before their husbands for supper, as a broad hint that it
was time to be out riding for plunder so that their children might
eat, crops and cottages having been burned for the fifth harvest
running.

Gareth drifted back and forth in the marches. He went to Carlisle
for a month in midwinter, when the snowstorms made travel
impossible for any save suicides. Having confessed and prayed
diligently over Christmas, he rode into the marches again.

Towards the end of January he found himself on a wide empty
moor. Even for the borders, it was desolate. Nothing grew but the
rare blade of rank grass, cockle, spurge and thistles. He hadn't seen
so much as a thornbush in a mile. Now he rode past a strange,
bulbous formation of grey-white clay that looked as thought it had
broken out through the skin of the earth like a mass of boils.

Puzzled, he looked around him. The land stretched flat and
sere all the way to the world's edge. There had been hills in the
distance, and they ought to have been closer now. Pressing on for
another league, he encountered no features other than a barren,
twisting ravine.

A falling meteor streaked across the sky. Lifting his face to watch
it, he noticed that the stars themselves looked peculiar. Although
thinning clouds moved across the sky before a lost wind, the gaps
between them never revealed Orion or the Wain. Gareth would
vow, too, that he'd never seen that group of stars yonder, which
somewhat resembled a bat and whose brightest member glimmered
a tarnished yellow.

What part of the marches was this?

The attack took him quite by surprise. He had not supposed
that anything big enough to menace him could hide in ambush
for at least a mile around, but the creatures sprang out of meagre
hollows in the ground and clumps of rank weed where somehow
they had lain concealed.

Gareth reacted quickly enough, and so did his charger. The big
grey seized the nearest assailant's arm in great white teeth. Lifting
him high, he shook him hard before dropping him, then stamped
his ribs to pieces with iron forefeet. Gareth drew his sword and
clove another from ribs to breastbone.

A score of them surrounded Gareth. Naked except for leather

kilts and harnesses, they lacked any weapons and seemed to care nothing for death or maiming. Teeth and eyes glimmered white from their grey, hollow-cheeked faces.

In the end they dragged him down. Three pulled his sword from his grip, indifferently cutting their hands to the bone on its blade. Others stripped him bare, throwing his casque and mail shirt aside. They tied his arms and legs before carrying him off.

Gareth's grey steed charged several times in an effort to rescue him. His captors hurled large stones with deadly accuracy to drive it away, while Gareth cursed them in a blazing fury. After a couple of rocks had struck its legs it ceased to attack, but trailed behind its master, limping.

His captors remained mute. Their eyes stared blindly, their white teeth were dry, and the grey hands on his naked body were cold as the frosty earth. His horror of them grew. After a while, he realized something.

They no more breathed than they spoke.

They came to a black stream, foaming and leaping down from a height. The silent liches carried him through dark dog-willows and twisted alders. As they forded the stream one of Gareth's feet dipped into it. The chill snapped at his flesh.

Next they mounted a rocky path that led at last to a naked corrie beneath a height. On the height, Gareth saw their destination – a sprawling white heap of a castle with curtain walls, towers and buttresses rambling all ways.

Only when Gareth came nigh the main gate – it proved to be the single gate – did he see that the place was built wholly of bones.

Bones. White and clean as king's salt. Bones of rib and pelvis, head and thigh. They belonged to animal, human, giant and dragon, so it appeared, and some to monsters that none of the bestiaries contained. Entry was through the jawbone of a titanic boar. Behind it, a criss-cross of femurs large as saplings made the portcullis. Gareth heard the crash and felt the jar as it lowered behind him.

Four of the liches threw him at the foot of an ivory throne. The person who sat upon it at least was alive. Huge, black-haired, black-bearded and uncouth, he held a beef bone like a sceptre. Unlike his servants, he had not the look of a starved man, though his great swagbelly rumbled and churned in a way that could be heard across the chamber.

"Welcome to the Castle of Hunger," he said. His voice boomed. "I may tell you now that there is no leaving it."

"What lord are you that treats a knight so shamefully?" Gareth demanded. "I belong to the fellowship of the Round Table. I am Sir Gareth; my father is King Lot of Orkney."

The figure on the throne laughed harshly. "Much I care. I am in rebellion against a greater king than he, who was in former times my liege lord and is now known as Le Roi Pêcheur. Do not talk to me of Lot."

"The Fisher King?" Gareth struggled excitedly in his bonds. He managed to rise to his knees. "Again? This is his land?"

"Some in ignorance call him The Fisher King! I know better – as I should, who was his butler. Listen, Sir Gareth. *Pêcheur* means fisherman, but also it means sinner, and The Sinner King he is. Because of his sin he suffered a wound that cannot be healed in this life, and his realm became blighted and waste, as you see. Because of that I rebelled against him. Once he is defeated and cast down from his throne, then will the realm be whole and fruitful again."

Gareth said in disgust, "Ruled from a castle of bones by a traitor who usurped it?" He spat on the floor. "A butler not even anointed! Free my hands and I'll strike a blow for the true king."

"The true king? Look around you, Sir Gareth. I'm no necromancer to raise the dead. They rise in anger from their graves to fight against him of their own will. His sin brought the sickness and famine that slew them!"

"The like of you will never cure those ills."

The huge renegade leaned forward. His beef-bone sceptre dangled beside his knee. The other hand vanished under his beard, to serve as a prop for his chin. He stared long at the knight.

"So you say. So said every other knight of the Round Table who fell into my hands. They came to this land seeking the Grail. Instead they found their way to me – which says something, does it not, anent how worthy they must be?"

He laughed. "They refused my service, so now they lie in my dungeon. Oh, yes. You know them all. Pinel, Mador, your brother Agravaine, Tor and the aged Sir Lucan, to a full tally of twenty-six. With you it will make a round thrice nine. Satisfying."

"Shall I believe such a scoundrel?"

The butler gestured to his waiting liches. "Take him and show him."

They half-carried Gareth through twisting, winding passages to look at captive after captive. The butler had not lied. There was

Pinel, doubled up and confined within the bare ribcage of a gigantic ape; here Agravaine hung from a ceiling, swathed in chains made of knobbed vertebrae that galled and pricked; further along lay Tor, bent back and spread across an elephant's skull that almost filled his tiny prison chamber.

Not all the captives were knights or men. By the light of flaring torches set in an alcove, Gareth saw a lady and a young girl in a cage of crossed femurs, weeping. At the sight he struggled so fiercely that the dead men were flung back and forth across the passage before they could strike enough blows to subdue him. When they hauled him before the last and latest prisoner, he was so dazed he did not see clearly.

"Spine of God!" rasped a familiar voice. "Gareth!"

"Ironside?" he croaked, and for the first time was glad for the grisly support of his guards' lifeless arms.

The Red Knight's blood-coloured tunic hung in rags. He had been shackled between the pillar-like foreleg bones of some monstrous skeleton beast. With his great strength, he might well have pulled free. However, the boulder-heavy skull hung above him, knobbed, blunt-horned and twice Ironside's length. Did he pull the legs from under it, the skull would crash down to pulp him like a beetle.

"Damn that butler's soul!" Ironside snarled, but there were tears unpredecented in his eyes. "He has you too!" Then he forced a callous shrug. "Ah, then . . . welcome to our company, Gareth. This is a cheerful place, as you can see."

Gareth was given no time to answer. Nor could he think of much to say.

Tossed, bruised and bleeding, before the throne again, he heard the butler say gloatingly, "You credit me now, I dare say."

"You foul dog. Lancelot or Gawain will call you to account for this! Two dozen of Arthur's knights you may hold captive here, but you have not encountered the best."

"I have one of the best now, or so it is said. How many champions of the Round Table surpass Sir Gareth? By report, no more than nine or ten out of the hundred and forty."

Grinning like a tomcat with a new mouse, the butler fingered his immense black beard.

"Hear me," he said at last. "I am willing to exchange them all for you. Even Tor and Lucan."

Gareth was puzzled. "But you have me. What game is this?"

The butler chuckled meanly. "A game I like. Tell me, young

knight, with a fair lady and children at home who will miss you – would you tamely submit to a shameful death by hanging?"

"Never! It's you who shall have that shameful death, when your lord returns to his whole might."

"That will not happen soon," the butler assured him. "Let me tell you what is in my mind. It's most simple."

"It would be." Gareth couldn't resist. Pawky response, out of place and beneath his knightly dignity, but oh, how he enjoyed making it.

The butler only grinned more coldly yet. "Agree to the gallows, take the noose around your neck willingly, and I release all your comrades. Else they must stay where they are till death frees them."

The insult and the insolence were all Gareth could hear at first. Finally he said, "How should I believe you?"

"Ah. That's all that prevents you?" the butler fleered. "You would offer your life and dignity for your comrades at once, if you were only sure you could believe me? Of course you would." The smirk grew until it covered his broad face. "You find a way."

"Make your oath by the Grail to keep any such bargain, then," Gareth said in disgust. "I do not believe you would dare break it."

The smirk departed. The butler's skin turned as grey as his dead servitors'. At last he said, "I swear by the Holy Grail itself to abide by my terms."

"By any terms we make together," Gareth stipulated.

"I'll abide by any terms on which we agree. I swear it – by the Grail."

"I saw the lady and young girl in your loathly prison. I saw others. Free all your captives, each last one – no matter what their degree or condition, no matter why they are here. I would so require."

"You ask too much! I hold captives more important than the knights. No. The knights of your fellowship only, young sir, and that is a generous offer."

"Master butler, I dinna think you would ken a generous offer. What one is." In his bitter scorn, Gareth turned to the accents of his boyhood again. "Turn loose a' the captives, else there's nae bargain."

"No? Twenty-six knights of the Round Table, your brother among them, and you would leave them in durance for the sake of strangers?"

"The twenty-six, and mysel' too, pledged oor lives tae deliver ladies. Besides, I've quarrelled wi' the Red Knight and I'm none sae fond of Agravaine." Pausing, Gareth collected himself, and spoke again as the knights of Arthur's Court spoke. "Therefore let it be my terms or none, and I lower myself to make any terms at all with such a traitor recreant."

The butler pondered that, his brows knotted with anger. At last he said thickly, "And if I consent, will you?"

Gareth hesitated. The shame and disgrace of the gallows was no light thing. It was a scurvy death, a death for felons even when done cleanly. Besides, it was *not* always done cleanly; he had seen men dispatched by clumsy hangmen. But there were twenty-six knights with whom he had sworn fellowship, and ladies held captive whom he was bound to assist by vows made before the Virgin's altar.

He forced his stiff mouth to say, "I consent. Yes."

The butler's great coarse face fell. Was he disappointed? Why? Gareth did not know, but he saw the man fall to pondering again.

"You're young," he said, with false, unctuous mercy. "Too young that I should grant you no time for further thought. Hear me, then. I have no gallows here. Take thought to our bargain while I have one built out in the courtyard; nay, you may go there and watch it shaping. Until the last second you may reconsider and renege.

"You will be free to go where you like, with your horse and mail. Yes, and I promise that you will soon find your way back to your own country." He pointed with the beef bone. "Let all be done as I have said."

Battered and sickened, Gareth waited with bound arms in the courtyard. He watched the dead men erect his gibbet out of odd pieces of skeleton, working with care. The task took them hours. To Gareth, burningly aware of the sweetness of life, it seemed like decades.

Life called to him strongly; the world called. Leontyne and their children. Lancelot, whose friendship he might regain, whose pardon he was ready to ask – his and Guinevere's. When had Gareth been appointed their judge? If Lancelot du Lac had not been able to command his passion for the queen at last, it surely had not been for want of trying. Gareth felt more understanding for lapses from honour in his present situation.

That scurvy butler. Why had he done it? Why make Gareth

wait like this? It wasn't necessary to build a gallows; he might have swung his victim from the castle's overhanging battlements quickly enough and been done.

Gareth was slow to perceive the motives of cruel men, but in time he saw the butler's. The man wanted to torment him. More than that, perhaps, he longed to see Gareth break his word.

He would show the cur. It lay within his power to redeem all those captives from their bars and bonds. His brother, Ironside, that nameless lady and the sobbing little girl – all of them freed because of him. Gareth of Orkney would not be forgotten. He would have done a great thing.

The thought brought an eerie, heady exultation. Then Gareth looked again at the rising, growing platform. He imagined the close grip of hemp around his young throat. All high fancies of self-sacrificing virtue blew away like thistledown. Shameful life might be far better than shameful death.

Why not? Ah, why not? It occurred to him that his blood might not require him to behave with such rectitude. Lot of Orkney was known as a spineless, lazy king, his queen as a witch and harlot. It was astonishing that all Lot's sons were men of energy and prowess. All brave too, no matter what else they might have wrong with them. The youngest two, Agravaine and Mordred, were downright warped, and Gareth's mind shied away from wondering about the part of their mother Morgause in that.

It didn't matter. Did it? Brother Gawain was known as the model of knightly honour. When Arthur's life had been saved by the hideous lady who asked for marriage to a knight as her reward, not one had been prepared to pay the price and redeem the king's honour – except Gawain.

It had been Gawaine's gentle courtesy and kindness that broke the enchantment his bride suffered and restored her to her lovely self. Gawain of all men would be shattered to know that his brother had broken a knightly oath.

Even that didn't matter when one looked at it closely. All Gareth's brothers could be perjured as the devil, and it would not lessen the force of his bargain. A man's honour was his own.

So it went, and so it went. All too soon the gallows was finished, and the butler came with his ponderous stride to see it used. Then it came home to the core of Gareth's soul that he was to hang.

"You remain here, eh, fool?" the butler jeered. "It's more than I expected – but cast a glance in front of you. The portcullis is high and the gate open to its fullest. You can still run."

Gareth clamped his teeth against sickness and fought to stop his legs shaking.

"Well, then, if it suits you," the butler grumbled. "I find I'm bored with this. It isn't even worth gloating. Mount the ladder."

The Orkney stubbornness and pride came to Gareth's rescue. He went up rung by rung. Grey hands fitted the noose. Gareth still had time to scream that he recanted. Let me go, let me go. Let your captives rot! He shut his teeth hard against the traitor words. Another second and they would burst through.

Hands shoved him. He fell. The rope tightened, tightened, blood roared in his ears and his feet kicked. This was it, this was death, the end of hope and joy, the end of love, all he was and wished to be, and oh, Blessed Virgin, no . . .

The courtyard jarred his heel and knee. He saw a tower and the new moon above it, blurred to a silver smear. The noose unravelled from Gareth's neck. The gallows rocked. Posts lurched drunkenly, the crossbeam fell and rebounded a foot in front of his nose, quivered and settled. From the bone castle's depths to its highest turrets there were noises as of doors breaking outward and fetters bursting.

Gareth struggled to his feet, too far gone to wonder. The butler approached, looming like a mountain, and went down on one knee before the man he had condemned to hang. His face looked different. When he spoke, his voice had changed too.

"The prisoners are yours, Sir Gareth. I am indeed butler to the household of Le Roi Pêcheur. I never rebelled against him. I might not slay you even if I would. Depart with honour, for here in the Castle of Hunger you have been tested and found true."

The words did not penetrate – would not for hours. Gareth could only think, I'm alive. Then the captives, free, thronged into the courtyard. The castle servants accompanied them – and they did not look like dead men any longer. In another moment the Red Knight was supporting Gareth on one side, his brother Agravaine on the other. Tears ran down Agravaine's face.

"Gareth, you delivered us!"

"Aye, that you did."

Ironside seldom if ever wept, but his tears flowed now. After helping Gareth dress and arm himself again, he rode beside him from the castle at the head of a blissful line. He rode a long way before he looked back.

Gareth turned his head also, despite the rasp of mail on his chafed throat. The castle of bones appeared to be crumbling, as though its walls had become partly ruined. Perhaps he had been tested there, and perhaps, one way or another, all the captives had landed in its dungeons through their own sins, but he still loathed and despised the place. Turning his head, he urged the grey charger onward.

IV

Gareth and Ironside sat by a crackling fire in a cheerful inn near Carlisle. They had punished the flagon until they became maudlin and intimate. The other prisoners had all gone their ways, except Agravaine, and he had never been able to hold his liquor. He lay snoring on a bench.

"I'm Ironside, Turquine's son," the Red Knight said abruptly. "Not often felt helpless since I was a brat with a raging fever and thought I'd die. By God's Passion, though, I felt helpless fettered to those stinking bones! There's not another man breathing who would have done what you did to enlarge us. I'll swear it. Not one."

Gareth did not dispute it. Rueful, he said, "Then I've done one worthy thing. Meseems I'm no closer to the Holy Grail than when we started. I do not believe I thought about it once in that monstrous castle."

"Nor I. Wasn't even searching for the Grail when I stumbled upon the place, but for you, Sir Gareth."

"For me?"

"Yes."

"Why?" Gareth smiled wryly and stretched his legs towards the fire. "Had you decided to kill me after all?"

"No! Devil's horns, no! I wanted to – Ah, burn it, to unsay my red words and mend our quarrel."

"I wanted that too. Well I remember that I was first with the insults and blame."

"Can you forgive me that I nearly slew you?"

"Sir Ironside, you had your chance and forbore. The man who besieged the Lady Leontyne's castle had never done so. It's much to your credit and honour that you held back your hand. Under provocation too." Gareth extended his own hand. "Now maybe we have spent words enough on the matter. Let's forget it, and begin a new flagon."

Ironside took the offered clasp across the table. "Done!" He shook his scarred head. "By every bone in that charnel castle, youngster, a man has to look at you twice sometimes to be sure you are real."

They began the new flagon, and cup by cup approached the bottom. Gareth said in his wine haze, "I searched for you also. It may be that I even heard of you – though those men did not ride your horse or display your arms."

"No. I left Flambeau at a friendly castle for his leg to heal. He's still there." Ironside leered happily. "The knight's wife was friendly too. Most. I copied you by riding unknown for a while, with a borrowed shield and surcoat."

The flagon became empty. They embraced and swore brotherhood, that neither should ever be against the other and that always they should come to each other's aid in trouble. Then, gravely, they talked of the Grail.

"I suppose this ends the Quest for us," Ironside said. "The measure of worth is beyond me. Pardie! Christ Himself did no more than stand ready to hang on a gibbet for others, and you cannot even get near His chalice?"

"Easy. Sir Ironside, I love you as a brother . . . Gawaine or Gaheris, I mean," Gareth added, seeing the Red Knight cast a dubious glance at the snoring Agravaine, "but you blaspheme too easily."

"You should have heard my sire," the other retorted, not at all abashed.

"I believe you. And I think I know why I failed now."

"Do you care to speak of it?"

"No."

"Bah! It can't be that monstrous a sin."

"It isn't, but it concerns only me."

Gareth felt sure by now that he had not been ejected from the Turning Fortress for any solecism of Ironside's. The fault had been his own. He recalled his smug thoughts on Lancelot's sin and his own comparative virtue; a sin in itself, of course, the sin of the Pharisees, of claiming that one is "not as other men".

In the Castle of Hunger he had redeemed himself, maybe, but at the end he had succumbed to despair. Plunging from the scaffold, all hope and faith gone, he had been convinced that even God had abandoned him. He had been allowed to rescue the captives, but for his loss of faith he had been denied a further vision of the Grail.

Achieving it would be hard . . . perhaps beyond him.

"I've been to confession," Sir Ironside said. "My penance is a pilgrimage to Glastonbury."

"Then to Glastonbury we'll go," Gareth said promptly. "I cannot see that we'd be trifling with the Quest on that account. We've seen that the Grail Castle can appear anywhere, just as men say. But if we should hear any word of it, see any sign, I'll turn aside and follow it, though I'm within sight of Camelot. Agreed?"

"Agreed!"

In the morning they rode south, into the Cumbrian mountains, to the small castle where Sir Ironside had left his charger. The big flame-coloured beast seemed well recovered. The lord of the castle had put Flambeau to stud with a mare or two while he was there, and said he hoped for good results.

Gareth noticed that the lady was tall and bold-eyed, with a fine shape, and the way she looked at Sir Ironside indicated that he had not been bragging idly in his cups when he'd mentioned her. The knight as well as his charger, it appeared, had seen stud service in Cumbria.

Gareth felt a strong yearning to be at home with Leontyne again. Or at least freed from the pure demands of this tantalizing Quest.

Riding down out of the mountains, they saw little but ferns, grass and a golden eagle drifting on ragged wings. Reaching a bracken-covered shore beside a lake, they spent the night there.

Gareth awoke in the morning with a sense of something eerie and sacred. The spring bracken seemed to glow, and mist as delicate as a child's breath over frosted silver covered the lake.

Gareth had seen wondrous sights since he began the Quest, but neither the Turning Fortress nor the Castle of Hunger had been as wondrous as this. It was peaceful, with a beauty that partook of the divine. Somehow he was not surprised when the mist parted and a ship came softly to the lakeshore, a slim purple ship with a blue sail bearing the device of a chalice surrounded by rays.

Gareth knelt for a moment. Then he rose and nudged the sleeping Ironside with his toe. "Awake and see, comrade! The Quest goes on!"

Ironside rolled to his feet, sword in hand, then stood blinking at the empty ship. Slowly he opened his fingers, dropped the blade and crossed himself. This miracle disconcerted him the more for being a quiet, gentle one compared with the others he had witnessed.

"Are we to go aboard?"

"Surely we're intended to. This is a third sign, a third chance, and we failed the first two. I dare not shirk this one."

Gareth waded into the water, his heart alight with gratitude for the favour he had been given. Behind him, Ironside said lugubriously, "Are we to abandon our horses yet again?"

"They are tethered, and won't wander far even if they break loose. This lake is scarcely more than a mile long."

Gareth hauled himself over the gunwale, legs dripping, and looked down the narrow length of the vessel. It had neither oars nor steerboard, its purple timbers carried a scent like incense, and amidships stood a small cabin with a four-panelled door. Each panel was carved with a symbol of one of the gospel saints; bull, lion, eagle and man.

A slight push opened it. The cabin proved light and airy, with three pallets on the floor and as many low stools. A mantle of distinctive blue and white weave lay on one of the pallets. Bending, Gareth touched it.

"I'm almost sure this was Percival's."

"Percival." Ironside thought of the naïve knight, raised in the deep forest. "He was before us?" He thought further. "He was not in the dungeons with me and Mador and the rest."

"No, that he was not." Gareth grew excited. "Look, Ironside, three pallets! Did three knights rest here?"

"Maybe we will know," Ironside said grimly, "when this ship takes us – wherever it is going."

A tiny breeze rose, blowing off the mountains, barely swelling the blue sail. The ship almost drifted. As it moved down the lake the dawn mist thinned from the hills.

"There, Ironside," Gareth said reverently. "*There* is where we are going."

A castle stood at the lake's far end. Neither square and solid, like the Turning Fortress, nor a sprawling shambles in the fashion of the Castle of Hunger, its walls of marble and porphyry rose cleanly perfect.

There was no drawbridge, moat or portcullis to guard it. The gateway stood wide open. On the stones of the arch

above, lilies were carved, alternating with roses, and above
them again, the relief of a chalice surrounded by rays. Stretching
down to the lakeside before the gateway was a green expanse
of clovery grass.

"The end of the Quest?" Ironside asked, and answered himself.
"It has to be."

"I think so. It cannot be other. A third chance, Ironside! Come
on! I'll enter this castle no matter what test awaits!"

Gareth sprang over the side without his helmet and rushed
ashore, his shield with its device of clasped hands on one arm,
his sword sheathed beside him. He ran lightly up the gentle slope
towards the arch. Sir Ironside ran beside him, all suspicion and
wrath asleep in his soul for once, as moved as Gareth by the castle's
tranquil loveliness.

Then they both halted dead. Two mighty lions rose from beside
the gateway to stalk across their path. A hoarse oath ripped from
Ironside's throat. He drew his sword. Gareth set hand to hilt and
half drew his before thinking better of it. With all his strength of
will he halted his arm.

"No, Ironside! Don't strike. Think where we are."

Sweat broke out on the Red Knight's furrowed brow. With
an effort perhaps greater than Gareth's, he lowered his violent hand. The sword with which he had ravaged and killed
across three counties shone in the sun, but remained pointed at
the grass.

Gareth tried to sheathe his weapon again. It would not slide back
into its scabbard one inch, but remained half-drawn. The lions
shook their manes and roared. Others appeared from around the
sides of the castle; three younger males and about a dozen lionesses
– the rest of the pride. With an easy, dignified gait they converged
upon the two knights, then lay down in the grass, watchful. The
warning was plain.

Gareth's heart felt scalded. Turning to Sir Ironside, he said in
anguish, "We've failed once more! But why?"

This time he imputed no blame to his fellow.

"I don't know."

There was movement in the gateway, and a tall figure came out.
His simple tunic bore the emblem of the Grail, and his leggings
were horsehide. Reddish hair hung down to his shoulders. He
seemed ordinary enough, except that looking into his eyes as he
approached, Gareth saw God's peace there.

"Welcome, Sir Gareth of Orkney and Sir Ironside of the Red

Laundes," he greeted them. "I am the porter of this castle, which is called Carbonek."

"Hah! We've come down, haven't we?" Ironside growled. "First the Seneschal, then the butler, now the porter. What was it all for? Just to humble us? I haven't any need to ask why I couldn't achieve the Grail. But why not my friend? He's a mighty champion, and withal so gentle and pure-hearted my stomach sometimes rebels."

"Only because it is such a choleric stomach," Gareth said. "Master porter, is this the true Grail Castle before us?"

"It is, Sir Gareth – and so were the others. The Grail Castle takes many forms. It never appears to any but those who have it in them to be worthy, and to none save you and Sir Ironside has it appeared three times."

"And still we never saw the Grail. Or its guardian, Le Roi Pêcheur. Is it possible that we may know why?"

"It is possible that you, Sir Gareth, may enter the court-yard, though not fare beyond. This is granted because your sword was only halfway drawn, but Sir Ironside must remain without."

Gareth looked at his companion. His heart did not appear to be breaking at the news.

"Go. I trust him. The lions will keep me company." Sir Ironside gazed at the lions with eyes as fierce as their own. In that moment, too, they seemed as innocent. "And while it may be a sign that I've lost my wits, I trust them too."

Gareth followed the porter. Beyond the archway, aspens and sycamores lined two sides of a broad courtyard, a row of columns the other. A fountain played brightly.

"Sir Gareth, you have won the right to drink from this fountain, though it is forbidden that you enter the castle. And many would give a hand to do so much."

"What is it, this fountain, and what is its nature?"

"Its water gives clarity. Clear sight, clear thought, clarity of spirit and a clear heart."

"That is a drink worth tasting." Gareth cupped his hands, filled them and drank. The water poured into him like cool light. He filled his hands again, and then a third time.

The porter had spoken the truth. It was as though clouded, tainted veils had lifted from his mind and spirit, letting him see without care or prejudice. His smug judgement of Lancelot and Guinevere had been one thing barring him from the Grail, indeed, and his lapse into despair on the gallows another, but more than all had been his commitment to the world. It was not wrong, or less than good. It was only that utter faith and devotion to the spirit, a gaze unwaveringly fixed on Heaven, were needed to find the Holy Grail.

Gareth loved other things too much. His commitment was given on earth – to his lady and children, to his brothers, to his king and the fellowship of the Round Table, which, although the noblest on earth, was still *of* earth, and thus flawed, and holding within it the causes of its own dissolution.

When someone reached the state in which the Grail could be achieved there remained nothing to do in the world, and, indeed, it became impossible to remain therein for long. Gareth saw this truth and conceded that he was not ready for that.

The fountain did give clear sight. He leaned on its rim of malachite and marble for a space, then shook himself like a swimmer coming up from a deep dive. Although he looked long at the castle, he no longer dreamed of entering its inner keep. Turning, he followed the porter out in silence.

Beyond the gateway, he thought of questions to which he did not have the answers, and which he must ask at Carbonek or nowhere else.

"Master porter? You declare that only to us has the Grail Castle appeared three times. But have others been here before us? Sir Percival, for one? And was the Grail revealed to them?"

"That question it is permitted me to answer." The porter leaned on his staff. "Sir Percival was here. He entered Castle Carbonek and achieved the Grail. Sir Bors and Sir Galahad were with him on the same ship that carried you today, and they also saw the Grail uncovered."

"Then it's in my mind that I will see none of them again in this life."

"Sir Bors will return to tell what happened, but then he will become a holy hermit, until his time on earth is finished."

"And those three only achieved the Quest?"

"Sir Lancelot came before them."

"Ahh." Gareth let out his breath in a sigh. "And he?"

"He came into the presence of the Holy Grail and knelt in its light, but he saw it only when it was cloth-covered, through a half-open door."

"I'm well served for thinking I could do more in such a Quest than he." Gareth meant it. He felt no jealousy, no secret condemnation. "Of all worldly knights, he's the greatest and noblest."

"And so will he be remembered, Sir Gareth; yet neither will you or your brothers be forgotten."

"I've another question," Gareth said, "or several. Who is Le Roi Pêcheur? Does his name signify The Fisher or The Sinner? If the butler at the Castle of Hunger did not lie, then what was the nature of his sin, and where lies the realm that was wasted thereby . . . and what is the meaning of the riddle for us, here in Britain?"

"You ask wisely, but, alas, to you I may not reveal the answer. Bors or Percival or Galahad, I might have told. Yet none of them thought to ask. Their minds were wholly set upon the Grail."

Gareth was haunted by his questions as he travelled south. They troubled his sleep and came into his dreams, where he saw a wounded king with a shadowed face. His pain-racked voice whispered, 'My wound may never be healed in this world, and I must leave it.' And always there was the sense that his wound had come from some long-ago, unnamed sin, while the ruin and waste that engulfed his kingdom had the same source.

However, Gareth was young, and he had other thoughts to distract him, as more and more they did; thoughts of Leontyne and his brothers, of what he would say to Lancelot when they met. There was also Sir Ironside's brash, abrasive company, which in the circumstances he found as good as a bracing medicine.

The day came at last when they saw the spires of Camelot once more. Their Quest was over, and Gareth knew with a sober new wisdom that he and Ironside, and all those of the fellowship who had survived, would be needed more than ever. As Arthur had said, there would be too many empty places at the Round Table.

On the last mile of the road they saw two young men riding towards them at a canter, one of them waving. Gareth recognized his brothers. He rode to meet them. Agravaine clutched him in an awkward embrace while the other waited his turn, languid, easy, self-contained.

Gareth looked at him, and at once all the dread and tragedy of his dreams returned, vivid and piercing, the more so for being experienced in waking daylight.

He forced the feelings away; he was becoming like an old

woman. His youngest brother always had made him uneasy, but he could have nothing to do with the matter of Gareth's recurring nightmares.

"Hello, Mordred," he said.

THE LEGEND OF SIR DINAR

Arthur Quiller-Couch

At the turn of the nineteenth century, Arthur Quiller-Couch
(1863–1944), often known simply as Q, was a leading figure
of the establishment, an excellent teacher and lecturer, a poet,
writer and editor. He was knighted in 1910. Today his name
is little remembered, although many will have probably delved
into The Oxford Book of English Verse (1900), which he
compiled. Born and raised in Cornwall, of a noted Cornish
family, Quiller-Couch used Cornwall as the setting for much
of his best work, including Dead Man's Rock (1887) and Troy
Town (1888). The following story, which shows how some of
the remaining knights must have felt once the leading contenders
had set off on their Quest, comes from his collection Wandering
Heath (1895).

A puff of north-east wind shot over the hill, detached a late
December leaf from the sycamore on its summit, and swooped
like a wave upon the roofs and chimney-stacks below. It caught the
smoke midway in the chimneys, drove it back with showers of soot
and wood-ash, and set the townsmen sneezing who lingered by their
hearths to read the morning newspaper. Its strength broken, it fell
prone upon the main street, scattering its fine dust into fan-shaped
figures, then died away in eddies towards the south. Among these
eddies the sycamore leaf danced and twirled, now running along
the ground upon its edge, now whisked up to the level of the first

storey windows. A nurse holding up a three-year-old child behind the pane, pointed after the leaf –

"Look – there goes Sir Dinar!"

Sir Dinar was the youngest son and comeliest of King Geraint, who had left Arthur's Court for his own western castle of Dingerein in Roseland, where Portseatho now stands; and was buried, when his time came, over the Nare, in his golden boat with his silver oars beside him. To fill his siege at the Round Table he sent, in the lad's sixteenth year, this Dinar, who in two years was made knight by King Arthur, and in the third was turned into an old man before he had achieved a single deed of note.

For on the fifth day after he was made knight, and upon the Feast of Pentecost, there began the great quest of the Sancgrael, which took Sir Lancelot from the Court, Sir Perceval, Sir Bors, Sir Gawaine, Sir Galahad, and all the flower of the famous brotherhood. And because, after their going, it was all sad cheer at Camelot, and heavy, empty days, Sir Dinar took two of his best friends aside, both young knights, Sir Galhaltin and Sir Ozanna le Cœur Hardi, and spoke to them of riding from the Court by stealth. "For," he said, "we have many days before us, and no villainy upon our consciences, and besides are eager. Who knows, then, but we may achieve this adventure of the Sancgrael?" These listened and imparted it to another, Sir Sentrail: and the four rode forth secretly one morning before the dawn, and set their faces towards the north-east wind.

The day of their departure was that next after Christmas, the same being the Feast of Saint Stephen the Martyr. And as they rode through a thick wood, it came into Sir Dinar's mind that upon this day it was right to kill any bird that flew, in remembrance that when Saint Stephen had all but escaped from the soldiers who guarded him, a small bird had sung in their ears and awakened them. By this, the sky was growing white with the morning, but nothing yet clear to the sight: and while they pressed forward under the naked boughs, their horses' hoofs crackling the frosted undergrowth, Sir Dinar was aware of a bird's wing ruffling ahead, and let fly a bolt without warning his companions; who had forgotten what morning it was, and drew rein for a moment. But pressing forward again, they came upon a gerfalcon lying, with long lunes tangled about his feet and through his breast the hole that Sir Dinar's bolt had made. While they stooped over this bird the sun rose and shone between the tree-trunks, and lifting their heads they saw a green glade before them, and in the midst of the glade three pavilions set, each of red sendal, that shone in the morning. In the first pavilion slept seven knights, and in the second a score of damsels, but by the door of the third stood a lady, fair and tall, in a robe of samite, who, as they drew near to accost her, inquired of them.

"Which of you has slain my gerfalcon?"

And when Sir Dinar confessed and began to make his excuse, "Silly knight!" said she, "who couldst not guess that my falcon, too, was abroad to avenge the blessed Stephen. Or dost think that it was a hawk, of all birds, that sang a melody in the ears of his guards?"

With that she laughed, as if pacified, and asked of their affairs; and being told that they rode in search of the Sancgrael, she laughed again, saying –

"Silly knights all, that seek it before you be bearded! For three of you must faint and die on the quest, and you, sir," turning to Sir Dinar, "must many times long to die, yet never reach nearer by a foot."

"Let it be as God will," answered Sir Dinar. "But hast thou any tidings, to guide us?"

"I have heard," said she, "that it was seen latest in the land of Gore, beyond Trent Water." And with her white finger she pointed down a narrow glade that led to the north-west. So they thanked her and pricked on, none guessing that she herself was King Urience' wife, of Gore, and none other than Queen Morgan le Fay, the famous enchantress, who for loss of her gerfalcon was lightly sending Sir Dinar to his ruin.

So all that day they rode, two and two, in the strait alley that she had pointed out; and by her enchantments she made the winter trees to move with them, serried close on either hand, so that, though the four knights wist nothing of it, they advanced not a furlong for all their haste. But towards nightfall there appeared close ahead a blaze of windows lit and then a tall castle with dim towers soaring up and shaking to the din of minstrelsy. And finding a great company about the doors, they lit down from their horses and stepped into the great hall, Sir Dinar leading them. For a while their eyes were dazed, seeing that sconces flared along the walls and the place was full of knights and damsels brightly clad, and the floor shone. But while they were yet blinking, a band of maidens came and unbuckled their arms and cast a shining cloak upon each; which was hardly done when a lady came towards them out of the throng, and though she was truly the Queen Morgan le Fay, they knew her not at all, for by her necromancy she had altered her countenance.

"Come, dance," said she, "for in an instant the musicians will begin."

The other three knights carried awhile, being weary with riding; but Sir Dinar stepped forward and caught the hand of a damsel, and she, as she gave it, looked in his eyes and laughed. She was dressed all in scarlet, with scarlet shoes, and her hair lay on her shoulders like waves of burnished gold. As Sir Dinar set his arm about her, with a crash the merry music began; and floating out with him into the dance, her scarlet shoes twinkling and her tossed hair shaking spices under his nostrils, she leaned back a little on his arm and laughed again.

Sir Galhaltin was leaning by the doorway, and he heard her laugh and saw her feet twinkle like blood-red moths, and he called to Sir Dinar. But Sir Dinar heard only the brassy music, nor did any of the dancers turn their heads, though Sir Galhaltin called a second time and more loudly. Then Sir Sentrail and Sir Ozanna also began to call, fearing they knew not what for their comrade. But the guests still drifted by as they were clouds, and Sir Dinar, with the red blood showing beneath the down on his cheeks, smiled always and whirled with the woman upon his arm.

By-and-by he began to pant, and would have rested: but she denied him.

"For a moment only," he said, "because I have ridden far to-day."

But "No" she said, and hung a little more heavily upon his arm, and still the music went on. And now, gazing upon her, he was frightened; for it seemed she was growing older under his eyes, with deep lines sinking into her face, and the flesh of her neck and bosom shrivelling up, so that the skin hung loose and gathered in wrinkles. And now he heard the voices of his companions calling about the door, and would have cast off the sorceress and run to them. But when he tried, his arm was welded around her waist, nor could he stay his feet.

The three knights now, seeing the sweat upon his white face and the looks he cast towards them, would have broken in and freed him: but they, too, were by enchantment held there in the doorway. So, with their eyes starting, they must needs stay there and watch; and while they stood the boards became as molten brass under Sir Dinar's feet, and the hag slowly withered in his embrace: and still the music played, and the other dancers cast him never a look as he whirled round and round again. But at length, with never a stay in the music, his partner's feet trailed heavily, and, bending forward, she shook her white locks clear of her gaunt eyes, and laughed a third time, bringing her lips close to his. And the poison of death was in her lips as she set them upon his mouth. With that kiss there was a crash. The lights went out, and the music died away in a wail: and the three knights by the door were caught away suddenly and stunned by a great wind.

Awaking, they found themselves lying in the glade where they had come upon the three red pavilions. Their horses were cropping at the turf, beside them, and Sir Dinar's horse stood in sight, a little way off. But Sir Dinar was already deep in the forest, twirling and spinning among the rotten leaves, and on his arm hung a corrupting corpse. For a whole day they sought him and found him not (for he heard nothing of their shouts), and towards evening mounted and rode forward after the Sancgrael; on which quest they died, all three, each in his turn.

But Sir Dinar remained, and twirled and skipped till the body he held was a skeleton; and still he twirled, till it dropped away piece-meal; and yet again, till it was but a stain of dust on his ragged sleeve. Before this his hair was white and his face wizened with age.

But on a day a knight in white armour came riding through the forest, leaning somewhat heavily on his saddle-bow: and was aware of an old decrepit man that ran towards him, jigging and capering as if for gladness, yet caught him by the stirrup and looked up with rheumy tears in his eyes.

"In God's name, who art thou?" asked the knight. He, too, was past his youth; but his face shone with a marvellous glory.

"I am young Sir Dinar, that was made a knight of the Round Table but five days before Pentecost. And I know thee. Thou art Sir Galahad, who shouldst win the Sancgrael: therefore by Christ's power rid me of this enchantment."

"I have not won it yet," Sir Galahad answered, sighing. "Yet, poor comrade, I may do something for thee, though I cannot stay thy dancing."

So he stretched out his hand and touched Sir Dinar: and by his touch Sir Dinar became a withered leaf of the wood. And when mothers and nurses see him dancing before the wind, they tell this story of him to their children.

GALAHAD'S LADY

Phyllis Ann Karr

In the last story, Sir Dinar encounters Sir Galahad on his Quest. Now we turn to Galahad's own Quest, which is central to the Grail story. Phyllis Ann Karr (b. 1944) should be no stranger to devotees of Arthurian fiction. Besides the fact that she has appeared in all four of my Arthurian anthologies, she is the author of The King Arthur Companion *(1983) and the delightful murder mystery* The Idylls of the Queen *(1982).*

Have I betrayed my virginity? she thought. Her blood, perhaps her life, was dropping from her wrist into the silver bowl; and if she had betrayed her virginity she must die the most villainous death that ever woman had died.

Her thoughts went back to the visions.

The first vision had come on the eve of Pentecost, and might have been a simple dream but for its coherence – the history of the Sangreal, as the Queen of the Waste Lands had taught it to her from the ancient book, seen as if she were an angel hovering in the air to watch it happen:

Saint Joseph of Arimathea and his son coming to Britain with their followers, their family and the Holy Grail; travelling through the land teaching and being martyred; planting the Flowering Thorn that blooms in winter in the holy Isle of Avilion and leaving Sir Josue, son of the saintly priest Nascien, as the first of the Fisher Kings to guard the Grail in Listeneise.

From Sir Josue, Amide's own father, King Pellinore, brother to the present Fisher King, had come, in direct descent.

The second vision had come on the feast of Pentecost itself, the four hundred and fifty-fourth year after the Passion of the Lord Jesu Christ. Amide saw the court of King Arthur at Camelot as clearly as if she were present, except that she could not see one face – the face of the newest knight, he who sat without peril in the Siege Perilous that would burn any other with fire.

She watched as the Sangreal, veiled with white silk, entered the Great Hall, though all the doors and windows were closed tightly, – even as the Holy Spirit had entered into the womb of the Virgin Mother. Ever veiled, it fed every knight with the food he loved best. Then, when the Holy Grail was gone as it had come, through closed doors and as if it moved through the air of itself, the knights swore their oath to quest a year and a day for a clear sight of it without the veil.

Nascien, the priest and hermit, who had lived five centuries to bring the knight of the Siege Perilous to Court, warned them.

They must confess their sins and purify their lives; they must not undertake this quest as they undertook other adventures, lightly and with much careless bloodshed, but rather in penance and constant prayer, and he who undertook the Quest of the Grail unworthily would return a worse sinner than when he started. Better, said Nascien, for a man to break his newly made vow than to keep it and enter the Quest of the Sangreal unworthily.

Yet none of the knights who had vowed chose to stay behind.

Then the damsels and ladies of King Arthur's Court came into the hall, weeping and begging to go with their husbands and lovers. But Nascien told them sternly that no woman, neither wife nor maid, was permitted to accompany her lord on this holy Quest.

Amide woke weeping, holding her hands to her breast and wondering why a damsel might not search for the holy mysteries as well as a knight. Had not the bearer of the Holy Grail, when it had rested in her uncle's keep at Castle Carbonek, been a pure damsel?

The third vision came that night, and was of King Solomon's Ship. Amide knew of this ship from the story of how her uncle, Pellam, the Fisher King of Carbonek, had once found it, entered it, and tried to draw the sword. Now she saw its history as she had seen that of the Sangreal in her first vision.

King Solomon's wife was called a wicked woman. Yet, when Solomon learned in a vision of the perfect knight who was to be the last of his line, it was his wife who advised and directed the building and furnishing of the ship – a new ark, made of wood to outlast the Temple itself and drift through the centuries of the world until it brought the sword of Solomon's father to Solomon's last descendant.

King David's Sword – newly pommelled by Solomon's craftsmen with gold and precious stones, inlaid with the scales and bones of the marvellous beasts Ertanax and Calidone, and sheathed in a scabbard fashioned in part with wood from the Tree of Life – lay on a silk-covered bed safe within the ship. Above the bed hung the three spindles carved from the wood of the Tree of Knowledge.

In a vision within the vision, Amide saw Eve, about to be exiled from Paradise, break off the bough on which the fatal fruit had hung. Eve planted the bough again in the earth outside the Garden, so that it grew into a great tree, virgin-white all through. It grew quickly; it was already a large tree when God instructed Adam how to lie with his wife and beget the human race. When Adam and Eve coupled beneath the tree it turned green, the colour of generation. It grew green all the while Eve's first sons grew to manhood, but when Cain slew his brother beneath this same tree it turned blood-red, and so remained evermore.

Solomon's wife brought a workman to take wood from the ancient tree. It bled when he cut it, but still she insisted he cut off one of its largest and oldest branches. The crimson layer of growth on the outside was the thickest, the green inner ring the thinnest, and the pure white centre was exactly the right circumference for a spindle. The green spindle had to be pieced together, the red and white were each carved from a single block of wood. Solomon's wife joined the three spindles into the shape of an H, or a cross with two cross-pieces, symbol of the easy and noble Yoke of Christ.

To the scabbard of King David's Sword Solomon's wife fastened a belt of hemp, the one tawdry thing in all that splendour. When King Solomon complained, she told him that a pure maid would replace the hempen hangings with others more suitable at the proper time. The night, when the ship was ready to be set adrift, King Solomon saw in another vision how an angel came and wrote letters on the sword, the scabbard, and the ship. And Amide saw King Solomon's vision anew.

In the morning, Amide cut off her long russet-brown hair and began to plait it with golden threads and a golden buckle to make a fit sword-belt for the scabbard of King David's Sword. She understood the risk; if she were the maid who was meant to replace the hempen belt, then she must ever guard her virginity or else die such a death as would horrify all who heard of it. But she, too, was descended from King Solomon, and her uncle was the latest of the Fisher Kings.

The churchyard of the Chapel of the Leprous Lady was filled with tombs – threescore white marble tombs above the bodies of kings' daughters and the kinswomen of kings, maidens all, who had bled in vain to cure the Leprous Lady of her disease. Though none of their blood had healed her, the place where they lay buried was fragrant as the fairest garden, and birds sang there even while tempests raged and knights did battle outside. Yet King Pellinore's daughter prayed she would not be buried there among the others.

Not all died who gave their blood to the Leprous Lady. Some recovered. With God's grace, perhaps Amide would live also, to continue seeking the Holy Grail with her three knights – Sir Percivale, her brother, the old, wise Sir Bors de Ganis and Sir Galahad, the last – and purest, after the Virgin herself – of King Solomon's line.

Amide gazed into the silver dish. The surface of crimson liquid rippled slightly with each new drop that fell from her wrist, and the red blood became the dark sea of Collibe, where she'd first seen the ship with two of her knights.

The sea and sky were each as blue as the other on that day when she looked down from the hermitage-castle of the Queen of the Waste Lands, where she had been raised, and saw the little ship riding near the white sand. It was not King Solomon's Ship; she would have recognized that from her vision, still clear in her mind though months had passed and the new sword-belt was long completed.

Nor did she recognize the two small knights in their silver-flashing armour and white surcoats, who rode in the ship without rowing or guiding it, but she knew them for good men. And she knew, even before she went to the chapel to pray, that the time had come to leave her preparations and ride out into the world.

In the chapel, the sun shining through the stained-glass window of the Five Wounds formed the coloured panes into a map – the map of the valley above Collibe, where Amide had spent her life. A bubble in a piece of crimson glass showed her where she must go – not to the ship in the haven, not yet, but to the hermitage of Sir Ulfin, a little further than she had ever gone in her seventeen years.

She saddled the silver-grey palfrey herself, as she had always done, before putting on her whitest gown and riding south-eastward, away from the sea and into the forest towards the hermitage of Sir Ulfin, who had once been a brave knight of King Uther Pendragon. Darkness fell before she reached the place, but a dove flew slowly ahead of her, silver-white as a silken veil against the clear indigo sky.

Amide seemed to ride in a waking vision, flowing into God's will for her moment by moment; she knew she was riding to find a knight helpmeet to go with her to the High Mysteries. She did not know his name, not yet, but as she rode the wind in the leaves and the plants beneath her palfrey's hooves seemed to rustle over and over, "Lancelot . . . Lancelot."

But it was not Lancelot, not that noble, life-scarred man who had slept with Amide's cousin, Elaine of Carbonek, and engendered a child on her – Amide knew the story, though it had happened before her own birth. The Queen of the Waste Lands had told it to her, at the time of her first bleeding, as a mystery, as a sin that, like the disobedience of Adam and Eve, was happy because it had brought about so great a redemption.

Lancelot had had a different christened name before the Lady of the Lake took him to raise. He had been christened Galahad, and that was the name of his son and Elaine's.

When she came into the glade and saw the dark hermitage, Amide's palfrey leaped towards it in a gallop, and the rhythm of his leap sent the name through her: "Galahad! Galahad!" So that was the name she called when she came to the hermit's door, and her waking vision held true, for Sir Ulfin brought him out to her.

Her cousin Galahad, little older than she herself, who had already seen much of the world, had been made knight by King Arthur's own hand and sat safely in the Siege Perilous.

He wore a sword already – the sword of Sir Balin le Savage, who had dealt King Pellam of Carbonek the Dolorous Stroke long ago, in retribution for his attempt to draw King David's Sword.

After Balin's death, Merlin the enchanter had put the sword into a block of red marble, to float down to Arthur's Court on the Pentecost of Galahad's arrival. As only Arthur had been able to draw that other sword from stone and anvil to prove his kingship years before, so now only Galahad could draw Sir Balin's sword from the block of floating red marble. Amide had seen this too, in her vision of last Pentecost, when the Sangreal had fed the knights of Arthur's Round Table.

Sir Galahad's shield was the white shield of King Mordrains, who had come to Britain with Joseph of Arimathea. The red cross on that shield had been painted by Joseph himself on his deathbed, with his own blood, and the shield had waited four centuries in its abbey for Sir Galahad to come and find it. The young knight's armour and surcoat were also red – the colour of the Holy Ghost and Pentecost, of fire, of the devotion unto death and of the blood of life.

His hair was such a pale gold it seemed white, like a nimbus round his head in the moonlight. He was beautiful as the Archangel Michael, and for a moment Amide could not speak. Then she said only, "Arm yourself, Sir Galahad, and follow me. Within three days I will show you the highest adventure any knight has ever seen."

Why she promised this, or what the adventure was to be, she could not say, but the Holy Ghost seemed to speak through her, as through the saints of old. She listened to the promise as she spoke it with as much surprise as did the knight and the hermit – perhaps with more – and the words echoed in her mind through no effort of her own, for all she could think of was Sir Galahad.

She turned and put her palfrey into a gallop again, almost before Sir Galahad had time to mount and follow her, but she could not ride away from her thoughts. How like the Archangel he seemed to her! How had *she* seemed to him? What adventure could she show him on the third day, if she had deluded herself and the Lord God sent no marvel?

She brought him home by night to the castle of the Queen of the Waste Lands, waited on him with her own hands as he ate and saw the servants lead him to the finest bedchamber. Then she sought advice from the Queen. "Madam, shall he stay here all night, or two nights, or three?"

The old queen shook her head. "I have watched the ship all day. Let Sir Galahad sleep a while yet, but he must leave before dawn."

"Madam, shall I go with him?"

The Queen of the Waste Lands smiled and laid her hand on her pupil's shoulder. "Child, you shall go with him to the end of your quest."

"Madam, the Quest is not for women. I heard the holy hermit Nascien say it, in my vision."

Amide had been like a daughter to the Queen of the Waste Lands. The old recluse bent forward and kissed her cheek. "My child, the hermit Nascien is but a man, for all his centuries, and he spoke then as a man, not as a saintly prophet. If the Quest were not for you, you would not have had your visions. May the Holy Mother forgive him for forbidding the Quest to her daughters."

Amide pressed the old woman's hand and returned her kiss. She did not speak, for her throat was too swollen with tears. She rose and went to her chamber, but she could not sleep.

Shortly after midnight, she took the belt she had woven with her hair, put it into a silver box and tied the box carefully in a blanket, with an extra shift, two clean wimples, her needle, her comb – for though her hair had only grown back to the middle of her neck, it must still be combed – and a few other small necessaries. Little as she took, it seemed like much to her, much more than her knight had brought with him in the holy Quest, and yet she carried neither armour nor shield, and the weight of her bundle, with the silver box as its precious heart, would sit very lightly on the palfrey's back.

Then she went with the torchbearer to call Sir Galahad. She waited, shivering in the draughty hallway, while he dressed and armed himself. When he was ready, she led him down through the night, they two alone, with neither squire nor damsel to attend them, guided only by the moon shining like a white dove above the waters of Collibe. Down to the pale ship that had drifted in close to shore.

The two knights aboard it were asleep, but woke to their hailing.

"We must leave the horses here," said Amide, finding a rock to stand on while she unsaddled her own.

They waded through the knee-deep water to the ship, Amide carrying her palfrey's saddle and bridle as Galahad carried those of his charger; but he had arms and armour as well, while she had only her light bundle, tied safely to her back. The waiting knights helped them up, welcoming them into the ship.

Scarcely were they aboard when the dawn wind started to blow, moving the ship out to open sea again.

As the sun rose Amide looked one last time at the castle of the Queen of the Waste Lands, where she had grown to womanhood. The two horses were already halfway up the slope to it, the silver-grey palfrey leading the great white charger. The sun rising up over the land crimsoned them all – castle, horses, trees, every familiar stone and fold in the hillside, seen now from a new, strange angle.

On the highest tower Amide thought she saw the figure of the Queen of the Waste Lands, in her grey gown and wimple like a nun's. She waved, and thought the woman on the tower waved back. Then she turned and looked westward, at the encircling cliffs the ship had almost reached, and at the open sea beyond the dawn.

A single dish of blood from a maiden's arm, though the dish was large and deep, hardly seemed a great deal when compared with what so many men had shed to win it for the Leprous Lady. Threescore and ten knights had come out of the castle to force Amide to yield to its custom, and her three knights had slain a score of them in one afternoon. Amide had looked on from one side and the gentlewomen of the Leprous Lady, the tallest holding her empty silver dish, had looked on from the other.

On the third day after Amide had brought Sir Galahad to join Sir Percivale and Sir Bors, they had been blown to a pair of huge rocks jutting up from the sea, and had found between them, safe as if in harbour, King Solomon's Ship. But Amide dared not remember that day – not yet.

She thought instead of yesterday, of bright metal turning slick and wet with men's blood, of her three knights, anonymous in their armour and helmets – two in white surcoats, one in red – striking down man after man.

Her memory blurred for a moment, and the din of yesterday merged with the battle of several days ago, the only other time she had ever seen her knights kill. Then her mind cleared and the two scenes separated, but she remained caught in the mystery of bloodshed.

They had returned from King Solomon's Ship into their first vessel, and the wind had blown them back to the mainland. They beached in the northern marches, and, having no food left, went ashore.

Sir Bors, who was old enough to have been father to his companions, pointed to the fortress on the cliff above them. "Carteloise," he said. "The castle of Earl Hernox. I saw it once before, in my youth."

Amide looked up at it, only the second castle she had ever seen in her life, and felt the strange sight of waking vision begin again

... but this time the chill was more of foreboding than awe. "Is he a good man, the lord of Carteloise?"

"A good knight and a friend to Arthur."

Amide looked again and saw a party of mounted knights start down the cliff from the castle. Their armour flashed against the dark rock like fire-glow caught in flecks of soot, and she could not hold back her warning, be it false prophecy or true. "If they learn you are of Arthur's Court, my lords," she said, knowing that her knights would never deny the truth, "they will strike to kill you."

They did not question her warning. They seemed to regard her not as a gentlewoman young in years and younger in experience, but as a saint and true prophetess. Sir Galahad took her hand and held it a moment. Even armoured in his steel gauntlet his fingers were gentle. "My lady, the Power that has kept us until now will deliver us from greater dangers than this."

In their full armour, but carrying their helmets, they began walking up the path, Amide in their midst. A squire was the first who met them. She supposed he was a squire, for he wore rich clothes, although his face was smudged with dark stains, his eyes were red and his nose swollen.

"What are you?" he said, as if he were challenging them. When Sir Bors answered that they were of Arthur's Court, the squire sneered and spat onto the ground between him and them before turning his horse and riding back up to the armed knights.

There were few folk in the castle-hermitage of the Queen of the Waste Lands. All lived together according to their proper rank but not imprisoned in their rank, as befitted God's creatures. Amide had never seen such rudeness in the lowest churl of her home as she saw in this squire of Carteloise Castle.

Nor, at that time, had she seen bloodshed by sword or lance or any other weapon.

They continued upward. A horn sounded, hoarse and melancholy, above them. They passed a shadow that seemed to be the mouth of a cave and a gentlewoman came out of it to them, pale and beautiful, clad in a white garment covered with crimson and black stains. Her hair hung loose to her waist and looked white in the sunlight, despite the youth of her face. The skin of her face and hands seemed almost transparent against the rock.

"Turn back!" she wailed to them, stretching forth her arms. "For God's love, turn back – lest you die and come unshriven into Purgatory!"

Sir Bors took a step forward to comfort the lady, but Percivale
held him back. "God give you rest, good lady," said Sir Galahad,
gazing at her with compassion. "We come in the service of God,
who will both help us and give you ease."

The pale lady pointed upward with a scream that sounded more
of grief than fear. They looked and saw the first knights from the
castle coming round a turn in the path.

Amide had time to help fasten her lord's helmet, while her
brother and Sir Bors quickly helmed themselves. Then she retired
to the mouth of the cave, standing beside the pale gentlewoman
in stained white, careful not to touch her.

Amide and her knights had neither charger nor palfrey, for there
had not been room for horses in their small ship. The knights of
the castle rode fine warhorses. They stopped twenty paces from
Amide's three knights, and the foremost one shouted in a husky
voice, "Yield or die!"

Another opened his visor and leered at Amide in a way that she
knew was evil, though she had never seen anyone look at her so
before. She could not tell whether he also saw the gentlewoman
in white. A third, who wore a black claw instead of a plume on
his helmet, added, "You may find it more unpleasant to yield."

"Then we will choose the more pleasant way," said Sir Bors.

"With God's help, we will neither yield nor die," Sir Percivale
added.

Sir Galahad said nothing, but stood with his first sword, the
sword of Sir Balin le Savage, in his right hand, and his second
sword, the Sword with the Strange Hangings, loosened in its
sheath. It was the first time Amide had seen him prepared for
battle. She missed the sight of his grey eyes and high forehead
with its single crease, but even in the lines of his armour she could
read his tension.

The knights of the castle spurred forward down the narrow
path, horses at the gallop and lances lowered. Percivale was the
first to be threatened.

Stepping aside from the driving lance, he thrust his sword up into
one of the joints of his opponent's armour. There was screaming
and a crash of metal. The saddle was empty for a moment, and
then Percivale was sitting in it, turning the horse, kicking the foot
of the fallen knight free from the stirrup, where the bloody spur
had caught and dangled him.

Her brother had been the first by so few heartbeats that when
she looked at the others Amide saw Sir Bors and Sir Galahad had

already done the same thing to their attackers. For a moment she felt cheated that she had not seen her lord unhorse his foe and swing up into the saddle, lightly for all the weight of his armour. Then all her joy in the victory vanished in the blood of it.

Her knights had no lances, but they charged with swords in their right hands and shields carried high on their left arms. Sir Galahad let his shield hang down his back, out of the way, however, while he brandished Sir Balin's sword in one hand and King David's Sword in the other.

The knights of the castle had lances, but the three were close upon them before they could use the long weapons. The knights of the castle turned in confusion and fled before Amide's knights with screams and a great noise, many of them falling even before they were out of sight behind the rocks.

The pale gentlewoman screamed again, and sank down upon the rocks – not quite sitting, not quite kneeling, but crumpled somehow, without support. "The devils are taking them. The angels do not fight for them!"

Amide looked once more at the narrow road. The air smelled of blood, and a stench worse than blood, large swatches of earth were soaked and rocks spattered crimson; but to her eyes the battle had moved much further up the mountain, and to her ears the din was already lessening in the heights above, leaving only corpses and the silence of death. And the black claw on the helmet of one knight now quiet at last, after scratching in the mire of dust and blood.

To the eyes and ears of the woman beside her the worst battle of all was still raging – the demons and the angels of the dead men struggling for their souls . . . No, the gentlewoman had said that the angels were not fighting. They were weeping, perhaps, or soaring away and abandoning those who had been their charges.

Angels would not behave so unless there was no hope – unless the dying were utterly beyond salvation. So the screams which the pale gentlewoman heard were not of souls in fear, but of souls already damned, being borne away and down.

The vision did not come to Amide, and she was grateful. But enough sense of vision reached her that she understood her companion groaned only for the newly dead, and not for herself. Amide turned back and watched the pale woman fade from sight.

"Gone, gone," she murmured, her voice vibrating with thousands of tiny echoes. Then she lifted her face to the sun, raised her hands towards Amide and whispered, "Pray for me," just before vanishing completely.

Left alone, Amide knelt and prayed that the gentlewoman's soul would soon be released from Purgatory into Heaven, as it had now been released from Earth into Purgatory. Pray for the knights who lay dead on the path she could not. She rose and followed the trail of corpses up the mountain to Carteloise Castle. The rocks were often slippery with blood, and sometimes she had little space to pick her way around a heap of armour grotesquely crumpled and oozing at the joints.

The battle was finished when she reached the fortress, but it could not have been long over. Her three knights stood in the hall, in the midst of a great number of dead men. Percivale, Bors and Galahad had not yet removed their helmets, so their faces were hidden as they turned their heads to look at the desolation around them.

The evil stench of damned souls departing their bodies, which had dissipated quickly in the air outside, hung heavy in the hall, and clouds of black smoke whirled near the roof for a few moments, as if seeking the air vents, before seeming to sink back through the stone floor, pulled down by unseen demons.

Sir Bors unhelmed at last and shook his head. "If God had loved them, we could not have slain them thus. Their sins must have been so great that Our Lord sent us to end their rule."

Sir Percivale leaned wearily on his sword and said nothing.

Sir Galahad knelt and shook, as if weeping. "Vengeance was not ours to deal out to them. Has God no power to avenge sin but through the arms of sinful men?"

Sir Bors and even Sir Percivale had killed men in battle before this, but Sir Galahad never. The knight of most skill and prowess in the world, he had always until now stopped at unhorsing or otherwise defeating his opponents – even the seven murderous brothers of the Castle of Maidens. Nor had he so much as killed a man by mischance.

Amide knew this from their days on the sea together. She went to him now, drew off his helmet and held his head in her arms, so that the blood on his armour stained her gown as well.

A priest came out into the hall from a side-chamber, holding up the Host and Chalice before him like protective talismans. When he learned what they had done, he blessed them for it.

Sir Hernox, the good Earl who had ruled Carteloise as Sir Bors remembered, had had three sons and a daughter. The sons had burned in sinful love for their own sister, had forced her and murdered her when she cried out to their father. Then they had wounded and imprisoned the Earl himself, gathered a great number of unbaptized men-at-arms and begun to slay priests, burn chapels, force nuns and gentlewomen – spreading even more terror than had the seven brothers of the Castle of Maidens.

The priest who told them this story had come there that day to shrive and anoint the dying Earl, who had told him deliverance was near at hand, that three servants of God were soon to end his sons' rule. Thus had Earl Hernox approved before the time the deaths of his own sons.

The priest agreed with Sir Bors that the slaughter had been God's will and Heaven's just vengeance. Earl Hernox called himself blessed to die in Sir Galahad's arms, and Galahad accepted the blessing, kneeling in the hall amid the corpses and holding the old, sick Earl until his soul had gone to meet his daughter's in Purgatory or Heaven.

But Galahad was not made cheerful again until they left that place, and Carteloise still ran with blood.

Within three days, Sir Galahad had killed again, and this time the slaughter was meaningless. Amide's champions had killed a score of knights to save her from the custom of the Castle of the Leprous Lady. But when the evening's truce was called, and they learned that her blood was wanted to heal the castle's mistress, who had lain sick for many years, Amide chose to submit of her own will.

Thus, further bloodshed had been avoided, but the knights who had already died in the service of their lady need not have done so, and their souls seemed to sit around the rim of the deep silver bowl, watching Amide as the soul of Earl Hernox's daughter had watched the men who rode down from Carteloise Castle.

Could the blood of a woman – virgin or not – who had been the cause of so much death bring back health to the Leprous Lady? Was not Amide's life dripping from her wrist to no purpose?

She turned her head away from the silver dish, now more than half filled, and groped weakly with her left hand. Sir Galahad took her fingers and held them. She saw his face above her, worried yet already resigned. He did not speak today, but she remembered his words of last night, when she had announced that she would submit to the custom of this castle.

"My lady, if you bleed so much, you will die."

She had answered him. "Better for me to die than for the battle to begin again. And if I die to heal this lady," she had gone on, though she was speaking not in vision but in simple mortal reason,

"I will win great honour and my soul's salvation. And it will be to the honour of my brothers and my parents' lineage," she had added, as Sir Percivale had bent forward to speak to her.

"Surely this Leprous Lady is a great sinner," had said Sir Bors, "or God would have healed her before now."

But Amide had turned back his own argument upon him. "Has not King Pellam our uncle waited as many years as this lady to be cured? Has not King Mordrains waited more than four centuries for the knight who is to heal him? God means my lord, Sir Galahad, to heal King Pellam and King Mordrains. May I not be Heaven's instrument to heal the lady of this castle?"

"God may use us for good as well as for vengeance," said Sir Galahad.

"Vengeance also is good, if Heaven wills it," said Sir Bors. "And sacrifice may be evil if Heaven wills it not."

"You adventure your lives daily to win praise and honour, my lords," said Amide. "Allow me to adventure mine this once."

So she had won her will, yesterday between Vespers and Compline. Now, in silence, she seemed to hear her lord say directly into her mind, "We could have slipped past the castle in the night, sweet love."

She sent her thought back to his mind. "For the blood of the men we have killed here – perhaps even for the blood spilled at Carteloise Castle – this is necessary reparation, my love."

Closing her eyes, she remembered King Solomon's Ship before the carnage at Carteloise, that day when Earth had seemed one with Heaven, and yet when she had, perhaps, brought down upon herself the villainous death of the prophecy, as Kings Mordrains and Pellam had brought down vengeance on themselves – though they were good men – by trying to draw King David's Sword.

It was time to remember that day. She dared wait no longer.

It was a fair ship, a noble ship, fashioned of the cedars of Lebanon a thousand years before the death of Jesu. The sail was of pure white silk and the cabin hung about with silk of white and gold. In almost fifteen centuries of sailing about the waters of the world the cloth had never been frayed nor stained.

The ship was as fair and clean as Amide had seen it in her vision, on the night when it was newly finished and King Solomon had seen the angel sprinkle it with water from a silver bowl and write the letters on sword, scabbard and ship.

The angel's words were still there, bright in letters of gold on the prow: "Beware, thou man who would enter me, for I am Faith, and therefore be in steadfast belief, for if thou fail, I shall not help thee."

Not even King Solomon himself, reading those words, had dared enter his own ship after the angel had written them. King Mordrains, King Pellam and King Hurlame, who had ventured in and tried to draw the sword, had all been wounded grievously for their presumption.

When Sir Percivale hailed the ship, he had no reply. There was neither man nor woman aboard.

The Queen of the Waste Lands had told Amide her brother's name and story, but they had been raised apart, the children of different mothers, and he did not know her. Now, in their own vessel, with only a few inches of sun-rayed water separating them from King Solomon's Ship, she recognized the moment for which she had been waiting without knowing why she waited.

"Percivale, have you guessed who I am?"

"No," he said, looking at her. He was pledged to purity, but even a man so pledged might look with pure pleasure on a woman's face, even as a woman pledged to purity might look on that of a handsome man. Amide saw by her brother's gaze that she was beautiful, more beautiful than she had used to dream of being in her silly childhood, when she had sat alone looking into still ponds or mirrors of polished iron and dreaming of court and a lord to love her. And Percivale was the most handsome man she had ever seen or could imagine, except one.

"Percivale, I am your sister, King Pellinore's daughter, and so you are the man I love most in all this world." At the moment she said this it was true, for he was her brother and Galahad as yet no more than friend and comrade. "And so I tell you, Percivale, if you have any doubt, if your faith is not perfect, sweet brother, do not enter this ship. Do not risk the danger."

He had smiled and held her hand.

At that time, she had seen in his smile only the joy of knowing her, and, perhaps, of suddenly knowing his own faith from within. Now, lying on a bed in the Castle of the Leprous Lady, with the danger of the worst death that ever woman died intruding into her memory, she wondered if he had smiled because, until that moment before King Solomon's Ship, her beauty had tempted his vow, and because learning who she was to him had released him from the temptation.

"Fair sister," he had told her that day, still holding her hand, "I shall enter this ship and test myself. If I am no true knight, better for me to perish at once."

But it was Sir Galahad who crossed himself and stepped aboard King Solomon's Ship the first of them all, his golden hair shining, his crimson surcoat bright as though the stains of travel had been washed away by sunlight. On the deck between side and cabin he waited, extending his arm and helping Amide up into the Ship of Faith beside him. Then Sir Bors followed, and Sir Percivale last of all.

In the cabin they found the bed with the spindles made of the wood of the Tree of Knowledge hanging above it and King David's Sword lying on it – the pommel set with precious stones, the haft glistening with the bones and scales of Ertanax and Calidone, just as Amide had seen it in her vision. The blade was pulled half a foot from the rich sheath, as King Pellam had left it. Otherwise, no one except themselves seemed ever to have entered here since King Solomon had sent his ship forth on the seas of the world.

Sir Percivale bent and read the words on the sword. "Now, in the name of God," he cried, "let me make the attempt!"

Amide watched half in fear. Her grandfather, his father before him, her uncle King Pellam and King Mordrains in the time of Joseph of Arimathea had all drawn King David's Sword, or tried to draw it, and had been killed or maimed for the attempt – not for their wickedness, for some had been very good men – but for their attempt to handle this sword unauthorized.

She did not try to stop her brother, but in her fear she sent up a secret prayer; and perhaps it was heard, for Sir Percivale was favoured. He could not so much as grip the handle firmly, and so he escaped all punishment for attempting to draw the blade.

He stepped back at last, saddened and humbled, but safe. Then Sir Bors made the attempt – less, Amide thought, because he hoped to succeed than because he wished to comfort Sir Percivale. Again she prayed in secret, and the older knight, too, was unable even to close his fingers round the hilt.

Last, Sir Galahad came to the bed and studied the warning on the sword: "Let no one attempt to draw me but the one who is hardier than all others: and he who is to draw me out shall never be shamed nor die of battle wound."

"In faith," said Galahad, "who would not desire this sword for its beauty and its promise? But the warning is too great. I will not try."

Yet one of Amide's three must be the one meant to draw King

David's Sword, or else her own vision had been vain and her effort and sacrifice wasted when she'd cut off her long hair to plait the new belt.

She had thought it might be her brother, Sir Percivale, who should draw his ancestor's sword, for he was descended from King David through their father, King Pellinore. And Sir Bors, who was Sir Lancelot's cousin-german, might also have been the chosen, for he also was descended from David, through a brother of King Pellinore's ancestor in the direct line – Josue, the great-grandson of Nascien the Holy Hermit.

But now she knew, and seemed always to have known in her heart, since the night she had followed the silver-white dove to the hermitage where he lay, that it was Sir Galahad for whom King Solomon and his wife had made their ship – Sir Galahad, the last of his own line, descended from King David on both his father's side and his mother's, in the twelfth generation from Jesu Christ.

"Galahad, Galahad," she told him, "the drawing of this sword is forbidden to all men save you alone."

As he still hesitated she told them the story of the three who had grasped King David's Sword: how King Hurlame the Saracen, who had wrenched it out to kill King Pellam's grandfather, had died even as he returned it to the scabbard; how King Mordrains, their ancestor's brother-in-law, and King Pellam himself had been maimed for their attempt to draw it.

Then she told them of the ship itself, how King Solomon and his wife had made it, what things these were in it – the great sword of Jesu's ancestor David, holding the mystic properties of Calidone, which guarded the sword's user from heat, and of Ertanax, which lent him singleness of purpose for his present task; and the three spindles, white, green and red, carved from the Tree brought out of Paradise and tied together in prophetic symbol of the Yoke of Christ.

She did not speak in present vision but in the strength of remembered vision, hardly aware of what words she chose to describe the wonders that filled her mind.

And when she had finished Sir Galahad slowly lifted King David's Sword, still sheathed, and read the words written on the scabbard: "He who is meant to wear me shall never be shamed while I hang by his side. But let none take away my belt except she who is meant to replace it; she will be a king's daughter and a queen's, and she must be a maid all her life, both in will and in deed; and if she break her virginity she shall die the most villainous death that ever died any woman."

"It seems no one may wear this scabbard and draw the sword," Sir Galahad said slowly, "until the maid is found who will replace the hempen belt."

When first they had seen King Solomon's Ship waiting between the rocks Amide had recognized it even from a distance as the ship of her vision. She had taken the small silver box from her bundle and put it carefully into her mantle while the three knights had gazed constantly at the ship.

She should bring it out now . . . her life was gathering into the moment for which she had been born . . . but although her faith in God's Mysteries was firm, her faith in herself was not.

While she hesitated her brother found a scrip lying half-hidden beneath the spindles. The scrip held a parchment that told the story of King Solomon's Ship and all it contained from the time Solomon and his wife decided to make it until they were ready to set it adrift. It told nothing of the warnings on ship, sword and scabbard, for David's son himself had not dared go back aboard after the angel had written those warnings. But what it told proved Amide's visions to be true.

"My noble lord Sir Galahad," she said, after they had read King Solomon's parchment, "with God's will, I shall replace the sword-belt."

She brought out her silver box at last, opened it, and lifted up the sword-belt with two fingers and thumb, as reverently as if she had not braided it herself, using her own hair. It was no longer her own. It was now a thing that had always belonged in this ship – that had, indeed, been here since King Solomon's wife foresaw its making and left the poor rope belt to keep its place through the centuries. It was part of the Mystery, as she herself was part of the Mystery.

But it was also a belt of fine craftsmanship. When she realized that her three knights were admiring it for the beauty of its crafting and materials, as well as for the Mystery, that did not displease her. Nor did it displease her when Sir Galahad pushed aside her wimple, gently, as if he were arranging robes on a statue of the Virgin, and held the swordbelt up to the shorn fringe of her deep russet-coloured hair.

"Yes," she said, "I loved it well when I was a worldly woman. But when I learned this adventure was for me, I clipped it off and made this sword-belt for the glory of God."

They were silent while she unbound the old rope belt from the scabbard and fastened on the new belt of her own hair. As she completed the task, however, Sir Bors said, "Now it will be called not King David's Sword, but Sir Galahad's Sword."

"No," replied Sir Galahad. "Let it not be called after me. If it must have a new name, do you give it one, my lady."

She hesitated a moment, looking at the old hemp sword-belt on the bed and the new one, russet and gold, attached to the scabbard. The name which had come into her head did not seem solemn enough, and she was unsure whether she moved in inspiration or in mortality; but even the holy angels in Heaven must smile sometimes. "Truly," she said, "its name should be The Sword with the Strange Hangings."

She lifted it up and turned to them, holding it before her like a cross, with the belt hanging down in a graceful loop that touched hilt, scabbard and her hands. In that scabbard was a fragment of the Tree of Life, a fragment from the same beam that had later been made into the Holy Cross and stained with Jesu's blood. None whose blood still flowed in their veins could tell which piece of the scabbard it was.

"And the name of the scabbard," Amide went on, speaking now in what must have been inspiration, for it was not mortal reason, "is Mover of Blood."

Moving slowly, she brought the sword to Sir Galahad and held it out to him. Centuries and heartbeats melded together, and had this moment never ended, as she stood and looked into Sir Galahad's grey eyes, Amide thought they must have been translated into Heaven.

Then one of the knights – she was too far from the senses of mortality to know whether the voice belonged to Bors or Percivale – said, "In the Name of Jesu, Galahad . . . draw it and wear it!"

"Pray for me, then. If I succeed, the sword and the success will be yours, my friends, as well as mine." Sir Galahad closed his right hand around the jewelled hilt, put his left hand over Amide's hand on the scabbard, and drew out the blade.

He held the sword straight up for a few moments. It gleamed as if in sunlight, although they were enclosed in the cool twilight of the ship's cabin. At last he returned it to the sheath called Mover of Blood and held his arms away from his body while Amide bent and buckled her sword-belt around his waist. Now he was the Knight with the Two Swords, as Sir Balin le Savage had been before him. But Balin le Savage was to Galahad as Adam had been to Christ.

As Amide finished Galahad took her hands in his, and so they stood a moment longer. Her brother Percivale had told her that, raised in ignorance of knighthood and chivalry, he had mistaken the first knights he ever saw for angels. In Sir Galahad, Amide saw knight and angel both. Even so must the Archangel Michael have appeared in the moment before he led the hosts of Heaven against those of Hell. But who had girded the Archangel Michael with his sword?

"Now I care not if I die, for I am one of the blessed maidens of the world and I have girded the worthiest knight!"

"Live, sweet lady, live." Galahad kissed her hand. "And I shall be your own knight all the days of my life."

She should have died in that moment, and it would have been a glorious death.

She had not yet seen the blood of battle.

Although she girded herself with the poor hemp belt that King Solomon's wife had first attached to the scabbard Mover of Blood, Amide did not yet realize that after the moment of glory came the long days of suspension in the world. She did not yet understand that as early as that hour on King Solomon's Ship she had, perhaps, broken her virginity in will.

The silver dish was large and deep, and now Amide's blood lacked hardly a thumb's-length from its rim. Yet not all the damsels who had filled that dish for the Leprous Lady had died of it. The damsel who had come to this castle with Sir Balin le Savage had filled the dish and ridden away on the morrow laughing.

But she had been a woman who lived in the world, who had had a lover and who had helped Sir Balin avenge the lover's death – who had, perhaps, not been a virgin when she gave her blood. That damsel had perished when Sir Balin dealt King Pellam the Dolorous Stroke and a part of Carbonek Castle fell down upon them, but she had ridden away healthy and laughing from the castle of the Leprous Lady.

Amide had thought of herself, before her first visions at the start of this Quest, as a worldly woman; and yet she wondered, now, if she had ever guessed what it truly was to live in the world. She had woven childish dreams of courts, lovers, deeds of arms and feast-day merriment . . . but the only part of all this which she had seen – the deeds of arms – were not as noble in reality as they had been in fancy. The rest of it, too, might have been ugly, like the deeds of arms.

Only Sir Galahad was as she had dreamed . . . better than she had dreamed . . . gentler and nobler, when his two swords did not run with blood. Her knight, her lord . . . And if the Grail had left them room, he might have been her lover. As she might, in her secret heart, be his.

But perhaps she had already broken her maidenhood with an unknown lover, in the daydreams of her worldly youth. If so, why had she been granted her visions? And why this adventure of King Solomon's Ship and the Quest of the Holy Grail, which the hermit Nascien had forbidden to all women?

She had been the tool of Heaven – a soiled tool, serviceable but doomed. The price of that moment of glory in King Solomon's Ship was the villainous death of the curse. She must be taken early from her three knights.

She accepted it. She would have bought her brief glory even had she known ahead of time that by daring to replace the hempen belt with her own she was already doomed. She might have gained a few more days of life had she and her knights slipped past this castle in the dark, or had she allowed them to fight again in the morning and kill more of the Leprous Lady's people.

But the villainous death must still have come before her companions could find the Grail, for it could not be that a sinful creature like herself, a mere fountain-shaft for the miracle to flow through, would be granted to see the Sangreal clear and unveiled. She would have bought only a few more days of witnessing the bloodshed that was the price her knights paid for their honour, and then come quickly to a death more painful, perhaps, than this.

Yet there might also have been another hour like that of the day before yesterday, another hour when Heaven and the Holy Grail had seemed very close, and sin very weak and distant.

After leaving Carteloise Castle, on horses that were gifts from the grateful folk of that place, they had come into a waste forest, a wilderness far from people, far from murderous brothers and knights whose souls left their bodies with an evil stench.

The forest seemed good, soothing and healing, like the prayer of Matins in the hours of night, after a day of labour and a sleep of evil dreams. Shafts of sunlight came through the leaves and the air was sweet and unperfumed. They rode slowly, for there was no path, and much of the ground was covered with tall green plants.

Midway between the hours of Prime and Tierce, they saw the white hart and his four lions.

Other knights through the years had seen these marvellous animals wandering in the savage forest – the pure white deer who walked with four lions flanking him, front, back and at each side, like a cross, guarding rather than attacking. All who had glimpsed them reported that the sight brought a feeling of deep peace.

Most had stood quietly to watch the five animals pass, as if to move might break the fragile strand that seemed somehow to join hart, lions and beholders tenuously to Heaven. A few had tried to follow the hart and lions, but either they had quickly lost sight of them or the forest growth had blocked their way. So none knew where the animals came from or where they went, but they had wandered the woods longer than the natural lifespan of their race.

When the hart came abreast of the four adventurers, he turned his head and seemed to look at each of them. They watched him pass by, surrounded by his lions. Then, without speaking, they turned their horses and followed him, Amide first.

As long as the hart and lions walked slowly, they followed slowly. As the marvellous animals began to run, faster and faster, the horses followed pace, almost without urging. The dense forest growth parted before the leading lion and did not spring back until after the last knight, Sir Bors, had passed – how long after he had passed, they did not know, for they never looked behind. There might still have been a passage through the densest part of the waste forest, waiting for them if they had chosen to return the way they came rather than to go on forward.

They rode for an hour or more, and none of them tired. At last they came to a valley with a small hermitage in the centre. The hart and lions slowed again to a walk and entered the chapel of the hermitage. Amide and her knights dismounted, tied their horses in the churchyard and followed.

The hart stood behind the altar, with one lion sitting on each side of the holy table and two lying in front. At the altar stood a priest, fully vested, ready to begin the Mass. He nodded to the knights and damsel, but did not seem to notice the animals, though the hart stood at his very shoulder. His vestments were red and he recited the Mass of the Holy Ghost. Red was the colour of the Holy Ghost, and also of the holy martyrs, the colour of fire and of blood, both divine and human.

When the priest reached the secret mysteries of the Mass, the air wavered and the animals changed. One remained a lion, but now he shone as if he were gold lighted from within. One turned into an ox, one into an eagle, and the last into a knight kneeling beside the altar with arms crossed over his chest.

The hart became a man robed like a prince, in white and gold. Now he sat in a throne on the altar. They had not seen how the throne came upon the altar, and, though it appeared substantial, they saw the priest also, in the same time and the same place, bending over the bread and wine to make them into God's own Body and Blood.

The prince and his four companions, once the white hart and the lions, remained in the chapel until Mass was done. When Amide and her knights ate the holy mysteries, the prince lifted his hand above them and smiled. Then, when the priest raised his arms to give the final blessing, the knight, lion, ox and eagle moved up around the prince on his throne. All five continued up and passed out through the high glass window, leaving not a single pane broken.

Amide did not hear the last words of the priest. She heard instead a voice, man's or woman's she did not know, speaking directly into her mind without penetrating through her ears: "Even so the Son of God entered into His mother's womb and issued from it, leaving her virginity unbroken for ever."

Amide felt as if she were being drawn up after the figures, lifted towards the window. All was white. There was an ecstasy in her soul that seemed ready to burst free of her body, and a pressure against her skin that held her flesh still together . . . In a moment she would either slip up through the glass, as they had done, or it would break and fill the white purity with her blood . . .

She did not know she had fallen, not floated, until she woke on the chapel's floor. Galahad was just sitting up also. Percivale and Bors were still lying on the floor, their eyes closed. She realized they must have heard what she had heard and felt what she had felt.

The priest, still in his vestments, gave them fresh water and helped them up, asking eagerly what they had seen. He had seen none of it, but he understood what they had seen, and why. The white hart was a living symbol of the Lord Jesu, and the four lions were the four evangelists who had set a part of his deeds in writing.

"I doubt that any knights will ever see them again," said the hermit priest, shaking his head happily. "To you God has given to see the mysteries of the hart and lions to their end, in promise of the greater secrets that await you. Surely you are the knights meant to achieve the Holy Grail."

When they asked his blessing, he gave it; but he insisted that Sir Galahad, although no priest, should bless him in return.

Why had she been granted to share with them in the mysteries of the white hart, if she, also, were not meant to find the Holy Grail with her knights? She might have been blind to the prince enthroned on the altar, as had the holy priest been himself.

Perhaps the deeds of mortals sometimes cancelled out the plans of Heaven. Perhaps God had meant her knights to fight and save her from the custom of this castle.

It was too late now. The silver bowl was almost filled. She was ashamed the draining had made her so weak . . . Could it be that she had lost so much more blood than a knight in battle, who, for all his bleeding, had strength left to strike again and defeat his enemy at last? White moonlight seemed to flow in her emptied veins.

The priest of the Chapel of the Leprous Lady stood near, to give Amide her Saviour and then take her away to be buried in his churchyard with the threescore other maidens who had died for his mistress. Amide longed for the white bread upon her tongue, but she dreaded the churchyard and the new white marble tomb.

Her lord Sir Galahad still sat beside her. She felt the pressure of his fingers on her unpierced hand, but as though her own flesh were already far away. She dared not look at him again, lest she grieve for what had never happened – lest she regret that, if she must suffer for the will alone, she had not enjoyed the deed as well, though she soil him with herself.

She looked instead at her brother, who knelt on her right side, just beyond the silver bowl. "Percivale, I am dying to heal this lady."

"No, Amide – sister, dear sister, live!"

"Who will guide us?" she heard Galahad ask.

She would not remind them of the curse on her, nor tell them why she must die before they could achieve their Quest. "If I die," she said, gazing at her brother, "let me not be buried here. Put me . . . put me in a boat at the next haven, and let the waves take me at adventure."

As the waves had taken them at adventure from the Castle of the Queen of the Waste Lands to King Solomon's Ship, and thence back to the harbour of Carteloise Castle, so she would go on her last adventuring alone.

But not alone. As she lay, looking at her brother and the priest behind him, who held up the Body of the Saviour, she glimpsed another beside the priest, an angel, who took her into her last vision – a dreaming vision not of the past or present, but of the future. She could not see it clearly; she could only see the blurred outlines of what Heaven intended . . . as a mortal might intend a deed . . . but knew that Heaven is stronger than mortal man or woman to bring about its will at last.

Her boat would not drift unguided. "I will go before you," she murmured. "I will go before you, and when you come to the island city and achieve the Holy Grail, bury me there. Perhaps you will lie there beside me, brother . . . and you, Sir Galahad, my good lord, in that same place."

"We will drape your barge in silk," said Percivale, "rich as King Solomon's Ship itself, with a writing to tell all who find you of your honour. But, sister, do not die."

The bowl was filled. The handmaiden of the Leprous Lady took it away and bandaged Amide's wrist with white linen. Then she lifted the dish of blood and stood with it, obscuring Amide's sight of her brother and the priest.

But not of the Host that the priest held in his hand. That fragment of Jesu's Body showed white and glowing through the flesh and gown of the gentlewoman. The gentlewoman faded . . . Amide saw only the silver dish, with her own blood shining through it as if the silver were translucent glass, and the holy Body of Christ poised in the air above it.

It began to move around her, floating as if by its own power. She knew the gentlewoman must be carrying it, but, fascinated, feeling her heart beating ever faster and lighter, with so little blood left to beat, she turned her head to keep the vision in sight. She did not know whether it was truly a vision, or only a dream of weakness and death, but she no longer feared.

This could not be the most villainous death ever died by any woman.

The floating silver dish came to a stop on the other side of her cot, behind and above Sir Galahad. She looked again at his face, no longer afraid. She saw the beauty of an archangel, all blood-guilt wiped away by his repentance . . . or perhaps by her sacrifice here.

She lifted her gaze once more. The silver dish came nearer, like a chalice. The Host came nearer yet. For a moment she understood that the gentlewoman and the priest had crossed the room together, that the gentlewoman was standing with the dish of blood while the priest knelt beside Sir Galahad to give Amide her Saviour. But the only mortal she saw was Galahad.

It seemed that he was the one who put Jesu's Body into her mouth, while the silver chalice floated above them both. Which was true did not matter, for both were true; Amide lay balanced between the world of flesh and that of spirit, and in the world of spirit it was Sir Galahad who gave her the Body of her Lord.

And in the world of the spirit she recognized the silver dish that she had bled into. It was the sight which all the best chivalry of Britain were seeking. Her own three knights did not see it yet, but they would.

It was the Holy Sangreal unveiled.

An hour afterwards, a cry of joy went through the castle. The Leprous Lady, anointed with Amide's blood, had been healed at last. Amide did not hear it, having died – as knights must who die in battle – without knowing whether the cause for which she had died would fail or succeed.

But she had died with the Holy Grail reflected in her eyes.

That same evening Percivale, Bors and Galahad carried her body to the harbour and laid it in a barge, hung about with black silk. As they were returning a sudden tempest fell over the land, and they watched from a distance while lightning struck the Castle of the Leprous Lady again and again.

They spent the night in a hermitage. When they came to the ruins of the castle next morning, they found no person alive. Only the churchyard, where the threescore maidens lay beneath their white marble tombs, was left untouched by the storm.

"It is God's vengeance on the Leprous Lady for putting her own health above the lives of all these maidens," said Galahad.

"Then my sister died in vain. She died to heal the Leprous Lady, and the Lady is dead," said Percivale.

Both knights were weeping, but Galahad was able to reply, "Our Lord Jesu died to save all sinners, yet many perish despite his death. The glory of the sacrifice is to the victim who gives himself – or herself – generously."

The hermit Nascien had forbidden any lady to travel with a knight in the Quest of the Holy Grail. Yet of more than a hundred knights of Britain who entered that Quest, the only three who fully achieved it were the three who did travel for part of their journey with a woman.

Sir Lancelot partially achieved the mysteries of the Sangreal, but only after he, too, had journeyed with Amide, drifting in the silk-shrouded barge with her body, which remained uncorrupted after death, like the body of one of the holiest saints.

SHROUDED IN MIST

Lawrence Schimel & Mark A. Garland

Lawrence Schimel (b. 1971) is a new writer who has rapidly established himself in a very short period with his clever and ingenious ultra-short stories in which he provides new twists on old themes. Here he collaborates with Mark Garland in a slightly longer story than usual which brings together the twin themes of the Holy Grail and the Shroud of Christ.

The damp pervaded everything, and as my foot sunk through to the bog I wondered if perhaps I were headed towards the fabled realm of Atlantis rather than the castle which held the Sangreal. I felt I would never again be dry, that the sensation of dryness was a phantom of my imagination, the memory of it merely the remembrance of my dreams, where the strange and the fantastic were commonplace compared to the dark creatures who haunted this fen.

The wasteland seemed to stretch from one end of England clear across to the other, if the weariness I felt from plodding through it these past fortnights were any indication of distance. And, bizarre though this haunted realm was, I was weary of the monotony in its never-ending succession of twisted roots and branches that clutched at my skin and hair and clothes, of snakes and insects and other creatures that sprang from the dank swamp waters.

But there was no rest, for the wasteland held no end, no dry land where I might pause and catch my breath. To stop moving was to begin to sink through the moss into the fetid waters below. I slept clutching the roots of trees, and more often than not awoke half-submerged, my limbs sore both from their nightly grasping and from the cold, foul water.

I thought occasionally of abandoning my Quest, but, the truth be told, I was afraid I could not find my way from the swamp, so I might as well continue on. I had no idea if I weren't travelling in circles; there was nothing to distinguish one fen from the next.

I often lost heart.

It was at one such time that I was wakened from my gloomy spirits by a peculiar sound. I thought, at first, that it was some creature of the swamp, but, listening more closely, I realized it was a human voice. I trailed after it, taking pains to tread as softly as possible when each footstep made a loud sucking sound as my boot pulled free from the bog.

Soon I came upon a fellow knight errant, kneeling on a cloth he had spread upon the bog. He was deep in prayer, and I found myself lost in the sound of his voice intoning Vespers. It had been many days since I had had human contact of any sort, and the Latin he spoke was additionally comforting in its familiarity.

I realized he must have found a patch of dry ground on which to spread his cloth. As I approached I could see that the cloth had not soaked up the bog water as my own clothes did whenever I laid myself to rest at night, though it was tracked with a few spots of mud from his boots and hands as he spread the cloth.

I waited until he had finished his devotions before I alerted him to my presence and approached. He was not in the least alarmed by my sudden appearance, and I wondered if perhaps he had noticed me during his devotions. Or perhaps I seemed an answer to one of his prayers, though what that prayer was, I could only guess. Surely one prayer, at least, we shared?

With very little struggle I ascended to his small earthen perch, the only such oasis that must exist in this place. He wore not armour, but was dressed simply in a tunic bearing a royal crest, a worn coat and well-made but sodden boots, and he had known no grooming for some time, much as I. My own clothes had been far grander once, though in their present condition that fact was lost, and I had abandoned my armour many days ago.

He looked up at me as he knelt on the cloth, and his eyes seemed filled with tears that would not flow. I did not recognize him, but that mattered little.

"What do you want of me?" he asked, his voice thin and dry, despite the moisture that pervaded everything else.

"Might I pray with you?" I asked.

He nodded.

I stepped forward, testing the ground with my sodden foot, then knelt quietly, carefully, still uncertain of what lay beneath the cloth. The ground felt solid enough; it was a sensation I had thought I might never know again. I wanted to stay there on that spot for as long as the fates would let me. I waited for him to introduce himself, as I had accepted his hospitality, as it were, but no name was forthcoming. He seemed determined to remain as anonymous as his garb now was, and as I was loath to relinquish this dry spot I accepted this decision, and did not offer my own name to him. We shared a common quest, I was certain, and that bound us more firmly than any more mundane loyalties.

Instead, I asked him, "Why are you here?"

"Perhaps," he replied, "we have each come here to die."

It was then that I looked down, and saw the face of God.

Though it lacked hard detail, the image was clearly discernible, like a shadow burned into the cloth – a bearded man with gentle features, a crown upon his head. A crown of thorns. It was this that made me realize what I must be kneeling on, and I leapt to my feet and stepped from it reverently, though after so many days and nights in the bog this thought seemed almost unbearable. The Shroud was legend, like the Grail itself – one had held His Blood, the other once held His Body – and no true believer doubted the existence of either. Just as no follower of Christ could look upon this face and hold any doubt that it was indeed the Saviour's own.

Indeed, as I sank into the muck, examining the cloth more closely, I noted that an entire shadow-body was outlined on the Shroud's surface. I felt a surging sense of wellness and elation, of direction, as one who finds himself suddenly near home after wandering long on unfamiliar roads. Yet at the same instant some part of my mind grew fearful of sacrilege.

Though my actions had been unwitting, I had found my sodden feet standing on the body of Christ!

The other knight rose to join me, and I realized that, profane as I had been, the sin was his as well. More so, perhaps.

"Do you know what this cloth is," I asked him, "which you have lain in the mud, and allowed us both to tread upon?"

"Do you?" he countered.

"Of course," I said. "It is the Holy Shroud, the very cloth that was wrapped about Our Lord as they laid Him in His tomb."

"And you are a man of God?"

"Sworn so."

"Then it is well you should share it with me."

"Or a great imprecation! To use so holy a garment in such a manner is to beg damnation by all the saints of all the ages!"

"I use it to pray," he said calmly. "Would you ask that I not accomplish my devotions? Would you forgo your own? Yet one can hardly kneel and give fullness of mind and heart to God while sinking into the muck. The Shroud serves us in many ways, as do we serve God."

"But the Shroud is nearly as sacred as the Grail itself! A divine treasure which must be properly kept and protected, not exploited. If I found the Grail tomorrow, I would not use it to drink mead with my supper. Yet you use the Shroud as a mat!"

"You would drink from the Cup to remember the Lord, as He asked when He held the Cup himself, and I would use the Shroud to protect my life, so that I might continue to serve Him, much as it was used to protect His Body when He was laid to rest, so that He might return to serve us all. And would you not use the Cup to give life? For that is surely one of its greatest abilities. I would use the Shroud thus. As will you."

He had said this last with a tone that gave rise to the hair on the back of my neck. The man was no novice at theology, but I was suddenly more certain than ever that he did not understand the fullness of his actions. The Land itself was now a wasteland, because a sacred object had been profaned, and now both he and, unwittingly, I had blasphemed the cloth which retained the image of the Lord Himself, perhaps further preventing the Land's redemption.

"How can steeping the Shroud in muck be a part of its purpose?" I demanded.

"Pray with me," he said. "Then we will travel on, to those destinies which await us."

"You are a dreamer," I told him, "and a fool. The Shroud is a sacred thing of unimaginable power. It can bring great goodness – look how it is able to restore the Land to its natural firmness – but used incorrectly it can bring destruction. Like the Grail itself. Like the Sword of David – as holy a relic as any, yet it is the very thing which brought these wastelands upon us all when it was used to wound the Grail King, Pelleam."

"The Dolorous Stroke," he said.

"Yes."

"But I am a holy man, and I use the Shroud only as I must – and to holy purpose."

"You don't know what holiness is!" I told him, frustrated now. "You imagine yourself to be in a state of grace, but I fear –"

"Do not fear me," he said. "The knight who maimed the Grail King was warned by an angel not to use the Sword of David so, yet he chose to ignore the message. If you heed the message, heed the miracle that has come to you, your fate, and that of this Land, will not be his."

I blinked. Whether it was a trick of the gloom or merely my own pressing fatigue I could not say, but as I looked at this stranger he seemed almost to fade just a little, to become nearly transparent. I looked once more, and saw nothing unusual.

"The angels may speak to Arthur, this I believe," I said, "but I do not believe they speak to one such as you, who could so profane the Holy Shroud, or likely to me, who follows your wicked example."

"It is all in how one listens."

"My ears, my mind, my heart – all know how to listen, and I have never heard the angels."

"But do you listen with faith?"

I stared at him for a moment, unable to respond, then turned and looked out into the wasteland again. The bog stretched endlessly – mist and muck and the foul plants that somehow thrived in such a place. I imagined never leaving this swamp, never finding its end. I imagined the Shroud being lost here, perhaps for ever, being swallowed up by the swamps, and this knight along with it. I would not fulfil my Quest for the Grail. I would not see the Shroud delivered to safety. I would not see the world I had known again.

Yet I could not accept this without questioning: To what end? What holy purpose of either God or man might be served by any of this, should it come to pass?

I could not answer these questions and I felt a need for them to be answered, a need which made this man's last question lie heavily now in my gut, like the death of a loved one finally realized.

No, I answered him, though I could not find voice to do so. "I believe I understand much of what you are saying," I said at last, trying one last time to enlist his aid in my struggle to do so. "And yet how can you look down at the mud upon your boots, at this place, and still say that you know truths greater than mine? Are you not mortal, as I? Are you not of these lands?"

"I hail from Byzantium," he said, not answering the meat of the question. "But I need not explain any more. You are indeed a man of faith, and more. As to the Shroud, the wasteland will awaken you to its nature."

"How the wasteland?"

He stepped back off the Shroud. As he began to sink into the muck once more he took up the cloth, revealing the small square of earth that lay beneath. Before my eyes, the ground drew water, and quickly became indistinguishable from the bog around it.

He placed the cloth over a different soggy tangle of roots, leaves and mire, waited a moment and then stepped back onto it. He beckoned to me, and I hesitated, but soon joined him. We stood on the Shroud as before, firm ground beneath us.

Even as I relished the solidity beneath my feet I felt the moral world shift beneath me. I still held my trepidations about whether we should thus use the Shroud. And guiltily I thought that perhaps this was why I wandered lost in the wasteland, why I had not yet come to the tower which held the Sangreal and salvation. But if this was how I responded in the presence of a holy miracle, how would I react if I did find the Grail?

"Come," the knight said as we stepped from the Shroud once more, and once more began sinking into the muck. "You must continue on towards that for which you search. And you must take the Shroud with you."

I followed after him, trying to resolve for myself the quagmire of my own faith, where all my ideals which had once been clear as a glass windowpane were now shrouded as the thick mist rising from the swamp.

Then my mind was filled with the thought of the Shroud somehow being used to restore the Land. The idea seemed impossible to ignore, and yet, as remarkable as the small miracle I had seen seemed to be, the ground the Shroud had restored was but swamp once more, now that it had been moved.

"Take the Shroud," the other man said, and a chill swept my neck once more. As we moved back again I grasped the Shroud with both hands, then lifted it. The ground beneath it remained. "Take it with you to all men of faith, where it might become the salvation that is needed. Redeem yourself, redeem them – and this Land as well."

I touched the dry, hard ground, then I stood up slowly and gathered the Shroud to my side, holding it as if it were the newborn God Child Himself. I raised my eyes at last, and found myself alone, shrouded in the mist.

THE UNWANTED GRAIL

Darrell Schweitzer

Like Phyllis Ann Karr, Darrell Schweitzer (b. 1952) has appeared in each of the four volumes of this series, and he can always be relied upon to contribute something out of the ordinary. No straightforward Grail Quest for Darrell. Yet he still highlights the core challenge to understanding and belief. Schweitzer is a prolific American critic, editor and writer, mostly of fantasy, including the novels The Shattered Goddess *(1982),* The White Isle *(1990) and* The Mask of the Sorcerer *(1995). His short stories have been collected as* We Are All Legends *(1981) and* Tom O'Bedlam's Night Out *(1985). He was the editor of the latest incarnation of the magazine* Weird Tales, *and is the editor of its spiritual successor* Worlds of Fantasy & Horror.

He had slain three giants. I never knew their names, so in this tale, in which names are so important, those three must remain anonymous.

On a bitter winter's evening I found them, as the sky faded from steel-grey to purple to black, as the killing wind rattled the ice-coated trees. In the twilight I beheld the first giant, lying face-down in the snow like a dark continent rising above a white sea. The second knelt strangely, impaled on a broken tree as on a spear, his head twisted around so he might look down his own back in blank-eyed astonishment at the enormous splash his blood had made on the snow.

The third rested peacefully, as if asleep with a log for a pillow, his death betrayed only by the frozen tickle of blood that seeped from his eye, where perhaps a poignard had slipped in and pierced his brain.

There was nothing to be scavenged from any of these, for giants are of the fairy kind. Their metal burns the hand, and crumbles like old leaves with the coming of the sun.

Far more promising was the knight, the author of this carnage, who sat frozen where he had fallen amid briars, a fairy spear sunk deep into his side. I could still see where the spear-shaft had dragged in the snow, and the blood had trailed.

I grabbed him by the ankles and hauled him urgently out of the briars, then started to work. What I envied most were his thick hide boots. I had only rags this season, beneath which my feet were no doubt black and bloody. I, a scarecrow of a boy pretending to be a man, a thing of flapping tatters and stinking hides and limbs like sticks, would look ridiculous clumping around in those big fine boots, but I would have them.

My fingers were too numb to untie the laces, so I got out my knife and started cutting.

The knight's eyes snapped open.

I crouched at his feet, transfixed by his gaze, the knife in my hand a seeming confession of every possible crime. I couldn't understand the feeling. I knew then that he was like no other man I had ever met, and I was afraid of him.

"Would you murder a helpless man?"

I couldn't meet his gaze. I stared at the knife.

"I ask you again, would you murder me?"

I cut through his laces and yanked off one boot. Beneath, he wore thick woolen hose. I would have those too.

"I ask you –"

I flashed my knife in front of his face. I trembled, tears on my cheeks, trying to seem very tough. "I've killed a lot of people already."

He let out a long sigh, then smiled, like a father responding to a child who had just admitted some childishly heinous crime. *Have you, indeed? Naughty, naughty.*

Now his gaze was far away, and he seemed to be remembering or quoting something. "A third time I say unto you –"

I started working on his other boot. I spat in the snow. "I could just wait for you to freeze to death."

"Then you would be no murderer, indeed, no human criminal

– merely a carrion-robbing animal, a beast in the form of a man. Which might be an improvement in your circumstances, since beasts are without sin."

He was raving. I assumed his mind was dying, a little bit at a time. I tried not to listen to him as I worked.

"I do what I must," I said.

"And what must you do, Theodorus? That means 'gift of God'. Did you know that? You are a gift of God. To somebody."

Again I was transfixed. I glared at him with venomous hatred, closer than ever to slitting his throat just to shut him up. But I was too much afraid.

"How do you know my name? Nobody knows my name. I'm called Vermin or Badger or Crow, or Murderer's Get. Yes, yes, I can murder as easily as I can breathe."

I stood up. Maybe I was going to leap on him and kill him right there. But my knees buckled and I fell over backwards, arms flailing, and the knife went flying off into the evening dark.

I crawled back to him, caught hold of his belt and stole his poignard, and lay beside him with the tip of the poignard beneath his chin.

"You had better explain yourself," I said, gasping from hunger and exhaustion and cold. "Make it good."

His eyes rolled down to regard the blade and he *laughed*, but there was sorrow in his laughter, and, I think, a touch of madness. And something more than that: *recognition*. Somehow he seemed to be saying to himself, *Yes, this is the one. This is the answer. It's not what I expected, but this is what I've got.*

Only after a long while was he able to speak.

"Your name came to me in a vision. A white bird, with fire circling all around its head in a ring, like a haloed saint, alighted on a branch above a battlefield while black birds pecked at the corpses. The white bird spoke to me as I leaned on my shield, wounded full sore and weary, and in a voice like that of the fairest maiden the creature bade me seek out God's gift and understand fully the mysteries of knighthood."

I sat up in the snow and slid the poignard under my own belt. "I know all about knights. A knight raped my mother and hanged her man when he tried to protect her. He and the other knights slew many men and burned their houses. They did it in the name of God. Therefore I hate God and all his knights."

He laughed again, and I wondered if he even knew why he was laughing. Perhaps it was because the deeds of knights were told in tales, and no poet would ever tell a story that ended like this, with me in it. Here I was, the terminal blot on the page of chivalry and all such pretty lies. So be it.

I wondered if he might have raped my mother. If he might be my father. He was about the right age.

But his laughter told me something, something mere words could not have: *No, the story is not over. It continues.*

Once more I reached to cut his throat with the poignard.

"Do you suppose," he said, "that we could remove ourselves to a more comfortable place and continue this discussion?"

Maybe I was going mad too. I slid the poignard back into my belt. Then I put on his second boot and lurched to my feet. I took him under the arms from behind, and, with every ounce of strength I had, with surprising reserves I hadn't known I had, began to drag him across the snow, his bootless feet trailing. Every once in a while the spear-shaft hit some obstacle, and he cried out in pain.

Once I stopped and made to pull the spear out, but the knight commanded me not to touch it, lest his guts and blood pour out all at once and he die too soon, as if there were a specific, appointed hour for his death and he knew what it was.

It was a desperate, terrible struggle, and I didn't even know why I was doing it. Some force compelled me, like a wind filling a sail. My mind wandered, and I wasn't even sure any more if I really was that Theodorus who was the get of a knight, or if I'd made that story up just to cause pain or to explain it. Maybe I was a badger, or a crow – or some clod of earth anointed with the blood of warriors and somehow come alive in the mocking semblance of a man.

In full darkness beneath the starry sky I dragged him, while wolves howled not far away and the frigid wind whispered in my ears like ghosts and told me tales of chivalry and monsters and dying knights.

All this while my burden muttered to himself. I think he was praying.

I must have been near to death myself when I reached my hermitage. Call it a hovel and give it glory; a cleft scooped out of a hillside, the opening covered over with mud and stones and dead branches, a little place for a fire and a hole in the roof for the smoke to go out. This was my castle and my domain – the Siege Ridiculous, at which a knight might have laughed.

All I could do was haul the both of us inside. The knight screamed as the spear caught and dragged. I reached for it. I smelled my hand burning as I touched the metal shaft, but my hand was too frozen for there to be any pain. It must have been burning inside his wound too.

I uncovered the fire pit and blew on the ashes to get a little flame going. After a while, pain returned to my hands, and even to my feet inside the knight's warm boots.

I hunched over him, unsure of what to do next, and could only stare at him while he babbled on – about many adventures and the great King Arthur, who dwelt, in Camelot, who had himself done wondrous deeds –

"Are you listening, boy?"

I made no reply.

"Sometimes I feel as if I'm talking to the walls," my guest said, and yet he continued on – about the Holy Grail, how it had appeared in Camelot at Pentecost, and how all the knights had sworn themselves to Quests of great holiness, which had caused King Arthur to weep, for he knew they were not holy men, and would suffer and perish in the questing; therefore on this Pentecost he saw them assembled together in feasting for the last time and the Grail fed them, providing each man with the meat he desired most; then it passed out of Camelot and vanished, until such knights could, by their chivalry and worship, achieve some fleeting glimpse of it in the course of their adventures.

"Do you understand any of this, boy?"

I shrugged. I was afraid.

The wind rattled in the walls of my poor dwelling.

"The thing about a Quest is," the knight went on, "that the author is not the knight at all, but God, and God is like a smith, who works with his hammer, then his tongs, then his pliers – whichever tool he chooses – and then lays each aside to pick up another. Even as he has laid me aside while working to some greater end."

He was silent for a time, and there was only the wind, and the wolves outside.

He closed his eyes. I thought he was asleep, or perhaps, finally, to the relief of all concerned, dead.

But he spoke in a whisper, as if in sleep, "Theodorus, go outside. Then return and tell me what you have seen."

And I got up and went outside, and came back in to report that I had only seen the stars, and the trees bending in the wind, and the swirling snow.

"Ah," said he. "We have a little time yet. I must confess my sins ... to you, I suppose ... and beg your forgiveness, since you are my host and have treated me with kindness. I have been lacking in courtesy, being as I am far from home, burdened by sin and filled with sorrow. Those giants, I think, were my sins made flesh, and I overcame them, and may hope for Heaven . . . But they were the undoing of me, and the ruin of my Quest . . . Much of what it means to be a knight is that you have a duty, a goal, and *no excuses accepted* . . . Therefore I ask you to forgive my sins then go outside again, and come back in and tell me what you have seen."

I muttered some words, afraid and bewildered, and certain that I had no business forgiving anybody's sins. Then I got up and went outside once more.

The moon had risen, a pale, dying crescent, flickering through the icy branches, and by moonlight in a little clearing I saw a knight, all in black, with his sword drawn and his visor raised, so to reveal a face which was only a bare skull.

I returned and told what I had seen.

"That is only Death, who has been my companion on the road for a long while. We still have a little time."

Still he spoke on, his tale like a tangle of thread which no one could ever unravel, a muddle of haunted castles and temptresses, of holy men who gave blessings, of demons who led knights astray and to their dooms, of a hundred white knights and a hundred black ones, who fought until not one was left standing and then all stood up and fought again. And once, on a lonely, dark night like this, in a wilderness, when my own knight – my guest or victim or whatever he was – felt himself giving over to despair, he looked up and saw what he thought was a single star shining through a cloud.

But it was not a star, and the cloud settled to earth and he beheld the Grail, but far away, like a lantern in a window seen from across a mile of darkened countryside.

One of the more confusing aspects of the story was that I didn't even know the hero's name, and sometimes, as he told it, the hero was called Theodorus.

I huddled by the fire, clasping my knees and resting my head on them.

So I asked him directly who he was, and he was startled, as if the walls had spoken back to him.

"For this discourtesy, too, I ask you to forgive me."

And I forgave him – for all the good that did.

"I am called Ufilias," he said, "one of the hundred and fifty who were there that fatal Pentecost. I am a knight of the Round Table, if not one of the more famous ones. I am mentioned only in the chronicles as 'many more were there', or 'also included'. I swore a Quest with the others, and – well, here I am. I think that is all I have to tell. Therefore, good friend, I beg you to go outside yet again, and return and report what you have seen."

And I went outside, and saw in another clearing, near at hand, a knight with sword and shield at ready, in armour gleaming golden like the sunrise. His raised visor revealed a face sculpted out of living flame, and I could not look on it.

I reached for my stolen poignard, as if to defend myself. The burning knight turned towards me, and, at once afraid, I ducked back inside.

Crouched down again, I listened to the wind and the wolves and to Sir Ufilias's laboured breathing, and I whispered to him what I had seen.

"I think it is the time when God puts down one tool," he said, "which is old and broken, and picks up another so that his labour might continue."

Then, from outside, I heard many sounds, all of them muted and far away: the thunder of countless hooves, a maiden singing, church bells, trumpets and clangour of arms, the cawing of crows as they pecked at the slain.

"Theodorus," my knight said, "here's what you have to do. You must put on my armour and take up my weapons and continue on the Quest. Win glory for yourself. Become a famous man, a hero, not merely one of the knights who was 'also there'. The labour goes on and on – God hammering away in His smithy of our lives, beating the sins out of us."

And I believed every word he said, and was very much afraid. It was a kind of death that came over me then, for merely by listening, and believing, all that I had been must die.

Angrily, desperately, I shoved the stolen poignard back into Sir Ufilias's belt.

"No! I am *not* a knight! I *don't* go on quests!"

"What are you, then?"

"Nothing. I am a rat and a carrion-dog and a maggot-worm!"

"Is that what you really want?"

After much hesitation, I finally said, "No, it is not."

"Even a dog or a worm can be a miracle, if God wills it. Go outside, Theodorus, one last time, and see what you may see."

I went outside, and it seemed I was a small child again, running in terror, barefoot through the snow, while all around me houses burned and black knights with demon-masks struck down everyone I had ever known. The snow became fire, and swirled up and formed great castles of living flame, tier upon tier, with towers higher than the sun at noontide and windows like gaping mouths out of which came bewitching songs, which drew me into the fire, and screams, which drove me away.

And I covered my eyes and ran, burning and naked through the snow and the winter woods, clothed only in flame, in terrible pain but not consumed; and I heard the hammer of God clanging away on His terrible anvil; and the blood of men hissed as hot metal touched it.

Then I came, at last, to the shore of a lake, where the touch of the waters healed me and the fire went out. I stood there, shivering, while a white ship drew near, draped all in white samite, with lanterns hung from its masts like stars. And within the ship I saw maidens dressed all in white, and a wounded king, drawn and shrivelled with suffering, and a bleeding knight whose name was Ufilias, and likewise another knight who held aloft a bloody spear.

Then came someone holding a covered vessel, which shone through its cover so brilliantly that I could not see, and I fell down, dazzled, amazed and afraid; and a commanding voice called out to me, "Rise up, Theodorus, and follow after."

And I rose, and followed, and ran naked and barefoot on the surface of the water as if over smooth marble. But the ship drew away from me, like a star setting behind a hill, until I was alone in the darkness once more and the water would not hold me up. I fell, splashing, into the frigid lake, and struggled desperately to reach the shore.

Many times I thought I would not, and would die here instead, but somehow I *had* to. I *had* to tell Ufilias what I had seen, as if it mattered terribly in some way I could not even dimly understand.

When I got back to my miserable domain, I was indeed naked, and almost dead from cold. Sir Ufilias lay waiting for me, and I knew that he would die very soon.

There was no time to tell the tale. I tried to. He seemed already to know it, and hurried me on about my business as I stripped off his armour and his clothing and girt myself as a knight.

"But this is a *joke*," I said. "I am a species of carrion-beast, not the stuff of which knights are made."

And he repeated to me again that part of being a knight is that there are no excuses accepted.

"Let me take one more thing," I said, having put on his armour, which did not fit, and his sword, which was too heavy for me. "Let me take also your name."

That was the heaviest burden of them all.

I heard God's terrible hammer, clanging.

But Sir Ufilias was already dead. I drew the fairy spear out of his side, and no blood issued forth, only a little water. The spear burned my hand, and always as I carried it I was in pain, but I never put it down while on my Quest.

Outside, I battled the two knights. The black knight feigned to yield, and drew off, but circled around behind me and crept into the hovel to steal away the soul of Ufilias. There was nothing I could do about that.

But the other and I fought all throughout the morning twilight, as the sun rose, and my spear did not crumble away, like a fairy thing, but burned like pure flame. Strength filled me, like wind filling a sail, propelling me on, into this battle, as arms clashed on shields like terrible thunder.

And as I fought I seemed to pass into a dream, in which the boy Theodorus walked through Camelot's halls barefoot, in stinking skins and rags, while all around him the elegant knights and their ladies feasted. No one noticed him, even when he protested that he didn't belong there, and in time his voice faded away, like the wind rattling among frozen branches, growing still.

And I awoke from that dream, into another, which was the dream of Ufilias, which has not ended, even yet.

When the sun rose I transfixed the flaming knight with my spear, then smote off his head and saw that his pained, frightened and utterly bewildered face was that of a boy – of one Theodorus.

One last time I heard Ufilias cry out, in pain and surprise. I searched for him, but could not find him.

Nor could I find Theodorus.

I searched for them both through many lands, through many adventures and perils, through much pain, while the hammering of God thundered in my ears and the burning spear seared my hand.

Only once did I ever encounter other knights on the Quest. Three of us came together at a crossroads, on a cold winter's evening, and we spoke together there with much longing and sorrow and in endless weariness; yet we did not despair, for all of us had seen the Grail, at least once, that Pentecost at Camelot.

I called myself Ufilias then, and no one questioned me, or asked about Theodorus; and I spoke through my lowered visor, that none should see my face. I suppose the others thought I was fulfilling some sort of vow.

Therefore, when the chronicles are written and the tales told, it shall not be recorded that one of the heroes who met there was an impostor.

Possibly we were all impostors – we, who heard God's hammering.

THE FIGURE IN DARKNESS

Ken Alden

The Grail Quests continued over a period of years. Almost all of the knights were unsuccessful, though they would try, try and try again. It was only when they realized they had to learn something about themselves that they could start to move towards their goal. One of the most fascinating knights in this respect is Sir Bors. We encounter him more than once in this anthology. In this story, Ken Alden, the alias of aspiring author and scriptwriter Alan Kitch (b. 1951), considers one such episode in Sir Bors's Quest.

Sir Bors stood by the monastery door and listened. Could it be dawn yet? Surely it must be close.

Could he allow himself to open the door and check? No, he had better not, he told himself. His duty was to stand guard here and wait, not to worry and fidget and be continually checking to see if he could leave. And since it was his duty he would stand here all night, stiff and unmoving, just as he had stood by the door every night for the past month. The moment he allowed himself any weakness the demon was certain to appear and try to gain entrance to the monastery.

He sensed a movement and turned his head. Was that a monk disappearing around the corner at the far end of the dark corridor? There was only one flaming torch attached to the corridor's walls. The jumping shadows it cast could easily be mistaken for a figure.

The monks had kept their distance from him. Their vows kept them silent and their cowls hid their faces. To him they had almost been ghosts. Indeed, it was now six weeks since anyone had responded to what he said.

The monastery itself had puzzled him ever since he arrived. There were few signs of Christianity about it. Instead there were images of the Green Man, and of animals that were half-human, and most of all there were images of a large, full-bearded man who had antlers on his head.

He had not recognized many of the ceremonies that the monks carried out, either. Their chanting was often accompanied by heathen drums, and they even used animals as part of their ritual.

When he had approached the bishop to ask permission to stay here the man's unease had been obvious. There had even been some hostility from the bishop's underlings.

Nor had it been that easy to find someone who could direct him to the monastery itself. He had never seen a land so empty of farms, or indeed empty of life in any form. What was more, the one shepherd he had found had refused even to speak to him.

He had spent a day travelling over brown half-dead moorland before reaching the forest that surrounded the monastery. It had then taken him another day to force his way through the expanse of small trees and large bushes intertwined with brambles. Their leafless branches had jerked around in a cold, drizzle-filled wind, and as he'd ridden along the extremely narrow path that led to the monastery those spear-like branches had been continually poking at his armour. It had been difficult for him to keep his dignity.

Stop that, he told himself.

He was letting his thoughts wander from the task. He had to be continually on the alert for the demon's footsteps. Every time he let his attention wander he was failing in his duty to King Arthur.

He listened hard. When would they come, those footsteps? He had heard them four times in the last month. They always came on the darkest nights. He would be standing by the door when he would hear faint sounds out in the depths of the ugly wood. They would not sound like footsteps at first, but as they got closer the sounds grew clearer and more recognizable. Somebody out there in the darkness would be running frantically through the brambles. They would come racing out of the forest, across the grass-covered yard beyond the door and up to the door itself. And there they would abruptly stop.

Each time he had wrenched the door open and lifted up his sword, but each time there had been nothing there to attack. Nor had he felt an invisible presence or heard the footsteps moving away. There had been only the shadowy darkness and an unpleasant, almost threatening silence.

Would the creature have tried to enter the monastery if he had not stood guard every night? Surely the answer was yes. It would be the demon's duty to seize the monastery's precious visitor, and it was his duty to stop that demon entering.

He turned his head again. There was somebody moving around in the darkness at the far end of the corridor. He could hear them even if he could not see them. The monks must have risen. It would soon be dawn.

For the first time in hours he moved. He reached out, took hold of the handle and pulled the heavy door open.

The first hint of dawn was glowing among the stark branches of the forest's trees on the far side of the grass yard. His task was over for this night. He had kept the demon away.

Should he do more? Should he try to drive the demon from the forest? Then maybe the monastery's visitor would once again return to the chapel. The demon's very presence showed that the visitor wished to return, and that presence had to be what was stopping it.

Maybe he would spend the next night outside the door, and then when those footsteps came running towards him, he could raise up his sword and remove this barrier to the Grail.

Near noon a monk appeared in the doorway of Sir Bors's cell and beckoned to him.

"Wha – ?" he started to ask before remembering that this figure would not tell him what it wanted him for. "Very well," he said instead.

The monk turned and went off down the corridor. Sir Bors rose stiffly from his hard bed and followed as the figure led him to the tiled courtyard in front of the monastery's main entrance. There the monk pointed at the footpath through the forest.

A small carriage was being pulled along the path by a white horse. The carriage should have been far too wide for such a narrow path, yet it rolled along it without difficulty. It was of a design that Sir Bors had never seen before.

It was very close to the ground – in fact it was little more than a large casket on wheels, that rose no higher than a tall man's chest –

and it was woven out of wicker. Its weaver had left a multitude of small holes through which the figure inside it could be seen, and that occupant was the only one *to* be seen. There was no sign of a driver. The white horse strolled along of its own will, and when it reached the tiled courtyard it came to a halt before the monastery.

The side of the strange carriage opened. Out of it stepped an ancient man. He wore the garb of a senior monk, yet the three chains around his neck each bore a symbol that Sir Bors had not seen before. The old man looked around him in a bemused manner. His mouth hung slightly open. Eventually his gaze found Sir Bors.

"You are the questing knight?" he asked in a weak voice.

"Yes," Sir Bors responded curtly. He had thought it was obvious what he was.

"Then I have come to help you."

The old man began to shuffle forward. He went slowly across the courtyard and into the monastery.

Help him? How was this old man going to be able to help him? Still, the monk could be more than he seemed, he decided. He had better treat him with respect.

Sir Bors followed the old man at a slow, dignified pace until they reached the main chapel.

He had not been allowed in here before. It was as gaunt as everything else in the monastery. There was no altar or crucifix. Only the much older symbol of the fish hung on the wall.

"I have come to help you," the old man repeated, once he had sat on a stone block that was the chamber's only seat. "I have come to show you how you will fail today, so that you will not fail in some tomorrow."

Sir Bors stiffened. What was all this talk of failure? He had no intention of failing. Everything that could be done he would do, no matter how long it took or how difficult it was.

"Some tomorrow?" he asked.

The old man showed no sign of having heard him. Instead he stared blankly at the chamber's granite walls.

"Who will find the Grail?" he asked, without looking at Sir Bors.

"I don't know," said the knight. "One who is pure of heart."

"Pure of heart, yes." The old man nodded, while now staring up at the ceiling. "One who is without failings, yes?"

"Yes," Sir Bors agreed.

"And what are your failings?"

Sir Bors frowned at the old man. What were his failings? Was this monk seeking to insult him? He had worked hard to remove every weakness and cultivate every noble attribute.

"Only those without failings will find the Grail," the monk repeated. "All others will find that their very failings take the Grail from their hands."

"Yes, I understand," said Sir Bors.

But what were his failings? he wondered. Could he say he was without failings? No, he could not say that. Yet he could not think of even one he could list.

"The Grail has appeared to these monks," the old man said. "It has appeared to holy men. And you think that when it returns it will appear to you?"

"Yes," Sir Bors said defiantly.

"It has appeared before them here only four times – here in this very chamber – four times within a hundred years."

"Yes, four times," Sir Bors repeated.

"But even these monks were not without fault, and the Grail faded from their sight."

"Yes," Sir Bors said.

He was beginning to feel foolish, and he did not like that. Why couldn't he say more than a simple "yes"?

"Yet you expect it to appear before you?" the monk asked.

"It has been predicted that it will return to the monastery," said Sir Bors.

A small smile slowly spread across the old man's face. "And who has predicted it?" he asked.

"A forest monk. We do not know his name."

Sir Bors stared at the monk. He had not seen the forest monk who had made the prediction, but he had been told that the man wore three chains around his neck.

The old man nodded slowly as he stared down at the rough floor. "A forest monk," he muttered. "A forest monk, is it?"

"I am here to protect the Grail," Sir Bors said, and he spoke slowly in order to appear dignified. "It was predicted that a demon would try and stop it entering the monastery."

"A demon? I don't think this 'forest monk', as you put it, would have said the word 'demon'."

"An evil one, then."

"All mortals are evil. None are without failings."

"Yes," Sir Bors said again. Only he did not want to return to the subject of failings. "I am here to bar the way to the one who would bar the way to the Grail," he said instead.

"And you are sure you can recognize this evil one?" the monk asked. .

"It was described by the forest monk."

"Described? Ah, I see. And you have thought about this description?"

"It will be a figure clothed in black – one who hides in shadows."

"And you are sure this is the figure that comes to the door at night?"

"It cannot be seen because it is clothed in the black of night, and it hides in the shadow of invisibility. That is what King Arthur's own wise men said."

"And you do not doubt them?"

"Why should I?"

The old man once again slowly nodded, while continuing to stare at the ground. "Very well. If you are sure, then you must, indeed, protect the monastery from this intruder."

Sir Bors stood in the shadows. Shortly after the old man had left he had decided that tonight he would wait outside the door. The monk had irritated him and made him all the more determined to resolve this matter.

At sunset he had put on his black-painted armour, slipped silently out of the ugly door that the invisible visitor was so interested in and stood in the shadow of one of the larger trees. There he had waited, without moving, as the long winter night passed.

A couple of times he heard noises. They were probably made by animals. Though since his arrival at the monastery he had seen no sign at all of wildlife.

For once the cold wind was not blowing. The spear-like branches were still. Drizzle had fallen earlier in the night, but now it had stopped.

His eyes scanned the grass yard. They were the only part of him he had allowed to move. Just shifting his weight from one foot to the other was enough to make his armour creak, and in the total silence of this night that creak would carry some distance.

He spotted a movement over to his right. Dared he lean forward to get a better view of it? No, perhaps he had better not. Besides, now he had concentrated on it he was half sure of what it was. One solitary leaf was, for no obvious reason, twitching around on an otherwise stationary tree. He had seen it happen several times while he was walking in the forest. It need not mean anything sinister. Still, why should just that one leaf move and not all the others?

His attention went back to the monastery. It was no more than a mass of ominous shadows. The monks had not risen. Dawn must still be some way off.

He stiffened. Something was over to his right. He could hear branches being very gently pushed aside. Something was trying not to make any noise. Would an animal do that?

Yes, it might, but it was highly unlikely that any animal would attack a human. A more probable candidate was another human – or something supernatural. Anyway, whatever it was he would deal with it.

Wait until it gets closer, though, he told himself. That way it will be exposing itself to danger.

And where exactly was it? The noises were surely coming from somewhere to the left of that large bush. Only he should be able to see something. The noises sounded quite close, and there was not much over there to block his view.

The noises stopped.

What did that mean? he wondered. It might have seen him. It could even be creeping up on him.

No, he must stop this. Such useless speculation was not helping him.

He listened. There was a quiet rustling that could have been almost anything. It was not coming from the same direction as the louder noises either. It might be a breeze moving the forest's branches. Only somehow he did not think that it was. He certainly could not feel any breeze.

A cry came from far off in the forest.

That was a wolf, he told himself. Though it was a rather strange cry for a wolf. It was also the first time he had heard such a cry in this forest.

The louder noises started up again. More branches were being pushed aside. That thing out there was running, and it was running away from him. It must have been an animal after all. The wolf's strange cry had frightened it.

He studied the area the other noises came from. There was something else there now. It was faint and distant, but, yes, that was a glint of light among the branches.

What should he do? Should he investigate that light, or should he stay here by the door?

That light had to have something to do with what was happening. There was surely no other reason for it to be out there in such an inhospitable forest during the darkest hours of the night. The only question was whether it was of human or supernatural origin.

He stepped out from underneath the tree. He had to know what that light was. After all, it was right that he should search out any possible threat. Just standing in the shadows was the coward's way. And if it was a threat he could take the advantage by attacking first.

He drew his sword and held it out in front of him as he moved carefully forward. His armour made some noise but not much. Only the practised ear would hear it. As he pushed his way through the first bush the noise inevitably grew louder. However, once through he had a better view of the light.

It was not flickering as a burning torch would. It was a steady light. What could possibly cast such a light? Every flame flickered.

He paused and listened. There was something nearby. He could not say what it was. There was nothing to see or hear, yet he was sure there was something. Instinct told him that – instinct and fear.

He shivered.

Yes, fear, that was what it was, and it was not the normal fear that a warrior felt in battle. This was a fear that came from the soul. His soul sensed danger even if his senses did not.

Fancy, he told himself. This was pure fancy. He was rationalizing a fear which no knight should allow himself.

He took a few unsteady steps forward. He was not going to give in to this fear. He was going to face it.

Yet the silence was strange. It was more than a normal silence. There was something oppressive about it. It was as if the darkness was smothering all sound.

He stopped. There was something else. He could sense it. Something large was close to him, even if he could not see it.

Everything seemed so dark here under the trees. There were just various shades of black and that was all. The only light was that glow, and that lit itself, not the forest around it. There could easily be something standing close to him and he would not see it.

He heard a new noise. Breathing. It was breathing. Something large was slowly drawing in air and letting it out. And it was close. If he reached out he would probably feel it.

But he did not need to feel it. He knew it was there. It was both close to him and above him. That breathing was coming from above his head. The thing had to be leaning over him. He could sense it. It was bending down towards him. It was going to reach out and take hold of him.

His sword moved. Something had pulled at its point. It had been a gentle pull, yet something was definitely holding his sword. This was not his fancy.

He jerked his weapon back. It came free of the grip without difficulty.

At the same time pain went up his arm. All the muscles in it were cramping.

"Dear Lord, protect me," he murmured.

The sword shuddered. Something had brushed against it this time. A coldness passed over his face. It was a cold wind, or at least he thought it was a wind. It was somehow far colder than any normal wind, though. This was a coldness that brought intense pain. The muscles across the lower part of his face twitched and contorted as they too began to cramp.

That was its breath, he suddenly realized. It had been the thing's breath which had passed across his face.

"Protect me, Lord," he repeated.

He sensed a new presence. Something else was in the forest with him. Had his prayers been answered so quickly?

He looked away from the shadows. The light was much closer now. But he still could not see it clearly. There remained bushes between him and it. Yet it had moved close to him.

He took a deep breath. He felt better. Some sort of pressure had lifted from him. It was as if the darkness had been solid and heavy and now it had been lifted. The breathing had gone as well. There was no creature standing above him now. He was certain that if he reached out he would feel nothing.

What power did this light have? He must continue to investigate.

He started to move around a bush. He should have a clear view once it was out of the way.

The light moved away. It did not want him to get closer. He took a few quick steps forward, and at the same time the light moved faster. He caught a glimpse of it. Then it was gone behind some brambles.

What could that have been? He could not really say. He had not seen it clearly enough.

But there were just the brambles in his way now. He need take only a few quick steps and he would see it.

He dashed forward. His sword caught in something. The thing was back. It was grabbing his sword. No, listen to that rustle. The sword was caught in the brambles, that was all.

He wrenched the sword free. It was brambles, all right.

But the light was moving on. He was going to lose it.

He slashed out at the brambles and pushed his way through them. They scraped at his armour. Some entangled his feet. He stumbled, nearly fell, but steadied himself. One more slash at the brambles brought a whole mass of them down. His view cleared. There in front of him was the source of the light.

It was a sphere, a glowing sphere of light that was floating in the air at about the level of his head. The Grail? Was this the Grail? When it had appeared to the knights at Camelot it had floated in a sphere of light.

But this time there was no sign of anything inside the sphere.

It was also moving away from the monastery.

No, that was not the Grail. The Grail would head towards the monastery.

He came to a halt and stared at the light.

This thing was trying to lead him away from the door. Yes, that made sense. He was being tricked.

He turned and hurried back the way he had come.

He had broken his own rules, hadn't he? He should be ashamed of himself. He was meant to be the one who would stand forever on one spot if that was what loyalty demanded, and yet he had let himself be led away from his duty.

That was his weakness. His failings were being used against him. His impetuosity had been used to trick him.

He pushed his way through the bush, not caring what noise he made.

The wolf howled. It was closer now. And there was fear in that howl. That was what made it sound strange. The creature feared that glow.

Something clutched at his feet. He kicked out at it. Only it did not give and he fell.

How could he have let this happen to him? Dignity was gone. All he had now was shame. He had forgotten the stiff unbending rules for one moment and this was the result.

He looked down at his feet. He could see nothing but shadows. There was no creature there. Yet something had tripped him up.

He lifted his leg.

It was brambles. He had fallen over brambles like some stupid clod.

He pushed himself up into a sitting position. He could not worry about that now. He had to get back to the doorway. It still might be possible to stop the demon entering the monastery.

As he got to his feet his armour let out a loud screech. But then stealth and secrecy were not important now. As he ran for the doorway it screeched again.

He pushed his way through the last bush. A thick branch blocked his way. He snapped it off, and as it fell to the ground the monastery came into view.

The first thing he noticed were the lights in the windows. The monks had risen. His gaze then went to the door. It was shut.

Was there anything else?

Quickly he scanned the whole area. There was nothing unusual to be seen.

It was all right. Nothing had happened. His humiliating failures ended here.

He listened.

There – that faint noise. That was the footsteps he could hear. The demon was coming.

The tree he had hidden under was just paces away. Three quick steps and he was back in its shadow.

He listened. It was definitely the footsteps. They were approaching fast.

What did he do now? Did he stand and observe? Did he rush forward?

He froze. He did not know what to do. He was failing, wasn't he? He was failing in his duty. He was failing King Arthur. He had to do something. He could not simply stand still while he sank into panic.

The footsteps were coming through the bushes and the brambles. Nothing natural could get through such a dense thicket at such a speed. The demon would be here at any moment.

His sword – he was letting it droop down to the ground. What was he thinking of?

He raised the sword. It rose a fraction, then it met resistance. Something was pushing down on it.

Pain went up his arm. His muscles were cramping again.

But he was not giving in to this pain, and he was not giving in to fear.

He wrenched the sword upwards. The resistance suddenly went. The sword shot high into the air.

Now he must regain control. He was a knight of King Arthur. He was the perfect fighter. Such knights did not lose control of their emotions.

The footsteps grew louder. They had left the forest and were crossing the grassy yard. Yet he could see nothing.

He had to act now.

He dashed forward. If he blocked the doorway the demon would retreat. And he was going to make it. He was sure of that. He had to make it.

The door was in front of him. Two more paces and he was standing under its arch. He turned and faced the demon.

It was still running towards him.

"Back!" he shouted.

It was in front of him, no more than steps away.

"Back!"

The footsteps stopped abruptly. It was stopping in front of the door, just as it always did.

He swung his sword through the air. It met resistance. There was a scream. Then he heard a new noise. Something had fallen at his feet.

He looked down. There was a body there in front of him. He could clearly see it in the shadows. It gave off a faint glow of silver light. It was a woman who lay there. Her face had a purity and innocence that not even a child possessed. Only now it was a face that was still with death. In her hands was the Grail.

He reached out for it. The tips of his fingers touched cold metal. Then it was gone. The Grail had faded from his sight and with it had gone the innocent corpse.

The Grail Bearer. He had killed the Grail Bearer. The purest of innocence had fallen to his sword.

He let out a cry of anguish.

He had stopped the Grail reaching the monastery. It had been before him and he had attacked it.

He looked down at himself. He wore black, didn't he? And he had hidden in the shadows. Here was his demon.

"And you were so sure that you were right," said the monk.

He took a step backwards. His back collided with the door. The monk had left that day. There was no one in the yard. Yet that voice had been close to his ear.

The strength went from his legs. It would be so easy to let

himself fall to the ground, but he could not allow that. He was a knight.

The wind blew for the first time that night. With it came a faint, distant whisper.

Learn from this. Was that what it said? He could hardly hear the words.

He strained and listened. The gentle breeze blew again.

Learn from this. That was what was being said. He could hear the words now. Yet he was not sure if he heard them with his ears.

Learn from this and the next time it will be yours.

THE TREASURES OF BRITAIN

Heather Rose Jones

Let us just pause awhile in this turbulence of Quests, and look at the story from another angle. The Grail Quest as we know it came from the French romancers, particularly Chrétien de Troyes and Robert de Boron, but they owed their origin to the Celtic myths and legends. These tell of the thirteen Treasures of Britain of which the magic cauldron and the chalice were but two. In this ingenious story, Heather Jones (b. 1958), an American editor, fantasist and folk singer, gives us a Celtic perspective of the Holy Grail.

Gwenhwyfar looked out over the Hall and muttered, "If it's not one thing it's another!" But it never failed. No sooner had knife gone into meat and drink into horn than some lack-wit came knocking on the gate. That business with Culhwch and the boar-hunt had taken *years* to clean up after, but had Arthur learned his lesson? No. Now he was convinced that anyone who showed up in the middle of dinner was a Destiny to be dealt with. The queen sighed as the porter was sent scurrying back to the gate to escort the travellers in with a proper semblance of reluctance and trepidation.

All through the Hall heads craned forward to see the visitors as they were led within. The man was tall and noble-looking, with dark curly hair that held just a hint of grey. He bore before him in both hands a golden cup of wondrous workmanship, set with pearls and precious stones and polished until it seemed to glow of its own accord.

The woman who followed him had skin as white as sea-foam and hair like a raven's wing. Her lips curled in some secret smile. From her shoulders hung a mantle of shining gold-brocaded silk that fell to sweep the ground about her feet. But few in the Hall spared a glance for the two travellers; their eyes were riveted to the golden chalice.

"Can it be?" Arthur muttered under his breath.

"Is our search ended at last?" Bedwyr asked of Cei.

"Is there no purpose left to the Quest?" Owein sighed, with just a hint of petulance.

The stranger bowed when he felt all eyes upon him and advanced to stand before Arthur. "I am Caradog Strong-arm, and I have come to your Court because I have heard that you are fond of wonders," he began.

Fond to the point of an entire barn-full, Gwenhwyfar thought.

"That is why I have brought you this . . . chalice," he continued. "The vessel has a peculiarity: it cannot abide impurity and faithlessness. And I thought, only here at Arthur's court will I find men who would dare to be tested, who would set it to their lips and see if the drink it contains is for them."

Owein was the first to step forward. "I am the chief of Arthur's warband. Let no man question my faith to him. I will drink."

Then Bedwyr pushed forth, saying, "I will hold my purity against any man's – I too will drink."

And Cei, who never lagged where Bedwyr led, demanded his turn. Then the others, Gereint and Gwalchmei, and all of Arthur's men, were shouting and demanding that they be allowed to test themselves.

When the noise had quieted some little bit, Caradog spoke again. "I think you have mistaken my meaning. This vessel cannot abide impurity and faithlessness – it will not contain the drink of a man whose lady has violated her marriage or her virginity. For such a man, the contents would spill to the ground."

The men were quiet then, for a moment, but once again Owein was the first to speak. He laughed and held out his hand to the lady at his side. "Then I have nothing to fear. Denw has always borne true faith to me. Yet will I drink."

He did not see the whiteness of her face nor the anger in her eyes.

"And I," Gereint echoed him. "My Enid kept true to me no matter how I tested her. I will drink."

Enid drew a fold of her headdress over her face and turned away.

One by one the bold boasts were repeated, until the men were nearly coming to blows for the right to drink from the cup first and prove their ladies' worth.

But then Gwenhwyfar came and stood before her lord, the king, and said, "Will it come to bloodshed before the meal is even begun? This is no fit welcome for guests." *Though it seems what the quest intended*, she thought. "Let us set the cup aside for now and wait for a more fitting time." *"Never" seems good.* She turned to the stranger and spoke more sharply. "It seems your test is one-sided. What of the ladies?"

He smiled craftily and beckoned his companion forward. "My lady, Tegeu Gold-breast, wears a garment with wondrous qualities." Tegeu bowed her head modestly and slipped the mantle from her shoulders to hold it before her. Her husband continued, "The peculiarity of her mantle is that its length will change according to the qualities of its wearer."

"Ah," Gwenhwyfar said. "It will be ill-fitting on a woman whose man has broken faith with her?"

"Not . . . precisely," he answered. "It will be ill-fitting if she has broken faith with him."

"*Delightful*," Gwenhwyfar muttered. She turned back to Arthur. "Surely such a marvel as this deserves a better setting – a grand feast, perhaps. And there are those who are absent from your Court today; should they not be called back to participate?"

The king frowned slightly. "Will the ladies of the Court be more virtuous tomorrow than they are today? We have just held our Easter banquet but days past. Where will you find provisions for a great feast now?"

"Though you think it is difficult, I will not find it so," Gwenhwyfar answered.

"And what of sufficient drink?" Arthur asked. "The brewers' vats are but dregs after our recent feasting. Where will you find enough mead and wine to fill Caradog's chalice for the testing?"

"Though you think it is difficult, I will not find it so," she said again. "There will be enough wine for all who choose to drink it from this man's cup."

"Many of my men have already left after my Easter Court," Arthur said. "How will you bring them back?"

"Though you think it is difficult, I will not find it so," Gwenhwyfar said once more. "All will be in readiness in three days' time, if you will consent."

And so Arthur gave his consent and they set a date for the feast and the test.

The next morning, Gwenhwyfar was sitting with her ladies by the windows, sewing on embroidered garments, when Denw, the Countess of the Fountain, came and asked for speech with her.

Gwenhwyfar drew her aside so that they might speak freely.

"O, Queen," Denw began. "You must not let this test go forward. It will only bring shame and ruin to this Court."

Gwenhwyfar smiled a thin-lipped smile and nodded for her to continue.

"You know I have been faithful to Owein, my husband, since first I pledged myself to him. And that despite his own faithlessness, when he left me behind for three years and forgot that he had ever loved me." A hard look came into Denw's eyes. "But which marriage will this cup test? Will it brand me faithless to my first husband because I wed his slayer? Will I be blamed for the way Owein deceived me at the first? I have asked him to refuse the test but he told me he dared not, after what he said before the others yesterday."

Gwenhwyfar placed her hand on the other lady's and said, "Have no fear. I will arrange matters so that it will not come to that. Meet me in my chambers this evening, when dusk has fallen." And then they went back and joined the others at their sewing.

And after a time, Enid came to the queen and asked for speech with her. And again, Gwenhwyfar drew her aside so that they might talk freely.

"Do you recall," Enid asked, "the tale of that time when my husband so despised me? How he feared I would betray him, and so he abused me and reviled me and tried to drive me away, and yet through it all I followed him and never ceased to love him?"

The queen nodded silently, though she shook with anger at the memory.

"And do you recall the tale of how he bade me entertain the Dun Earl, and how that one set his heart on me and tried to win me, first by promises and then by threats?"

Again Gwenhwyfar nodded.

Enid's voice dropped to the barest whisper. "The tale does not tell how he forced me." She looked pleadingly into Gwenhwyfar's face. "How could I admit it? Gereint already thought me faithless; he would never have believed I had not . . ." She paused a moment to regain her composure. "For three years now he has loved me again as he did at the first. If this test betrays me, that love will turn to gall within him. I have begged him to refuse the test but he says he will not, for then the other men would think I had something to hide."

The queen drew Enid into an embrace and comforted her. "Have no fear; it will not come to that. I will arrange matters otherwise. Come to my chambers tonight, when dusk has fallen."

And then they went back to join the other ladies and took up their sewing again.

In the afternoon, when the light was beginning to wane, Morfudd came to the queen and asked to have speech with her, and the two drew away from the others so that they might converse freely.

"This test will bring only sorrow," Morfudd said bitterly. "I have gone to beg Cynon, my betrothed, to refuse it and he says that he dares not be the only one to refuse."

"But what have you to fear?" Gwenhwyfar asked. "I have never seen two who loved each other more completely and wholeheartedly than you and Cynon."

"Completely, in truth," she answered. "For he has taken me to his bed, though we have not yet been married. Will the chalice make allowances for that? Or will it know only that I have violated my virginity and will not go a maid to my wedding? And will Cynon admit that it was he who had me, or will he repudiate me for fear of being mocked? O, Queen, you must prevent this!"

And Gwenhwyfar took her by the hand and answered, "You must rest easy. I will arrange matters so that it will not come to that. But come to my chamber later this evening, when dusk is falling."

And then they went back to the other ladies and Gwenhwyfar told them the time for sewing was done.

And when the evening meal had been eaten and the boards taken up, and dusk was falling, four women met in the queen's chamber. Gwenhwyfar drew out a shining cloth that she had kept bundled in her arms.

"Arthur's cloak, Gwen," she explained. "It will keep us from being seen while we are at our business, for that is one of its peculiarities. Although," she added, half to herself, "I'm more fond of the property whereby it will not abide having any other colour on it. It saves a great deal of grief for the laundresses, for he *will* use it as a carpet and set his chair on it and all manner of idiotic things."

Then she wrapped the cloak about the four of them and led them down to Arthur's treasure-house and past the Treasurer who stood there on guard.

Once inside, she lit a small lamp and set it on a chest while she contemplated the jumbled heaps of wonders surrounding them. There were swords and spears of cunning workmanship, horse harness and harps, cauldrons and collars, gameboards and gold rings, chariots and chests of gems. All the spoils of Annwn – and several mortal lands besides. Gifts received and gifts to be granted. Gwenhwyfar went to one corner and began pulling things off a dusty wheeled cart.

"The Chariot of Morgan Mwynfawr," she explained briefly, coughing a little at the dust that was raised. "I knew it would come in handy eventually. You have but to stand in it and wish where you want to be and you will come there quickly. Denw, you will take it and go collect those who have left the Court. They will listen to you because you are a countess and have authority."

The Countess of the Fountain helped pull the vehicle free of its encumbrances and turned questioningly to Gwenhwyfar. "How will this prevent the testing?"

"Leave that to me," the queen answered, "and I will arrange it."

Then Gwenhwyfar pulled a large basket from under a pile of embroidered tapestries. She handed it to Enid. "The Hamper of Gwyddno Garanhir – I don't think we've used it since Culhwch's wedding feast. I don't know why. It's such a practical thing; put food for one man in it and you will find food for a hundred when you open it again. That should solve most of the problems with provisions, though we may have to start with food for three men to get the right amount."

She pulled a silver-banded horn from the next pile, frowned, then tossed it back. "The Horn of Gwyn ap Nudd that he blows to summon the Wild Hunt is a fine horn indeed, but not the one I want. Ah!" She pulled a second horn from the pile, this one banded in gold and set with red gems. "The Horn of Bran Galed: it will pour out whatever drink you might wish for. That should keep our little company from thirsting."

That too she handed to Enid, who tucked it under one arm as she wrestled with the hamper.

"But I thought you meant to prevent the feast and the test," Enid protested.

"Leave that to me," the queen answered. "I will arrange everything."

She turned then to the far corner of the room, where the treasures were heaped up the highest. And though the lamp was flickering she could see well enough, for a glow seemed to come from somewhere in the heap.

"We'll need this, for certain," she said, rolling a large bronze cauldron towards Morfudd, who caught it before it could clang on the floor and alert the guard. "And this, as well," she added, taking a large whetstone from where it hung on the wall and tucking it into Morfudd's girdle.

Gwenhwyfar frowned and looked around until she spied a bit of scarlet cloth tucked inside a pitcher. "And here is the last of it," she said triumphantly, shaking out a finely embroidered tunic. She laid the garment over Morfudd's shoulder and then whisked Arthur's cloak about them all once more – chariot, hamper, cauldron and all – and took them out under the blind eyes of the Treasurer.

In three days all had been prepared, with the stragglers gathered in, and piles of food pulled from the hamper and set out on tables in the courtyard, and the fires burning under the cauldron in readiness for boiling the meat, and Bran's horn pouring out a steady stream of mead and wine into the waiting casks and tubs. Gwenhwyfar gathered her ladies about her for their instructions.

"Have you done as I told you?" she asked Enid.

The woman nodded. "I've made certain that Gereint's knife is as dull as I could make it – and I will have the whetstone close at hand."

And Morfudd added, "I've made certain that Cynon is wearing only a thin shirt – and I will have the red tunic close at hand."

Then Denw said, "And I will see that Owein is standing close by when it is time to put the meat into the cauldron."

"Then it is time to announce the feast," said the queen.

It was announced, and all the people of Arthur's Court gathered around the tables in the yard – for they were too many to fit in the Hall at a single sitting. And when they were assembled, Arthur called forth Caradog Strong-arm with his chalice and asked if he would begin his test.

"Indeed, I will," he answered. "And it would not be fitting for any other to take it unless I tried it first." And then Caradog filled his golden cup from the wine that flowed unceasingly from Bran Galed's horn and emptied it in a single draught, without spilling a drop. He looked over at Tegeu Gold-breast then, and she smiled proudly and looked around at the ladies of the Court. "Who will be next?" he asked.

"I will," Owein said.

But the Countess of the Fountain laid her hand on his arm and said, "If the drinking begins before the meat is even cooked you can be sure this day will end in quarrelling. Come, help us lift the joints of meat into the cauldron and let us have it served before the drinking starts."

So Owein heaved the meat into the bubbling cauldron and they settled down to wait for it to cook. But however long they waited, and though the water boiled and bubbled merrily, the meat remained as raw as ever.

Then Gereint stood up and said, "Enough of this waiting – I will drink from the chalice."

But Enid laid her hand on his arm and said, "We can wait a while yet. And you will need to be ready to carve the joint when it is done. I thought your knife seemed dull when last I saw it. Here is a whetstone you can use to sharpen it while we wait."

So Gereint took some oil and the stone and began whetting his knife. But, however long he scraped it across the stone, it remained as dull as it had been before, so that he could not even have cut butter with it.

A shiver ran through the crowd, for they knew that there was some form of magic at work.

And Cynon turned to Morfudd and said, "Run to my chamber and fetch me warmer clothes. It seems to me the day has turned cold of a sudden."

But Morfudd said, "If that is all the problem, I have a fine tunic here that you can put on. I thought it was foolish of you to wear such a thin garment." She held out the scarlet tunic to him, but though it seemed of a large enough size when he held it before him, no matter how he tugged and pulled it would not fit.

Gwenhwyfar smiled behind her hand to see Owein prodding and swearing at the joint of meat, and Gereint scraping and swearing at the whetstone, and Cynon swearing and tugging at the garment.

But Caradog Strong-arm was not smiling, and finally he turned to Arthur and asked, "When will you put an end to this? Shall your men be tested with the chalice or not?"

Arthur frowned, and called to the Countess, saying, "What ails your cauldron?"

"My lord King, I do not know," she answered. "Unless it could be that this is the Cauldron of Dyrnwch the Giant, which will not cook meat for a coward. But if a brave man's meat is put in it, it will be cooked on the instant."

When Owein heard that, he turned pale.

Then Arthur called to Enid, saying, "What ails your whetstone?"

"My lord King, I do not know," she answered. "Unless it could be that this is the Whetstone of Tudwal Tudglyd, which will not sharpen the blade of a coward. But if a brave man uses it, his blade will be sharp enough to draw blood from the wind."

When Gereint heard that, there came a roaring in his ears.

Then Arthur called to Morfudd, saying, "What ails your tunic?"

"My lord King, I do not know," she answered. "Unless it could be that this is the tunic of Padarn Peisrudd, which will never be the right size for a coward. But if a brave man wears it, it will fit perfectly."

When Cynon heard that, a weakness came over him and he shook like a leaf.

But Caradog Strong-arm became angry, and shouted, "Enough of this foolishness. Will none of you dare to test your ladies' faith by drinking from my chalice?"

Owein looked at Denw, and remembered all she had borne for his sake when he had abandoned her. Then he turned to Caradog and said, "My lady's faith needs none of your testing. I will not drink."

And Gereint looked at Enid, and remembered with shame the time that he had doubted her and the ill-fame it had brought him. Then he turned to Caradog and said, "If anyone here doubts my lady's chastity it is my sword that will answer his doubts, not your cup."

And Cynon looked at Morfudd, and his heart was filled with more love for her than even before. And he turned to Caradog and said, "Take your cup and mantle elsewhere. We neither want nor need them here."

Caradog Strong-arm looked around the Court, but now no one would step forward to drink from the cup or admit that he had doubted his lady's faithfulness. He thrust the cup into a pouch at his belt and took Tegeu Gold-breast by the hand and led her from Arthur's Court.

And as they left through the gate they might have heard the Countess of the Fountain calling out, "Dinner's ready!" And if they had looked back, they might have seen Gereint carving the joints so fast you would have thought his knife went through air, while Cynon served the first platter to the king, wearing his fine, well-fitting red tunic.

When dusk fell that evening, Gwenhwyfar gathered the three ladies once more, and the treasures with them, and cast Arthur's cloak about them so that the Treasure-keeper would not see them. They carried everything back into the treasure-house and set it all more or less in order – though who could really tell?

"But what if Caradog's chalice really was . . . what they have all been looking for?" Enid asked as she passed the items to Gwenhwyfar one at a time, to be returned to their places. "Perhaps such a marvel *would* test us and find us wanting. Have we truly done right?"

"There are some things that are better in the seeking than the having," Gwenhwyfar answered as she took the scarlet tunic and leaned over the stack of treasures in the farthest corner of the room. "Trust me – it wasn't," she said, carefully dropping the garment over a small cup in the back of the pile. A cup that shone softly of its own accord.

HONOUR BEFORE GLORY

Steve Lockley

Steve Lockley (b. 1958) is an English writer, now resident in Wales. He is the editor (with Paul Lewis) of the Cold Cuts *series of horror fiction anthologies. He has recently completed a children's novel and is working on an adaptation of the legends of Twm Siôn Catti, the Welsh Robin Hood. In this story Steve unites the Grail legend with that of the Wandering Jew. The connection is an obvious one, but one that has tended to be overlooked. The Wandering Jew was a man who admonished (some stories say pushed) Jesus as He staggered with the Cross on the way to His crucifixion. Jesus is supposed to have told the man that he would tarry on earth until Jesus came again. As a result the Jew, who in the early legends was called Cartophilus, and later Ahasueras (and in this story is Isaac), has wandered the world since, awaiting Christ's second coming. Many books have been written about the Wandering Jew, but the only novel I know of to bring him (or in that case her) and the Arthurian legends together is* The Grail of Hearts *(1992) by Susan Schwartz. But it's an obvious link. Here, Steve Lockley takes the story to a logical conclusion.*

Two men sit beside a fire, steam rising from their cloaks drying on branches staked into the ground. They are tired from their long journey, much of it on foot, and at last it is almost over. Above them, set into the hillside, stands a castle, imposing yet barely substantial.

They remember a conversation which took place months earlier around another campfire, when they were in better spirits. A time when they had not had the opportunity to become tired of each other's company, annoyed by the constant repetition of familiar complaints that is the root of friction in any fellowship. A time when the soles of their feet had not grown sore and bleeding inside boots that never dried.

The younger of the two, his full beard heavily tinged with grey, hankers for those times. Over the months he has come to wish that, despite the hatred that had originally spurned him on, he had remained in Camelot. Better still, he could have swallowed his pride and followed in the footsteps of his King, as his allegiance dictated. Now his mind drifts back to those happier days.

"I could have been king, you know," slurred Sir Kay, his face sweating not from the heat of the fire but from the rough wine the old man had given him. He had left Camelot in search of solitude, but on finding the old man had joined him by his fire.

"So you said," replied the old man, his face brown and weatherbeaten. "But I was there. I saw Arthur pull the sword from the stone before riding as if the devil were at his back to bring it to you."

Sir Kay belched and wiped grease from his greying beard. "I should take my sword to you, old man, and hang your gizzard out for the crows. It does not pay a man to cross me. It never has."

"Is that why you have always hated Arthur? Did he cross you by taking your place at your father's right hand? Or perhaps Sir Gareth? Did you treat him so badly because of the way Arthur agreed to feed and keep him?"

"What of Gareth? I did not know he was Gawain's brother. How could I? Gawain himself did not know him. Besides, I gave him everything Arthur asked of me."

"Not knowing who he was does not justify treating him as poorly as you could. Arthur agreed to feed and shelter him. He did not intend having him put to work in the kitchens and treated no better than a village boy. But that is it. You begrudge having to answer to Arthur. Yes, you obey his orders to the letter, as is your obligation to the king, but there is no dedication; no love. Had there been you would have insisted on riding on Rome with the others."

"What do you know, old man? How come you take such an interest in my affairs? Who are you, some confederate of that cursed Merlin?"

"My name is of little importance. It will mean nothing to you."

Kay rose to his feet slightly shakily and started to pull his sword from its sheath. "I am done with this, old man. Tell me your name or let us end this conversation."

The old man shrugged and poked the fire. "My name is Isaac."

Kay dropped back to the ground again, relieved that he would not have to carry out his threat, and raised the winesack to his lips. "So, Isaac, how come you know so much about me? I do not recall having seen you at Court. Is your knowledge based on rumours and whispers?"

"Not at all, Sir Kay. Our paths have crossed many times, although I can understand you not wishing to remember those events."

"Remind me."

"I was in Carlisle when you accepted a challenge to ride through the forest until daybreak. You also vowed to kill anyone who opposed you."

"That was a trick by Arthur to belittle me. He laid a band of vagabonds in my path, determined to stop me. I could not have killed them all."

"Gawain did," said Isaac. "Or at least enough to help you make your escape. I helped tend your wounds when the delirium took hold."

"Gawain. Always Gawain. Gawain the adventurer; Gawain the lover; Gawain the finder of the Holy Grail."

"Do you hate him as much as you hate Arthur?"

"I do not hate him. I might be jealous of his good fortune, but I do not hate him. Sometimes I would just like the opportunity to wipe the smug grin off his face. But enough of me. Why do our paths keep crossing in the way you claim?"

"A curse," replied Isaac.

Kay laughed. "Is my presence so offensive?"

"No, that is not my curse. The spell placed on me is far more wearing. My curse is never to rest, never to find a place I can call home."

"And the name of this witch who placed the curse on you?"

"It was no witch," said Isaac. "I once stopped a man from taking a rest in my doorway when He most needed it. He told me that while I could prevent Him from resting for a while, He would do the same to me for all eternity."

"A powerful man to place such a curse with a few simple words," said Kay. "Perhaps you should have slain him and avoided your penance."

"It was not the time for killing," said Isaac. "He was on His way to Calvary, bearing His own cross."

"You jest with me, Isaac. Do you take me for a fool?"

"Not at all," said Isaac. "A fool would have drawn his sword against me long before now."

"It is not too late for that," said Kay. "But I thought the tale of the Wandering Jew belonged in the tales told around the campfire. Perhaps that is what we are doing. Yes, you lay a good jest."

"Believe what you will, but it is no jest."

"Why should I believe you?" said Kay, staring at the old man, his interest captured by the way in which his companion did not try to convince him.

"You do not have to believe me. You asked my name and I gave it. I came to this country in the same ship as Joseph of Arimathea, when he came to establish his religious order. There were people in Jerusalem who had heard of what I had done and hounded me out of the city. For the first year I did little but travel from village to village, unable to find work. It was not long before I was reduced to being the beggar you see before you now.

"I met Joseph when I was at my lowest, having been without food beyond frozen turnips for weeks. I did not even know what country I was in at the time, nor do I know now. He made me part of his party and gave me passage, promising me a new life. In exchange all I had to do was ask Christ for forgiveness and accept Him as my Saviour."

"The Grail Bearer?" asked Kay, enthralled by the story as it unravelled.

Isaac nodded. "Yes, he carried the bowl you call the Grail."

"Did you see it? What did it look like?" The questions tumbled out of his mouth in a torrent.

Isaac shrugged and poked the fire, sending a shower of sparks into the darkening sky.

"I believe your tale, Isaac. I have seen too much these last years to dismiss anything. But is there no way to lift your curse?" asked Kay. He knew without needing proof that he was hearing the truth.

"If only there was," said the Jew. "I am a man of peace and yet I have been attacked on my travels more times than I can remember. It seems no number of sword-cuts can stop me drawing breath."

"I had not meant anything so drastic," said Kay, surprised at the calm in the old man's voice.

"I know of no way to lift the curse. The curse your Christ made on me seems fixed tight."

"My Christ? Do you deny Him?"

"I am a Jew, Sir Kay. I was not one of the rabble taken in by the blasphemy He and His followers peddled. They are the ones who drove me from my home."

"Yet you accept that it was His curse that led to your present position? If you accept that, then surely you know of His power over others?"

"I have no doubt about His strength, but I deny He was the Son of God."

"And perhaps there lies your problem," said Kay.

"How do you mean?"

"I am not a man of intellect, Isaac, nor do I claim to be pure of heart, but I have seen the effect of belief in others."

"You think that I would find release by denying my own religion?"

Kay shrugged. "Perhaps your journey is your own Quest – as fruitless as that for the Grail. Even Gawain could not realize what was within his grasp. Now he does not remember where the castle lies. If it were mine to take I would not relinquish it as easily as I did the Sword."

"Then the man is as big a fool as you believe, Sir Kay," said Isaac. "If a man is unable to retrace his steps he will never be able to learn from his own mistakes. I retread my own steps unerringly, day after day, month after month, always repeating the same patterns. I know where the castle you speak of lies. My path draws me by it constantly."

Sir Kay laughed and rose to his feet. "In that case, my new friend, you will act as my guide. I will gain the Grail and prove to Arthur my worth. Perhaps in doing so we can also bring your journey to an end."

Dawn was breaking, bringing the castle into full sunlight, and Sir Kay kicked earth over the dying embers of the fire. High above them the castle overlooked their crude encampment, with mist swirling around its granite outer walls. The inner keep was almost hidden from view by the height of its battlements. Kay shielded his eyes against the rising sun and stared at the building, eager yet wary of what he might find.

"It is time," he said.

Isaac rose in silence and dragged his few belongings together.

"Leave them," said Kay. "They will be well guarded." He pointed to the armour which lay half covered by overgrowth, housing only the bones of a fallen knight.

"If we succeed we will return to collect them."

"And if we fail we will have little need of a change of clothes and a pile of ragged sacking," his companion replied. With that they took one last look at their surroundings, as if to remember their position, then started their climb up the hill.

"I have never been this close before," said Isaac as they walked. The sun began to beat on their backs as it rose in the sky.

"Have you never been curious?" said Kay. "You must have known how highly the Grail is prized. Look around you at the wreckage of failure. These brave souls gave their lives in trying to find it." He indicated the human debris and decay which became more evident the closer they came to the castle.

"Then why are we doing this? Why are we putting ourselves in peril if so many have died before us?"

"I cannot speak for you, but as you seem to have little to lose, the fear of death can mean nothing. For myself it would be a stake worth wagering."

The Jew began to stoop as they climbed, as if a weight pressed heavily on his back and shoulders.

"It is nothing," he said, seeming to shift his burden when Kay questioned him on it. "This happens whenever I am near this place."

"Then why keep coming? Is this all part of the curse?"

Isaac shrugged. "I am drawn like a moth to a flame. I have no control over the path I take other than when I take the decision to walk away from this place. Sometimes I feel it would be easier to give in than continue to resist."

Just as it appeared as if they were close to their destination they found their way blocked by a dense overgrowth of thornbushes. Despite the hacking of Sir Kay's blade it would not allow them passage.

"Do we need to go further round?" asked Kay.

"I know no more than you, yet I feel as if we are on the right track."

"If you can feel your way then perhaps we are trying too hard to find the easiest way. Lead on."

"Just because I seem to be able to feel whether or not we

are on the right track does not make me a guide," rebuked Isaac.

Kay sensed his companion's growing anger. "Close your eyes. Try to make the journey one step at a time. I will follow."

Reluctantly Isaac obeyed, and, ignoring the thorn barrier, took tentative steps forward. Kay followed. He concentrated only on Isaac's feet and followed close behind, one step in front of the other. He lost count of how long they weaved through the thorn, but when they finally broke through Kay looked up for the first time and saw that the sun was almost overhead. When they looked back they saw behind them a single thorn bush. Their path to the castle was now clear, although steep, and Isaac strode on despite his burden.

The weight appeared to become heavier as they tackled the steeper part of the climb, and yet Isaac did not complain, despite Kay's offers of assistance. At last they reached the entrance of the castle, where heavy wooden doors hung open, leading into an empty courtyard.

At first in awe of the emptiness Kay began to look around, until dismay began to creep into his heart. All around him he could see nothing but a state of decay. Here the stone courtyard floor had cracked and crumbled, falling into disrepair; there a dead bird lay unheeded and crawling with maggots; and all around the bases of the wall was scattered wind-borne debris.

"Is there anyone here?" Sir Kay called, but without reply. He glanced across to Isaac, who stood by his side. His face bore the strain of his invisible burden.

"Is it over?" asked Isaac through clenched teeth.

From the square stone keep three women dressed in white approached them; with each step the stone flags seemed to crumble beneath them. Each carried a golden bowl of differing shape and design.

"You may set your burden down now, Isaac. You have carried it long enough," said the woman in the centre, her voice echoing around the stone wall without losing its clarity. At once the weight was removed from the old man's shoulders and he stood upright once more.

"For both of you your Quest is over, and yet your journeys have just begun. First, if you seek the Grail then you must make your choice."

Sir Kay looked at the three bowls presented before them, staring at each in turn. The bowl held by the woman nearest to him looked closest to the description given by Gawain. Its value was obvious from its bright gold lustre and the jewels embedded in it. This was a bowl suitable for use by the King of Kings, and he was about to reach out to touch it when Isaac knocked his hand away and touched the bowl in the middle.

"This one," he said. "I have seen it before."

The woman took a step closer. "Do you accept Christ as your Saviour," she said, echoing a question that had been asked of him before.

The weight had been lifted from his shoulders, and Kay could see that his companion's spirits had been lifted with it.

"I do," he said.

Sir Kay waited while his companion looked into the bowl. Was this the Grail? Was this simple bowl on a short pedestal what they had travelled so far to find? It did not fit the description Gawain had given, nor were they being welcomed into the Great Hall he had talked of. But then his tale seemed to have been dressed in wild trappings that could so easily have been drawn from his imagination. Or perhaps that splendour too was fading.

Kay had almost decided to step forward and seize the bowl. Three women would not be able to stop him. Even on foot he would able to make his escape, especially now that he knew the thornbush was nothing but an illusion.

Unable to see the contents of the bowl, he contented himself with watching the expression on Isaac's face. The old man wore a look of surprise, which changed to astonishment before he started to sway unsteadily on his feet.

The woman stepped away from him on the instant that his legs gave way and he fell heavily to his knees. By the time Kay had taken the four strides to his side he was lying face-down on the ground. Kay tried to shake him, but it was as if the life had vanished from him.

"Isaac. Isaac!" he shouted, but the man did not respond.

"Let him be," said the woman. "At last he has found his resting place."

Kay stood and moved away from the body. "No. We have come so far together. It cannot end like this."

"But is this not what you wanted for him?"

The body twitched and Kay was about to rush back to him when the woman held out her arm to restrain him. The body seemed to become weightless, lifting from the ground slowly until only its knuckles scraped the ground. A shaft of sunlight broke through the cloud and illuminated the body, burning a shadow into the courtyard floor. The body then rose along the shaft of light, higher and higher, until the cloud closed around it and he was gone. Only the shadow remained to mark his passing.

"Now it is your turn, Sir Kay," the woman said, stepping towards him. "That is if the notion of stealing the Grail has now passed."

"That was never my intent," he said. The lie sprang automatically to his lips, and he knew how foolish he must sound. "What has happened here?" he said, gesturing at the signs of decay. "If the Grail is so powerful, why is this happening?"

"The fate of the Grail, and of this castle, at least for the immediate future, is linked to that of Arthur."

"Arthur? What does he have to do with this?" He felt the familiar heat rising with the surge of hatred.

"Look into the Grail and you may receive your answer," she said.

"What will happen to me?" he asked.

For the first time in his life he was afraid for his own safety. Until now this had been an adventure, one that he had never really thought he would complete. In the past, the glory others had taken for granted had been beyond him. Now he had reached that threshold he feared for his life.

No answer came. No indication of his fate. Only the proffering of the bowl. A sound came from within, and he felt himself drawn to the dark liquid it held. Slowly a picture formed, and the sound of battle rang in his ears. Arthur. Arthur in danger from a blow about to strike his head from his shoulders. "No! Not that!"

He wanted to shout, to scream at the scene in the hope that Arthur would be able to hear him and defend himself.

"You can save him," said the woman.

"How? How can I save him?" he asked.

The woman indicated a black stallion which had appeared at his side. "Keep the picture in your mind, and with your eyes closed ride for the rest of the day and all night. By morning you will be at his side."

"But that will be too late. Arthur will be dead."

"Ride through the night without rest and you may yet save him," she said.

"What of the Grail?"

"There is a choice to be made, Sir Kay. Take the Grail, and glory, or save the man who has protected you. But take the Grail and this place will be no more. It only exists to house the Grail, and without it the castle becomes nothing. Its end has already begun, but it is not irreversible."

She was right; he knew that. Arthur had been his protector, and without him he would have been nothing.

There was no choice. No matter how much he hated, or thought he hated Arthur, he could not let him die if fate had put in his hands the opportunity to save him. He took one last look into the bowl, then swung himself onto the horse. He squeezed his eyelids tight and dug his heels into the horse's flanks.

The horse flew like the wind, its hooves barely touching the ground, and Kay pressed himself against its neck for speed and shelter. He did not know how long they rode, but the sun moved from being above him to beating down on his back again. After it had set, the horse's hooves skimmed effortlessly across water.

From time to time he almost dozed, but at the least sign of the horse dropping its pace he was awake again and driving on. Always he held the picture in his mind of the blade swinging towards Arthur's neck.

They were approaching battle; the sound of metal on metal was growing louder. He opened his eyes for an instant to find himself in the midst of the fighting, and instantly the horse fell beneath him. Dead.

Ahead, a sword was rising behind Arthur, but the noise prevented Kay's cries being heard. He ran, despite the cramp in his legs, and in the instant before the blade fell threw himself between Arthur and his assailant. Weaponless and without armour, he could do nothing but take the blow that had been destined for his King.

"Peace," came Isaac's voice above the sounds of violence. "Peace comes to us all in the end."

THE KINGDOMS OF THE AIR

Tanith Lee

Tanith Lee (b. 1947) is one of the most respected writers of fantasy fiction working today. She is able to draw upon the very substance of myth and legend and imbue it with her own inimitable treatment, making the story just as relevant to today as it might have been in centuries past. You might like to sample her Tales from the Flat Earth series, starting with Night's Master *(1978), which presents a modern interpretation of the Arabian Nights; or her retelling of popular fairy tales in* Red as Blood *(1983). Tanith Lee's stories strike not just at the heart but at the soul. You will not be left untouched by "The Kingdoms of the Air".*

– Who is he, that Knight riding by?
  – His name is Cedrevir. He has been Questing.
  – Pale as death, and his eyes looked blind. I thought, a good thing the horse knows its way. I thought, there is one wounded by unseen arrows.
  – They are an ancient Fellowship, these Knights. It is in their vows to invite the Quest, whatever it may be, whatever its peril or strangeness. But many return home as you have seen.
  – This Cedrevir: What Quest then was his? Do you know it?
  – Yes, and I will tell it you.
  At the Midsummer Feast they met as it is usual for them to do, this Fellowship of Knights, up there in the Castle of Towers.
  In the Castle's heart there is a great hidden hall, the entrances

to which are known only to an Initiate. The hall is built as a perfect circle, its floor and walls paved with blocks of polished stone. From the high dome of the roof hang down the thousand swords and shields, banners and devices, of all the Knights who are and have been of the Fellowship. High on the walls the torches burn in iron cages of curious shape, so they resemble the heads of serpents and monsters which breathe fire. In the floor is set, in fine mosaic, a huge round sun-disc, and on the rayed rim of it stand the Knights, repeating the circle of power a third time, in flesh and steel.

For each man comes to that place fully armed and in mail, though each surcote is of undyed and unembroidered linen, and the visor of each helm lowered, and though every man carries in his gauntleted hand a sword, it has no mark.

(There are ways of knowing a man, even under these circumstances. From his height and build, his voice, his manner, or by some expression in his eyes.)

There they stood, then, at this Midsummer near to midnight, in the dark light of the dragon-torches. They performed their rites, and reaffirmed their vows. In turn they confessed any of their transgressions against God, Man, or the Fellowship. They told, in turn, of their feats, and furnished proofs, which might be anything, from a lady's scarf to the severed hand of an enemy.

There is one further property in that hall. On a tall stand to the east is a clock, in the form of a golden sword and a marble heart on water. As the liquid drips down through the basin, the weights go up, and all morning the golden sword lifts slowly, until, at noon, it strikes a golden chiming apple in the summit of the clock. Then, as the water gradually refills the basin, the weights sink, the marble heart floats up and the sword descends, until at midnight its yellow blade pierces through the heart, which gives out a long singing note.

Shortly before midnight at Midsummer, when the sword is just grazing the marble, an Invocation is spoken by all the Knights of the circle. There are those that say a certain wine is then drunk, a wafer eaten and an incense burned. Every man bows his head and awaits what will come to him.

Then the sword enters the marble heart, and the heart sweetly cries.

Cedrevir heard the note of the heart, as he had previously heard it, twelve times in all, for he had been six years a Knight of the circle. At first he had been strung, expectant and eager, but year by year these emotions dulled to patience. He had undertaken

between whiles many adventures, all successful. As a warrior he
was valiant and accomplished, and as a priest – for the Initiate of
the Fellowship is both – he was, equally, chaste and passionate.
He had done no wrong, he had fought with honour and skill, but
yet nothing had come to him at midnight of Midsummer, or in
the dark Midwinter either.

Now however, as the note faded from the water-clock, Cedrevir
began to hear another sound so like, that for a moment he thought
the heart cried out a second time. Then he became aware that what
he heard was the voice of a maiden, singing. Her tones were pure
and thin as beaten silver, and her words were these:

> Primo dolens lancea est
> Corona dolor de Dominus
> Est secundo et tertio
> Gradalis cruenta fulgero

The voice rang all round the hollow chamber, and in the hollows
of helm and skull it rang.

Cedrevir raised his head, sure that every other Knight did in like
fashion, and looked with wide grey eyes. There, at the centre of the
mosaic sunburst, a column of light so sheer and bright it dimmed
the torches rose up from floor to roof. Even as Cedrevir stared
into this radiance, half dazzled, uncannily half not, he began to
make out objects moving, there within the column. For a moment
he did not know what these things were. Then, though never before
having seen them, he recognized each, and a low faint groan burst
from him.

He fell to his knees, and wild bells began to ring, and mildly,
terribly, the aching voices sang *Primo dolens lancea est corona
dolor de Dominus est secundo et tertio gradalis cruenta fulgero.*
And down the pillar of white fire came drifting like a cobweb a
spear of silver with a burning tip that shone even more fiercely
than the light, and from it fell ceaselessly petals of crimson that
became butterflies as they faded. And after the burning bleeding
spear, a garland of fiery thorns which also bled, and as the drops
burst from it they changed to roses of gold that opened on hearts
like the moon and stars themselves. Lastly there weightlessly fell
a chalice of a deep clear flaming green, a colour whose depths
seemed bottomless as the sea. And from the lip of the chalice
there ran a stream of blood, but the blood was like liquid gold
and it blazed brighter than the sun.

Then, another voice spoke at the Knight's right shoulder. It seemed to him it was the voice of a man, but before them, on the ground, a glowing shadow showed with folded wings. "Seek then these things, Cedrevir. The Lance of Pain, the Sorrowing Crown, the Cup of the Life's Blood. That is your Quest, and may you be true to it."

After that came darkness on the wide grey eyes of Cedrevir.

Cedrevir knew well enough what he had had revealed to him in the vision. And when he came to himself in the Castle of Towers, and recounted what he had seen – for no other but himself had been made witness to it – no man of the Fellowship was in ignorance.

In the great light had passed the three holy relics of the Sacrifice of Christ: The Spear that had pierced His side, the Thorn-Crown that had garlanded His brows, the Chalice in which had been shared the sacred blood-wine of the Last Supper, and in which the true blood of His wounds had subsequently been caught.

These articles, long reverenced as aspects of the Martyrdom, are, we say, supposed to have remained on Earth. Indeed, their whereabouts, as you may hear, is known, though not by situation. A fortress, called the Castle of the Jewel of Goodness (which is, Carba Bonem), that is where they are lodged, and tended there by mysterious guardians. All about Carba Bonem stretches a vast waste that has no seasons in it save only heat or cold, but that is named, for its looks and barrenness, the Winterlands. And in the waste is a dead forest as old as the world, which is named the Wood of the Savage Hart. But the way to it, the forest, the wasteland, the secret Castle of the Jewel of Goodness, they lie off the edge of any map, beyond the memory of any traveller. It is not possible to come to them either by accident or by design. And so the quiet priests told Cedrevir as he kneeled before them, with his dark head bowed and beautiful hands upon the hilt of the sword which bore his device, a couched sarpafex.

For many days then he fasted and watched, and kept by himself or with these learned ones from whom he sought counsel. All this while, the images of the vision stayed clear before him as if he had seen them only a moment ago, and in his ears the voices sang *Dolens lancea, Corona dolor, Gradalis cruenta fulgero.* And the last voice told him, waking and sleeping and watching, *This is your quest. Be true to it.*

Then at last there came an hour just before sunrise, when the birds piped over the meadows, and the sky was pale as a shell. And Cedrevir came from the Castle of Towers.

He rode as if to a battle, sword, shield, and lance at their stations, clad in mail of steel. Both he and the blond horse were trapped and clad in his colour, the blue-grey of distances. And worked on the saddle-cloth, and enamelled on the shield and sword-hilt, the snake-lynx of his blazon, silver and blue and gilt.

In the fields, where the women and boys were labouring, they raised their heads among the tall corn, to watch Cedrevir go by. There is a Knight of the Fellowship, they said, he goes Questing. For the look of setting forth is, though unlike, as unmistakable as that other look with which, often, they return.

So he rode across the Near Lands, towards the North, for north lies the House of Winter, and in the North there are mountains, the high places. And that was all the guide he had to find a spot that is of the Earth but not on the Earth; a spot that some wise men say is a myth, although also a certain truth.

Beyond the Near Lands lie others less known, but all were wrapped in the late richness of summer, and it may be supposed that human tasks went on there much as they do everywhere. In the orchards, vineyards and fields they would be making ready for harvest, toiling on into evening under the wide golden skies. At the streams and wells the women gathered with their washing and their buckets, and by the rivers they cut reeds. Where the castles stood up on the hills, or some massive tower thrust from the woods, the sentries would remark a riding Knight. Some challenge or greeting might be offered him. And now and then, at a lonely chapel, the priest would render lodging, blessing, bread and wine, most frequently in silence.

Perhaps two months Cedrevir travelled, going always north-wards, questioning on the way those he met, where it seemed the sign of knowledge was on them, here a hermit in his cell, there an old peasant woman, or a little child even, with a freckle like a star on its forehead. Otherwise, sometimes, the Knight himself would be petitioned for his help, and so would fight, a champion against some wrong. And then again there were those who sought to tempt him aside, to view a wonder, which might be a mysterious flower that grew in a ruined pagan temple, a thing which would work miracles, or a fountain that gushed from a rock at the striking of his fist. Or there were, from time to time, those who desired to corrupt, such as a white-shouldered woman in a red gown, who leaned from her window so her long hair, scented with a strange spice, brushed the face of Cedrevir as he rode by. But for her he did not stay.

One dusk, when the light still hung like a dome of crystal high up in the vault of heaven though all the landscape darkened, Cedrevir came on a broken tower beside a lake. Through the windows of the tower the shining afterglow ran like spears, and the lake itself lay like a great pool of sky fallen on the Earth. Not a breeze stirred and not a cloud marred the surface of air or water. Then the stars began to dew and daisy out; and one lit more brightly than the rest upon the strand against the lake. It was a torch, that burned in a cage of bronze before a pavilion. And as Cedrevir rode close, other lights bloomed in the pavilion's heart, and turned it to a bulb of softest fire.

Presently two Knights stepped from the pavilion. They were of another fellowship, and on the shield of one was the device of a falcon, and on the other a white bull with wings.

"Where are you going, Knight-at-Arms?" said he of the falcon-shield.

"Northward," replied Cedrevir. "It is a Vowed Journey."

There is not a fellowship, they say, that does not honour the Quest, or the bond of it.

The two Knights nodded. He of the bull-shield spoke next.

"We guard here the Lady Marismë our sister."

"I do not challenge that, nor offer any threat to her."

"No. But she is a seeress, trained in the Luminous Arts," said the falcon-shield Knight.

"If you would confer with this lady, our sister, I believe she will do her best to help you," said the bull-shield Knight. "Only this morning, by her art, she descried you, and said, 'Here we will linger and await a traveller from the South. He seeks a key to his Quest, which I, maybe, shall find for him.'"

Now the two Knights stood in shadow beyond the torch, and their faces were hidden under their glistening and dark helms. It came to Cedrevir that he did not credit all that they had said to him, and yet they had spoken no lie. It was the deep shadow of occult things on them, but not of wickedness, as it was only night had darkened the lake.

Just then, the draperies of the pavilion parted with a flutter, and a woman came out. On her the torch shone full, and she was young, and fair, with clear wild eyes. Her white gown was bordered with gems like water-drops, and on her dim hair drifted a net like silver spray.

She said nothing to Cedrevir, and her eyes looked into him and through him. It was a terrible gaze, for she seemed to see his very birth and death, and all other matters that might come between. Then she beckoned, only once, and drew back into the pavilion.

"Follow her," said the falcon-shield Knight. "She is honourable, as are you. And if you were not, she is well able to protect herself. Besides, we are here."

So Cedrevir, in a sort of trance, for her eyes had curiously affected him, dismounted and entered the tent after the lady.

There was a woven carpet on the ground within the tent, and the lamps hung in clusters from posts of bronze. But the lady stood in the centre of the pavilion where there was a pedestal of carved wood. And on the pedestal before her, a golden bowl filled with water.

"Come here and see," said the Lady Marismë.

Cedrevir went to the pedestal, and looked down with her into the bowl.

At first there was only the clarity of the water over the gold. Then there came a turbulence that was in the water and not in it, and a veil seemed to be torn away. There in the bowl, as if miles off, a great host was fighting in the sky. It was a gorgeous and a fearsome battle, for a setting sun, and also bolts of lightning, flashed upon the gems and metals of the warriors, caught upon swords that blazed with inlay, and catching the crests and banners showed devices so mystic and so strange they were not at once understandable. But the sun was going down and the clouds, amethyst and purple and scarlet as the trappings of the Knights, began to lower and smother the scene. Then a trumpet sounded, unheard – but perfectly to be viewed – a long line of fire as from some comet. At the signal, through the cloud-mass there came riding two mighty lords, and all the host drew back away from them to give them room. And this was very dreadful, for it was plain at once that these two Knights were brothers. Each was golden, each as clearly beautiful and as sparkling as something made of the sun itself, and as hard to look on. But one was clad all in gold and white, and on his helm was a crest like stars, and on his shield a device for which there was no name at all, it might not be expressed or written, yet Cedrevir, glimpsing it, was filled by joy and terror. The other Knight was arrayed in the colours of heat and fire, and in his crest burned a green jewel so marvellous the eye seemed to drink at it. His shield had no device, but on his banner, that one bore behind him, were embroidered the words: *Non Serviam.*

They met with a clash, these two, that shook the sky; their lances splintered and the pieces rained down like blood and lava on the world. Each sword came from its scabbard like a lightning stroke that lit all heaven. And as they dashed once more upon each other, the last of the red sun fell, and on a cloth of gold, dead black yet shining bright, they fought, on and on, as the moon rose under their chargers' feet.

There was no telling how long the combat lasted; time had no meaning there. Cedrevir watched with awe and misgiving, in pity and dread and triumph. It was the First Battle, when the angels of God had fought together. The golden Knight was the Archangel Michael. He clothed like fire, whose banner proclaimed his rebellion – *I will not serve* – was Lucifer, before his fall.

When the final blow sang home, ever expected, ever impossible, needful and terrible for all that, the sky seemed to crack from end to end. Cedrevir did not behold the fall of him, Prince Lucifer, yet he saw flung out from the clouds a green shooting-star. It smoked and flamed, tearing downward to the earth. Over hills and heights it ripped its path, and there the ocean spread, glittering and unresting in the moon's sway. And here, in the sea, the emerald meteor went down, hissing. It was the jewel from the helm of Lucifer, the Prince of Hell, quenched in water.

But it was only the clear water in the seeress's bowl that Cedrevir now saw, and the Lady Marismë standing on the other side of it, who spoke to him.

"That spiritual jewel was the green ruby, his pride and pleasure. It lay in the sea, lost to him, as all else had been lost, until, with the centuries, it was washed ashore. Men, seeing it a stone beyond price, fashioned therefore a chalice. So to the lords of the Earth it passed, after the fire, the air and the water. Solomon the Wise drank from it. And through a line of kings it entered the possession of the Prince of All, Jesus the Christ. You are seeking His Grail. In the world or out of the world."

"Lady, I am. And have always wondered at the tale, that the ornament of Satan, the Evil One, should become the holy Cup of the Christ."

"But is He not," said Marismë, "called the Redeemer?"

Cedrevir bowed his head. "But," he said, "do you know the road to Carba Bonem?"

"I shall tell you its name," she said. "This road is called *I will*."

Cedrevir sighed. Then, surprised a little, he saw the lamps had burned away and that the soft light in the tent was dawn coming in from without. The moments of the magical revelation had consumed an entire night.

"If you wish," said the Lady Marismë, "you may now accompany us to our kingdom."

Then she spoke a word, and the whole pavilion lifted as a ball of thistledown lifts. It blew up into the air, and all its appurtenances and furnishings with it, and vanished quite. There they were, then, on the strand of the lake, and nearby the lady's Knights leaning on their shields, while on the hill-slope under the old tower the blond horse cropped the grasses.

At this minute the sun rose between two eastern hills, and threw down its rosy sword point-foremost straight across the lake. And out of the sun's glory, there might be seen a slender raft with a transparent sail coming slowly towards them, guided by no agency that Cedrevir could discern.

As Cedrevir stood pondering, the Knight of the winged-bull approached him and said, "Your horse is safely penned within an ancient wall, no longer visible, for this was the stronghold of magicians, and power remains. Come now with us, if you will."

Then the raft drew against the shore. The lady stepped on it, and after her the two Knight-brothers, and the three stayed, waiting courteously. So Cedrevir went after them, onto the raft, which hardly looked stout enough to uphold the lady alone. But when he was on it, it began to move again, its sail turning to the morning breeze, and went back the way it had come.

The lady was foremost of the craft, with the sunlight on her, and she said to Cedrevir, "You must know that in time past, we dwelled on shore, where the tower leans, which is all that remains of a great castle. One season, the waters of the lake rose and overwhelmed the land. We, swept away, outlasted the catastrophe. And now, live there."

"Where is that, lady?"

"Beneath your feet, bold Knight. Under the water."

The raft had reached the middle of the lake, and suddenly it stopped, with only its swan-white wake fading behind it.

Then Marismë laughed, and she went out, on to the very water, and after her her two brothers. And the liquid of the lake buoyantly held them up, and then gently drew them in. And as she slowly sank, Marismë called to Cedrevir. "Bold Knight, will you make bold to follow? We are your protectors in this. I, by the Arts called Luminous, will ensure you against harm. But you must be trustful, fearless, and swift. Follow now or do not follow."

Then Cedrevir also laughed aloud. "Say then I will," said he. (But his eyes, by turns, were black or blazing.)

Blithely as they, or so it seemed, he stepped onto the water, which held him upright with only a little motion, just such as the raft had, then gradually began to take him in, in company with the other three. Thus they sank together under the mirror of the lake.

This was the curious property either of the lake, or of the lady's magic, that there was no sensation of wetness, only of a silken levity, and that Cedrevir found himself enabled, as did his hosts, freely to breathe the water. Also, that he might hear and see, touch and taste, and in every other way respond and act as if he were above the surface on dry land. Yet everything was, too, transmuted and different. All speech, for example, now sounded to him like the sweetest singing. (And he heard besides the songs of the fish which darted here and there like linnets, as he descended.) As for vision, a dark radiance hung over all things, and proceeding through the kingdom beneath the lake, every movement was swathed in the sleeves, robes and veils of silver eddies.

Under the water was a land that, in many ways, resembled the country of the Earth. There was a road there, which led to a castle on a hill, but the road was paved with great round pebbles washed smooth and lucent as glass, and above, the castle glimmered green as peridot. All about the road were orchards and groves, where fruit grew shining, like apples of milky gold. The fish sat singing in the branches of the trees, whose foliage was fine and etiolate as strands of a girl's hair. Under the castle clustered a town of stone, and sometimes men and women passed to and fro. Seeing the Lady Marismë, these persons bowed to her. There was also something shadow-like about them, and it seemed to Cedrevir that here, too, though nothing was hidden, all was not shown.

As they neared the castle, the doors of the building opened and a Knight rode forth. He was clad in black, even to the plumes of his helm's high crest. The horse he sat was black and thin, but it was armoured all over, and its legs braced by black iron. And when they climbed and came up with the Black Knight, he turned his head to look at them, and he had no face, only a skull.

"It is Death," said Marismë, and she saluted him, and her brothers with her.

Death nodded, and made to pass on. Then, apparently noting Cedrevir, he spoke to him.

"I shall meet again with you, in another place," said Death. "But that is many years hence."

Cedrevir crossed himself. But he would not be shamed, and looked long on Death, and it began to seem to him that behind the skull, there was a man's face, and two sombre eyes that regarded him. No sooner did he think this, than the apparition raised his hand and lowered the black visor of his helm. Death rode away down the hill on the iron horse.

"Do not be concerned," said Marismë. "Our kind, though we live, are also numbered with the drowned. He has some rights over us, being in part our king." And in the open doorway of the castle, she turned to Cedrevir and said, "There are three mighty citadels of Powers. The Powers of the Water, which are inconstant and eternal. The Powers of Earth and Fire, which mingle, and are of the passions, and by which most wrongdoing is invoked. The Powers of the Air, whereof there are many kingdoms, for they lie closest to God – not in that they are in the sky, but in their permeation of everything, and their invisibility like breath, and life itself."

When she had said this, she went forward into the castle, entering a huge hall there that had looked empty and dark before, but lit up at her coming.

Presently, as it would happen in a sort of dream, Cedrevir found himself seated on a dais at the lady's right hand, before a board draped with damask. On this every delicacy that might be got from the dry world, or that might be found in fresh water, was displayed on dishes of gold and silver, while servers processed ceaselessly through the hall bearing jewelled trenchers and long-necked ewers of wine. And in that ambience of water, not a morsel of food was lost, or a drop of liquor spilled out or mixed in the currents of the lake, but flowed from beaker to cup, from cup to lip. Down from the roof hung gilded wheels each with a score of flaming candles in them, and in the walls torches burned, and not a fire was quenched, though the smokes wove endless patterns through the water.

In the body of the hall, not a place was vacant at the long tables. A full company of Knights and ladies dined together. And while they dined, proud dogs with collars of pearls lay by the tables or prowled about for scraps. The servers carved and the pages hastened on their errands, and the minstrels woke their harps. And on everything lay the iridescence of the lake. But under everything there lay a dimness and a shadow.

Perhaps several hours passed at the feasting. After this time a trumpet was sounded and a silence fell. Up the hall there walked a page clothed in black, pale as a plant of the deep woods, and carrying a dish of horn and onyx. On the dish lay a fruit from the aqueous orchards below the castle. Coming to Cedrevir, but no other, the boy kneeled: "Will you eat of this fruit, Knight?"

And Cedrevir hesitated. "Do you not come from Death?"

"If I do, it is not himself he sends you."

"What then?"

"The fruit, which is not forbidden, yet which is a fruit of knowledge. Perhaps a warning, perhaps a prophecy, perhaps a symbol or a test of heart or brain. Take the fruit, and see."

Then Cedrevir took the fruit, and at once the boy vanished. Cedrevir gazed long at the apple's satin skin, as he had outstared Death himself. And in the core of the fruit the Knight thought he saw a fire, but it was not impure or poisoned. So he put it before him and cut it open with his dagger.

Cedrevir started back in horror. For from the apple came a scaled worm, a serpent, which his knife had severed. Yet, it did not bleed, and both parts of it ended in a head, each having cold sad eyes that looked at him.

"You have wounded me," said the snake.

"Pardon me for that," the Knight answered. "I did not do it knowingly."

"You lie," said the snake.

"Not so."

"Do you not recognize me, then? I am the Serpent, that creature cursed of God and man. I am the Beguiler. I am Satan, your Enemy. Say now you do not wound me knowingly."

"If you are he," said Cedrevir, "then, knowingly, I would cut you from me, mind and body and soul, a hundred times over."

"It has been easy for you, this once," said the snake.

And then it shrank and shrivelled until it was no wider than a thread, and the thread went to ashes and crumbled, and was gone.

"What is the message of this, lady?" asked Cedrevir of Marismë.

"That you are already on your road. For no tempter would come to you if you had not entered the sphere of his sight."

Then she rose to her feet and the great hall grew vague and silent, as if a huge cloak had been thrown over it, and every light was smothered.

But at her side her brothers waited.

Marismë took Cedrevir by the hand, and led him out of the hall, and up a curving flight of marble stairs, into the well of a tower. At its summit was a chamber in which the windows were pillared by stone, but the casements were water where the fish swam in and out as they pleased. The two Knights took their stance, as at the pavilion, on either side the door, which then closed fast of itself.

"Now, Cedrevir," said the Lady Marismë. "You are young and you are thralled in my spell. You are here with me, and blameless, and who is to see us?"

And she showed him a bed, scented with flowers and soft as snow, and hung with heavy curtains of silver stuff. Next, she threw off her gown, and stood in her shift, as translucent as the lake itself. But when she had done this, he saw through her, through shift and skin and flesh and hair, and she was made of bones, as the face of Death had been.

"Lady," he said, "I will lie beside you, but in no other way."

She nodded, as Death had done, and drawing back the covers of the bed, she revealed to him that a barrier of upturned blades ran down the middle of it, a palisade of steel. Marismë stretched herself to one side of this, and he and on the other, the blades between them. And all at once Cedrevir slept, in that bed of swords, and in his sleep the fence grew higher and touched the roof of the chamber, which caught alight and fell down on him, and at that he woke.

He lay beside the lake, on the shore in the sunrise, and up the slope, where the ruin was, the patient horse cropped the grasses.

There was no sign of any other thing, for his hair and garments had no trace of wet. He was hungry and thirsty. The feast under the lake had not sustained him.

Yet, on opening his right hand, he found lying in the palm a little coal-black shell, and there fell from it one water drop, like a single tear.

The Knight of the Fellowship of the Circle rode northwards another month or more, and the summer waned from the land. He came among places of sterility where the trees were thin as famine, a burned country. In the valleys they had long since stripped the white corn, and the sun had withered off the grass and leaves. Only crows stood sentinel on the bald hill-tops. In the north, miles distant, were clouds that did not move, and these Cedrevir took for the mountains.

One noon, when the barren heat was very great, Cedrevir saw a church below him in the downlands, by a stream. The banks were shared by walnut trees, and the water was fresh. The fruits

on the walnuts were like stones, however, and when he smote on
the church door it sagged wide. No one was there but lizards that
rushed away like the scorched leaves over the floor. A window
shaped as a wheel hung in the east wall; before it an antique
banner dipped from a rafter, dark red, the fringes rusty. The
altar was singular, a block of quartz, and in the depths of it
might imperfectly be seen a war-axe, though how it had come
there there was no telling.

Cedrevir, going out again, tethered his horse, and stretched
himself among the trees to rest through the heat of the day.

No sooner had he closed his eyes than he heard a weird wild
pagan chanting, and shouts, and the tramp of feet coming towards
him along the valley.

Cedrevir started up – and as he did so, the noises died on the air.
Only the stream lilted in its narrow bed and the horse whispered
to the plants under the wall's shade.

Cedrevir sat down again, and leaned his head on his hand and
shut his eyes. Instantly he heard the chanting and the outcry, as
before but louder still. Now he did not stir, but only waited, and
presently shadows began to flicker and dance over his eyelids, as
if a company of people passed.

Cedrevir opened his eyes a second time, and wide and grey they
gazed on nothing but the arid afternoon.

A third time he withdrew his sight, and past him the people
tramped, and bells rang and women shrilled. Now Marismë, the
lady in the lake, had said to him: The name of your road is *I will*.
So then Cedrevir said softly to himself, "It is to be seen if it is to
be heard, and I will see this thing and what it is."

And as he had smitten on the church door, so he smote open
his own eyes with the thought.

Then he saw this: Across the valley floor, following the course
of the stream, came a band of men and women. They were
summer-tanned, lean and ragged, but they had garlanded their
heads with twisted briars. The women rang bells and the men
brandished staves. In the midst was a cart which they pulled
violently along, and in the cart was bound a young maiden, wan
as if near death, though in her dark hair too was caught a crown,
of vine-leaves and poppies. Plainly, she was to be a sacrifice.

Cedrevir got to his feet and loosened the sword in its sheath. It
transpired that, as he had formerly not seen these people, they could
not even now see him; he was invisible. Unhindered then, he trod
behind them, and when they mounted a nearby hill, kept after.

There among the stubble was a ring of lifeless trees, from which the carrion birds rose at their arrival like flung, screeking stones. The ground under the trees, where they had been feeding, was littered by bones and bits of rotted meat. The spot smelled of death. As the men lifted the girl from their cart, she began to weep, but she did not beg for any mercy, judging it, seemingly, beyond them. They tied her fast to one of the trunks. She drooped there like a dying lily on a black branch. The maddened crowd ran about the tree, wailing and calling, and then an ancient man, cackling at the curtailment of youth, crept around the ring, sprinkling from a censer on to the ground. It contained blood, which smoked and stank, and the crows, which had returned to the upper boughs, clapped their wings in greed.

When the ancient had completed his ritual, the people plunged together and swirled suddenly away. They went by Cedrevir, where he waited at the tree-ring's edge, without a look, and some even stumbled against him, but paid no heed to it. Their noise, which now had something more of fear than celebration, diminished and was gone. A vast silence settled on the hill. At this, the girl raised her drenched eyes and looked all about her. Her tears fell and she shook with terror, but nor did she make any sound.

Then there came a rumbling in the earth, under their very feet, and Cedrevir unslung from his shoulder the shield fronted with the sarpafex, and drew his sword.

In another second the ground bulged and split, and out of it there burst, flaming like a molten thing, a huge lizard, a dragon.

It was the colour of brass, and in size half the height again of a man. It bore up with it a fearful smell of sulphur and decayed matter, and as it grubbed and pawed, discarding the soil, searching for the accustomed offering, from its jaws ran a venomous breath tinctured with fire.

Cedrevir stepped forward, and lifting his shield against the exhalation, called to it.

The dragon turned at once, and its orbs of eyes, that looked blind with unthinking malice, yet appeared to take him in.

"Before her, first you must be done with me, Devil-spawn," said the Knight "Now God be at my side, in Christ's Name." And he went forward straight at the dragon, but, as he did so, covered his head and breast with the shield. A wave of the filthiness and heat seared Cedrevir like a furnace blast. Yet he came on, and struck with his sword, upward, against the underside of the ribs. But the cage of ribs was a monumental thing. He bruised it, for the monster roared, and in the trees the waiting crows exclaimed and took flight. But no more than that he did.

Cedrevir fell back now, for the awful breath and fire of the dragon were greatly weakening.

It slunk after him, and raking at him with its forefeet continuously, inflicted instead horrid wounds in the earth, for he was too quick for it.

Then again, he struck at the breast, at its jaw that weaved above him, and one of the huge teeth in its mouth was broken at the blow.

Down the hill they passaged, the dragon sweeping with its claws and pouring out its bane-breath, Cedrevir avoiding its attack as he could – and here and there a tree stump or a boulder sprang alight in lieu of him, or cracked in pieces.

But it was in the thoughts of the Knight that he would lead it down, away from the damsel, to the stream below the church. The dragon's element was fire, but there lay water.

Among the walnut trees they passed, and Cedrevir stepped back into the stream and felt, through his mail, its blessed lesser warmth like coolness. The dragon baulked. It would not come on. It snarled, and the small stones of the walnuts might be heard popping and snapping.

"Is it water you spurn, or the holy church above?"

Then the dragon spoke to Cedrevir.

"You have wounded me. Is that not enough? Let me return to the maiden who is meant for me. I would not slay you. I honour your valour. You did not mean to wound me."

"Is it you?" said Cedrevir. "You were before a little snake."

"I? Who knows me, or what I have been, or may be?" said the dragon. The words came from its mouth, in a pure voice, shining like an organ-note in the flaxen air. The words came from it, yet no man could be sure it was the dragon which uttered them.

Cedrevir answered: "You are the creature of Satan, let him protect you. I call upon my Lord. You are the weapon of the Enemy. Oh God!" cried out Cedrevir, "send me a weapon here to meet this foe."

At that, the ground quaked, even as it had when the dragon erupted out of it. Above the stream, where the church stood, there came a sound of rending, and up into the air shot a beam of light. Cedrevir did not turn; he held his eyes on the dragon, and covered himself over with his shield. But also he let fall his sword, and raising his right arm high, opened his hand. And into it there came a heavy rounded haft, and at the haft's end a wedge of brightness like a jewel. It was the axe he had seen bedded in the altar.

"I will," repeated Cedrevir. He lifted up the axe and whirled it.

The dragon coughed out a spurt of livid fire, which enveloped Cedrevir, and seemed to touch his heart and shatter it. But yet still he let the revolving axe fling free and even as he sank down, he saw the axe-head meet the dragon's skull, and cleave it and become embedded in it. And he saw too that the skull seemed made of a substance like quartz.

The cool water laved the mail, the hair and flesh of Cedrevir. He lay under the stream, dreaming of the dragon's death. But he could not breathe the water of the stream as in the lake he had. He must rise up again and shake it from him.

He climbed the hill wearily, and the crows berated him high above. (The dragon's corpse would be difficult eating.) Going to the dead tree, he cut the ropes which bound the maiden. She saw him clearly, as she had seen the battle for her life. She dropped at his feet. She clasped his ankles, and the garland of poppies slid from her shadowy hair.

"You are at liberty," he said.

"Yes, and I thank and bless you for it. But do not leave me here, for those savages of the region will themselves kill me. They have worshipped the dragon all the years of their lives." And she looked at him with the blackest eyes, and her mouth was red as the poppies. "I am called Melasind. A great lord is kin to me. Take me only to his kingdom. It lies northward. It is not far."

Cedrevir set the girl before him on the horse. She was slender and silent, no trouble for them, but for her beauty – which did trouble the Knight. For her beauty was of a subtle and uneasy sort, like smoke.

She gave no direction to the home of her kindred, the kingdom of the lord she had not named. Northward, she had said, northward they rode, and she was content. She did not question Cedrevir on any matter.

At night they slept upon the ground and gentle Melasind made no complaint. She wrapped herself in her mantle and lay down, her cheek pillowed in her hand. Her slumber was discreet, but her hair strayed as she slept; it coiled and shimmered on the earth. She had been the dragon's bride, and her power over desire came from that, her virginity burned under the skin.

By day the sky was brazen. The landscape became a desert, flat-tabled plains where drifts of minerals sparkled. Not a tree grew. Water, where it was to be had, lay still in the cups of stones, and tasted of metal, granite, or cinders.

Then, as an evening came on after the sunset, the girl said to the Knight, "Do not pause now. For another hour's riding will bring us to the kingdom I told you of."

Cedrevir looked before them, to the north. He saw dim, folded plateaux and the vault of light. There was no sign of any road, any wall or tower.

"Where, lady?"

"There," she said. "Where the stars are coming clear."

Then Cedrevir beheld a strangeness in the sky. On the height of it some stars were flashing out, a whole constellation, but it had a form which he had never seen before in any land, or place, nor ever heard spoken of.

It was like a spear or sword, but winged, the clustered stars thick like diamonds at its centre, raying away to glinting dust at the huge pinion-points, and the whole dazzling more fiercely than any other star of the sky, or the full moon even.

Cedrevir said nothing else to the maiden, and she nothing more to him. They rode on towards the winged sword of stars. And an hour passed, as she had said it must, but with no feature of the plain altering. Then, "Draw rein," said she. And when he had done so, she leaned forward and cried in a high voice thin as a wire:

"*Ex orio per Nomine.*"

That done, she bowed her head meekly and clasped her hands.

But on the plain a mighty wind rose up. It seemed to lift the very corners of the world up after it; shards and dusts flew into the air, and in the welter of these things, soundless as an opening flower, Cedrevir saw a castle rising out of the earth. Its battlements and towers were pierced with lights, and banners curled about the tops of it. All was stillness as the wind died down. Then from the castle's walks the trumpets clamoured.

"Do not delay, we are expected," said Melasind.

So they rode forward, and as they went, the starburst of the winged sword was eclipsed behind the stoneworks, its point seeming to stab slowly to the castle's heart.

There was a gate, with torched turrets either side. The portals of this now began to open, and a Knight rode out. In the torches' light he was dressed in red, his mail red as new copper, and he was mounted on a red horse.

"You are welcome," he said courteously, and to the Lady Melasind he bowed.

With great surprise, Cedrevir heard her give a shrill merry laugh, and felt her shrink away between his arms. He looked, and saw that as the torches found her now, Melasind was a slender girl-child, some seven or eight years of age. She turned to him her laughing face and said, "In the world, I am wise. But here, in the house of my kin, I am as a child. Help me get down, Sir Knight."

So Cedrevir dismounted and lifted her down.

With misgiving, yet ever with the purpose of the Quest, he followed her under the great gate, into the castle which had risen from the Earth.

A night and a day Cedrevir remained, the guest of an unknown host, in the Castle of Earth and Fire. And so it was. For by day, only the slightest sunlight entered through the embrasures, that were closed besides by panes of thick glass tinted with cinnabar. Constantly the lamps and torches and candles burned there. It was a place of great heat, and of leaping fire-cast shadows.

The servants of the Castle waited on Cedrevir, as, in the mansions of his own land, he was wont to be waited on. There seemed nothing uncommon in it, though they did not speak to him of anything, nor did he interrogate them. At the ending of that first day, sunset filled the windows, and the Knight in red mail came to Cedrevir, greeted him with all proper forms, and asked him to descend the Castle to a hall of feasting.

Together they went down countless wide stairs of burnished basalt, by passages and chambers red with sunset and fire, and going always lower, until Cedrevir believed they had now passed under the ground. But he made no remark upon this fact, nor did the Red Knight speak of it.

At length the last stair ended at a door, which opened itself at their approach. Beyond lay a garden, most unusual and enigmatic in its looks. No daylight ever came there, it was far beneath the earth, but in the midst of it was a pool of ebony water from which proceeded a sourceless glowing light. On the water the whitest lilies rested, and sometimes, in the lighted dark, the gold fin of a fish would blink. The walks of the garden were laid with opals and other pallid fiery gems. Herbs and flowers stood in the beds, but they had no hue nor perfume. All across the garden, nevertheless, a tall rose tree had spread itself, and every rose on the tree was crimson. But when they came near to it, Cedrevir saw that these roses were made of rubies, garnets, and spinels.

Beyond the tree was another door, and through the door a hall.

They left the gardens and entered the hall, and stood on its threshold. A million candles were burning there, above tables covered with cloth-of-gold, and against hangings that ran with gold, shining on cups of sheerest crystal and platters trimmed with precious stones. But none sat down there, and presently Cedrevir perceived that the dust of years had gathered over everything. And, as the fish had winked in the pool, now and then a black rat would flicker under the draperies.

At the room's far end, the child Melasind sat on the flagstones. She wore now a gown of yellow scarlet, and her hair was crowned with the colourless flowers of the garden. In her lap she held an agate bowl and a knife of bone, and she wept.

Cedrevir went to her and kneeled down before her.

"Lady," said he, "why are you crying so bitterly?"

"The lord, my kindred, is sick," said Melasind. "Only this bowl, brimmed by the blood of a virgin, can revive him at such times. See, I have been nerving myself to it, but am afraid."

Cedrevir frowned. The Red Knight stood at his left shoulder, and said. "It is as she tells you. For long ago my lord, who is the lord of this kingdom, received a grievous wound. It does not heal. Only virgin blood can make him well, and that only for a little while."

"I do not ask the nature of the wound, nor how he came by it," Cedrevir replied. "The voice of fate, shouting or murmuring, is always to be heard on such a journey as mine. My vow is also of chastity. I have never joined with a woman, or committed any carnal act. I am as virgin as this child, and far stronger. Therefore I offer your lord instead my blood, without fear. For my soul is in profound safekeeping."

The lord's Knight, hearing this, bowed very low. "He will receive your gift with thanks," said he. And he withdrew from the hall. But the child-girl only stared at Cedrevir.

"You must attend me," he said. "When it is done, take your scarf and bind the cut tightly. Now give me the bowl, and if you wish, look away from what I do."

So Cedrevir opened a vein in his left arm with the bone knife, and filled the agate bowl with his blood. When the deed was finished, the child-girl ran to him and bound his arm tightly, not looking at the cut. But then, she dipped her finger in the blood.

"You shall take him this yourself," said Melasind. "I will guide you to my lord's chamber."

Cedrevir felt a little weakness from the loss of the blood, and he remembered how he had lain down in the stream after the dragon's death, and heard the water singing in his ears, but not as it had sung under the lake.

"Where does your lord lie?" asked Cedrevir. "In one of the great towers of the Castle?"

"No. He is below us, here."

Cedrevir followed her, as she bore the bowl of bright blood, and her steps were quick and light, his slower and less gladsome.

She took him through a narrow door, and beyond the passage sloped and widened, lit only by the raw torches in its wells. Till suddenly Cedrevir could see they were entering among huge hollow caves underground. Soon enough, the lighted corridor fell behind them, and on all sides unfurled the shining dark, like eternal night. Yet nevertheless he could tell their path, for a hot radiance beamed out from the agate bowl.

Shortly, Melasind led him over a bridge of flint, under which, miles down, an unseen river clashed its furious way. On the other side of the bridge was a front of granite, in which a tall door of dull metal stood weirdly ajar. Through this slit went the maiden-child with her bloody lamp, and Cedrevir after her.

At once he seemed struck nearly blind. For though no light came out from the place beyond the door, yet light blazed there within. The means of the light Cedrevir could not discern, but the cause of its power he could barely miss. For the cavern that plunged away before him was piled with such treasures it would seem to beggar the richest kings of the world above.

"Come, follow still," said Melasind, and she led him on now up hills and along mountainsides of piled gold, made all of coins and chains and casks, crowns and swords and rings, and furnishings of every type. And through the gold ran streams of silver, and down its slopes rattled slips of jewels that their feet had disturbed. Until, coming over a ridge of this colossal wealth, Cedrevir looked upon a lake of sapphires, emeralds and rubies, so blue, so green, so bloodmost red, it seemed to boil and to flash lightnings. But in the centre of the lake, as the dragon lies upon its hoard, lay stretched a man on cushions of silk. And he was a giant, clad in black armour, his face turned away, so his locks of hair, that outshone the gold, flowed on the silk like fire.

Then Melasind gave a cry, and she ran down into the lake of jewels, and over it, and came to the giant and leaned above him. After a moment, she called to Cedrevir again: "Come, Sir Knight."

So Cedrevir walked out across all the jewels and when he reached the giant, gazed on his face. It was a countenance of such hideousness that none could look at it unmoved, nor without shrinking. For it was not the ugliness of any fleshly deformity, its horror stemmed from some inner twisting and torture. Then the eyes opened, and filled the face instead with an appalling beauty, but it was the endless beauty of agony that never ends.

"So you behold me, Knight," said the fallen one, and at his voice, no more than a sigh, stone and metal, skin and bone, heart and mind, were ravished and trembled and grew shamed and sick. "See what I possess," said the Lord of the Castle of Earth and Fire, "see what is mine. And see what I am brought to, that a child must fetch me gruel. I thank you for your charity, Sir Knight. Say now, may I drink?"

"Drink," said Cedrevir, "but I must turn away," and leaning on a mace of silver that protruded from the lake of jewels, he hid his eyes with his hand.

After a moment, though, the wondrous horror of the voice whispered again.

"Your gift does me good. There is great vitality in you. Whom then, do you serve?"

"Only my Fellowship," answered Cedrevir. "And God."

The fallen giant drank again. The bowl was drained.

He said: "I serve none. I will not serve, and so may never be free. Do you think my punishment has lasted sufficiently long? No, I am not punished. I need cry out humbly only once *Ut libet*. But will not do it. It is my pride, not your *God*, that binds me. *Ut libet. Nunquam. Ut qui libentum.*"

Cedrevir, unable to prevent himself, had gazed once more into that awful face of a fallen dragon, and in the deeps of the golden eyes he saw printed those words – *Ut qui libentum*. (Seeing that *I will*.)

"Go now," said the mouth that had drunk his blood. "Go take your reward with this damsel. For I would not see this special virtue of yours wasted on another after I have had benefit from it."

"Lord," Cedrevir replied, "you know I may not take any pleasure with her in that way."

"That is to be seen."

And then there came up in the golden eyes a redness, like two dead suns that rose underground, and over the mouth, and all the features, went a ghastly flaring, as if wax melted in flame, and the being roared, and all the cavern seemed to break apart and the jewels rushed up over their heads like a storm of water.

Melasind took to her heels, and catching at his hand, she pulled Cedrevir after her. And in his terror, which was like no other fear in the world, he also allowed her to do it. Together they escaped the cavern of riches, and up the slopes of stone into the passage, and so back into the banquet hall with all its places laid and not a single guest. And beyond that they ran, to the subterranean garden, and here both the doors slammed on them, and cold silence fell.

Cedrevir felt a longing for water, and leaning to the lily-pool, he raised some to his face and lips. As the rings settled in the pool, he saw reflected, between the white chalices of the flowers, Melasind, and she was no longer a child, but a damsel again, with sweet high breasts and a rosy mouth, and hair that poured to her hips.

Then Cedrevir drew his sword and smote that image in the pool, so it smashed in pieces.

The damsel laughed.

"But did he not give me to you," said she, "and here I am and we are prisoners of this garden. Who is to see?"

"I should see it," replied Cedrevir. "I am both warrior and priest. I will not break the vows I made. They have fashioned me, in water and fire, on the anvil, as this sword was fashioned. Though I desire you, lady, which you, and he, both know too well, I have another duty, and a better lust than for your love."

"Alas," said Melasind, and she hurried to him, swift and sinuous as a snake, and threw her arms about him and sought his lips with hers. But he remembered her, how she had been a child, sexless and innocent, that cried at the notion of a wound. And desire left him and he put her away, though the heat of her body burned him through. Lifting his voice he cried out then, as she herself had done on the night plain: "*Ex orio per Nomine!*"

But the Name invoked was now Another's, and all the power and passion of Cedrevir, which that place had stirred, turned otherwise, tore wide the enchantment.

With a screeching and thunder, the Castle of Earth and Fire seemed to burst, and up from the garden rushed the whirlwind, and taking Cedrevir in its grasp, hurled him through disintegrate stone and iron, glass and fire, on to the surface of the tindered land.

And as he lay on the breast of the world, the ground shook, and on the horizon a fiery crack, the shape of a serpent and two or three miles in length, healed itself, and thereafter everything was darkest night, without a beacon or a star.

But transfixing his palm, even through the steel of the gauntlet, was a blood-red thorn. And plucking it out, it left no mark on him. (And the cut from which he had filled the agate bowl had also vanished, leaving only a scar, a broken circle like the sickle Moon.)

In a dream, then he heard the voices sing:

> First the Sword of Painting
> Second the Sorrow's crowning
> Third the Blood-Grail shining.

As, in the Castle of Towers they had sung, dulcet as silver bells.

And after these he heard the seeress Lady Marismë, who said, "Water inconstant and eternal, Earth and Fire that mingle, and the many Kingdoms of the Air."

When he wakened, the land was changed, as if swept by a mighty broom that had tumbled boulders, and the sky of earliest day showed the strokes of the broom in long riven skeins of cloud.

But northward, now, he saw the mountains sharp and clear as swords. Partially transparent they seemed, and hard as forged steel. Yet before the mountains was a vast forest lying on the land like the smoke of an old burning.

Now, this might be that forest called the Wood of the Savage Heart, and since he looked on it and found it there, Cedrevir so named it. Mounting his horse, which wandered docile on the plain, he rode north again, and in a few hours entered under the tangled branches.

In the stories, the trees of that forest were all dead, but the towering trees of the forest Cedrevir had entered, though leafless and often leaning with half their clawed roots from the soil – which was itself only of dust and stones – yet seemed to pulse and throb with liveness, as if with the very beat of hearts. And even those trees which had fallen seemed quickened by a strange force, and here and there the roots had driven back into the unnourishing ground.

There were no birds, nor any truly living thing which Cedrevir might see, or hunt for food. But, as a Knight of a fellowship, he was accustomed to fasting. As the noiseless days and silent nights went by, his thoughts grew only flawless and crystalline, and as for the horse, it survived by sometimes chewing on a kind of mastic that exuded from the trees. Of water there was no scarcity, for the nights were chill and brought a frost which, in the sunrise, melted in quantities, dripping off the boughs and gathering in the stones until midday.

The only flowers of that forest were the sun and the moon. There was, too, an overcast which hid the stars, and also that constellation of the winged sword. But probably this had been, in any case, a sorcery.

One dawn he woke from a deep sleep in which the bell-voices chimed. Not the length of a spear away, a creature was drinking at one of the water-puddles in the stones. It was a hart, cold white, but between the forked horns of it a gold blossom seemed stamped upon its forehead.

It appeared to Cedrevir that this was a magical beast, the genius of the wood, and so he rose and began to go towards it, but at that the hart tossed its head and ran away. Yet it ran only to a clearing some score of trees distant, and there again it stood, flickering in its whiteness like a candle-flame, as if awaiting him.

Accordingly Cedrevir untethered and mounted his horse, and rode slowly after the hart which, seeing him come on, began to trot before him.

In this manner the morning and the noon passed, the Knight following and the white hart dancing before him. If Cedrevir should spur his horse, then the hart would run, so fleet the man seemed likely to lose it. However, if Cedrevir should lag, or pause, the hart too stayed itself, browsing on the dark mastic of the trees as the horse did.

When the afternoon came down into the forest, still the hart went on and the Knight rode after. It was a cheerless day, the season was no longer summer, nor anything, cool and dry, and without kindness.

There seemed no changes in the woods but for the natural alteration of the light. Later a pale amber westering glow flowed through the trees. Later yet, the dusk began.

Where did the creature lead him? In the crystal thoughts of Cedrevir, from which the fast too had sloughed most of the need for sleep or rest, the motive of the pursuit of the hart shone indivisible and immaculate. On a Vowed Journey, such things had all a reason.

Night won the land.

They had reached another of the hollow clearings, and now the hart stopped of its own accord and turned to face its pursuer. It gleamed dimly, even in the utter dark, and between its horned brows the golden flower was like a lingering speck of day. Then, a fearful metamorphosis occurred. The hart leapt abruptly high into the air, so its feet no longer touched the Earth, and as it did this, it seemed to leap out of its own skin, which pleated away into nothing behind it. From the skin of the hart there emerged a huge white lion, with a grey hoary mane like the spun frost, and eyes of flame. And in mid-air it sprang at Cedrevir, for his throat, and for his soul too it seemed.

The horse neighed in terror and plunged aside. The lion-beast, meeting the horse's flank in its spring, ripped with huge talons, but only the cloth and leather of the caparison were breached. The lion hung then from this vantage, glaring in the face of the Knight. And in the black silence of the forest, the hatred and blood-craving of the lion were like a torch. But Cedrevir had by now freed his sword. He swung it over and thrust it down, into the lion's jaws, until the hilt, where was engraved the sigil of the sarpafex, grated on the fangs. And the eyes of the lion turned to blackened coals. It fell away, and lay on the earth, still faintly shining, so Cedrevir beheld it was now only a flaccid pelt, without sinews, flesh or bones.

Cedrevir did not marvel, for he had come into a state of the marvellous, where nothing surprised him. But he bowed his head and gave customary thanks to God. Lifting his eyes again, he saw glow-worms in the wood, and then that they were not glow-worms, but the lit tapers of a procession of men and women, which wandered through the trees into the glade. As they drew closer, he noted also that they were garbed, the men as priests, the women as nuns. Reaching the spot where the skin of the lion sprawled, two of the priests raised it and bore it off. They spared no glance to Cedrevir, but passed him, chanting softly some litany he could not recognize.

Cedrevir leaned from his horse. He caught at the mantle of one of the nuns.

"Where is it that your mysterious company goes?"

She answered, "The Earth is fading. The sky will fall. You may follow us if you wish."

"But where, holy lady?"

"It is true, all places are as one in the World's death."

And with no more reply than that (though that perhaps reply enough), she slipped from him. And all of them had left him, the lion's skin carried in their midst.

Cedrevir dismounted and, leading the horse, went after.

Soon the way ascended. They climbed, the religious procession, and behind it Cedrevir. The trees thinned. The Knight looked about him, and saw they had emerged on a range of cliffs, which might be at the foot of the northern mountains, although these he could not make out. Though the forest had been stricken and non-verdurous, these cliffs were bare of everything but the rock itself. Presently, however, he might see the destination of the travellers. It was a skeletal chapel, roofless and wrecked.

A curious light came down. At first, Cedrevir took it for the glow-worm sheen of the tapers. But then, thinking over the words the nun had spoken, he looked up to heaven. And there was a strange sight, and one which filled him with a deep and sorrowing fear.

The night above had become a canopy, opaque and impenetrable, empty of moon or stars. Yet it was a canopy wonderfully adorned. Across the whole length of it, which stretched to the twelve quarters, ran scrolls and frettings of gold and silver, not in motion but still, as if painted there. And as Cedrevir gazed at this, the whole of it seemed always sinking a little nearer, so that indeed the sky, or this entity of the sky, was falling, by slow inches on the earth below. And from it nothing alive could fly away, but must be crushed beneath. Yet so beautifully fashioned it was, the great black coffin-lid of heaven, that now he saw gems of exquisite lucidity set into the metal, lilies of pearl and asphodel of the clearest topaz, and hyacinths of such purple corundum he could hardly bear to look at them. In his heart, Cedrevir wept. God, dismayed by the unrelenting wickedness of Man, let down the sky to end His creation. Yet, too, He honoured it with beauty. Not cruel water nor ravening fire would be the quietus of mankind, but black air flowered with jewels. Yes, Cedrevir's heart wept, and overflowed with pity for the Creator, and love and an anguish of fear, and resignation, also.

And so he followed the company into the chapel, and here they doused their lights, and were illumined only by the falling slow lights of the sky.

But where they had laid the lion's skin, suddenly there was also a fire on the earth. The pelt blazed up, and the flames divided. Out of them came daintily stepping a little snowy fawn, with a golden cross between its brows. For a moment it was clearly visible, and then it vanished and the glittering ashes of the fire snuffed out to nothing.

A wind blew through the chapel, among the silent watchers there. It was fierce yet strengthless, all the winds of the world flattened under the lid of the sky. After the wind had passed, dew or rain fell, but it died to dust even as it touched the ground.

Looking up again, through roofless walls, Cedrevir saw the canopy had come so close that every flow and decoration might be measured by the eye, huge in dimension, with gems set within gems. Then again, he bowed his head. And Heaven fell.

There was neither heat nor cold, nor sound nor vision nor thought. There was no pain or smothering. A vast *un-ness* covered all, and all was absorbed in it.

After the darkness, there was light. After the death of sleep, a second awakening. The Knight Cedrevir was as you have yourself seen him, well-made, and fair to look on, and he stood as formerly, clad in mail and full armed, but alone, upon a mountainside. The world lay far beneath, or it was gone entirely to a ring of palest most insubstantial brightness, like the sea. The sky was all around, roseate blue with dawn, and clouds passed below and on all sides, moving leisurely as swans on a morning lake. And the sky too was full of golden flowers and silver flowers, like those which had fretted the lid of the Annihilation. But these flowers hung, as if woven in a tapestry, and as he began again to climb, now and then they brushed his face or shoulders, and they had only the touch of flowers, but they did not break or fall.

Above there was a castle which grew up from the mountain, and as it grew it changed to gold, so it was a thing of fire like the sun, and he could not keep his eyes on it. There was a road also under his feet, and it was laid with lapis lazuli and sapphire. While, at the roadside, trees sprang out of the mountain, and their boughs were all blossom, yet fruit hung from them that shone like mirrors and gave off a perfume like no fruit or bloom of the Earth.

By accident or by design it is not possible to come there, but by faith and will, sometimes, it is.

For Cedrevir had entered a kingdom of the Kingdoms of the Air, and before him rose Carba Bonem, blinding him with its glory.

As he approached the gate a horn blew within the Castle, a

long and liquid note, and the doors of the gate opened without a sound.

Within lay a court. It was paved with marble, and on every side the towers went up blazing, and one tower above the others like a shaft of flame, whose head was not to be distinguished. At the centre of the court stood a tawny willow, the curved trunk of which was braced with silver. From its boughs depended the helms and swords, spears and shields and colours, of many scores of Knights, marked with their various devices, so it was a gaudy object, this brown tree. Under it there waited a maiden dressed in sackcloth. Her hair was white as salt, and her eyes the pallid green-azure grey of glass, but she was thin and twisted, and her face beautiless.

"Stay, Knight," said she. "You must leave your weapons and your colours here."

"As others have," said Cedrevir, "and not reclaimed them."

"Not all reclaim them, it is true," said the maiden. "But you have entered the *Azori Mundi Regna*, the Kingdoms of the Air, and must obey their laws."

Cedrevir unsheathed his sword, and unslung the shield from his shoulder, these he gave her, with his war-helm. And she raised the items as if they were no weight at all, and hung them on the tree.

"Who guards you, lady?" he asked her then, "are you alone, and still make this harsh demand of any man that comes here?"

"There is protection, though invisible. I am Morgainor, and it is I myself who guard this place, and its treasures, which you seek."

"So I do," he answered very low.

"Enter the tower then, the tallest of all, and go up the stair."

At these words Cedrevir went pale, and his heart thundered. He said "Is there no other preparation?"

"What is to be can only be."

So he left the maiden who had called herself Morgainor, and crossed the court, and the door of that tallest of the towers opened for him. He saw beyond a stair ascending. It was of polished ebony, inlaid with ivory. And in the tower too, the flowers of gold and silver hung in the air, brushing his face and shoulders as again he climbed upward. And he was filled by feverish lightness, and tears stood in his eyes.

Now as he climbed the stairs of ebony and ivory, it did begin to suggest itself to the Knight that, aside from the flowers which he might see and feel, the air thickened with unseen presences, and sometimes they too brushed him, as if with draperies or wings.

Where the stair curled about itself, as it did very often, it seemed to him he detected voices also, soft and melodious, but they spoke in a tongue he had never heard.

At last he saw the light of the sky again before him, but, as he stepped off from the stair, he found the way was closed with a palisade the height of three men, and made from the bones of men, and the day streamed through them and through the eyeless skulls, which were very white and pure, as if fashioned of alabaster, but they were not.

This door would not open for Cedrevir. He paced before it, and saw dimly through its eyelets radiant day beyond.

Then a shadow moved in an inner corner of the door, and there was a stooped, gross woman there, dressed in sackcloth, her pale hair matted and her face very ugly, though her eyes were the eyes of the maiden in the court.

"You must give me a gift," said she, "or I may not open the way for you."

"What would you have? For I have nothing."

"Give me," she said, "a coal-black shell and a blood-red thorn."

Then he considered how he had remained true to himself and to his vows at the castle in the lake and the Castle of Earth and Fire, and how, waking, he had on both occasions found tokens left him, the shell and the thorn. So he took them from his belt and placed them on the ugly woman's palm.

At that she smiled, and she shook her head, and closed her hand upon the things.

"I am Morgainor," she said. "Do you recollect? You have met me before."

"If you are Morgainor, then you are she. I have given you what you asked."

"Yours is a heart that has no stain, nor any occlusion," she said. "I see through it, therefore. Alas, did you never question what you have been given, to give it up so easily in turn?"

"A shell," he said, "a thorn."

"Knight, I will render you one thing in exchange, and then will open the door of bone." And she held out to him her other hand, the right, and on the palm lay a golden needle. Cedrevir took this, and as he did so the door broke at its centre and folded wide for him to pass.

Beyond, the day was itself standing open, like a flower; it dazzled him, that upper sunshine.

The atmosphere was rare, thin as silk, and fragrant, and cold. The place was by the turret of the tower, its topmost roof, and so high a place the Castle itself had now vanished in the cloud below. A pavement stretched on every side, a round space without a wall, and at the centre of the pavement was a ring of white stones, each about half the height of a man. That was all, and the sun's rays smote on the stones, the pavement, and the gold turret, so everything was caught in a brilliant haze.

Then, from the brilliancy, forms began to shape themselves. Cedrevir stood immobile, and next he kneeled, for these creatures, though never wholly seen, yet appeared like angels, gleaming, and clad in robes of samite, with great wings, and having every one a nimbus about its head. And these strange ethereal beings went to and fro in the air itself, not treading the pavement. (But they did not go inside the ring of stones.)

Cedrevir knelt and prayed then, for the dazzle of the sun and of the angel-beings had brought him all at once to a leaden weariness. As he prayed, too, every slight transgression, every weakness of his life, came into his mind, and he was ashamed. He began to believe that, like those others whose weapons and colours remained on the willow tree, he too would shrivel in this bath of light, and die. Flawed as man and as priest-warrior, he partly longed to leave the height, he could not bear the peerlessness he sensed hovering over him.

Then he heard the chime of bells, and startled, looked up. In the sky to the east he saw a sight.

A glistening barge came floating down the air. It had a sail that shone like red bronze, and the prow was carved like an eagle. A band of Knights rowed the barge through the ether with gilded oars, and young girls stood in the stern and rang bells in their white hands, and chanted dolefully.

Down and down the barge descended; it slipped over the ring of stones and landed weightless on the tower beneath the turret. When that was done, the Knights put up their oars. One, who was clothed in white, came from the barge, and with him an old, crippled, hag-like woman, dressed in sackcloth, who hid her face behind a veil. These two approached, and while the White Knight stood aside, the hag addressed Cedrevir.

"I am Morgainor. We meet a third time. Will you give me back now the golden needle, for if you do, I will then instruct you in the mystery."

Cedrevir rose from his knees. He looked at the White Knight, whose face was as splendid as sunrise and as unearthly. Cedrevir looked at the hag who peeped hideously from her veil with faded azure-green grey eyes.

"Lady, before, you seemed to warn me that I had given up to you too easily the shell and the thorn. Shall I relinquish as easily this needle?"

"You must. And since you must, you shall."

"I believe I have begun to guess the riddle," said Cedrevir. He lowered his eyes and said, "The shell was symbol of the Blood Cup, and the thorn symbol of the Sorrow Crown. The needle is the Lance of Pain. I am unworthy of the vision which was sent me and so, unwittingly but at the design of God, resigned the key to these sacred relics. Nevertheless this needle I still hold, and if I do not part with it, perhaps I shall be granted one further sight of the Lance. Or, I shall be granted clean death upon the lance of a Knight more worthy than I, maybe such a one as he that stands before me now."

Then the hag said this: "Cedrevir you must not presume. If God has chosen you, how do you dare to judge yourself unworthy? What is your knowledge beside the knowledge of Him? You see into your heart, but He sees much more. It is your soul He sees. Whatever is said to you, whatever you gain or lose, what do such things matter? Did the Christ not promise Heaven to a wretched thief?"

Cedrevir sighed deeply. He said, "I am in God's hand." And he gave the hag Morgainor back her needle.

She took it. She said, "Go to the barge. That is the mystery and the last test. There is no more to say."

Cedrevir went towards the barge, and as he walked, the White Knight with the archangel's face fell into step with him. And the White Knight said, "In the barge lies one under a curse, and you may free her from it." But his voice was remote, like distant music.

"What curse is that?" enquired Cedrevir, expressionless, and his heart ached within him, at the words of the hag Morgainor, at doubt, and *because* of doubt. He was not uplifted or comforted. His eagerness lay spent.

"That you shall see, the nature of the cursing. But to break it is, of itself, most simple. One lies within the barge. Embrace her, and kiss her, on the lips. All shall be well."

"That I may not do," Cedrevir replied, dully. "All and every intimate connection with women is forbidden me."

But now they had reached the barge. The beaked prow craned above, and the sail had netted the sun. At the stern the young

girls stood with folded hands, bowed heads. The Knights were
motionless. A ladder led into the midships of the vessel, and
Cedrevir mounted it and stepped down into the barge. There
lay a canopied bier, the hangings of which were blue silk.

"It is not to be, I can do nothing," said Cedrevir to the White
Knight.

But, "Look on her. Perhaps you will pity her enough to do
it."

Then, impelled, Cedrevir crossed to the bier and lifted aside its
hangings. At the view he recoiled, unable to repress a groan of
darkest loathing.

Then again, disbelieving, he stared, and could not take his
gaze away.

On the bier there spilled a faintly-stirring mass. If it was a female
it was the more terrible for that, for it was also reptile. The ripplings
of its curded flesh, shapeless under a swathe of silk, gave way at
the upper limbs to the little clutching arms of lizards, sheathed in
lustreless metallic scales. And from the waist its lower part was
a serpent, oozing in a slime. And round the whole slithered hair
that lived, fatted worms, the snake-hair of a gorgon. The face grew
from the torso – that had no scales. It was in truth a woman's face,
but old as mummy, all fissured and crinkled, lipless and having
no teeth but the four long fangs of its serpent side, these broken
and discoloured. An evil stink arose from it as it laboured there
at life, half-torpid and half-awake. And finally Cedrevir, sick with
horror, dragged away his stare from it, but just then it spoke.

"You are wounded by the sight," said the voice, "But I by the
existence."

And it was the voice of a lost child, that tore his heart.

"That is undeniable, lady," he answered.

"But you, if you would, with one kiss, might set me free. How
long does a brief kiss last? How long my life?"

Then Cedrevir looked again on the monster. His gorge rose,
but now for the first he saw her eyes. They had no colour and
seemed mostly blind, yet in the windows of them shone the well
of the world's tears. A hundred centuries of direst misery. Perhaps
a hundred more if he should stint compassion.

To kiss her was not lust or longing, to kiss her was a kind of
fearful death, and never sin.

So Cedrevir, keeping wide his eyes on hers, leaned down into
the stench and shimmering shadow. He put his hand under her
head, among the hair of worms, and he put his face to her face,

and his lips upon her serpent mouth, and kissed her the kiss of all the love-desire in him that never once had he bestowed.

It was as if he had grasped lightning or the rushing sea. He opened his eyes yet wider, and lifted his head, and saw there in his grasp a maiden so lovely and so fair that not even the wonders of the Castle would outshine her. Her hair, flowing over his hands, was like spring sunshine on wild flax, her eyes were like marine turquoise, her lips were red and her clear-water skin as white as may. And all of her was slim and sweet and human, but quite perfect, so her gentle fingers that touched his brow fell there like petals, and with her perfumed breath she said to him, "Kiss me again." And in that moment he could not stay himself, and he did kiss her, in her beauty and in his great irreconcilable lust.

"I too am Morgainor," he heard her murmur then, as the Earth and sky wheeled about him. "And now you have given up to me all."

There was no thunderclap or shaking of the stones, but the light entirely perished. Everything was gone. The tower, the sky, the angel forms, the Knights and maidens, and the barge. Morgainor too, melted like water from between his hands. And Cedrevir was left in anguish and the dark.

But not for long. For presently, a new lamp was kindled. It was like the intimation of sunrise under storm.

Cedrevir, in his despair, looked yearningly towards it, and held himself ready, nearly gladly, for chastisement.

Next, through the smokes of the cloud, he beheld a searing hint of gold, and then of silver, of crimson, and of a depthless ruby green. Up in the air, anchorless, they wafted. He saw them hang in space, as if a thousand miles away – the Spear, the Thorn Crown, and the Grail. And Cedrevir, in his agony, covered his face and wept aloud, for he knew very well that now the culmination of his Quest was denied him. Even as he thought it, and other things more bitter, a burning wind passed by and colours stained against his tight-closed lids. After which the dark returned, without, within.

From the dark a voice spoke at last, at his right shoulder, and it seemed to Cedrevir that he had already heard it once, at the coming of the vision on Midsummer Midnight. But nothing now was to be seen.

"Cedrevir, were you not warned, and did not heed? It is your presumption that has denied you the final prize."

"Lord," Cedrevir replied, "it is my sin which has kept it from me."

"Who are you, before God, to judge yourself or how you sin? Know this. In the moment of the second embrace, you had not lost the Quest. You lost it in the moment that you deemed yourself one fallen, and damned yourself."

"Fallen and damned I was. My vows were broken."

"And who are you to say you will never sin? Are you not a human man? Or are you a god, who is above sin?"

"I am a man. A sinner, and cast from grace."

"Since you must be perfect in your own eyes, Knight, perfect as God, it is your own grace that you have fallen from. It is not for you to know how God has judged you, blameless or to blame. But be assured of this, even the King of All cannot grant you what you stubbornly refuse to take. Go then, Knight. Go down again to the world. Believe this, your fault is forgiven, for a man has only to say *Forgive me* for his sins to be stripped from him. But you are proud. You say in your heart to God, Oh God, forgive me. But to yourself you say, *I* cannot forgive myself. *I will not.*"

After that the voice was silent, and a wan twilight came, and in the twilight Credrevir stumbled down from the high place, over the stair of ebony and ivory, perhaps for many hours, and came at length into the court, the darkness gone, and another lesser darkness come, for already night had shut its wings.

There the willow cascaded to the ground, and on its ghostly weft the trophies of the Knights eerily spangled and swung. No figure was near, but three times round the trunk of the tree was coiled a silvery snake, which hissed at him. When the snake did this, the shield and helm and sword of Cedrevir dropped to the marble. He went and took them up, and in heavy grief turned from the Castle and descended the mountains.

A night and a day he travelled, scarcely knowing what he did, and eventually he lost his way and his wits, and wandered some while.

In a valley of the world, kindly people found him, restored him as best they might, and brought to him a horse that was his own, lean and sad, which they had come on similarly wandering the valley a month before.

Of the Forest of the Savage Hart there was no sign, and the valley was set in verdant hills, flowered with fields and orchardland, though now the winter came on them.

Cedrevir rode south before the snow, which pressed behind him and covered the Earth with its white cloak. So, turning his head, he could yet see the snowy northern mountain-tops for several days, shining up in the sky like shed pieces of the winter moon.

He saw, however, no unusual sights, and no uncommon adventures befell him.

Cedrevir returned, as you yourself have noted. And as he seemed, so he is. The Quest is more often resolved in such failure than in death. For now he knows the colours and the weapons on the willow tree remained of those who journeyed on to some explicit bliss he is denied. Or that he has, as the angel told him, denied for ever to himself.

– But tell me, then, since you have told so much, how do you know it all? His journey and his grief and loss.

– How do I know? How could it be, but that I too, long, long ago, have gone Questing? I too have striven and failed and fallen. I too have heard those awful words and known – not in heart and mind, but in my soul – the truth of them. God it is not, who is cruel. But we ourselves. *Mea culpa. Mea maxima culpa.* I, too.

THE SECRET HISTORY

Peter T. Garratt

We have already encountered Galahad's quest for the Grail in the story by Phyllis Ann Karr. Karr viewed the story from the perspective of the French Romantics and brought her own individual treatment to the traditional story. Peter Garratt (b. 1949) looks at the more sinister aspects of the story, this time through Celtic eyes. The end may be similar but the motives and events are very different. Garratt is a writer and lecturer who reviews Arthurian literature and has given talks on the subject. He has a special interest in the historical authenticity of the period, and this provides substantial background to the following story.

Gwalhwavad came to Artor's hall on the eve of the Feast of Pentecost. This was planned, for the monks who had trained him to the sword as well as the cloister believed that a youth who joined the defenders of Christ on that day would flourish mightily in the Lord's service. Some had been warriors in the days when every man had had to carry arms against the enemies of God and the Roman way, unable to retreat from the corruption of the world till victory had been won over worldly foes.

The Scotti: raiders; worshippers of lifeless things, trees and fountains; merciless plunderers; the Picti: painted men; who pricked their skin under dyes to be forever graven with images, worshippers of carven stones; worst of all, the Saxenach: creators of the Wasted Land; worshippers and raisers of demons.

There was talk also of the Atecotti, the strange older race who had lived before the first true men, whom some said had vanished from the Earth, but whom others claimed still lived in secret places just out of view, in the corner of men's eyes. But scholars said these were trifling tales to be turned from.

Gwalhwavad rode through lands whence the citizens had driven their enemies, guided by Brother Illtud's map. He rode his large pony, wearing tunic and leggings of brown homespun and a simple circle-cross. The small pony carried his armour, mostly iron rings stitched to leather, carefully wrapped and oiled. There was also the bronze helmet, with its horsehair crest still just about red – the dark just-red of drying blood.

He stayed with monks where he could, but a few times had to lodge in cities. Great walls of mortared stone, leaning columns still flecked with white paint, half-blocked fountains, fine houses ill-repaired or falling down and used as dens for pigs, all showed what these cities had once been and had become. He avoided the baths where they were still open, for more even than the city smells of decay and pig-dung, he disliked the women who went there but could not be cleaned by water.

At the monastery of Ynis Witrin, the Glass Island, he met the preacher Gildas. This dour but educated cleric scorned the widespread view that Gwalhwavad was travelling to the greatest stronghold of Christianity in Britain. "These people are not what they seem. They may hang around the altar at Matins, but by noon they idle in luxury, listening to frivolous bards, drinking wine till they vomit like dogs."

Gwalhwaved was not convinced; indeed he was offended. "How could Defenders of Christ live like that?"

"The Bear defends the Roman way. By the end, Rome did accept the Light, so he will protect the Church, though only if it keeps what he considers its place. But he yearns for the older Roman times, when men worshipped not demons perhaps, but false Gods even they suspected did not truly exist."

Before Gwalhwavad could reply, Gildas warmed to what was clearly a favourite theme. "Nor is his personal life any less impure. It's well know that Artor allows his wife to sleep with his false friend Llancalot, while he himself, even worse, has dishonoured his sister's bed, she whom he should most protect!"

Next day Gwalhwavad rode the causeway over the swampy lake round Ynis Witrin, then on to the stronghold. He had seen hill-castels before, but none like this Caer Malat. There were sheep and half-grown lambs on other hills, but they seemed to avoid the steep slope of the fortress. The ditches had been cut deep into the hillside and the wall was of stones; not mortared but pasted in place with daub, reinforced with timber.

Over the gate stood a massive tower, wood also, he realized, though not till he was almost there. He caught glimpses of whitewashed buildings inside the fortress, but all the timber in the walls and towers had been painted the dull grey of the stones.

There were sentries at the gate, men who wore oiled iron rings on their leather even on a hot day in peacetime. They ordered him to wait for the Magister Militum, the legendary Llancalot. Gwalhwavad had to combat the sin of pride in his heart, as he realized so famous a hero would speak to *him*.

Llancalot was old for a warrior. His face was lined as that of a flesh-mortifying hermit, but he stood tall, straight and strong, walking with a spring that took years off him. His hair was a dull, dark brown, which could have been about to turn grey, and his voice seemed younger than his very correct Latin.

He read the message Gwalhwavad brought from Brother Illtud, stating that here was a pure youth who could be both monk and soldier, a Christian warrior untarnished by thoughts of the flesh.

"Why have you come here? This is no monk-house! We don't ask our men to live like monks, and we don't let them smother their knowledge of the real world with religious illusions!"

Gwalhwavad replied hesitantly, unsure how to deal with this strange test. "It's said you are modest men, who reject the sin of pride. But it's known this place is the best." He could not judge the other's reaction, so went on, "So says Brother Illtud, who was a soldier himself before he progressed to other work."

An odd look flickered in Llancalot's eyes, which might have been contempt, could such a man have felt contempt for Brother Illtud. "So! Describe yourself! Do you have any armour but a habit, any weapons sharper than Holy Books?"

"My grandfather's sword, lance, helmet, armour of leather and iron. He ruled the castel of Caer Banak. Do you know it?"

Llancalot nodded. "In the east. It was a Roman fort at the mouth of a river, on the border with the Saxenach. *Then!*"

Gwalhwavad said sadly, "I was sent to the monks when I was young. My grandfather thought Caer Banak was a bad place for a child. Already the Saxenach had laid Waste most of the land from which the soldiers drew their food. He himself was crippled in action, unable to lead his men, reduced to living by fishing. Now all that land is Wasted, barren, infertile . . ."

"Just a minute. The Saxenach are men. It's true they are worse than other men – they worship demons – but they are not demons themselves. They steal the land to till it, in their own crude way; the land itself remains."

"*Your* name was known at Caer Banak! As a demon-slayer!"

Llancalot shook his head. "I have never seen a demon. I am not even sure they exist, though I know the Saxenach worship . . . something dark. But as well as the defence of civilized lands, we do send expeditions to stop the pagans trying to *raise* demons. I suppose that's the kind of adventure you seek?"

"Why, yes! The Lord's work is the greatest adventure. The monks taught me that good work is done here, but better is waiting. I can just remember, from my earliest years at Caer Banak, the Holy Relics that were kept there. Wondrous things which have been lost, which must be found again."

Llancalot snapped, "Wait here!" He turned and strode into the fortress.

Gwalhwavad had extremely good hearing. Not only did he hear footsteps going up into the upper chamber of the gate tower, but he was sure he could hear voices whispering within. He could not quite make out what they were saying, save one snatch of Llancalot's voice: "Even so, I think it best to keep him here, where we can observe what he gets up to."

He found it hard not to be disappointed with his first days at Caer Malat. His quarters, in the small hostel given to the youngest warriors, were more comfortable than he had ever known. There were no leaks in the thatch, or bad draughts, and the mattress was full of fresh straw. But the lack of privacy distressed him, for some of the others committed the amazing sin of bringing their camp-followers into the hostel. The rank stench of their lust pervaded the place like rotten fish.

He prayed for them in the church. It was in the shape of a cross, an innovation he approved, but was the flimsiest building on the hilltop. The Great Hall, the hostels of the warriors, and the large fenced building where dwelled the Viri Modesti, the rulers of Caer Malat, were all more solidly built. The church was of thin planks, lightly tacked together. The draughts were an integral part of the penance one paid on vigil, but he worried that in a storm the whole structure could be blown away – quite the reverse of the message a church should have built into it. It smelled more of wind than incense.

Pentecost itself was a shock. He had expected a day of prayer, as happened among the monks. Instead, though there was a brief, unenthusiastic service, his new companions spoke only of the Feast. He found himself kneeling alone in the rickety church.

At length he became aware, perhaps just by hearing breathing, of someone else. He awkwardly stood up, became aware of a silent, hooded figure in the doorway, regarding him.

"You're new here, aren't you?"

He was shocked at first to realize the speaker was a woman, but decided it was scarcely Christian to be offended by her sex alone. She was tall and wore a long, loose garment of plain cloth, quite unlike the dresses of the camp-followers whose presence degraded the castel. He bowed and said, "Yes. My name is Gwalhwavad."

She tutted, before leading the way into the light, obviously anxious to avoid being compromised. "Hasn't anyone told you to use proper Latin names here? Artorius hates Vulgar nicknames."

"Gallus Habilis. Should I refer to . . . to Lanus Callistus?"

"Always. And to the Dux as Artorius. Never, ever, use the Vulgar name 'The Bear'." She had a round, innocent face, clear skin, no hint of face-paint – one he could trust. "I'm Viviana. Here at Cavella Belgorum, everything is Roman." She gave a delightful, tinkling laugh. "Why, I think Artorius would insist on living in the family villa still, if it was in a defendable position and he could find anyone to repair the tile roof!"

"*The* family? You are of the Modesti?"

"A distant relative. I am Artorius's ward. He likes me to take an interest in the new arrivals, especially those of special religious dedication." Before he could reply, she hurried on, "Come! It is time for the Feast!"

Gwalhwavad had never eaten so well in his life, nor drunk wine away from communion, even watered. He could not continue his talk with Viviana, who used a couch with the other Modesti, though he noticed she was the only woman modestly dressed. The meat was fresh and cooked with a rich, tempting spice, hot and sweet, with only wine or mead to wash it down.

Perhaps it was that which made his mind wander back to the warning of Gildas, and his heart was troubled as the Feast drew to an end.

His eyes kept flitting to the richly dressed group who reclined

on couches round a circular table on the platform at the top of
the Hall. He did not want to try and read the characters of the
women by looking too long, so he studied the War Lord. Artorius
was said to be very old, but like Llancalot he was a very tall man
whose careworn face was belied by a tough physique.

At length Artorius rose and indicated that he would withdraw to
discuss business with his most important guest. This was Cato, the
official ruler of all South-Western Britannia. Rumour was unclear
whether Artorius paid meaningful tribute to Cato.

But Cato did not turn to leave. He stood on his couch, and
shouted till he had the attention of everyone in the Hall. "I wish to
thank my host. I wish to thank him by *not* conducting our business
in secret, but here, where the warriors can hear what we say!

"I have spent this past year travelling and visiting the courts of
the kings and consuls of Britannia. One theme I heard everywhere:
Britannia is weary of peace, but unprepared for war. Men thirst
for action against the Saxenach, yet, divided as they are, success
is doubtful."

Men were starting to nod around the Hall. Artorius tried to
intervene, but Cato ignored him: "All the leaders, Aelius of
Corinium, Cuneglassus of Viriconium, Vortiporius Protector of
the West, Peredur of Ebrauc, who overcame the vile Pict Andru
map Roburt, agree that we need a High King . . ."

"Emperor!" Artorius interrupted.

"Use what title you wish! The kings want the victor of the twelve
battles to lead them!"

There was cheering and the banging of dagger-hilts on the
tables. Artorius's face was hard, unreadable. His voice was quiet,
but carried through the Hall and instantly stilled the noise.

"I am very old." He ignored the expressions of cheerful disbelief.
"So old I remember more of the true Roman way than anyone else
alive. Government should be by a Senatus of the great nobles of
the Republic. These should meet regularly, and elect an Emperor
from the most noble of them."

"None of the men you call noble compares to yourself!" Cato
shouted. "Most wouldn't attend the Senate you believe in . . ."

Someone yelled, "They fear the Saxenach!"

"They're just as afraid of their own heirs and officers!"

Artorius was shaking his head slowly, as though despite his
experience he was bewildered by this turn of events. "The Roman
Empire civilized the world for six hundred years. Centuries of
stability! What human institution has endured so well, for so long?

The Senatus was led by the most noble, and the great emperors came from their ranks. My family are minor landowners. Some would almost doubt our claim to be Viri Modesti."

He ignored the disbelieving shouts and ploughed on, "Only the gravest crisis of the Empire provoked us to a role above our station! When the plague laid low the heads of the noblest houses, Vortigern seized illegitimate power, invited Barbarians into this province, and tried to revive the ancient worship of demons – even planned to sacrifice the true heir to his mentors.

"*Then* a man of doubtful birth had no option but to act. I have fought many battles and seen more vile things than any of you: pestilence, superstition, the destruction of the Roman way even in Rome itself. Do not ask that my modest contribution be sullied by adding to the disorder and disrespect for rank!"

Heads were shaking around the Hall. Gwalhwavad could see that many of the warriors could not understand their leader's reluctance to usurp supreme worldly power.

Cato answered in a colder voice, "So! Where will Artorius stand, if Mailcunn of Guenedota, who already calls himself Dragon, should declare himself PenDragon of all Britannia? Or Medraut of Din Eidin, that wild man whom many say is kin of yours . . ."

Artorius snapped, "One thing is certain. I tell you this: Medraut will never be ruler of Britannia!"

Something took Gwalhwavad to his feet. Perhaps it was an awareness that Artorius was resisting the temptation offered by Cato but might be manoeuvred by fear of this Medraut, known as a warlord almost as savage as the Picts whose lands bordered his own.

"I . . . Gallus Habilis, am new to this stronghold. But I pledge on this Holy day that my sword belongs only, after God, to the leader who resists the temptation of worldly power!"

People stared at him in surprise. Some seemed to approve; he noticed Viviana smile. Inspired, he continued, "I was born in a land now Wasted and lost to the Saxenach. Lost with it were Holy Relics, even including the sacred chalice of the Last Supper, brought hither by Joseph of Arimathea.

"Two years ago, on a day just after the feast of Holy Valentine, the Lord granted us a sign. The sun was blotted out of the sky, stars appeared in daytime, and we were granted a vision of the Grail like a crown of fire in the sky where the sun had been: the most beautiful, the most awesome thing Man's eyes have ever seen!

"Now I know the meaning of that sign! With your inspiration to guide us, we will drive the pagans right out of the island, regain the lost relics, and make Britannia such a centre of Christian sanctity as has never been known before!"

Surprised at himself, he sat down. Many warriors banged the table and shouted approval; but he noticed that Artorius frowned at his presumption, and the rest of the nobles at the top of the Hall were slow and reluctant to join the applause.

The trees in the forest grew so densely that Gwalhwavad could not tell if the sun had actually risen. Above, he could just see the sky, whose mid-blue colour could have been that of pre-dawn light, but as he rode along the path towards the east, he fancied he could see much brighter, redder light through the tightly interlaced branches.

Though in most places dew was still visible on the leaves of the undergrowth, in others it was rising into mist, so trees would loom into the path and make him think of the ancient, immobile spirits men had worshipped before they were brought to the Light.

Gwalhwavad would not have chosen to ride at dawn, but Llancalot had insisted it was the key time to prevent the work of Darkness being done.

It was quiet for the hour, as if the birds were still asleep, but ahead there was noise – heavy, tuneless drums and the sound of voices singing – no, this wasn't like a psalm – shouting a chant. Then a man stepped into the path, and halted in shock at the sight of a mounted warrior.

He wore armour of a sort: black leather jerkin and helmet, a massive dagger, and a cape decorated with crude, leering images of faces. Gwalhwavad realized with a cold feeling that this was a Pagan, a man who worshipped lifeless things, who might be prepared, in despair at the unsatisfying nature of his cult, to raise demons. The man ran to a massive horn hung at mouth-height from a broken bough of a tree, placed it to his lips to blast a warning.

Gwalhwavad realized there would be no time to reason with the man, to bring him to the Light. That was a mercy the Saxenach did not allow themselves. The man was in spear-throw; he raised the lance, kicked his horse forward, and cast as he had been taught. The man had time to start his blast, a loud, strangely musical note, cut off into a hideous resonating gurgle as the spearhead pierced his leather and ploughed into his chest.

Gwalhwaved cantered forward to recover his lance, which

looked easy at first, as the man had collapsed backwards with the weapon wobbling upright in the wound, but as Gwalhwavad grasped it the man started jerking in wild frenzy, so the pony reared and smashed the doomed Pagan with its hooves.

There was more noise ahead, shouts and, he thought, screams. The rest of Llancalot's company had fallen behind, and the pony was small to gallop with an armoured rider, but he did not hesitate to urge it forward. There was little mist in that part of the forest, and he soon saw light ahead, between massive tree-trunks. The path ended in in a large clearing, surrounded by a ring of vastly old, pre-Roman oaks. There, he at once took in a scene he had dreaded, but had been warned to expect.

The clearing seemed full of people; he had no time to count. There were a few immodestly dressed women, though most were warriors like the one he had just struck down. Some cast around for the source of the alarm, but the majority were surrounding a young woman, the only one decently clad, and dragging her toward a rough altar of earth which he saw had been dug from a pit like a grave.

He saw two things which chilled; a cross on the girl's dress and, standing by the altar, a horrifying figure. This man was dressed all in red, he bore a huge knife like an axeblade and, worst of all, his helmet was decorated with the antlers of a stag, like the horns of a demon!

Now the girl was thrust onto the crude altar, and the devil-priest lifted his knife. Gwalhwavad was still galloping, but not near enough. Some providential force impelled him to raise his spear and again hurl it, though the range was great. For a moment he thought he had wasted the lance, but his extra speed and rage carried it on, and it struck the horned priest just under the shoulder of his raised knife-arm, so he dropped the weapon, swayed and collapsed into the grave dug for his victim.

Consternation reigned among the other Pagans. Gwalhwavad tugged out his sword and started striking out as he thundered among them. He never knew how long the fight lasted, but it seemed an age before he heard the hoofbeats of his companions enter the glade behind him. During that time some weapon had bounced off his shield, and another off his helmet, nearly stunning him, and he had struck down three or four more Saxenach. He didn't care if they were wounded or dead.

When they heard the others, the remaining Saxenach turned and fled. Gwalhwavad rode to the makeshift altar, where he found the girl collapsed after her ordeal. Her dress would have been decent, had it not been ripped right open at the top, but it was strangely woven, in bands of colour decorated with leaf-shapes. She was frozen in the last stages of terror, like a bird in the claws of a tom-cat, but at the sight of Gwalhwavad victorious, she jerked upright, then collapsed on her knees beside his pony, grasping at his boots to kiss his feet.

Red light poured through sudden gaps in the trees, as in a church which had kept its Roman windows of tinted glass, making the grass, the leaves on the oaks and the ivy seem greener.

Llancalot rode up. "You did well," he said gruffly. "But you got too far ahead. I thought we'd lost you in both senses." He glanced at the girl. "Still, you've got your reward there. She'll be all over you tonight."

Gwalhwavad blushed as he disengaged himself from the girl to dismount from the winded pony. He helped her to her feet, reverently touched the cross. "Dishonour a Christian woman!"

Llancalot shook his head. "That's not a real cross, just an ornament that resembles one. She's not Roman; she's a captive from another Pagan tribe; Anglish from the style of her dress."

"Even so, she's one of God's creatures. She might be brought to the Light if we treat her better than her kinsmen did."

Llancalot looked at him oddly, then said, "You were born at Caer Banak. Which daughter of the King of the Fishers was your mother? Was her name Elaina?"

Gwalhwavad nodded glumly, remembering that it had been years slice he had had news of his family.

"I knew her once, years ago, before you were born. She was a good woman. But be warned: we are living in an age of Darkness. For you, her goodness may not be a sufficient inheritance."

Gwalhwavad's second arrival at Caer Malat was more spectacular than his first. Word of his almost single-handed victory over the demon-raisers had been sent ahead, and the whole stronghold turned out to salute him.

Viviana wore a demure white dress, without a hood in the heat. She had decorated her hair with flowers, and had prepared a wreath of oak leaves for him. "The correct Roman wreath for a conquering hero was laurel, but that's hard to find in this climate."

In turn he handed over to her the rescued Anglish girl, who had informed him via Llancalot, who knew the strange talk of the Barbarians, that she was now his *churl*. Viviana would be more able to teach the duties of a Christian woman than he.

He hastened to the church, was not that surprised to find it almost empty. A single, habited figure knelt before the altar, but rose at the sound of footsteps, and he recognized Gildas.

"So! The new hero of the Bear's stronghold!"

"By God's Grace, I did lead our victorious charge."

"And gained an Anglish concubine to add to the Roman one."

Gwalhwavad was unused to talking back to the clergy, but on that of all days the preacher's words stung him. "If, Brother, you knew Lady Viviana as I do, you would not speak so!"

"I spoke of the future, as much as the past. Nothing here is as it seems, as you will see."

He had not thought what part Viviana might play in his future. He was not yet a monk, though he had always assumed he would eventually take vows. He said, "Viviana is a good woman, and loyal to the Dux. He resists more temptations than most of us could imagine. Truly, Artorius is a giant among men!"

"A giant?" Gildas raised one eyebrow and came close. He had an odd smell. It wasn't rank, for he cleaned and subdued his body by immersing it in the coldest hillside streams, it was a smell of old, half-rotten leather and papyrus, of long nights handling books. "Is it not written that in the oldest days, soon after the Fall, there were then giants in the Earth?"

"In those days, yes," Gwalhwavad answered at once, still at heart a young scholar. "Long ago, before even the Patriarchs."

"Indeed. But giants are children of Lilith, and, like all evil things, have the power to dissemble and alter their shape. Luckily, it is in their nature to exaggerate, so if you seek that which is most rotten within, look first at that which seems fairest. But do not look too long!"

"I don't intend to hang around here for too long looking at

anything! I intend to find the Sangrail of the Last Supper, which I saw when I was young and later in a vision."

"What! By yourself?"

"There are many warriors here who would join such a Quest!"

Gildas nodded slowly. "Aye, but for what purpose? Do you know that the Bear, like all warlords, extorts provisions and cattle, not only from peasants but from holy monks? Let me tell you that he also steals Holy Relics, objects of veneration and pilgrimage. He stole the beautiful tunic the Patriarch of Jerusalem gave to Brother Paternus, and the marvellous floating altar of Brother Carranog, saying he meant to trade them for Roman gold coins. Have you seen the fool's gold?"

Gwalhwavad had never seen any gold coin. None had been left at Caer Banak, or needed at the monastery. When he had set out, Illtud had given him a bag of ancient silver discs, so worn he could not read the inscriptions. To his surprise, these baubles could be traded for supplies. "No one could dream of selling the Sangrail!" he said now. "I will ensure that never happens!"

"Wise men say the Sangrail never came to these shores, that the tales told of it are the same the Druids told of their Cauldron of Plenty, in the days before the Light!"

That was enough. "Do not wise men say the Lost Tribes of Israel came to this Island? Why should all wisdom have been given to the one tribe which betrayed Our Lord? Do you say our ancestors were no better than the demon-worshippers?"

Before Gildas could confirm that he was indeed saying that, Gwalhwavad had stormed off to the Feast. An extra couch had been found for him to join the nobles at the high table; he looked at it suspiciously, for it was an old one, and looked perilously rickety, but, as the alternative was Llancalot's more dangerous suggestion that he share Viviana's couch, he used it.

Cato was there, and had brought his court bard, one Bryan ap Drustan, the most famous in the land. This man he requested to sing a favourite, "The Battle Song of Artor the War Leader".

Gwalhwavad was unused to profane music, but as the bard tuned his harp the chords thrilled him, prepared him for the words:

I sing of Artor, Leader of Men, Leader of Battles,
Leader of Kings.
He men call "The Iron Hammer of the Saxenach";
And the Sax call "Dreadful Bear", ravager of their lands,
The stolen lands.
I saw Artor, the man from nowhere,
Less noble than many, many said.
Lead the kings of Britannia in the wars.
First I saw Artor, at the mouth of the river
Men call "Clear Water"
Clear was the victor, muddy the water with red.
I saw Artor the second time, on the banks of
     the river
In Linnuis, called "Black Water"
The third battle, the fourth victory,
The fifth triumph of Artor,
The battles at the ford
Where Black Water remained black, clotted with
     heathen blood.
And I saw him again on the river men call "Bassas"
The sixth battle of Artor
Sweet was the mead in Artor's Hall, after the
     battle of Bassas
Truthful the boasting.
I saw Artor ride to Caledonia, the farthest part
     of Britain
Campaigning at the ends of the world, in the
     Silver Forest,
Putting the Painted Ones to flight in the Wood of Caledon
Blue was the paint that I saw on the heathen bodies,
Dark were their wounds, overpainted with blood.
I saw Artor don the image of St Mary, Ever-Virgin
In the Castel Guinnion, where the eighth battle was fought:
I saw the Pagans put to flight on that day
And a great slaughter made of them
By the power of Our Lord and His Mother
     the Virgin.
I heard the ring of soldiers' boot,
Drowned by their clamour of voices
Crying "Emperor", after the ninth battle
In the City of the Legion.
I saw the enemies of Britain gather

Crows upon the wind.
I watched the crows feeding, happy in gluttony
Gorging on Anglish blood
Fed by the sword of Artor, on the river men call "Tribruit"
After the tenth battle.
I saw the enemy shudder at the name of Artor
I heard the Anglish crying across the sea
Sending for kings to lead them, to the Isle of Angeln,
To Juteland and Saxeland; crying, those trusters in kings.
I saw the battle of Agned
The eleventh victory of Artor.
I saw the men of Artor march to Mont Badon, them
    alone I saw
Save for the enemies of our country
They at least were there.
I did not see you Medraut, little king, pretender to
    the name.
Any more than Aelius, taking the words
"Last of the Romans", better known
As the last of men.
I did not see Vortipor, Protector, by your title,
Of the land farthest from the enemy.
Or Cuneglass, before you were a king, my master's
    coachman:
The chariot-driver of the Bear's Stronghold.
And least of all did I see
Mailcunn, Dragon of the land of Guenedota, breather
    of fire
And mead: the king of air and shadow.
Three times three hundred Saxemen did I see
And threescore, and three
Slain by the sword of Artor
And no other brought them to the dew
And no other rusted their mail-coats
And Artor remains victorious in all his battles
The Anglish know this, if the kings do not:
He will be named in song, three times three
    hundred years
And three times three times threescore after that;
And those who are enemies to his name
Will be forgotten, and will sleep
As sleep his enemies!

The Hall filled with applause and the rattle of hilt on board; there were cries of "Artorius, Imperator! Artor, PenDragon!"

Artorius frowned; Gwalhwavad realized the warlord was too modest to be pleased. Seeing Cato about to rise, Gwalhwavad jumped up, called for silence.

"As guest of honour, let *me* speak. Let us not annoy our leader with the pressing of honours and offices he does not seek; let us dedicate ourselves to a higher purpose. The Sangrail, the sacred link between the light of Our Lord and the ancient wisdom of the Druids has been lost. Let us honour Artorius by pledging ourselves to find that Holy Relic. The Quest I predicted at Pentecost begins today!"

Artorius showed no gratitude; indeed, he lost his composure and for the first time showed his age, feebly worrying that the unity of his command would be damaged by the pursuit of a rainbow dream.

As the young warriors spread out in search of news of the Grail, Gwalhwavad determined to make the hazardous journey to Caer Banak, where it had once been. Llancalot insisted on escorting him – as, mysteriously, did Viviana.

For three days they rode east, along roads the Romans had left. On the third afternoon, instead of camping, they waited beside the river known to the Saxenach as Mercredsburn, "Frontier-stream", and to civilized folk as "Black Water".

Llancalot explained that here they had defeated the Saxenach four times in the old days, giving a kind of peace. Then he went to find the boat one of his agents kept hidden there.

Gwalhwavad turned to Viviana. "It'd be safer if you went back."

Her face was pale, but she did not look afraid. "Why? I'm too young to marry, but too old to cower at home. The Saxenach of the woods fear us. They will not attack two armed horsemen."

"So I hope. But this is dangerous work for a woman."

"It could be dangerous for you too, Gallus. You think because my face is fair that I am young and weak. But –" and hear she changed to a strange voice he had not heard "– there are dangers you cannot guess at; cannot dream of!"

For the first time he felt seriously afraid, but not of dangers that lay ahead. He remembered Gildas's talk of fair beings that were not as they seemed. He said roughly, "This Quest is not what I expected. Why, Warlord Artorius scarcely gave it his blessing!"

She hesitated, then said carefully, "That is why I am concerned for you. There are secret things ... I want you to know that I admire you very much, and for that reason I'll tell you a little of them. But only if you swear by your vision of the Grail not to pass my words on."

For the first time in his life Gwalhwavad felt terrified. He was being tempted to swear away his right to make public anything he might discover, and that would include the evil mysteries Brother Gildas had predicted. Finally he said, "In honour, I can only swear to conceal matters that do not contradict the True Religion."

She sighed and said, "What is the true religion?" Dreadful words that reflected those of Pontius Pilate. Before he could upbraid her, she went on sadly, "I know you are a man of honour. Therefore I will trust you this far.

"Not only is Artorius older than he looks, but our family records go back very many generations. We are Roman citizens, but our family was old before the first Roman brought his eagle to this land."

"Why should that be a secret?" he asked suspiciously.

"Because ancient blood, ancient claims – these are dangerous. They attract the attention of insecure tyrants. Because the family is so old, we have few allies, save others who are distant relatives. Like us, they prefer to study and live quietly. I could tell you ... at one time, our kind were much persecuted, till we learned to lie low. You know Artorius could be the Emperor of this island, but he resists that temptation."

"That's true!" Gwalhwavad muttered.

"He is very wise. There have been many religions, since the building of the stone circles and before. Perhaps yours is the most true. But Artorius fears you have an excess of faith, that too much devotion in the hunt for miracles can make the walls between the worlds weaker ..."

"May Jesus Christ protect us from the demons of the Otherworld!" he exclaimed, then realized he had referred to the ancient, superstitious lore of the island's tribes, not to the demons truthfully described in Holy Writ. "Can demons be stronger than the Light?"

She pointed to the late afternoon sun. It was not far above the level of the tree-tops, but had not yet started to turn red. She made a show of not looking directly at it, saying, "Could you stare right into it? Would you at noon?"

He flinched. Brother Illtud had warned him against exactly this. And monks did not embark on wild quests.

She went on softly, "You could be a great lord at Caer Malat. Not a king or emperor, no, but the Dux has no successor. Sometimes a promising young man may marry into the family . . ."

It was very tempting. To marry a respectable girl like this one hadn't been Gwalhwavad's plan, but it would be allowed. But it was a temptation, and he had been warned against those.

"I must keep my chastity till I find the Sangrail. Then . . . who knows? If I burn out my eyes, I shall have to become a monk. If not . . ." He could be the Warlord of the Island, married into its oldest family. Lord of the World. He said angrily, "Why were your ancestors persecuted? Were they giants?"

She snapped back, "For being ancient, and different, and here first!" In anger her face looked different, indeed wild, as if she had relaxed a disguise. Then she changed again, said playfully, "Look at me. Am I a giant? If you were to slay me, would the people hail you as a hero?"

He felt revolted at his own intolerance, at the suspicion that it might lead him to kill a woman – especially this one.

Llancalot returned with the boat. It was big enough to take them and their horses. They travelled all through that night.

By the early summer dawn, they were well within the great forest which ran through the Wasted Land. Here, men were few, but there were still passable roads. These were overhung by trees, so they sometimes had to lead the horses, but easier to ride than the forest paths. If there were Saxenach they saw none, only the occasional roe deer.

They pressed on till sunset, making good time. At last Llancalot called a halt. "We are all tired. Tomorrow we must cross another river, then it is less than a day's journey to Caer Banak."

"I hope so," Gwalhwavad said. "For we are near the longest day of Midsummer, which the folk celebrated when I was a child. Surely that day some vision of the Grail will be granted us!"

Llancalot frowned. "Be confident, but be prepared for disappointment and distress. My spies tell me no Roman fortress has held out against the Saxenach this far to the east. The Barbarians will not be dwelling there themselves, for part of their superstition is a terror of the spirits of dead enemies, but you must prepare yourself for one of the scenes of desolation no one who rides the Wasted Lands may avoid."

Gwalhwavad wondered briefly at the kind of man who could be

a spy, moving among the Pagans, perhaps sharing their hideous way of life. With a shudder, he asked, "If you have so little confidence in my vision, why have you joined our Quest?"

"Many saw the vision of the cup of fire. It is a natural thing the ancients often noticed in the sky. You are too young to have experience of such things."

Llancalot paused, then said heavily, "I spoke as I did through my own fear of what we shall see at Caer Banak. Many years ago I passed through the place, when I was young and loved to wander. I knew your mother and her kin, and once I made a promise, that I would do all in my power to protect her and hers. Other duties kept me from Caer Banak in later years, so all of the promise I can fulfil is to help and guide you, as if you were my son as well as hers."

They pitched Viviana's little tent and their larger one in a small glade, less regular and sinister than the oak-grove of the demon-raisers.

Viviana seemed to have lost her nerve at last; she produced a skin of spiced wine and drank from it, persuaded Gwalhwavad to do the same. It had an unfortunate effect on her. He remarked that she had pinned her dress with the odd cross that had belonged to the Anglish girl, and she at once unfastened it, saying the cross belonged rightfully to him.

The dress fell open so he could see the tops of her breasts in the firelight; something which should never happen with a respectable woman. Before he could decide how to point this out, she said, "Llancalot will go during the night to look for a boat. Will you not sleep in my tent to guard me?" She offered the wineskin again; it looked about half-full.

He shook his head vigorously. "That would be dishonourable. UnChristian!" He found he knew for certain what would happen if he did share her tent, was shocked by the intensity of his desire. Instead, he vowed to sleep in blanket and armour across the tent entrance, his sword driven into the ground as a symbol of respectful distance.

His sleep was heavy, but disturbed; sometimes he did not know if he slept or woke. Once, he fancied he heard voices, but could not stir himself to investigate them:

"I failed, as you see."

"The man must be made of iron. I would not harm him if it can be avoided, but how?"

"Give me one more chance. Please, I beg it!"

"One. Remember, he must not see what will happen tomorrow in the morning."

"Does it matter so much? He saw it once before!"

"He was nobody then! Now, already a hero, he could unleash the demons of fanaticism that have kept us in hiding through the ages! You have till noon. If all is well we can travel, and I doubt anything will come of this Quest; but whatever happens, he must not see what will come before!"

Gwalhwavad awoke bleary from the wine and stiff from cold. The sun was already in the sky, but dew had soaked his blanket. The camp was empty; neither Llancalot nor Viviana were to be seen. He worried, and remembering Gildas's words about the girl and her morals only made that worse. But he had his Quest. He broke his fast with bread and cheese, packed his own equipment, and rode down the old road towards the sun.

Mist was rising in glittering patches, so he passed through many zones of light: some with the warmth of morning, others chill with fog. It was not silent in the forest, morning birds were calling from their branches, but there was no sight or sound of the presence of men.

After less than an hour he came to the river. It wasn't wide, but was flowing fast and looked too deep to ford. The road ended abruptly in a patch of marshy ground without a proper bank; reeds extended into the river a little, then stopped abruptly.

He wondered how to proceed. Swimming was one of the few arts the monks had not taught him. He dismounted from the pony, which was certainly too small to carry him across. As he tried to decide if the Romans had used a bridge or a ferry, his acute ears became aware of something from upstream, hardly a sound, merely difference in the silence.

A bank of mist rose from the water there and he could just see a shape emerging from it. By straining his eyes, he was able to identify it as a ship or large boat: it was bigger than the coracles of fishermen, at least twenty feet long, of timber, with a peak-roofed cabin in the middle occupying half the length and the whole beam.

Viviana sat in the stern. She wore a light summer dress of a colour he could only think of as gold ochre as she emerged from the mist and caught the light of the sun, and she wore a crown and necklace of lilies. Gwalhwavad realized as the boat passed slowly, without oar or sail, through patches of sunlight and shadow, that he had never seen anything so beautiful, that a rebel part of his soul even compared this to the vision of the Grail he had been given two years before.

When she saw him, she smiled and waved, and made a movement which turned the boat towards the shore. She had a steering oar under her arm, but it was inefficient, for the boat ran right into the reeds and seemed to ground itself. Vivian jumped up, trying to paddle, overbalanced, and fell into the water; she struggled to her feet, being about waist-deep, grasped the gunwhale and only succeeded in pushing it much further aground.

He ran into the shallows. His first thought was to get her ashore, but she wanted to be helped back into the boat. He had to touch her body to do this, and was amazed at its suppleness and softness. She was flushed and sweating, and he caught the smell of her; strong, overwhelmingly sensuous, but with a hint of something alien. A scent that had madness in it.

In turn, she helped him aboard. The boat shifted, and he said, "We'll soon get this afloat."

"Later," she replied. "This river is tidal, and the water will be higher by noon. I'll catch cold if I stay in this wet dress." By now he was not surprised when she pulled it slowly over her head, nor that she wore nothing beneath it, so she stood naked before him save for her garlands of flowers.

She gave the dress a cursory check for mud, then spread it on the place where the sun caught the cabin roof. Amazed, he watched the way her body moved as she performed this mundane task, which her nakedness rendered extraordinary. Finishing, she gave an impudent smile, as if there was nothing in the world more natural than to undress merely because wet, then her expression became concerned.

"Gallus! You're soaking too! And me thinking only of myself!"

He shrugged, said lamely, "I'll be fine."

"But your armour! Your precious armour! Your mail-rings will rust if we don't ensure the sun dries it!" She stepped right up to him and started tugging at the ties, saying, "I know you're a modest man, but you can step into the cabin, and there's a big blanket we can both dry off with. We'll hang the armour over the door, and no one will be able to see in."

He looked at the cabin. It was solidly built, more so, he felt, than the church at Caer Malat. It was true that no light could get in; inside it was as dark as night. He glared at her in shame at his temptation, all his suspicions roused.

"Just a minute! How could you know the tides of this river, which flows through land long lost to the Saxenach?"

She did not reply directly, but, ignoring her own advice of the previous day, looked carefully at the sun, as though trying to tell the exact time. Doing that changed her mood again, and she seized his wrist with surprising strength, started pulling him forward. "Stupid man! Stop arguing and do as I say for once!"

"What are you?" he snapped. "You have the moral weakness of your sex, if not the physical!"

She made no reply, and continued dragging him forward, her nails digging now into his flesh like talons. Furious, he slapped her face hard, the first time he had ever hit a woman. At first it just reddened, like a bruised fruit, but then a more terrible change came over her countenance, and she snarled, "And what are you? Spineless, lifeless, superstitious thing! You're not even a man! You're less than a man!" Her voice had lost all trace of mortal woman, now full of the hideous scorn of a fury from Hell, which, to his horror, he realized was what she must be.

As if to prove it, she raked the nails of her free hand towards his eyes, an attack he only ducked at the expense of the skin of his forehead, which she almost ripped off.

Blood almost blinding him, he reached out with his free hand, found her throat, pushed her back viciously until she stumbled and her neck or head cracked against the peak of the cabin roof, which smashed and left her slumped and broken in the bottom of the boat. Blood poured briefly from her mouth and nose, then trickled to a stop.

He tried to brush his own blood from his eyes. Though she had not turned into a total fiend and leapt into the Pit of Fire, it seemed that in death she looked different yet. True, she had not revealed her demon shape, and vanished amid sulphurous fumes, but her dead face seemed again to be changing, starting to look like something which was only a cousin to a woman.

His eyes were blurring, and he could not be quite sure; it was as if darkness were spreading over the land. He did hear hoofbeats, and looking up, saw Llancalot riding down the old road.

The warrior must have guessed at something amiss, for he urged his horse into the water, right up to the boat, and vaulted aboard like a man half his age. He took in the situation at once, and cried in an anguished voice, "You madman! You have killed Vivie!" Now, like Artor, he did look his age, and tears appeared at the corners of his eyes.

Gwalhwavad again brushed the blood from his own eyes, said, "I am not mad. She sought to corrupt me and tempt me to Hell, in sight of the goal of my Quest. Look! See how the fiend's appearance is changed now her evil spirit is driven out!"

Llancalot said wretchedly, "Her sweet face is changed indeed, by murder! But that is nothing to the changes I have seen after death. It is only the bad light . . ."

He looked fearfully upward. Something was indeed happening to the light; a shadow had appeared over the sun, a black disc, growing as they glanced and then averted their gaze, reducing it to a crescent of fire.

Gwalhwavad breathed, "Again, a day shadowy as night! Oh, Dear God, You have delivered me today from the temptation of the Fiend, and now You show me a second time the Holy Sign!"

Llancalot shouted at him, "You fool! This is but a natural phenomena which can be predicted – has been for millennia!"

He replied, "Get thee behind me, Satan!" but without force, for he knew the fiend preferred female shape and had been vanquished in it. Instead, he fell to his knees, and a deeper silence settled over the land, as the birds were surprised by the unexpected night. Soon there was but a tiny rim of sun; stars were appearing in the daytime, and an owl, suddenly awake, hooted loudly.

Now the sun was nothing but a round shadow in the sky, like the base of some celestial cup, from around whose rim there shone an infinitely beautiful crown of light, both soft and wild against the blackness, as though the cup contained all truth and all mystery.

Even Llancalot felt he could have worshipped it, had he been a being capable of worship. Instead, he drew his sword silently. He was an old warrior, one who knew how to kill swiftly, almost without pain, so that Gwalhwavad, lost in the ecstasy of his devotion, hardly knew he was dying.

On the road from Black Water to Caer Malat, Llancalot met the preacher Gildas, who asked him what had become of his companion. He did not deign to mention Viviana. "Did he find what he sought?"

Llancalot nodded stiffly. "I believe so. Yet the holy thing was too much for him. He sought a thing no mortal man should seek."

He tried to read the preacher's face, and could not. He decided to speak clearly. "Preacher Gildas, men say that although you do not wear a bishop's robe, you are the most influential churchman in this Island. Furthermore, they say you are writing a book."

Modesty and realism clashed in the preacher's eyes, and in the end he nodded slowly.

Llancalot continued, "Men even call you, 'The Wisest of the Britons'. I suspect that is because you know well how far you can go in your preaching – who to attack and who to leave alone. If that is so, you will know to be discreet in what you write also."

Gildas absorbed this, pondering, no doubt, on the age-old problems of the churchman confronted with overwhelming worldly force. In the end, he sidestepped. "How about you? Did you behold the mighty thing which was too much for Gwalhwavad?"

"I did. But I only saw it from a distance."

————

This secret history is the only true record of the events it describes, for Gildas did ignore them, even leaving out the name of the ruler he called The Bear. But, according to the Anglo-Saxon Chronicle, *the sun was eclipsed on 16 February AD 538 and 20 June AD 540, both times around nine o'clock a.m.*

AN IDYLL OF THE GRAIL

Phyllis Ann Karr

Phyllis Ann Karr returns to bring us towards the end of the Arthurian age. This poem reminds us all too poignantly of the likely consequences of adventure and the effects on those left behind.

The lady Guenevere, who once was queen
And ruled all Britain with a gracious hand
Beside her lord, lived now a cloistered nun,
Her days a round of prayer, and work, and prayer,
Her nights a narrow cot, and memories,
Alone, unlighted, in her narrow cell.
And there were those among her fellow nuns
Who whispered that it must be mocking God
To clothe her in the same unblemished white
That marked their house of holy, prayerful dames.
But others bowed still to her former state.
And so the convent seethed in hushed ferment
Round one who wanted only to forget.
She who had helped to hold the very realm
In peace for years, now caused a petty war.
She had no power to quell it, for while some
Would hail her abbess, others would rebel
And cry their present Mother was a saint,
And Guenevere a slut who should have burned.

Thus power itself would fuel the discontent.
Yet Mother Agnes was indeed a saint,
And she had always shown the queen that same
Due care she gave each daughter of her house.
But even she could not control the strife,
For in her presence, whisperers fell mute,
And Guenevere might weep, but not complain.
So while the abbess guessed, she could not prove,
But only point her daughters towards the One
To Whom they hourly prayed, and hope that they
Would follow in His steps.

                                      It so fell out
When Guenevere was in the second year
Of her new life, a peasant brought one day
An offering of honey fine and pure,
And milk still warm from richly pastured cows.
(So well this corner had escaped the wars
That followed Arthur's passing. Else the nuns
Had had small leisure for their small disputes.)
The golden sweetness of a hive at prayer
With insect praises for the perfumed flowers,
And satin whiteness called forth by new life
And for new life, into its mother's fount
In such abundance, there was overflow
To please the throat of peasant and of nun.
These gifts the sister kitchener had blent
Into a posset. There was just enough
That every dame might drink a dipperful.
That day the serving sister was of those
Who never had a kindly word to say
Of Guenevere, not though the queen had lived
For all these months in gracious courtesy
And patience like the Virgin Mary's own.
That graciousness her enemies called pride;
That queenly patience seemed to them contempt:
They used her as a mirror of themselves.
Six bowls the serving sister set with care
Before six nuns, and then another six,
And so on till she neared the queen. Then five
She set in safety – and let slip the last,
The one that should have been Dame Guenevere's –

It fell before the nuns could understand
That it was fallen, all its contents spilled
And vanishing in lacy rivulets
Down through the rushes that bestrew the floor
(Strewn fresh each month). The sisterhood sat mute.
"Your pardon, Lady," cried the serving nun,
"I did not mean to drop it." But her words
Rang false: all present knew her heart too well.
The mother abbess glanced from face to face:
Some few looked horrified; and some abashed;
And some perplexed; and several novices,
As yet unserved, looked ready to leap up
And pledge their own sweet portions to the queen.
But far too many faces showed a smug,
Half-hidden pleasure at the queen's disgrace.
"Dame Guenevere," the mother abbess said, and rose,
And lifted up her bowl (for she had been
Served first of all as fitted her estate),
And left her place, and set her bowl before
Dame Guenevere. There passed a solemn look
Between the ruler of this house of nuns
And she who once had ruled the realm entire.
Both knew the mother's need to feed the child.
But Mother Agnes saw as well the chance
To point her wayward daughters towards the path
Of charity, as trodden by their Lord.
And, guessing at her ghostly mother's thought,
The queen inclined her head, and took the bowl.
(Although the notion flitted through her mind,
One tiny spoonful from each bowl would soon
Make up the loss; but such a compromise
Fit not the situation nor the age,
And, from her lips, would have been ill construed.)
Dame Agnes turned back towards her place. Before
She went three steps, they heard a little cry:
There in the doorway joining hall to court
The sister portress stood, supporting one
Who must have come a hard and tortured way
Through war-torn lands, in quest of peace and rest:
A withered hag, her sparse white hair in knots,
Her flesh like crumpled parchment, hanging pinched
Upon a frame of gaunt and stick-like bones.

Too spent to stand, she staggered through the arms
Of her supporting nun, and slumped, and sank
And lay there on the rush-strewn floor, like one
Bereft of strength, and hope, and will to live.
Dame Guenevere caught up her bowl of milk
And hurried to the fallen beldame's side,
And, kneeling, took the filthy, louseful head
Upon her lap, and with one gentle hand
She held the chin, and with the other hand
Tipped up the bowl, and fed the feeble dame
With slow and tiny sips of sweetened milk
Until the bowl was emptied. Then the crone
Smiled once, and tried to speak, and coughed, and died.

Or so it seemed. But when they looked again,
She stirred, and winked, and suddenly sprang up,
Aglow with vibrant, buoyant, newborn health.
And, as they watched, her long years peeled away
Until she stood before them, neither crone,
Nor child, nor matron, but an ageless form,
And sexless as an angel; while her garb
From dirt-caked rags changed into seamless white,
As smooth and lustrous as the inner shell
Of clam or oyster. Golden radiance
Played all about her, and her heavenly smile
Encompassed everyone, but most of all
Dame Guenevere, who knelt there still enrapt,
And Mother Agnes, standing poised in awe.
The vision bent, and plucked the wooden bowl,
Once full of milk, from Guenevere's limp hand,
And, rising upright, lifted it on high,
To close the circle of her upraised arms.

The serving dame saw none of this, but lay
Face-down, and sobbed into the muffling straw.
Those who remembered their unworthiness
And bowed their heads, saw that the angel's feet,
No longer touching ground, trod now on light.
But Mother Agnes, and the portress nun
(Who'd fallen to her knees), and everyone
Whose awe drove out awareness of herself,
And most of all Dame Guenevere, gazed up

To watch their imaged faces, one and all,
Appear as though poured upward from the bowl
In billowing flight to Heaven; and not theirs
Alone, the nuns', but everyone they'd known,
Or heard or dreamt of, or, undreaming, sensed –
The faces brown and yellow, blue and red
With nature or with dyes, of peoples gone
Long centuries ago, or not as yet
Encountered in the world. Beasts as well,
And even plants and rocks: creation all,
In vision flowing eagerly to God
Till all were swallowed in a golden glow
Like that of sunlight through a million leaves . . .
And then the flow reversed, and all this light
Of Godliness rushed outward from the bowl
To press the place with sense of the Divine
So tangible, so pure, and so intense,
That many sisters fainted of that awe,
And did not see Dame Guenevere raised up
Transfixed, and shining, like a holy saint.
But Mother Agnes saw, although without
Awareness of the glory round herself.
Drawn upward on a carpeting of air
She reached the queen, and wrapped her in her arms,
And with one hand received the bowl again
Back from the angel, in the final breath
Before the heavenly visitor dissolved
In heavenly light, and vanished from their sight,
Not to be seen again in earthly life.

They made a treasured relic of the bowl
That once had bathed their hall with Heaven's glow.
And, ever after, in her daughters' eyes,
Dame Agnes wore the golden aureole;
And Guenevere, the queen, found lasting peace.

LAUNCELOT'S GRAIL

Peter Valentine Timlett

Peter Timlett picks up from Karr's idyll to bring the Grail Quest to a close.

Great souls had walked the stage of life and now were gone to their own place. Galahad had become one with the Grail, and Percivale had been granted a glimpse of that wondrous vessel before he too followed Galahad into death – and even the Grail Maiden lay dead upon the Ship of Faythe. Darkness had fallen and Modred had stalked the land at the bidding of grim Morgan le Fay, and as a result the great Arthur Pendragon was no longer among the living, and even Excalibur had been returned to the ancient halls of Lake Avalon. Great moments had come and gone and great deeds were now the stuff of legend. Of all the great names only a few remained upon the earth plane, and soon these too would depart and leave the tale to the bards and chroniclers.

> The boy sat for a long time watching the old man. Occasionally the tired old eyes would flicker open and stare straight through him to some scene that only he could see, and then he would mutter and sigh and the eyes would close again. The monastery was poor. Here in this tiny stone cell there was no raised bed, no carven platters, no meat, no wine. The old man lay on straw and in the corner were scraps of bread. The cell was cold, and the boy shivered.

"Care for him in these his last hours," the abbot had said. "Moisten his lips, wipe his brow, watch over him as though he were your own flesh and kin, and do all this with great diligence, boy, for you know not whom you tend."

The boy's eyes drooped with fatigue, and then suddenly he jerked awake. The old man had raised himself up on one elbow again, his breath rasping in his throat, his eyes staring, the long matted hair thrown back, his free hand held out and upwards, imploring. "Forgive me," the old man whispered hoarsely. "Forgive me . . . forgive me . . ."

At Benwick in France Launcelot gathered an army of a hundred thousand to march against Modred, but before they could even embark from France they learned that they were already too late. The old monk, weary from his crossing, stood before the kings and knights.

"As I have said, my lords," he repeated patiently, "Arthur defeated Modred at Dover and again at Baron Down, and then marched to meet him at Salisbury Down. A hundred thousand on each side came together on Easter Sunday and such was the slaughter that few survived. Modred is dead and most of his followers, of that we are certain. Sir Gawain is dead, as you already knew, and so too is Sir Lucas at Salisbury. But of King Arthur and Sir Bedivere there is no trace. All we can say is that they were not among the dead and wounded at Salisbury."

"At Camelot, then?" said Launcelot.

"Perhaps, but I doubt it. We would have received word if they were there."

"And Queen Guenevere?"

"As I have said, she was at the Tower of London besieged by Modred when Arthur arrived at Dover. When the battle was over she went to Canterbury to see the Archbishop but he had already gone to the west country. She then dismissed all her knights save Sir Badouin, and the two of them set out westward. We have had no word since."

"But four such important people cannot just vanish like that," said Ector gruffly. "For sweet Jesu's sake, we are talking about your king, your queen and two of your most senior knights. Somebody must know where they are."

The monk spread his hands. "Perhaps. All I can say is that we have monasteries all over Britain and yet have received no word of any of them."

Launcelot rose. "Thank you for bringing the message. Go now and rest, for I see that you are weary."

When the priest had gone Launcelot turned to the others. "Tomorrow we must dismiss the army, obviously, but then I shall go to Britain – alone if necessary. This mystery must be resolved."

"I too dislike mysteries," said Ector. "I will go with you."

"And I," said Bors, and six others pledged their companionship.

When the army had been dismissed the nine knights set sail for Britain and landed at Dover. Before they began their search they visited Sir Gawain's tomb at the monastery and prayed for the peace of his soul.

"He was once our friend," Launcelot said to the Abbot. "Take this gold and see to it that his tomb is cared for and that masses are sung for his soul's welfare."

Then the nine knights turned their horses to the west and rode day and night for Salisbury, but when they were still many miles from their destination they began to smell the stench of death, and when they arrived at the scene of the battle they could only stare in nauseated horror at the heaps of dead that littered the plain.

"It has been a month since the battle," said Ector. "It will need a winter's snows and another spring to clear the air and hide this horror."

Sir Bors stared at the thousands and thousands of crows that hopped and plucked amidst the dead, gorged to bursting from their grisly feeding. "Sweet God in Heaven, is there no way these poor wretches can be buried decently."

Launcelot grunted. "There are too many. Let the earth take them in its own good time."

They left the field and rode to a nearby monastery and there found the grave of Sir Lucas. "Three days after the battle Sir Bedivere brought his brother here for burial," said the hermit.

"What of the king?" said Launcelot. "What of Arthur?"

The hermit shrugged. "I don't know, and nor does anyone else, I fancy. Bedivere came alone, apart from his dead brother, of course."

"But didn't you question him?"

"Yes, of course, but he was not disposed to answer. He remained here just long enough for the burial and then rode westward, I know not whither."

They stayed the night with the hermit and in the morning they split up. Launcelot and Bors rode south-west to Camelot, to seek news of Arthur there, and the remaining seven rode west to Glastonbury. "If Arthur is at Camelot we will send for you," said Launcelot. "If not then we will join you at Glastonbury."

Launcelot and Bors rode all that day, seeking news as they went, and arrived at Camelot late that afternoon, tired and dispirited. Arthur was not there, nor did they have any news of him, nor any of Guenevere. Only a few elderly knights were in residence, together with no more than half a dozen of the ladies of the court, and the number of servants had dwindled to a handful. Compared to the days of old, Camelot was as empty and lifeless as a tomb.

"Great names are soon forgotten, it seems," said Launcelot bitterly.

The following morning they went into the Great Hall and stood in silence before the Round Table. It was covered in dust, and indeed the whole hall had an air of neglect and even decay. "Do you remember the day that Percivale was made a Knight of Honour?" said Launcelot suddenly.

"Aye, and you rose and offered him your seat, and his name appeared in letters of gold along with all the rest."

Launcelot pointed. "The names are all gone now. All of them." The top of the table was bare of markings of any sort. Launcelot went up and took his old seat, and Bors did likewise. For several minutes they sat there in silence, and then Launcelot sighed. "It's all gone. There's nothing left. It's just a table."

Bors glanced up at the ceiling. "D'you remember the night the Holy Grail passed through this very hall?"

"Yes, and the way Galahad urged us all to follow the Quest." Launcelot looked down at the table. "I can still hear his voice even now."

Bors rose suddenly. "Come," he said firmly. "This is no time to wallow in memories. That is an old man's pastime."

Launcelot sighed. "But there is certainly something I can do about those memories." He bellowed for servants, and when they came running he said commandingly, "Gather as many men as you can. Take that table into the courtyard and burn it."

Sir Bors frowned. "Is this wise?"

Launcelot turned to his cousin. "In view of all it meant to us do you want to see it grow old and scarred? D'you want to see it used for feasting and drunkenness, with serving wenches spread upon it for the lechery of those who know not its glory or its meaning?"

Bors sighed. "Burn it, then, though it will grieve me to see it."

The broken table made a huge bonfire in the great courtyard, and it was while they were watching it that Launcelot overheard one of the servants mention the name of Sir Badouin. He had the man brought before him and questioned him closely.

Finally the man said, "I am sorry, my lord, but that is all I know. It is just a rumour that Sir Badouin was seen at the Abbey of Amesbury hewing wood and drawing water for the nuns."

Launcelot dismissed the man and watched the last of the table burn to ashes. "What d'you think?"

Bors shrugged. "Seems unlikely, but we have no other clues to follow."

"I agree. Tomorrow, then, we go to Amesbury just to put our minds at rest, and then on to Glastonbury to join Ector and the others." He turned to Bors. "But if it really is Badouin," he said softly, "he'll know where Guenevere is."

> *"It should have been you, Elaine," the old man muttered, and the boy bent closer to hear, but he could not make out the words. "If only it had been you . . ."*
>
> *The boy sat back, but was then startled when the old man suddenly raised himself up again upon one elbow and flung an arm aloft. "The Grail!" he cried in a weak and ailing voice. "The Grail! Oh, dear God, dear Lord, it was she who was my Grail. What mockery of a life was this!"*

They reached Amesbury late the following afternoon and Launcelot sought audience with the abbess, leaving Bors to wait for him outside, but she had little news that could help them. "Yes, Sir Badouin was here for a few weeks, but then he left and I have no knowledge of his whereabouts."

"And he really hewed wood and drew water?"

The abbess smiled. "A little humility is good for the soul, Sir Launcelot."

He rose and bowed to her in a courtly gesture. "Thank you for giving me your time. If anyone should ask of me I shall be at Glastonbury, at least for a while."

As he turned to go he glanced out of the embrasure that overlooked the herb garden and saw a single nun tending the plants, and at that precise moment the nun looked up. Her hand flew to her mouth in shock, and Launcelot's heart seemed to stand still in his chest. For several long seconds they stared at each other, and then Launcelot turned to the abbess. "So, you lied to me."

"I did no such thing," said the abbess calmly. "You asked me about Badouin, not Guenevere."

"But you hid her from me none the less."

"Hid her? In full view in the garden?" The abbess shook her head. "Had I wanted to hide her I would have asked her to wait in her cell until after your departure. But nuns do not hide, Sir Launcelot. We face what God chooses to bring us."

Launcelot turned back to the embrasure. Guenevere had returned to her task but even at this distance he could see that her cheeks were flushed with shock. "Enough of this talk. Send her to me, and have her horse made ready immediately."

The old nun's eyebrows lowered to a frown. "You presume too much, Sir Launcelot. I will ask her if she wishes to see you. If not then I must ask you to leave."

"Just do as I command," said Launcelot coldly. "Send her to me and prepare her horse. I don't know how you persuaded her to take this foolish step but she will be leaving this place with me today, this very hour."

"I did not persuade her. She came of her own accord. I tried to deter her but after being with us for some weeks it became obvious that her reasons were sincere. I was glad to welcome her to our Order, and as such she is now in my care and under God's protection."

"Just send her to me. I will soon demonstrate how sincere her reasons were."

The abbess rose. "You have just had one shock, Sir Launcelot," she said gently, "and I think you are about to receive another. I will ask her if she wishes to see you."

A few moments later he saw the abbess come into the garden. The two nuns spoke to each other and then Launcelot saw Guenevere nod and move away through a side door. He smiled triumphantly. But Launcelot had not been able to hear their words.

"This day had to come sooner or later, my mother," Guenevere had said sadly. "He has the right to hear it from my own lips."

"Then see him in the chapel," the abbess had said. "Perhaps he may not be so demonstrative before God's altar."

The abbess returned to Launcelot. "She will see you for a few moments only. Be gentle with her, I beg you. She is in the chapel on the far side of the cloisters."

Launcelot ran across the grass square of the cloisters and burst into the chapel. Guenevere was kneeling at the altar. Launcelot closed the carven door and strode down the aisle. "Guenevere," he called. "Guenevere."

She rose and turned to face him. Her cheeks were now pale and drawn. Her eyes flickered over him, remembering. How handsome he looked, how powerful, even though he was no longer a young man. She raised her hand. "Stop there, Launcelot," she warned. "Don't come any closer."

He stopped, puzzled. "I have come for you," he said simply. "All matters are now resolved and we can be together."

She shook her head. "This moment has come too late," she said quietly. "I have given myself to God."

"Then let Him give you back again. Gawain is dead, and so too is Modred. The way is clear."

"And my husband, the king?"

"We don't know. But even if he has survived we can come to some arrangement."

"It is too late."

"Nonsense," he said firmly, and moved forward.

"Stop!" she cried. "You don't know what you do. I have given myself to God, I tell you."

He stopped short and grunted disbelievingly. "But why? Was it because you didn't expect to see me again?"

"No."

"Then why?"

"Don't make me say the reason, for you know very well what it is."

"But I insist. After twenty years you can't dismiss me without a reason."

She was silent for a little while, and then said quietly, "I have confessed to God and to the mother abbess, and now it seems I must confess to you." Her face was pale, but never had he seen her look more beautiful. "Our love was adulterous," she said slowly. "We did not have the courage to declare it openly but continued to deceive my husband and the Court for twenty years. That of itself should answer your question."

"There were reasons for our actions, good reasons, as you well know, but now those reasons no longer apply. We can now declare ourselves openly and live together in honour."

"In honour?" she said bitterly. "Are you still using that word? God in Heaven, Launcelot, the adultery was bad enough, but because of our actions countless thousands have died."

"Their deaths are not our fault. Others used the situation for their own ambition."

"As we always knew they would, yet we did not change our ways. My soul is stained with these deeds, not because of you, but because of my own weakness, and I would make my peace with God."

"Fine words," he sneered, "but they cannot change your nature. Beneath that black robe of virtue is a woman's passionate body, and I know every inch of it, as you know mine. Look at me, Guenevere. Don't you remember what it felt like to be in my arms, to have my hands caress you, or remember the way you used to groan with pleasure and cry out my name?"

She looked down at the flagstoned floor, her face red with the memory of it. "Yes, I remember," she said quietly, "and I am ashamed. I have incurred a great debt but I will not add to it." She looked up at him. "You were the finest knight in Christendom, Launcelot, but you were refused the Holy Grail because of your passion for me. Let it end now and let there be a new beginning for you. Go out on the Quest again. You found it once and can do so again."

"It's too late for that now," he said. "We cannot change what we are. For all your fine words I need only kiss you once and you will come to me as you always did."

"No!"

"Then prove it. If your vow is so strong then one kiss will not harm it." He walked towards her and his eyes grew hot and dark. "Just one kiss and you will willingly lie with me, even here."

"No! This is God's house. Keep away from me!"

He smiled at her and reached out his hand. "Guenevere, you would lie with me before the throne of God itself, and you know it." He took her in his arms and forced her head back. By God, how soft she felt against him. She was his Grail and always had been.

"Launcelot!" cried a voice behind him. "For God's sake stop this blasphemy."

He turned and saw Bors come striding down the aisle with the abbess behind him. He tried to clear the fog in his head. He looked down at Guenevere's pale face and then released her and stepped back. His glazed eyes cleared and he stared wildly from the altar to Bors and back again. He then buried his head in his hands. "Sweet Jesu, what have I done?" he burst out.

Bors put his hand gently on his cousin's shoulder, but Launcelot gave one long, shuddering convulsion and then turned and ran like a madman the length of aisle and burst through the chapel doors to the outside.

Guenevere had fallen in a heap in front of the altar and was weeping bitterly; the old abbess knelt by her side.

"Is she all right?" said Bors anxiously.

"Yes. She has been tested and has triumphed."

"Unlike Launcelot," said Bors bitterly. "I never dreamt that he could be capable of anything like this."

The abbess looked up at him. "You are a Knight of the Grail, or so I hear. Go to him and deal with him gently. I have never seen a soul in such torment. This was his blackest hour and he will need a friend. Go quickly or you will lose him."

Bors hesitated. "Yes, you're right. I will send you word." And he turned and ran after Launcelot.

The abbess bent over Guenevere and stroked her brow. "It's all over now," she said gently. "He's gone." Great racking sobs shook the body under her hands. "Shh! Gently now." She pulled Guenevere into a sitting position and cradled her in her arms. "It's all over."

"But you don't understand," said the muffled voice.

"Yes, I do. I understand, believe me."

Guenevere raised her head. "But I wanted him. He was right. I wanted him there and then." She buried her head in the older woman's shoulder. "Oh, God, I wanted him!"

> The door to the cell creaked open and the abbot peered in. "How fares he?"
>
> The boy shrugged. "He lives, but oft cries out with strange words."
>
> The abbot stooped over the old man, and then, shaking his head slightly, he straightened and made to leave. "Tend him well, boy, for in his day, long before you were born, his deeds rang throughout the land."
>
> "And he has come to this?" said the boy dubiously. "Better to die, surely, at the height of one's deeds than live on into useless old age?"
>
> The abbot raised his eyebrows. "The rising sun will speak different words ere it sets, methinks. No matter, just you tend him well."

Bors had to chase Launcelot for nearly five miles before he caught up with him. He urged his horse alongside and grabbed for the reins. Launcelot tried to beat him off. The horse swerved and Launcelot pitched out of the saddle and crashed to the ground. Bors caught the runaway horse and led him back to where Launcelot had fallen.

He slid from his own horse, and as he did so Launcelot came charging at him like a maniac. "Defend yourself, traitor!"

Launcelot was clearly demented with rage and self-disgust, capable at this moment of almost anything. Sir Bors drew his own sword and flung it away and spread his hands wide. "I am unarmed," he said calmly. "I will not fight you."

"Pick up your sword, coward, or I will kill you where you stand!"

Bors stood his ground. "I know how you feel," he said, more calmly than he felt. "You want to kill me, and the abbess, and Guenevere, so there won't be anyone left to know what you've done." He shook his head firmly. "But that won't work. You will know, and God will know. Killing me will solve nothing."

In berserk rage Launcelot raised his sword high above his head. For several interminable seconds he stood thus, and then he turned and flung the sword away and strode over to the other side of the glade.

Beads of sweat stood out on Bors's forehead. Of all the battles he had ever fought, that was as close to death as he had ever come. Launcelot was now sitting on a grassy bank, unmoving, his face as impassive as stone. Bors ignored him. He tethered the horses, collected the two swords, and then sat down on the opposite side of the glade to Launcelot.

An hour passed, and in all that time Launcelot barely moved, and then Bors saw him put his head in his hands and heard him uttering great racking sobs. Bors waited for two or three minutes to let the pressure die down and then he went over and put his hand on Launcelot's shoulder. "It's all right. It's over now."

Gradually the sobs died down, and then there was silence. Bors did not quite know why it should be so but he was certain, beyond any doubt, that the tie between Launcelot and Guenevere was broken. For twenty years it had bound them together and now it was gone.

"It's all over, Launcelot," he said quietly. "Come, we must be going." Launcelot did not reply, but he allowed Bors to lead him across the glade and help him onto his horse.

They rode to Glastonbury in silence. As they neared the hamlet Bors saw the camp where the others were waiting and he guided the horses towards it. "Are you all right now?" he said anxiously. "We will be with the others in a few seconds."

Launcelot nodded. "Yes," he said, in a voice so low that Bors could barely hear him. "I will not forget what you did for me today. My action has incurred a debt that I shall spend the rest of my life repaying."

Bors smiled. "On the contrary, I believe you have just repaid a monstrous debt that has been hanging over your head all your life."

They came into camp and Bors shook his head warningly to stop the others saying anything. Launcelot muttered a greeting and then led his horse over to the far side and spread his blanket for the night.

"What's the matter?" whispered Ector.

"Nothing – not now. He's been through a somewhat chastening experience. I must leave it to him to decide if he wants to tell you about it. Don't press him. And what news of you?"

Ector shrugged. "No news of Arthur, or Guenevere."

"We found Guenevere," said Bors. "She's now a nun at the abbey at Amesbury. We've just come from there."

Ector glanced over at Launcelot. "Oh, I see."

He didn't, at least not entirely, but Bors let it ride. "So it would seem that we have come to an ending, then."

"Not yet," said Ector. "We've heard that Bedivere is lodging at a monastery nearby, but we waited for you."

"Good, excellent. We'll ride there first thing in the morning."

The erstwhile Archbishop, now abbot of the monastery, and Bedivere were astonished and delighted to see them, even though Bedivere knew that now he would have to give a full explanation. He had been with the Archbishop for nigh on a month and had said nothing of Avalon all that time, but now he would welcome the chance to share his doubts with others.

But as soon as they were seated Launcelot said simply, "There is something I must tell you, all of you." And he spoke of what had happened at Amesbury, omitting no detail whatsoever, including the fact that the queen had been his mistress for twenty years. "And now you must decide whether you want me in your company or not."

Bors prayed that no one would say the wrong thing, particularly the gruff and usually tactless Ector, and yet it was Ector who said precisely what was needed.

"If you go, then I go," he said bluntly. "And if you stay, then I stay," And the others nodded their agreement.

Launcelot raised his head. "Thank you," he said simply.

"And there is another here who has a secret to share," said the abbot, and looked at Bedivere. "The time for speaking out has come."

Bedivere sighed and then told them of the battles of Dover and Baron Down, and of the senseless slaughter at Salisbury Down, and of how he had seen the fight between Arthur and Modred, and had seen Modred die. And then his voice grew quieter as he described the journey to Avalon and what had happened there.

The abbot then spoke of Merlin's prophecy, and of how the body of Arthur had been brought for burial, and he showed them the words that he had carved on the tomb with his own hands.

They were silent for some time, and then Launcelot said quietly, "It has been an age of magic and wonderment and of high affairs beyond our understanding, and I thank God that I was permitted to play a part." He paused for a moment. "Nothing awaits us in France save kingship and affairs of state, and those kingdoms cannot compare to the kingdom that was Arthur's. I propose that we remain here at this monastery and dedicate the rest of our lives to God." He stepped forward and inserted his sword beneath the block of stone over the tomb and broke the blade in two. "And there is the token of my vow."

Bors stepped forward and did likewise, and one by one the others followed suit.

Some weeks later Launcelot went alone to Amesbury, and when he returned he would say little save that he had made his peace with Guenevere and with the abbess and had conducted a vigil of prayer in the chapel that he had defiled.

For six years they lived thus, growing lean and pale such that few would have recognized them for the lusty knights who had won fame for their prowess at arms. Then one day came news that Guenevere was dead, and they brought her from Amesbury and buried her with Arthur.

Launcelot looked into the face of the queen one last time before the tomb was sealed and wept a little and sighed. That night he read the service himself, and in the morning sang mass. But on the death of the queen a light seemed to go out in Launcelot. Thereafter he barely ate or drank, and slept but little. He spent most of the time in prayer and none could console him, and he became too weak and ill even to kneel at the tomb and he had to remain in his cell.

The boy's eyes drooped towards sleep, but he jerked himself awake. The old man was peaceful now, quiet. No longer did his eyes roll and stare, and no more wild words burst from his lips. His face was lined and the skin of his cheeks sagged like empty purses. He was old, so very old.

The boy leant forward, and with the sleeve of his tunic he dabbed the last tears from his eyes. The eyelids were closed now and he seemed at peace. The hands lay open atop the cloak, palms down.

Easing himself away, the boy stepped from the cell and stretched his young body to ease away the aches of the night's long vigil. It would be dawn soon. Already the sky was lighter there in the east. Suddenly, from a nearby cell, he heard the abbot give a great shout of joy, and then he came running, and others too from the other cells.

"What is it?" cried Bors, and the others gathered round, their faces anxious.

The abbot rubbed his eyes and stared round at the ring of faces. "I was dreaming," he whispered. "I saw Launcelot in the Holy City of Sarras. I saw him welcomed by Galahad and Percivale, and saw Merlin himself lead him up to the Holy of Holies wherein lies the Grail of God, and as he went in I saw a great light and I heard a paean of joy and wonder rise up from the whole city."

Bors spun round and ran into the cell, with the others crowding in after him, but they were too late. Sir Launcelot, the most human of all the knights, had at last found the Holy Grail.

EPILOGUE

All had gone – save one.

It was still dark, though the new day was not far off. Painfully she hobbled from her cell and skirted Chalybeate Well until she came to Lake Avalon, and there she rested. The sky to the east was wreathed in pinks and yellows, heralding the dawn. She gathered her cloak around her and propped her chin in her hand.

"Still plotting, Morgan le Fay?" said a voice behind her.

She turned and saw a figure robed in white. "Ah, Merlin. Yes,

I thought that you would come to me sooner or later." She turned and looked across the lake. "Plotting? No, not any more, there is no need. The tale is done."

"And are you satisfied?"

"I made a few mistakes," she admitted, "and some of my methods will be questioned, but the main result was achieved." She looked up at him. "History will speak of me as the villain of this tale, as indeed do you."

"Not any more. I used to think of you as my enemy, when I was involved in the events as they took place, but now I have a broader view."

She raised her eyebrows mockingly. "Ah, then there is hope for you yet, Merlin. What, then, think you of me now?"

Merlin smiled briefly. "Without those in opposition, and without the final act of betrayal, there would have been no Crucifixion, no Resurrection and no Ascension."

The priestess nodded. "Yes, the Christians don't seem to understand the great part that Judas played. And obviously neither did he, since he hanged himself. Are you comparing me with him?"

"No. It is the principle I am comparing."

She looked up at him. "Be careful, Merlin. Are you saying that evil is necessary?"

"No, don't try to trap me into that. I am saying that humanity seems to need the spur of opposition to prick them to great deeds."

"And I was the opposition?"

"If you like."

She smiled. "Clumsily put, but there is the seed of an understanding there. As I say, there is hope for you yet, Merlin."

He walked down to the water, and as he did so the barge came silently across the lake and nudged into the shore where he stood. He held out his hand. "Would you like to come with me?" he invited.

She rose and walked towards him. "Why not?" she said. "It's not often that you and I travel together." She took her place in the prow and the barge moved away. She looked back at the shore and saw a crumpled figure lying by the water's edge. "Look there – who is that?" But then her eyes changed and she smiled. "Yes, of course." She turned to him. "You're a cunning old devil, Merlin, but thank you. It hasn't always been as easy as that."

"A lot easier than mine," he said drily.

"Yes, I did not like doing that, but you were so pig-headed you had to learn the lesson the hard way. Do you bear me a grudge?"

"No. I recognized the motive. It was then that I began to think that there might be some hope for you yet, Morgan le Fay."

She smiled and looked back at the crumpled figure. "And now the tale is really ended."

He shook his head. "Nonsense. It has barely begun."

RELIQUARY

F. Gwynplaine MacIntyre

And so we move from legend to story. The Grail Quest may be over, but the story and the memories live on. Although the following story is set in Cornwall, MacIntyre (b. 1947) was inspired to write it while visiting the Strata Florida abbey in Dyfed, which is one of the suggested resting places of the Holy Grail. Although now resident in the United States, MacIntyre was born in Scotland and was raised in Australia. He has been writing science fiction and fantasy for over twenty years, though much of his work has appeared either pseudonymously, or as uncredited ghost-writer or reviser. For instance, he co-authored Pinball *(1984) by Jerzy Kosinski. Here, for once, is a story under his own name.*

"The Old One howled again last night," said Gowek to Tebelwas, as their errands intersected in the forest. Gowek had been sent by Brother Morgelyn to gather cammock-greens for the monastery's evening meal. The cammocks were more plentiful on the sunlit hill, Gowek knew, than in the darkling woods. But, since he had a burthen of fresh gossip weighing heavy on his tongue, young Gowek had contrived to wander into the woods, so that he could unloose his rumours into the eager ears of Tebelwas.

"Speak quietly, lest others overhear." Tebelwas gathered his robe about himself, and bent to search the forest floor for wood. Father Derowen had sent the youth Tebelwas to fetch kindling for the evening's fire, and – since the Order's sacred vows forbade any monk of their brotherhood from stripping the branches or bark of a tree – Tebelwas had to content himself with collecting the windfalls that had already dropped to the ground. The proscription against harming a tree was left over from Druidic times, of course, but as there was nothing in the newer faith which contradicted it Tebelwas was obliged to follow the laws of the old faith as well as the new. He bent to pick up an especially large branch, and groaned at the slight effort. "The Old One howled, you say? That is no revelation. He often howls."

Gowek shook his head, even though the two youths were not facing each other. If any of the friars chanced to pass this way, it would be well if Gowek appeared to be engaged in his tasks; he reached towards a bright yellow cammock-blossom underneath a nearby rotting log, then snorted in disgust when he saw that it was a dead leaf instead. "At the horn of midnight," Gowek muttered as the two young postulants pretended to be working, "I awoke with full bowels and went into the forest to cloiter myself. As I passed the Old One's hut I chanced to hear him howling as he slept."

"He often howls," repeated Tebelwas.

Gowek nodded. "But this time there were words to his madness. I heard them."

"Heard you, aye? What did he say, then?"

"He said . . ." Gowek paused, and made an effort to remember the fitful words that he had heard emerging last night from the hermit's cell. "I am uncertain. But I believe that the Old One shouted: 'Arthur! The Grail is rejoined with the Christ, and I only am returned, alone, to tell thee.'"

This time it was the turn of Tebelwas to snort in disgust. "The Old One is *gorbollak*. A proper loony, that one." Tebelwas touched his forehead and then tapped the side of his nose.

"A madman, perhaps. But not a liar," said Gowek. "I heard him, I tell you. He spoke of Arthur."

"Many men speak of Arthur," said Tebelwas, as he gathered his bundle of kindling and turned towards the priory's gates. "Perhaps even a hundred years hence there will be men who speak of Arthur."

"But this time was different," said Gowek, bending to uproot a very small and unpromising cammock-root. He straightened up, and discovered that he was alone in the autumning woods. "This time was different," he repeated.

* * *

Father Ydfran was astonished that evening, when the young postulant Tebelwas requested the honour of bringing the nightly bowl of *cawlcennin* to the hermit's cottage. Tebelwas had a reputation for laziness, and it was surprising that he volunteered to do this task. Grudgingly, Father Ydfran ladled the meagre portion of *cawlcennin* – ostensibly a soup, but as prepared in Father Ydfran's humble larder it was more truthfully a broth – into an earthenware bowl, and gave it to the eager postulant.

"Thou'lt take this to Brother Bohort directly, then?" asked the friar dubiously.

"I will that." Tebelwas nodded.

"And none of Brother Bohort's portion will, perchance, find its way into thine *own* greed-a-guts gullet between here and his doorstep?" Father Ydfran persisted.

Tebelwas shook his head, and the friar reluctantly let him go. Tebelwas tightened the cincture of his thin robe as he stepped out of the warm, firelit kitchen and into the cold, autumn dusk.

"'Tis dark tonight. Take a candle with thee." Father Ydfran handed Tebelwas a small clay dish filled with sheep's-liver oil, in which floated a thin, burning wick. Tebelwas grunted his thanks and cupped this under the hood of his robe, so that the autumn wind might not blow out the flame.

The hermit's cottage looked the same as when Tebelwas had last seen it, half-again a fortnight past. The senior monks did not encourage young postulants to dawdle in this region of the forest . . . and in *this* stricture, at least, if none of their others, Tebelwas found himself quite willing to obey them. But Gowek's tale had made him curious, and now he was eager to see the Old One for himself . . . the Old One who had spoken of Arthur.

The door was latched, of course, and the cottage's only window lay shuttered. Tebelwas rapped the knocker, and for a time was rewarded only with silence.

Then at last came a wizened voice, dry as dust, asking: "*Pyu ys ena*?" in an accent from some region of Cornwall that Tebelwas could not recognize. Then, as the voice's ancient owner remembered to speak in the Vulgate dialect that was the favoured language of this Holy Order, the question was repeated, "Who comes?"

Tebelwas restrained a mischief's urge to answer: *Arthur*. Instead, he replied, "Your food is without, Brother Bohort. Shall I fetch it in, or leave it on the threshold?"

There was a sound behind the shutter, as of someone immensely old and infinitely weary somehow dragging himself across the room. An iron bolt was drawn back and the door was nudged open. Someone coughed within, but did not speak. Tebelwas interpreted this as permission to enter.

The Old One lived in nearly total darkness. A fire had burnt out on the bluestone hearth. Tebelwas knelt, unbidden, to rake the coals into a heap and rouse the embers into some attempt at a flame. When there was light in the cottage at last, he turned.

The Old One was, verily, *old*. He wore some ancient mouldy garment which Tebelwas failed to recognize; it was certainly not the familiar herringbone cloth which the nuns of Bodmin had provided for the Order's monastic robes. With deft, experienced fingers – Tebelwas had once been a pickpocket's apprentice, before arousing the attention of the authorities and strategically retreating into this Holy Order – he brushed against the hermit's garb, and then, just as swiftly, recoiled in disgust when his sense of touch identified the cloth: it was a *hevys*, a hair-shirt designed to mortify the Old One's flesh. With an effort, Tebelwas suppressed his revulsion.

"I have brought your meal, Brother." Tebelwas had already set down the bowl of soup on the hut's narrow table. He nodded towards it now, but the Old One saw him not. Instead, the hermit sniffed the air, then turned unerringly towards the scent of turnip and leek which told him of the *cawlcennin's* presence. As the man called Brother Bohort turned Tebelwas caught a glimpse of his face.

The Old One was nearly blind. Two veils of rheum concealed his eyes, as the folds of a wimple might veil a nun's gaze, and the Old One could only peer out at the world through rheum's tapestries.

"Thank you, my son," the hermit muttered with an effort. "Leave me now to my sup." Brother Bohort fumbled about within the folds of his garment and extracted a blackened tin spoon. Tebelwas turned away to depart, when of a sudden something else caught his attention.

A glint of metal. Tebelwas had seen it only for an instant, yet that instant was enough. *Silver*. He would know it anywhere. His training as a thief's boy in the markets of Penryn had not forsaken him. A silver box, with a red enamel triskele emblem upon its lid, dangled from a leathern cord about the hermit's throat. Yet already the Old One's crabbed hands had pushed the forbidden glimpse of silver back within his hair-shirt's depths.

How came an old and blind hermit – living on the charity of a

mendicant Order whose friars had all pledged vows of poverty –
to be in possession of *silver*?

The old man whom the monks called Brother Bohort had already
bent to his meal, and was noisily supping turnip gruel. Tebelwas
paused in the doorway and was about to depart when he felt his
earlier mischief bubbling to the surface again, and this time he
could no longer suppress it.

He swiftly whispered in Cornish, "*Myghtern Arthur nyns yu
marow.*" Just loud enough for the hermit to hear – King Arthur
is not dead.

The effect was miraculous. As Tebelwas watched, a gleam
awoke within the hermit's rheumy eyes. The old man straightened, and turned with an expression of majestic awe upon his
crumbled face.

"*Arthur! King! Lord!*" The hermit let fall his tin spoon as he
raised his right arm and saluted.

A gust of autumn wind was all the answer he received. Tebelwas,
not daring to push the jest any further, had fled into the night.

"He's not a hermit, you know."

Gowek had been told to wash the dishes. Because it was a fine,
clear day, and Tebelwas had been put to work sweeping the priory's
footpaths, Gowek had contrived to do his task outdoors, so that he
and Tebelwas might converse surreptitiously.

"The Old One, I mean. He's not a hermit," Gowek repeated.

"Of course he's a hermit," said Tebelwas. "He lives alone in an
old hut. He never goes out, and nobody ever visits him except to
fetch in his meals and to fetch out his cloiter-pot. If that's not
a hermit, I'm King Caractacus. Did you know that the Old One
wears a *hevys*?"

"A hair-shirt?" Gowek shuddered. "He has embraced a hermit's
ways, then. Yet Brother Bohort is no ordinary hermit."

"Hermits are hermits," said Tebelwas.

"Yet listen." Gowek spoke in a whisper; as a mere postulant,
he was not supposed to speak at all except in utter necessity. For
two postulants to hold a conversation – much less to be found
gossiping about a brother of their Order – would bring penitence
upon both of them, sure, if any of the monks should overhear.
"I'm a bit older than you, Tebelwas, and I came to the Order for
sanctuary nearly two years before your arrival. There were other
hermits here before you came: elder monks of the Order, too blind
and feeble to serve the Christ in any useful way, yet their bellies

still required provender. The Order fed them, cared for them, and then buried them. This fellow Bohort is different."

Tebelwas had not forgotten the glimpse of silver he had seen at Brother Bohort's throat. "Different how?" he asked warily.

"He has not a friar's ways," said Gowek quietly. "I've seen him more often than you have, and watched him more carefully. The Old One was a *soldier* once."

"What?"

"A soldier, aye. Or a knight." Gowek scrubbed a stubborn blot of patina from the round tin serving-platter in his hand. "Do you not see his military bearing? The way he speaks to Father Derowen – with respect, but not humility – on the few occasions when they meet? Oh, he is bent and old now, and his feet are unsteady. But his stride is measured and regular, as if marching to drumbeats, and he turns corners at a sharp angle. A man does not learn to walk that way by chanting plainsongs. He was a soldier once, I warrant you. Or a knight."

Tebelwas said nothing, but swept the path with his broom.

"I'll tell you another thing," said Gowek eagerly. "The Old One's name is not Bohort. I have seen the order's register. The *codex accepti*."

"That's a lie," said Tebelwas. "You cannot read, for you have not been clerked."

"'Tis true, I am not clerked," Gowek admitted. "Yet Brother Clogh ... you will admit that *he* can read, eh? I wanted to know about the Old One, so on a pretext I went in errand to the *tabularium*. Brother Clogh was grateful for my company – I don't wonder; he spends his days with only books for companions – and I pretended to find fault with his ink. Said that it would fade with time, and wagered him my day's portion of fruit that the older records were no longer legible. Then I hinted that his archives were disorganized."

Tebelwas had become aware that Gowek's talent for craftiness was nearly as ripe as his own. "Well, what happened, then?"

"He bit, of course." Gowek was pleased with himself. "Brother Clogh challenged me to name any event in the Order's history, and he would prove me wrong by laying hands on the proper document instantly and reading it off. So I challenged him to find the exact date when Bohort joined this Holy Order."

Tebelwas waited.

"*Anno Domini* 542," said Gowek triumphantly. "Why, that's *seyth vledhen deu ygans* – seven-and-forty years ago!"

Tebelwas suppressed a shudder. He was only nineteen summers of age, and Gowek was perhaps a year older. Assuming that Brother Bohort had been at least twenty-five when he entered the monastery's gates, then . . . seventy-*two* years old! It seemed impossible to Tebelwas that any man could reap so many years.

"And that's not all," said Gowek, so excited now that he did not even bother to feign the actions of his tasks. "The friars call him Brother Bohort, but that isn't his name."

"What, then?"

"I heard it. Brother Clogh stumbled over the word when he read it out of the *codex*, but he pretended that there was an error in the vellum – a palimpsest – and the second time he read it out to me as 'Bohort'. Yet that was not the name he read the first time." Gowek shook his head and bent towards Tebelwas. "The Old One's name is . . . *Bors*!"

Tebelwas could feel the hairs prickling on the nape of his neck. "I have heard legends of a knight named Bors."

"As have I." Gowek turned over the tin platter and scrubbed its underside. "Three knights, they say, went forth from Camelot in quest of the Grail: Sir Galahad, Sir Parsifal . . . and *Sir Bors*."

The mind of Tebelwas grew full with thoughts of golden Grails . . . and silver. "Did they find what they sought?" he asked.

"No man knows," Gowek answered. "Sir Galahad died, in a land yclept Sarras. Parsifal's fate is unknown. Sir Bors, they say, became the king of a land yclept Claudas."

"A *king*, say you?" Tebelwas had never heard of these lands before: Sarras, Claudas. Yet foreign lands were known to be ripe with gold and silver, and kings were generally possessors of wealth. "Sir Bors, a king? How comes this king of distant lands to end his days *here*, in a hair-shirt, mumbling into his gruel in a poor-vows priory in Cornwall?" Tebelwas asked.

"Arthur summoned him, I'll wager," said Gowek. "There was a battle for the throne of Camelot, and Sir Bors came home to aid his lord, King Arthur."

Tebelwas spat into the dead leaves as he swept them. "You expect me to believe that a king would yield his throne – and endanger his riches – to serve as any other man's knight?"

"Not *any* man," said Gowek, and his eyes were shining. "Not any man, but King Arthur! Even the date fits, I tell you. Brother Bohort joined our priory in 542. That was only *three years* after Arthur died in battle! With Arthur dead, and Camelot fallen, the fire went out of Bohort's life, and he has dwelt here as a hermit

ever since. I tell thee, Brother Bohort is Sir Bors: the only knight
of the Round Table who found the Grail and lived to tell of it.
The last living knight of King Arthur."

Tebelwas gave no answer. He had been thinking about a single
piece of silver, suspended round a hermit's neck. But now, at the
mention of kingdoms and Grails, Tebelwas had begun to think
about vast quantities of *gold* . . .

"Art thou busied, Brother Clogh?"

The monastery's archive-keeper, the withered *tabularius*, looked
up from his dust-covered volumes, eager for some human company
in his cramped library. "Busied? No, but 'tis fortunate that you
came to see me today instead of tomorrow." Eagerly, the librarian
cleared a sitting-space for his two visitors. "Tomorrow is the
Kalendae Novembres – the first day of ninth-month – and I will
be busy the day long, transcribing this month's accounts into the
permanent ledger. But sit! What brings you hence?"

Gowek and Tebelwas had decided their strategy before their
arrival. First came the bribe-gift, to allay Brother Clogh's suspicions
and to loosen his tongue. "Here, Brother, is the fruit that I promised
you." From a fold within his garment, Gowek produced a handful
of rowanberries and an apologetic-looking pear. The rowanberries
aroused no comment – this was the end of October, after all, and
the priory's meagre rowanberry crop had attained the peak of its
ripeness a month earlier – but Brother Clogh's eyes widened at
sight of the pear.

"A *pear*! I tasted one of these once, when I visited Gaul." In a
trice, the librarian's bright teeth bit into the fruit's dappled skin
and devoured its ripe flesh.

Gowek winced as the pear began to vanish; he had made a
forbidden trip out of the priory's grounds to one of the local
track-paths leading eastward to the Fosse Way, and on that road
he had given a pedlar three farthings – hard-saved wealth, indeed,
for a postulant monk – in exchange for what was possibly the only
pear in Cornwall. "Tebelwas and I have come to seek thine advice,
Brother Clogh," he began.

The monk-cleric seemed flattered; no one had ever sought his
advice before. "What is your problem, *ow mebyon* – my sons?"

"I am troubled by a dream," said Tebelwas, who had rehearsed
the lie until it fitted his tongue easily. "Each night, I see before
me a box made of silver – so big." He held his thumb and
forefinger apart, duplicating the width of Brother Bohort's

pendant. "A box of silver, aye, with the emblem of a red triskele in its lid."

Brother Clogh seemed astonished. Then, wiping pear-juice from his fingers with the sleeve of his robe, the cleric went to a shelf and returned with a dust-covered vellum. "Is *this* the object which you saw?"

The codex held several lines of neatly lettered half-uncial script, and Tebelwas cursed himself for his inability to read. But in the centre of the page was a neat rubric illustration: a silver box, with a triskelion emblem picked out in red. Tebelwas recognized it: the secret keepsake of Sir Bors.

Tebelwas nodded.

Instantly Brother Clogh crossed himself.

"'Tis no dream that you had, then," said the cleric. "'Tis a vision! You have seen the reliquary of the Holy Grail!"

Gowek and Tebelwas exchanged glances. By now Brother Clogh's tongue needed no further loosening; it was rolling downhill of itself, and gathering momentum.

"Do you know the reliquary's tale, then, *ow mebyon*? This box that you saw: 'tis no dream-thing. It truly exists. It was brought to our monastery seven-and-twoscore years ago by Sir Bo –" the cleric caught himself just in time, and stifled the name on his lips "– by a man whom I may not name. Nor may I tell you where the reliquary now resides."

"Is this . . . this what-ye-call-'em valuable, then?" asked Gowek casually.

"Well, 'tis silver – a few shillings' worth – but there are men who will kill men for less. 'Tis the relic *inside* the reliquary which has the true worth," Brother Clogh went on heedlessly, pleased at last to have a chance of impressing someone with his knowledge.

"Go on, then," said Tebelwas. "What's in the box that's so valuable?"

"A mystery," said Brother Clogh, sighing rapturously. "Some say the box contains a fragment of the Holy Grail itself."

"Then the Grail must be precious? Of gold, perhaps?" Gowek asked innocently.

"Let me see." The robed cleric scanned the lines of the codex, then found what he sought. "Here it is, in the words of Sir . . . *ahem*! . . . in the words of he who found the Grail."

Brother Clogh lifted the vellum towards the single shaft of sunlight begrudged him by the archive's only window, and he read aloud the words: "'*In the kingdom of Sarras I beheld the*

Sacred Grail: a great circular dish, gleaming a-silver, encrusted all about its rim with jewels, which once had been the serving-dish at the Last Supper of Our Lord Jesus the Christ. And I beheld the Face and Hands of the Christ, extending His Grail unto me as I –'"

"Thy pardon, Brother Clogh, but I require ... *What* is the meaning of this?" The door had opened, unheard by Tebelwas or Gowek, and now the head of the priory was standing there, glaring in outrage. "Do I see postulants tarrying here?" Father Derowen raged, as Tebelwas and Gowek hastily leapt from their bench and genuflected before him. "Ye sin thrice, then: the sin of sloth, for you should be at your tasks. The sin of pride, for you have disobeyed the monks who set those tasks for you. And the sin of avarice, for you have stolen the precious time which Brother Clogh must devote to his duties, and hoarded that time for yourselves."

Tebelwas, knowing that he would only make matters worse by speaking, bowed his head and made the traditional penitent's gesture by way of apology. Gowek followed his example. Yet Father Derowen was unappeased.

"This grieves me sorely, for you two of all our Order's postulants should feel the greatest urge to atone for past transgressions," Father Derowen went on. "Thou, Tebelwas, thou wert 'prenticed to a thief, and did enter our priory's gates pleading sanctuary and vowing to live for the Christ ... yet you came here not, I notice, until *after* the authorities became aware of your criminal career. And thou, Gowek, art worse than a thief for thou wert 'prenticed to a *jongleur*, a mountebank, a conjuror! A man who pulled miracles out of his sleeves and sold them to the hoodwinked populace. And thou too, Gowek, very conveniently came not unto the Christ until the day when thou wert only one step ahead of the authorities."

There was no possible reply to this, especially since the Order's postulants were bound by vows of silence. Agan, Gowek and Tebelwas repeated the gesture of penitence.

"We will speak of this matter again, after Vespers," said the prior, signifying that Gowek and Tebelwas might cease their genuflexions. "I have business here with Brother Clogh. Leave us now ... and return to your tasks."

"Mayhap we shouldn't be doing this." Gowek glanced about furtively as he and Tebelwas proceeded through the woods. "Should we not at least wait several days? A fortnight, say, so as to give Father Derowen's wrath a time to cool."

"No, it must be tonight." Tebelwas trudged resolutely onward. "Are you not minded that tomorrow is the Kalendae Novembres? Tonight, then, is All Hallows Eve: the perfect night for miracles."

"I doubt that our 'miracle' will deceive the Old One," said Gowek nervously. "His body is old, yet his mind is not stupid."

"The Old One is twice blinded," said Tebelwas. "Once in his eyes and once in his faith. He sees naught except what he wishes to see. When he sees *this*, I warrant you, he will behold the Grail."

Tebelwas reached into the sack he was carrying and took out the monastery's serving-platter, its tin surface now polished and buffed to a high gleam. Around its circular edge, freshly affixed to it with marsh-sap from the Bodmin moors, were rubies and emeralds and sapphires . . . or rather glittering fragments of stained glass, which Tebelwas had harvested from a rubbish-tip behind the priory whilst Gowek had fetched the marsh-sap.

While Tebelwas had disguised the platter, Gowek too had been transformed. A generous application of marsh-sap to the lower half of his face, augmented with hair unwillingly donated by the priory's milk-goat, had provided Gowek with a long and saintly beard. Red ochre in the palms of his hands, and on the backs of his hands as well, completed the disguise, parodied the Christ's stigmata. The remainder of Gowek's face and hands had been liberally dusted with crumbled portions of the ripest jack o'lantern fungus from the moors.

Some of the fungus-dust had found its way into Gowek's nose; he sneezed. "Might it not be better if we traded roles?" Gowek mumbled as they neared the Old One's cottage.

"Thou art more skilful than I in the conjuror's art," said Tebelwas, flattering Gowek with the truth. "And besides, thy likeness resembleth the Christ's more nearly than doth mine own."

"I like this not," said Gowek, covering his disguised face with the cowl of the heavy magician's robe that he wore. Unlike the thin grey herringbone weave of his priory's Order, this was a thick dark cloth with a barleycorn weft, dyed a nearly perfect black, its hem descending to the ground and thus concealing Gowek's feet. Gowek had used this robe in his days as a mountebank's assistant, and had kept it concealed in a safe place on the priory's grounds – not in his own cramped postulant's cell, of course – until now. He sneezed again, and hurried onward through the dusk. "Methinks your plan does mock the Christ, and bring dishonour to the Cross."

"The Cross, say you?" Tebelwas dug a thumb and forefinger into the secret flap which he had sewn into his robe and drew forth his life's savings: a Saxon threepenny-bit, a souvenir of his former thief-jaunts in the marketplaces east of the river Tamar. He turned the coin so that Gowek could see its reverse. "You see this mark? The crucifer? *That's* the only cross that men do worship: this one and its brethren on coins made of silver and gold. The cross that jingles!" Gowek repocketed his coin and nodded. "Sir Bors was a king once, and a knight of King Arthur, hey? That's two kings, then, and two kings' ransoms. The Old One is the only man who knows what became of the treasure of Camelot and the wealth of the Grail."

"Perhaps he spent it all," suggested Gowek.

"Spent all, yet lived another seven-and-twoscore years with his last bit of silver a-dangling idle 'bout his neck?" Tebelwas shook his head as he hefted his sack containing the counterfeit Grail. "I'll warrant those treasures are near . . . and yon reliquary round the Old One's throat holds the key to their discovery."

In addition to the sack slung over his shoulder Tebelwas had also filched a double portion of *cawlcennin* from the priory's kitchen, and – whilst Father Ydfran had been busy elsewhere – had hastily added some pungent leeks and cabbage to the turnip broth.

It was nearly sunset on October's last evening when they reached the Old One's cottage. The autumn wind was rousing all about them, and even the clouds overhead seemed to glow with a strange inner light. This sight gave Tebelwas an inspiration for the lie which he would tell to Brother Bohort.

Gowek, cowled and garbed entirely in black, placed himself against the darkest background he could find: an easy task, this, in a dusking forest.

Tebelwas rapped confidently on the door, and was granted the Old One's cry, "Who comes?"

"I have brought thy supper, Brother Bohort." Tebelwas spoke through the door. "An extra portion, for the parish has given us its tithe today."

"So early comes mine evening meal? 'Tis not the Vespers yet." From somewhere in the hermit's hut a shuffling sound came closer. Then the bolt was drawn back and the door opened.

Instantly Tebelwas thrust the steaming bowl of pungent broth as close as possible to Brother Bohort's nose without splashing him. The ancient half-blind monk – who had long since grown accustomed to relying on his sense of smell more fully than his failing eyes – was distracted by the strong odour of *cawlcennin*, long enough for the black-robed figure of Gowek to slip past him and enter the cottage. Tebelwas too entered, uninvited. "God rest you, Brother," he said, with loud voice and broad gestures, so as to distract the hermit's eyes and ears from Gowek's presence.

The interior of the Old One's lodge was just as dark as Tebelwas had remembered it to be; again, the fire within the hearth had dwindled low unto embers, but this time Tebelwas did not resurrect the flame. Darkness was more congenial for his stratagem.

"Hast thou heard the tidings, Brother Bohort?" asked Tebelwas casually, as the ancient monk found his tin spoon and bent to the bowl of *cawlcennin*.

"Tidings? Tidings? I hear of no tidings," rasped the Old One as he mumbled his soup. "I am an *ancaren*, a hermit."

"You have not heard, then?" said Tebelwas innocently, gesturing at Gowek to make ready. "All the monks of our order have seen it. Tonight, in the sky above our monastery, we beheld a *glowing Cross*. It came towards us and grew larger, and –"

"*I summon thee, Sir Bors*," interrupted a voice, emerging from the shadowed blackness at the far end of the hermit's lodge.

The Old One suddenly stiffened. He stood, and turned towards the voice. "*Pandr'a vynnough wy*? What do you want?"

"*In Arthur's name I summon thee*," grated the voice, and from within the folds of darkness – literally folds, because in the dim light of the cottage Tebelwas could see the folds of Gowek's robe, where the half-blind Old One saw only blackness – there now emerged a metal shape that gleamed like silver. It came edge on, and then it turned. "*Behold the Grail*."

A shining circular platter, gleaming a-silver, hung suspended in mid-air. Round its edge there glittered precious jewels. The Old One trembled, and with an effort he fell to his knees. His palsied hands clutched at his hair-shirt and drew forth . . . yes! . . . the silver box, the reliquary. He clutched it, yet he did not open it.

In the dimness above the floating Grail there now appeared a bearded face, and a pair of outstretched hands disfigured by two bleeding wounds. The face and hands glowed eerily in the darkness, with the same greenish phosphorescence that was sometimes displayed on the moors of Cornwall by certain species of decaying fungus.

"My Lord! 'Tis I, Thy servant Bors!" As Tebelwas looked

on in astonishment a change came over the Old One. His body seemed to cast off its burthen of age. For seven-and-forty years his soul had disguised itself as Bohort, humble monk of an obscure priory. Yet now – there was no mistaking it – he became again as once he had been: Sir Bors, the keeper of the Grail. The last knight of King Arthur's Camelot.

"*Here is thy task, Sir Bors,*" intoned the voice of the bearded visitor. "*Reveal unto me, in the presence of yon postulant, the location of the treasures of Sarras – aye, and Camelot. And give to my postulant that reliquary at your throat, so that I . . . I . . .* Achoo!"

Gowek sneezed, and the false Grail – which had been attached to the front of his robe by two black threads – fell clattering to the floor. At the same instant Sir Bors convulsed. He tore the leathern cord from his neck and broke open the silver reliquary.

Tebelwas caught a glimpse of some brightness unknown – some small object that glittered more fiercely than any metal or jewel he had encountered in all his thief's days. Swiftly, deliberately, the last knight of Camelot flung the small object towards the hearth – directly into the embers of the fireplace.

There was a flash of light within the embers. "In Arthur's name, Lord . . . *I come!*" cried the Old One. Suddenly Sir Bors gasped, and clutched his hair-shirt on the left side of his chest. His body pitched forward and fell.

No! The plan had gone wrong! In sudden panic, it occurred to Tebelwas that it might be prudent if he elsewhered himself. He turned and ran for the door, leaving Gowek to his own devices.

As Tebelwas rushed outside the wind hit him. A gale, a torrent of air was plunging through the forest. Twigs and dead leaves rose up and stung his face as he hurried away. He stumbled, turned and looked back . . .

Above the cottage of the Old One hung a single glowing cloud, gleaming a-silver and shaped like a vast, airborne platter or saucer. Round its edge, a row of jewels – or lights, or stars – winked and glittered like fireflies. Mayhap some unknown constellation in the night sky? And now, as Tebelwas looked on, a single shaft of light – a moonbeam, surely? – emerged from the centre of the disc-shaped cloud and pierced the thatched roof of the Old One's hut.

From within the hermit's cottage, someone screamed. Gowek? Or the Old One himself?

Tebelwas turned and fled. Halfway back to the priory's walls he heard the slap of sandal-clad feet. Brother Morgelyn and Father Derowen came pattering towards him. *"A'n gwelsough wy?"* shouted Tebelwas, ignoring the Order's vows of silence as he stabbed his finger skywards at the apparition. "Did you see it? This way!"

The two monks rushed onwards towards the hermit's lodge, and Tebelwas – feeling a pang of concern for Gowek's safety – came behind them.

Gowek was dead. He lay, face upward, on the dirt floor of the cottage, his eyes staring lifelessly. Father Derowen gasped and crossed himself upon sight of the Christ-beard and false stigmata that Gowek wore.

The Old One was gone. Alive or dead, his flesh had vanished. A mouldy hair-shirt, thick and rumpled, in one corner of the hut, was all that remained of Camelot's last knight. A hair-shirt and a shattered reliquary.

To Tebelwas, the cottage seemed more brightly lit than it had been when he had fled. Gazing upwards, he discovered the reason: there was a jagged hole in the thatched roof, slightly larger than the breadth of a man. Above the hole, the twilit stars hung winking.

"I saw . . . I saw . . ." Tebelwas gasped for breath and collected his wits. "I saw a silver dish within the sky."

"You saw the moon," said Brother Morgelyn.

"Around its edge there glittered flashing jewels."

"You saw the stars," said Brother Morgelyn.

"I saw a beam of light descend and touch a man, and now the man is gone," said Tebelwas.

"A moonbeam came," said Brother Morgelyn.

Father Derowen beckoned Tebelwas to come closer. The postulant approached the prior fearfully, yet Father Derowen's voice was surprisingly gentle.

"Come with me to the chapel, my son."

The Vespers were delayed that night while Tebelwas confessed himself, face downwards on the floor as was the custom of his Order. Afterwards, Father Derowen decreed a penance – a surprisingly light one. Tebelwas, relieved, began to clamber to his feet . . . until a gesture from the prior signified that he should remain where he was.

"I have given thee a penance, Tebelwas, but not a punishment," said Father Derowen. "Think upon thy crimes, then ask thyself: What penalty is fitting?"

Tebelwas, fully aware that he would not be permitted the luxury of choosing his own penalty, said nothing.

"Here is your punishment," said Father Derowen. "You are the youngest one within our gates. If you are kept healthy and strong by means of hard work, with no chance of trysts with Mistress Gluttony or Lady Sloth, you will likely outlive every member of our order. I intend to make certain that for many years to come you will have *plenty* of hard work, with no opportunities to overeat or oversleep. In this wise, so you will survive us."

Father Derowen's voice grew colder. "But other things survive as well. You have told a strange legend this night: of a Grail in the sky and flashing lights, and a vanishing man. Yet legends are the opposite of men; in the passage of time men dwindle and vanish, whilst legends grow larger. Only a few men grow larger with time; Arthur was one. That is why Sir Bors took holy vows, and became the Brother Bohort of our Order; he served Arthur willingly in life, yet after Arthur's death he wanted to escape the legend. To 'scape the burthen of being the last living knight of the Round Table.

"Another legend has begun tonight, my son, and you will preserve it in your most sacred receptacle: the one that God in His Wisdom has given to all men, yet denied to the beasts." Father Derowen tapped his own skull while pointing with his other hand towards the mind of Tebelwas. "In here: the reliquary of *memory*. But in time this legend will escape the boundaries of your memory, and the seeds of this legend will grow and ripen unbidden in the minds of those who were not here tonight."

Now Tebelwas began to sense what was coming. Father Derowen smiled cruelly, but there was pity in his eyes. "This is your penalty, Tebelwas ... and your curse. You will live all your days in our priory. And in distant years hence – when all the rest of us have died and been replaced by other men – when you have grown old – when time mocks you and your flesh has betrayed you – there will come into this place impatient young fools who will give you no peace, just as you gave no peace to Sir Bors. And these eager fools will plague your last years with their endless questions and other torments. They will all want to meet you, and speak with you, and pluck at you, and scavenge at your mind's reliquary. For you will be ...

the last living man who knew the last living knight of King Arthur."

Then Father Derowen turned his back upon the trembling postulant, and went away to chant the Vespers.

PERONNIK THE FOOL

George Moore

In The Merlin Chronicles, *I reprinted "The Castle of Kerglas" by Emile Souvestre. That was based on the same Breton legend that Moore uses in the following story. Both are based on the original story of Peredur or Perceval, but in the telling the tale has moved on from the Celtic and Norman-French origins. In this version you will find a timeless quest for the Grail. George Moore (1852–1933) is rapidly becoming a forgotten author, even though in his heyday he was every bit as well-known as his contemporary Irish colleagues Oscar Wilde, George Bernard Shaw and W.B. Yeats. His most successful work was* Esther Waters *(1894), a frank and powerful story of social degradation and religious salvation. In his later years Moore turned to more mythic themes, including a novel about Jesus and Joseph of Arimathea,* The Brook Kerith *(1916), a translation of* Daphnis and Chloë *(1924), the novels* Héloïse and Abelard *(1921) and* Aphrodite in Aulis *(1930), and the following Arthurian tale.*

I

Boy or youth, which was he? Héloïse could not remember, only that he was allowed to beg his living from door to door, everybody throwing him a crust when there was one by that did not seem wanted, and, when he grew stronger, claiming the right to send him to the well, to give him an adze to chop wood in the backyard, and to pay him for his day's work with broken meats and two sheaves of straw to lie on in a barn. Everybody's drudge, she said, and nobody taking thought to teach him a trade, not caring even to ask him who his parents were or what manner of life his was before he strayed into the village of Saint-Jean-de-Braie. A mere child of seven or eight, she continued as she sat in the convent library biting the end of her quill.

And, having recalled all she had heard in Brittany of his story, her pen kept pace with her memories of Peronnik – how he had wandered out of the forest and had since forgotten everything except the forest, whither it was still his wont to return (compelled, maybe, by some homesickness), sometimes staying away for three or four days, setting the folk talking, asking each other if they had lost their Peronnik for ever. She had heard that he once stayed away so long that the folk had gone forth to seek him, getting tidings of him as they passed through the fringes of the forest. He passed us by at daybreak, singing like a lark in the morning, the woodmen cried; and these tidings were enough for the searchers, who turned back, saying, We shall find him begging his breakfast from somebody, and from us he'll get the thrashing he deserves for having put us to such pains. Why, there he is! cried one, in the doorway of Farmer Leroux's house. Whereupon they stood waiting, fidgeting at their sticks, whilst Peronnik enjoyed such cheer as he could get out of a wooden bowl that all the spoons of the house had already been over. As he scraped and picked the clotted meal from the sides he talked so pleasantly, flattering the goodwife so well that she bethought herself of some crusts in her cupboard and returned with her hands full, throwing them one by one into the bowl, for which Peronnik was thankful, gobbling them up with such good appetite that a knight in armour riding by could not do else than rein in his horse to watch him.

Thou hast a hungry boy with thee, he said, addressing the housewife. And well might he be hungry, she answered, for not a bite nor a sup has passed his lips these three days or more. Which is it, Peronnik, three days or five? Peronnik held up his hand, for his fingers were his accounts. Five days, as much as that, said the housewife. And with nothing in my belly but berries, of that I am sure, said Peronnik; and the housewife began to tell the knight of the mischief, how searchers had gone forth to seek him in the forest. And are still seeking him, maybe ... But, in troth, they are back again, having gotten tidings of him. You see them at yon house, waiting till you've gone, sir, to come hither to enquire out his adventures. So he knows the forest? the knight asked. As none other knows it, she answered, laughing, and fell to telling more stories of Peronnik's rambles, the knight cutting her short, saying, If he be knowledgeable of the forest paths, he is the boy I am looking for; and, turning to Peronnik, he asked him if he could lead him to the Grey Castle. In the name of the Holy Virgin and God himself! cried the housewife, it cannot be that a noble knight like you, sir, should be going to the Grey Castle? By my faith, I am, the knight replied, if I can find it; for three months I have been seeking it, and for as many years my companions-in-arms have been on their way thither.

At these words Peronnik lifted his head from the wooden bowl out of which he was feeding, and with his eyes on the knight he hearkened, hearing that the Diamond Spear and the Golden Bowl were the greatest treasures the world could bestow on any man. For in the Golden Bowl, said the knight, he will find all food and drink that he may wish for and every kind of wealth. Faith and troth! That bowl is the bowl for me, said Peronnik to himself. Every kind of wealth, the knight continued, and also health, for if he eat and drink from the Golden Bowl he shall be healed, whatever his sicknesses may be; and though he may be dead, if not for more than three days, life will come back to him if the Bowl be put to his lips. What a wonderful bowl this is! said Peronnik. I would have it for myself. Well, tell us now about the Spear, good knight.

The Spear, the knight said, will destroy everything it touches. And who owns the Bowl and the Spear? asked Peronnik. Good knight, cried the housewife, you will not lead the poor boy astray? Ah! said the knight, so thou hast heard of the Bowl and the Spear. And thou too hast heard of them? he added, turning to Peronnik. And who would have heard of them if I hadn't? Peronnik answered, for I was born and bred in the forest and many's the time I've seen in the days gone by the enchantress Redemonde riding, the Spear in rest and the Bowl at her girdle. But would she ride about the forest with the Spear and the Bowl? the knight asked, and this time it was the housewife who answered him. Faith, said the woman, the sorceress would be of no high degree in her arts if she left the castle without the Spear and the Bowl, for without them she would be no more than ourselves and it would be easy to invade her castle. Thou speakest well, woman, said the knight; none can prevail against her while she have the Spear. She lays the Spear aside when she enters the castle, continued the woman. And the Bowl and the Spear sink down into a vault with a door that no key can open but hers, said the knight; and my plan is to make show to fall in with her humour and to steal her keys while she sleeps. I have heard of plans no better and no worse than yours, sir knight, from many of your company that have passed by my house asking the way to the Grey Castle, but none of them returned from thence. Thou sayest well, answered the knight; none of them returned from the castle, for none of them took counsel of the hermit of Blavet. And did you do that, good knight? asked Peronnik.

I did indeed, replied the knight; and was told by him that a hard task was before me, for out of the Wood of Deceits, he said, will come to meet me all kinds of fears and terrors, and if my heart be staunch and I do not yield to them, flowers will bend down from their stalks and sweet perfumes assail my nostrils; at the end of the vistas fair, shadowy forms will beckon me, and if I follow them they will lead me into deserts where I shall perish from cold and hunger, like those that went before me. But if I pass, as I shall pass, through the Wood of Deceits in safety, I shall meet a dwarf waving a fiery dart which burns up everything around it within twenty paces of the apple tree from which I must pluck an Apple. If I escape the flames and get the Apple, I shall have to go in search of the Laughing Flower, but to pluck this I must beguile a lion whose mane is of living snakes. I shall wait till the lion sleeps (the snakes are forever wakeful, but I must get the Flower); and having gotten the Flower I shall seek a passage through the dragon-haunted lake, and on reaching the thither side a fight will begin between me and the Black Man, whose weapon is an iron ball that returns of itself to the master after every throw. After that I shall enter the Valley of Delights to conquer every kind of temptation with which the Devil may assail a Christian. My courage will weaken, but it will become strong again, for I shall resort to prayers and fare onwards till I come to a river by whose bank sits a lady clad in black. She will say to me, Good knight, thou must carry me across the ford, for it is said I may not instruct thee on the hither side, but on the thither thou'lt learn from me what next thou hast to do. All these perils await me, said the knight, but I go to meet them without fear and asking no help from anybody but Peronnik, who will point out the path to the Grey Castle in the woods.

The goodwife would have stopped Peronnik from telling the knight the way, for her heart was moved at the thought that a man of good appearance and fair words should be lost to the world, which sadly needed such men, but before she could pluck the Fool by the sleeve he had pointed out the path to the knight, who at once pricked forward. Redemonde will get his life and his armour, the woman said, and was moved to pull Peronnik by the ears. But of what good to pull a fool's ears? she asked herself, and threw him instead two or three more crusts, bidding him go his way and never return to her again, for after his wanton words she hoped to see his face no more. Of reproofs Peronnik understood nothing, but he was used to being told to go his way, and he was about to do as he was bidden when the housewife caught sight of her husband coming across the fields. In an evil humour my good man comes to me, she said, his gait tells it to me plainly; and she began to ask herself, Has he come upon a lamb dead in the fields, or has the mare cast her foal? Before any words passed his lips Leroux's eyes fell on Peronnik, and he said, Now then, my boy, my neat-herd has gone for disobedience to my orders, and thou'rt the lad I want to take his place. At which the goodwife held her peace, for the time was not one to arouse his anger further; and she bethought herself of the great rise in life this was for Peronnik.

From that day Peronnik minded the farmer's cows, the white and the brown and the black, keeping them together in the pasture the farmer had told him they were to feed in, forgetful at first of the Diamond Spear and the Golden Bowl; stories did not stay long in Peronnik's head, and of all at the time he was in, for he had the weather to think of, and very bad weather it was, the country withering under a blue sky with never a cloud in it except the one that appeared about three o'clock every day and fled away southward, breaking Peronnik's heart. If the clouds do not gather and no more rain falls, whither shall I drive my cows to pasture? he said again and again, for there's little grass anywhere, and what there is is dry and crisped, with no diet in it. And whither shall I drive them for water? The pools that were are but baked mud, and the river that was is but heaps of hot shingle, with only a trickle round the middle rocks.

And it was as Peronnik said; the country seemed to have fallen out of its luck. Rain is our need and without it we perish, was the cry of man and beast and bird. Even when the chains of the deepest wells were lengthened the buckets came up but half filled. The spells of the sorceress have caused this drought, for we will not worship Satan with her, the folk replied to the knights who came riding, asking that the path to the Grey Castle should be shown to them, every knight gathering a crowd of villagers about his saddle bow, crying, Let the Spear and the Bowl be raped from the sorceress else we perish. At which words the knights pricked on hastily, promising to return with both. But none returned, and the villagers fell into steady despair, saying, We are undone; we thirst in our houses and the cattle thirst in the fields even unto death; our hens thirst, and the ducks and the geese return from their quest for water sadly; the flowers wither in the gardens, and no honey will be gathered by the bees this season. We are undone utterly if rain do not fall. We have neither catapults nor towers to lay siege with, and the armoured knights meet their fate, for whosoever has the Spear is all-powerful. Will no true knight by the power of God and his virtue release us from the sorceress? If we pray will he come? And the folk fell to praying till some began to doubt if God's power availed against Redemonde. The roads are empty, no knights come. Hast seen a knight? they cried to Peronnik, returning with his cattle from a distant river. Hast seen a knight journeying? Never a one, he answered; the sorceress has had them all. And in the river did thy beasts get their fill? They wetted their nozzles in the leavings of the birds, replied Peronnik, for thousands of birds have come down from the woods and have drunk up what remains of the Arduzon. We perish utterly, were the words that Peronnik heard wailed behind him, if no knight come to save us from the woman in the Grey Castle. Wicked above all other women she is, Peronnik said to himself, and continued on his way, asking himself why she sought to destroy the poor folk who had no castle to live in. What have we done, he said, to merit this revenge? And what have the poor cows, who in other days gave their milk so cheerfully, done to deserve her terrible hatred? And that he might think more fully he sat himself by the roadside. Another knight comes, he said, catching the sound of hooves, whom I shall direct to his doom; for Peronnik was not without a heart. But seeing that the horseman wore no armour, he said to himself, No knight is this one.

Why now, my lad, said the horseman, reining in his steed beside Peronnik, what grief is this that sets such young eyes as thine weeping? Grief there is enough in the world for men and women, but for lads and lasses the world should be naught but songs and flowers. For what art thou weeping? I am weeping, good sir, Peronnik answered, for the witch of the Grey Castle in the wood has laid a curse upon the land. And who told these evil tidings of the lady in the Grey Castle? the knight asked. Good sir, replied Peronnik, I am but telling the stories that are told in the village. It may be that her ladyship knows none of these things, and that the curse that has fallen is not her curse. But if no rain fall within the next few days my cows and young heifers will lie down and die and be eaten by wolves. But the wolves, too, have to drink, said the knight, and he asked whither they went for it and learnt from Peronnik that the wolves knew of pools untouched by the curse lying far away in the depths of the forest. Hearken, sir, to that poor heifer calling me from the well-head, but were I to let down the bucket again it might come up dry. I have no heart to disappoint her, nor have I heart to see her die. I grieve for my cows and for my master, who will be as poor as I am this winter if the curse be not lifted from the land.

At these words the horseman covered his face with his hands, and Peronnik guessed him to be weeping. You are weeping, good sir, he said, for my dying kine; and if the paths of the forest be not known to you I will point them out, and maybe (though a knight you are not, for you wear no armour) the witch of the Grey Castle will listen to your prayers and give back the Diamond Spear and the Golden Bowl, and the country be saved from famine. Alas, Peronnik, I know the paths through the forest and need no guide. Look into my face and tell me if thou rememberest me. And that Peronnik might judge him better the horseman stepped down from the saddle and, leading his horse by the bridle, stood by Peronnik, saying, Look into my face and say if thou hast not seen it before. Good sir, said Peronnik, you are the knight who stopped to watch me cleaning out the porridge bowl when I returned from the forest. For as many days as I have fingers I was with naught but berries in my belly, I was hungry; and the goodwife's hand was stretched to snatch the bowl from me, for my readiness to lead you to the Grey Castle, sir. That day was a dark one for me, the knight answered, but for thee it was a bright day; for I have not forgotten Farmer Leroux coming from his fields angry at his neat-herd's disobedience to his orders, and, seeing thee, he said, Vagrant though thou art, I will trust thee till I find thee disobedient. My luck came, sir knight, just as you tell it. And such luck never came before to a hind like me, for those in search of me were waiting to beat me, as I heard afterwards. But, sir, your countenance is so rueful that I guess a great grief must be upon you.

Overtaken am I by many misfortunes, the knight replied; a knight without sword or shield or lance is indeed unfortunate even amid the unfortunate. And who robbed you of your armour? asked Peronnik. Myself robbed myself, was the answer that he got, and Peronnik sat wondering, for the knight bade him keep

his seat, saying that it was he who should stand. But my crippled
knee forbids it, he said, and I will sit beside thee instead on this
fallen tree, and we will talk, Peronnik, of the day that I rode
away confident into the forest in quest of the Grey Castle. You
spoke, said Peronnik, about the Wood of Deceits and the Valley
of Delights, through which you would pass with your eyes closed
lest lovely shapen fairies – I have forgotten what the dangers were,
sir knight, but did you overcome them and reach the castle? I
did indeed, the knight replied, and so came into my misfortune.
I remember my cattle and would know them among hundreds,
said Peronnik, but have little memory for words, yet I have not
forgotten that you said that whosoever owned the Golden Bowl
would find in it all the food and drink and wealth he wished for,
and that whosoever owned the Diamond Spear would be master of
the world, for it destroys everything it touches. Whilst driving my
cattle from pasture to pasture I have often thought that if I were a
knight I would go in quest of the Spear and the Bowl and save my
country from the curse that the woman in the Grey Castle has put
upon it, without telling my thoughts to anybody, for were a word
to go forth that I was thinking such things I would have all the
village laughing at me. But you, sir knight, have not joined with the
village against me? Joined with the village against thee, Peronnik?
said the knight. Putting a joke upon me, answered Peronnik, for
it is hard to believe that you passed through all the great perils
you told us of and have come back from the Grey Castle without
the Spear and the Bowl. It may be, Peronnik, that thine eyes have
never dwelt with rapture upon a woman's beautiful face? Your
words, sir knight, are hard for a neat-herd, a stray come into the
village of Saint-Jean-de-Braie without a story to tell of his father
or mother.

A woman's beautiful face! Peronnik repeated, and he asked
the knight if all the beautiful ones were good and the ugly ones
wicked. To which the knight replied that he would not go so far
as to say that, but believed that a fine open countenance never
foreshadowed a base soul, words that were too hard for Peronnik
to find an answer for. Moreover, he was minded to ask the knight
how he might know beauty when it passed him by, if it were sinful
to be beautiful, and if men were beautiful as well as women, getting
from the knight the answer that beauty was not given to men and
women only, but was shared by the birds and the beasts. The
loving heifer approaching us, Peronnik, is beautiful. If you were
milking her, sir knight, Peronnik answered, you'd have a different

word for her, for however hard I pull at the teats I cannot fill the pail. Flowers are more beautiful than grass, said the knight. Not in my eyes, replied Peronnik, for I would give all the flowers in the world for a field of juicy grass into which I might turn my kine. Only great knights like you, sir, can praise milkless udders and set flowers above useful grass. Whilst seeking the Grail you turn verses as you ride about girls with rosy cheeks and white legs – Leaving the sallow faces and the tough skins songless, said the knight. But are there no lads in thy village whose hearts ache after rosy cheeks and white legs? There are many such, said Peronnik. But thou'rt not one of them? the knight asked. My mother may have kissed me, but I have no memory of her, Peronnik replied.

Rather than these things I would hear from you, sir knight, how you passed through the Wood of Deceits and the Valley of Delights. And cheated the dwarf, said the knight, who guards the apple tree, and the lion whose mane is of live snakes. To have overcome such a beast as that you must be possessed of a great secret, sir knight, said Peronnik; for those who went before you had doubtless stout hearts, but a stout heart is not enough to overcome a lion whose mane is of live snakes. It is as thou sayest, Peronnik, for the snakes are wakeful, and when the lion sleeps a snake is always ready to rouse him at the approach of danger. I went to the hermit of Blavet, who told me how I might deceive the lion and poison the dragons in the lake; but he gave me no secret to save me from the beauty of the Lady Redemonde, who came to my saddle bow to welcome me when I reached the castle, and held a goblet of sweet wine to my lips and pressed into my hand spiced cakes on a silver salver. These I might have denied myself, but not her sweet smile nor the sunny gold of her hair. But of these things thou knowest nothing, Peronnik. Nothing indeed, Peronnik, replied; much more of porridge and crusts, and not enough of them at the end of a hard day's work. But for the sake of my kine and of the village of Saint-Jean-de-Braie I would have turned my eyes from the cakes and wine and said, Sorceress, I have come for the Diamond Spear and the Golden Bowl. Then it may be, the knight said, that thou art the lad I am seeking. A mocking-stock, sir knight, you must be making of me, for why should a knight, even one who has trespassed, seek such a boy as I am?

Thou would'st hear, asked the knight, what happened to me? I would indeed, Peronnik answered, and the knight said, Besides the beauty of the Lady Redemonde there was music and dancing and sweet singing and fine linen in her castle. I dallied with her, and when the day came for me to ride round the castle ramparts, the last task through which a knight must pass before he claim the Bowl and the Spear, my will was not free to conquer, and I rode weakly at the great abyss; and myself and my horse were thrown into it, my horse being killed and myself carried a cripple to the castle, where my limbs were mended as best they might be. Since then I have had no will but the will of the Lady Redemonde, and her power over me is such that I go forth at her bidding to lure other knights, knowing well that they will fail in the Wood of Deceits or the Valley of Delights, not one having had care to go to the hermit of Blavet, who alone can tell a good and true knight how he may save himself from these dangers.

So you, sir knight, were the only one to reach the castle? Peronnik asked, and the knight answered that the others perished in the Wood or in the Valley, some, by the aid of heart-felt prayers, getting through those places, only to perish in the desert that lay outside. Thou'lt see their bones – But shall I have to go in search of the Diamond Spear and the Golden Bowl? Peronnik asked. If the country is to be saved, thou'lt have to go, replied the knight, but possessed of the secrets that will bring thee to the castle unscathed. For all secrets are in my power for giving save how to harden thy heart against Lady Redemonde's beauty. I have that myself, said Peronnik, so think no more of it. But while I am away seeking the Spear and the Bowl who will let down the buckets in the wells and wind them up again? Think not of thy herd but of thy country, the knight replied; thy herd matters little, for the herds of all the world will be thine if thou returnest with the Spear and the Bowl. I am but a hind, sir knight, and would be driven away from her castle. We can put knighthood upon thee, the knight said. But, answered Peronnik, I should never dare to ride through the streets of Saint-Jean-de-Braie with a shield on my arm and a lance in my hand and a sword by my side, none of which I have had any practice with, all the boys and girls throwing things at me, saying, Lord! there goeth Peronnik, a greater fool than ever he was before. To which the knight answered that he could give Peronnik his horse only. Armour he had none, neither sword nor lance. She having taken mine from me. But, said Peronnik, I know where there is a lance and a sword and a shield and a helmet. Then let us go in search of them! cried the knight. There may be no sword and there may be no shield and there may be no lance, answered Peronnik, but there's a helmet in a blasted tree on a heath. But this the knight could not believe, saying: How should a helmet have come down a hollow tree? It may be only one of Peronnik's thoughts, he said to himself, which are little considered in Saint-Jean-de-Braie; and they fared onward into the forest.

II

And through shady dells, over sunlit hill-tops out of sight of watchers, out of hearing of eavesdroppers, the twain wandered, the knight in deep thought, Peronnik leading the horse half forgetful of the Grey Castle and his approaching knighthood, happy in the enchantment of the forest, and at home in it even as the birds and animals.

At noon the knight dismounted, and whilst the horse grazed at tether he talked to Peronnik of the honour of knighthood and its duties, the chime of his words, of which Peronnik understood nothing, bringing sleep into Peronnik's eyes. But remembering, as he always did, that courtesy should be lacking in nobody, he struggled against the weariness that the warmth of the sunlight and the monotonous murmur of the forest imposed upon his eyelids, till the knight's talk became in his mind a green and golden mystery, full of vague sounds, with somebody talking whose voice Peronnik had heard before in the streets of Saint-Jean-de-Braie, but whose name kept slipping from his memory, try hard as he might to remember it. And this was the last that Peronnik heard of the pardoner, who had stopped in front of the knight to rest for a while, the afternoon being hot and his pack heavy, and who, sitting on a fallen bole, had fallen to deploring the evil times, saying that he had traversed many villages without selling a single relic, and in a country renowned for its plenty. And this pause of faith among the peasantry he set down to the drought, for having addressed themselves to God without avail the peasantry were now offering prayers to the Devil every evening in the Village of Saint-Jean-de-Braie, a favourite retreat for worship being a dusky garden or orchard. On the knight asking the reason for these conversions, the pardoner said that the folk had put aside the priest, saying that the same power could not be the creator of both good and evil. He had often heard mutterings among the crowd that collected about him: God is deaf; the Devil may have a readier ear to our prayers. He and the priest, though often at variance, were agreed that Devil-worship was of all sins the worst, and they had striven against the heresy. If he had had some relics of the evil one, some clippings of the hooves and a few bristles or hairs from his hinder parts, he could have driven a fine trade in Saint-Jean-de-Braie in these days of drought. But neither Satan nor Beelzebub nor any of the inferior fallen angels had abided on earth, so there was little of their bodies that he could collect; smells there were in plenty, but smells could not be collected. Moreover, he was not one of those who turned their backs on their benefactors. He had thriven in the belief that God was the creator of both good and evil, and in this belief he would abide, selling only relics of the saints and holy men and women.

On these words the pardoner began to vaunt his wares, and the rather a bit of sail from St Peter's boat. He displayed teeth from the jaws of nearly all the Apostles; and as these did not tempt the knight he continued his prattle unavailingly till he produced a bunch of feathers plucked from the cock that crowed the morning of the day that Christ died, adding happily that any one of these would keep the wearer safe from the curse of the sorceress. Now is this true what you are telling me? the knight asked; shall my thoughts be safe from her, for she is a great reader of thoughts? As long as you wear this feather your thoughts will be your own, the pardoner replied; and he picked the finest feather from the bunch and gave it to the knight in return for a piece of money. And then strapping his pack together he departed quickly, leaving the knight in a pretty humour of smiling satisfaction, for what he feared more than all else were Redemonde's eyes. But they will read no more from me, he muttered, for this feather I shall wear in my bosom. And calling upon Peronnik, who did not answer, the lad having rolled over asleep under a holly, he picked him up and bade him lay his hand on the bridle and lead on to the hollow tree where the needed armour was hidden. Is our way to the right or to the left, to the west or to the east, to the north or to the south? the knight asked. Such questions as these Peronnik could not answer, and the knight, angered by his dullness of wit, was about to bid him away from him back to Farmer Leroux to get beaten for his neglect of the herd. But before he could speak the words, like one bidden from within, Peronnik seized the bridle of the knight's horse, and they went forward till evening, seeing only hawks at hover above the tree-tops and foxes slinking through the underwood. Only hawks and foxes have we seen, said the knight, since we started forth this morning, and Peronnik answered him that in all his forest faring he had never seen before the trees they were among. Nor this boulder, he said, nor yon stunted pines; it is not my forest but another. And the knight was about to lay his lance about Peronnik's shoulders, but kept himself from doing so lest he should run away; and Peronnik could easily outstrip him by dodging from tree to tree, passing under the thick bushes and round rocks where a horseman could not go. And were this to happen, he said to himself, I am lost indeed; Peronnik is my chance to escape from the forest.

And as courtesy is always better than hard words in such circumstances he spoke encouragingly to Peronnik, who fared on at hazard till the night was nigh upon them, when he cried out, Sir, yonder are three ravens just come up from the rocks. Yes, the knight replied, I see three black birds of ill omen in the air. Not so, answered Peronnik, this evening the ravens are birds of good omen, for their way is to their roosting-tree, and we have but to follow them to come upon the buried armour. Nor had they fared far when Peronnik began to remember the part of the forest he was in, and he begged the knight to take courage, saying that they were within a quarter of a league, or less than that, of the helmet he had heard the birds speak about. And the knight, putting confidence in Peronnik's wood-lore, fared onward with him in silence until the evening star burst into flame in the heavens and the tree was before them with the three ravens on its branches. It was from them, said Peronnik, that I heard of the armour hidden in the tree. So thou hast told me already, the knight answered; but what knowest thou of the talk of birds? More than you think for, sir knight, for there is a raven in Farmer Leroux's yard that speaks as plainly as you do; when he has hidden anything he goes hopping about, crying to us, Look here, look there, look everywhere, and the very same words I have heard the ravens in yon tree speak before tucking their heads under their wings. Now give your ear to them, sir knight, and what I tell you you will hear.

The knight listened to the chatter above in the branches, but he could not divide it into words for a long time, and once more he began to think that Peronnik was fooling him; all the same, he could not do else than listen to the birds. Now, sir knight, Peronnik whispered, tell me what you think you hear; and the knight answered, Methinks I hear one bird say: Look here, and the next answer: Look there, and the three cry together: Look everywhere, for the — Helmet is in the tree, Peronnik whispered; put your hand to your ear, sir knight. The knight raised his hand, hearing this time, so it seemed to him, the word helmet in the birds' talk. It may be as thou thinkest, Peronnik, that we are within reach of what we need to win the Bowl and Spear from the sorceress. So now up with thee into the tree; as easy to climb it is as any ladder, and I will hoist thee into the first branches.

With a great clatter of wings and hoarse cries of anger the ravens flopped away into the forest, and Peronnik, reaching the hollow bole, looked down into it, crying to the knight, who waited below for tidings. The ravens have not lied to us; a helmet there is in the tree, and it being no more than six feet from the ground mayhap the rest of the knight is underneath it. Now why should the knight be underneath it and how could he be? asked the knight. None but a fool could think to find a live knight in a hollow tree. To which Peronnik replied, If he be not a live knight he must be a dead one. Thine answer is worthy of thee, said the knight, for a man is always alive or dead; and the helmet may have fallen from the knight's head as he looked down into the tree for buried treasure, to be caught midway. It may be that, answered Peronnik, or something worse, it being in his mind that the ravens would not trouble much about a steel helmet. Now what meanest thou by that something worser? And the two began to dispute together, the knight trying to persuade Peronnik to go down into the tree after the helmet, and Peronnik answering that if he did he might not be able to climb out of the tree again. Nor would you, sir, be able to lend a hand to get me out of the hole. My lame leg, it is true, replied the knight, unfits me for climbing. Whereupon they were friends again, with the knight taking advice from Peronnik, it seeming true to him that they would have to go to work with adze and saw to get the whole of the armour, if the whole of it – helmet, sword, shield, lance, and chain surcoat – were hidden in the tree. If you will remain by the tree, sir knight, said Peronnik, I will go whither I think I can buy an adze and saw; a hammer, too, it will be as well to bring. But without money thou'lt not be able to buy these things, the knight answered, so I will give the money for them and for the many other things that we shall need, among them a leathern coat to wear under thy surcoat of mail; and to escape the several dangers that beset the way to the castle, to overcome the spells with which Redemonde has surrounded herself, thou'lt need a linen bag, and let it be filled with larks' feathers – not sparrows, but larks, to be sure; some bird-lime, too, and a garland of roses – forget it not, nor a pipe made out of a stem of elderwood. These things come to my mind readily, but others will be needed, and I will tell them to thee and impress them upon thy memory as we journey to the village. Which is not far, Peronnik interjected. It will be well indeed that you accompany me thither, for – That I

should go with thee, Peronnik, is a thought that has been in my
head while speaking to thee. It's a good thought, too, for who
would believe that I had gotten so much money honestly as you
will have to give me? cried Peronnik. What story could I tell them,
and of whom should I tell it? My name, said the knight, is Sir
Gilles de Lacenaire.

Sir Gilles' straightforward speech reassured Peronnik, and he
kept pace beside the knight's charger all the way, now and then
clinging to the stirrup leather. And in this way they came into the
village, where they were followed by eyes open with admiration,
Sir Gilles' martial bearing overawing the women and children, the
men, whose shrewdness might have led them to ask what business
brought a knight and a shepherd lad to the village after sundown
to buy saw and adze, being away in the harvest fields. The larks'
feathers, the bird-lime, the pipe made out of elderwood, and the
garland of roses awakened astonishment, but it was enough to
remember that knights were not as other men. And so favoured
Sir Gilles and Peronnik returned to the heath with all they needed,
and once arrived they came to their work without delay on the
blasted tree, putting to flight the ravens, who had returned thither.
We are well rid of those croakers, who have tongues in their beaks
to tell all they see and hear, said Peronnik. Thou art not the fool
that I thought thee, Peronnik; a mind is awakening in thee. And
without more words Sir Gilles dealt the hollow tree some great
blows with the adze; but the tree was tougher than they thought
for and yielded but little. Our work will take us till daybreak, he
said, and spat upon his hands to get a better grip of the slippery
heft. Peronnik worked with chisel and hammer, and when he and
Sir Gilles stopped to take breath they saw the moon rising into
the pure summer sky, sending long shadows of the tree over the
heath. It may be that the evil birds are roosting in yonder wood
and watching us; if so, it would be well to drive them out of it, said
Peronnik. On this errand they went and drove the ravens farther
away lest they should have the story to tell to whomsoever might
listen to them in the morning; and hearkening from time to time
to birds winging their way high overhead to some pool or mere
known only to themselves, where they would stay till morning,
and to the footfalls (foxes and badgers, mayhap) they plied adze
and saw. Once the tread was heavier and Peronnik whispered, A
bear. My horse, said Sir Gilles, has winded him; and they clung
to the horse's bridle, striving to quieten him with words, but he
plunged out of their hands and nearly broke his tether. If we had

lost him? Sir Gilles muttered, leaving the rest of his thoughts to be spoken by Peronnik, who said, It would be a bad luck indeed if we were to lose our horse now, for if the morning light makes a knight of me I must have a horse to take me to the Grey Castle. And if we had lost mine, where should we have found another? Sir Gilles asked, for all my money is now spent. If that be so, said Peronnik, we would do well to light a fire, for if wolves be about (and there's no reason why they are not on the prowl) your horse will break his tether; there is naught that a horse fears like the smell of a wolf. Thereat the twain set to work to build a fire, and having done this they returned to the tree and worked for another hour or more.

We are just on daylight, said Peronnik, and when Sir Gilles asked him how he knew that daylight was high, Peronnik pointed to the stars, saying, They are no longer near us, Sir Gilles, for they follow the night; and he asked Sir Gilles if he did not feel a chilliness in the air. Sir Gilles answered that the sky was greyer, and Peronnik pointed to a heron flapping through the greyness on his way to the reeds that the ducks had left for the corn-fields, where he will bide all day. All the noises of the night have ceased, Sir Gilles said, and they fell once more to their work, chopping and hacking and breaking the old tree away in parts, without, however, being able to widen a hole big enough to allow the tree to be searched to the roots. And it was not till the line of the forest began to show under a streak of green sky that they discovered a skeleton in armour. So it was the smell of the corpse that drew the ravens to the tree, said Sir Gilles. And the birds mighty angry at not being able to get a bite out of him, Peronnik answered. Are we on the spot where some foul murder was done and the body hidden in a hollow tree? Sir Gilles said, speaking more to himself than to Peronnik. Or the knight may have climbed into the tree to take counsel from the ravens and toppled into the hole, answered Peronnik, and once down in it, it would take a chimney-sweeper, and the best in France, to get out again. It may be as thou sayest, Peronnik, and weighed down by his armour he perished. We all perish, said Peronnik, one way or the other, leaving our goods behind for another's use and benefit, maybe for an enemy's. The armour we have gotten is of more worth than the moralities, Peronnik. Now into it. Upon thy head I place the helmet and over thy shoulders the mail surcoat reaching to the waist. Thy shoon are stricken, but thy excuse to the lady of the Grey Castle will be that thou hast been long on thine errand.

With his sword by thy side and his shield on thine arm, kneel before me, and with a blow of my sword I will dub thee Sir Peronnik, and bid thee arise to start on an adventure in which many have fallen but in which thou'lt win renown. Hie thee into thy saddle, and as my broken knee does not allow me to walk far I'll seat myself behind thee, telling thee how to manage the charger, how to turn him to the right or to the left, how to rein him in, and how to escape the spells with which thy way will be beset on entering the Wood of Deceits and the Valley of Delights. To escape the dangers of the way I can help thee, but the greatest danger is the sorceress, and from her spell the purity of thy heart will save thee. It was then her beauty that caused your downfall, Sir Gilles? To which Sir Gilles answered furtively that it was the man within him that yielded to the wiles of Redemonde. Then there is no danger for me, Peronnik replied, for the man is not yet born within me. But I would hear of the wiles and the spells she casts upon the knights. The spell of her beauty, answered Sir Gilles, which is everywhere, in her hands, in her hair, in her eyes, in her foot; at which Peronnik was perplexed. But if you know not, sir, how the knights were beguiled, you can tell me what spell she cast upon you, for you are a true and valiant knight and must have yielded to some mightier force than her foot.

The traps, Sir Gilles answered, that the sorceress sets are manifold, and she never sets the same trap twice. But before telling of the trap in which I was caught, it behoves thee to hear that the Diamond Spear and the Golden Bowl were brought from Palestine in a ship by the Crusaders; and that tidings of the argosy were wafted to a great magician in Italy, Rogéar, brother of the Sorceress Redemonde, who by his spells called the vessel on the rocks, thereby possessing himself of a talisman that gives him power over the whole world. And how is it, asked Peronnik, that Rogéar has yielded his power to his sister? He has not yielded it, Sir Gilles answered, for they share it together; sometimes the Spear and the Bowl are in France, sometimes in Italy; at which answer Peronnik was perplexed and subdued. But, brightening a little, he said, Well, Sir Gilles, tell me of the trap that laid you low, to which Sir Gilles answered, She invited me first to a great feast, and after we had eaten and drunken she called me to her side, and, having confidence that my prayers would save me from the snare of her beauty, I gave ear to the lulling music of her voice, till in the middle of a story a great noise was heard – voices in the courtyard of the castle and afterwards trampling of feet on the stairs. My brother, Rogéar, has returned, she said, and if he finds thee with me he will kill thee or change thee into some animal shape. But I love thee and will not open to him, and he cannot enter against my will, my spells being as strong as his. And myself, unsuspicious that the tumult and Rogéar's voice was but an enchantment of the senses wrought by Redemonde herself to bring me to her purpose, shook with terror, half smothered by the stench of the Devil behind the door. At last hooves were heard departing, and we stood waiting till we could bear it no longer, and fell into each other's arms, my mouth upon her mouth.

I know not how the other knights were undone but I was undone by the lifting of the dread that followed after Rogéar's departure. But let not my downfall dishearten thee, Peronnik, for thine innocence will cast a shield over thee. I shall be near thee, and though I know not all the snares she will set I can divine most of them; and when the snare is set for thee I will awaken thee by the shuffle of my feet, by a cough, or by words suddenly addressed to her. Many victories, however, will have to be won before thou reachest Redemonde. Yonder is the Wood of Deceits, through which thou'lt have to pass; and here we part. At these words Sir Gilles slipped from the horse's quarters, and with his hand on the bridle he sought in his memory, afraid that he had forgotten some danger that Peronnik would meet on his way to the castle. But in his thoughtfulness his hand loosened on the bridle and the horse sprang forward, and no sooner were the first trees passed than the predicted dangers began to appear, and Sir Peronnik could think of no better way to save himself from the allurements of the flowers than to pull his visor over his eyes, in this way shunning the danger of sight. But the delicious scent of the flowers penetrated the woof of his armour, causing him to reel in his saddle, and he said, I must draw breath through my mouth, and he rode through the wood in safety till he came upon a great plain on the thither side littered with the skeletons of many men and horses and pieces of rusty armour. The bones of those, said Peronnik, who were beguiled by visionary hosts, so Sir Gilles told me, images of beauty to which my eyes have never been opened, and to which I hope my eyes will never be opened, for beauty must be in itself a gift from the Devil, since those who have it are wicked. Redemonde has it and she is a sorceress, and girls in the village that have it are often good for naught but decking themselves with ribbons, whilst those who have it not sit in the cottage doorways spinning their lives away in loneliness. Beauty therefore cannot be else than a gift from the Devil, since no good comes of it. From the beasts in the fields I learn the same lesson; the cow that gives but two pints of milk daily found more favour in Sir Gilles' eyes than the cow that gives two quarts. But what did he say? That beauty drew the world together, meaning thereby that without beauty the world would come to an end. But is that so?

And Sir Peronnik bethought himself of the spring season, which is always a season of bleating and lowing in the fields and singing in the woods. The ram and the yoe, he said, know naught of beauty, nor the birds in the branches, so it is not beauty that draws the world together. At that moment his eyes caught sight of two butterflies on love's quest high up in the blue air, and he said, Even the insects are drawn together, but not by beauty, for if I know little of beauty the butterflies must know less, for a fool is wiser than an insect. The beasts and the birds, and for aught I know, the fishes, he said, come to no harm, likewise monks and nuns; but not the good knights in search of the Bowl and the Spear, every one of whom has fallen, even Sir Gilles.

Sir Gilles had told him that though many had failed to get the Spear and the Bowl from the sorceress a pure knight would get them, one who had never looked yearningly into a woman's face nor sought a woman's kisses, if such a one could be found. Sir Gilles thought that he, Peronnik, was such a one, for he had strayed out of the forest without knowledge of his father and mother. Never before had the thought come to him that his father and mother met as all things that fly or walk, crawl or swim, meet, and that if his father and mother had not met he would not be. Only by the recovery of the Spear and the Bowl would God's purposes be justified. For God's ends he had come to be, and for God's ends Nature's secret was withheld from him. Would he live and die without knowing it, or would the knowledge that all possessed but he fall upon him suddenly? Let it not fall, he prayed, till I reach the castle and wrest the Spear and the Bowl from the sorceress. Till then, Holy Virgin, let me be without the knowledge, and, if it be your will, for ever afterwards. And as he rode he prayed to the Virgin for help, vowing himself to honourable chastity, saying, Let all be as you will it, Lady of Heaven; you'll be my guide now and for ever, he said, raising his eyes.

At that moment a scream hoarser than that of a sea-crow interrupted his meditation, and he saw a fair green meadow with an apple tree in the middle of it. The very apple tree, no doubt, said Peronnik, from which Sir Gilles told me I must pluck the

Apple; and there is the dwarf preparing to launch his dart at me. So he doffed his helmet, and the dwarf, who was not accustomed to such courtesy, hesitated, and Peronnik had an opportunity of addressing him. Let me pass, dear little friend, he said, for I am the new bird-catcher that my Lady Redemonde has engaged to snare the birds that are robbing her garden. She has told you of my coming? She has told me nothing about it, said the dwarf, and I read a lie on your face. If you continue to flourish your dart, good sir, my horse will rear and throw me, but if you'll lay it aside and come hither you will discover the Lady Redemonde's crest on the accoutrements that my horse wears. And these words seeming fair to the dwarf he laid aside his dart and examined them, and finding the Lady Redemonde's name engraved upon them he began with a changed mien to ask Peronnik if he had brought the bird-lime with which to catch the birds that infested the apple tree. You must think me a fool indeed to come without it, answered Peronnik, and alighting from his horse he began to smear the branches; and when this was done, pretending that he needed the dwarf's help to hold the end of the twine out of which he was weaving a snare, he said, Put your head into the bag, good sir. And the dwarf, being now unsuspicious, did as he was bidden, and as soon as the bag was over his shoulders Peronnik tied the snare up so tightly that the dwarf could not scream. His struggles grew fainter, for the holy water in which the bag had been dipped kept the knot tight, and Peronnik had time to pluck the Apple and ride on his way.

It was very soon after leaving the meadow and the apple tree and the dwarf dead beneath it that Peronnik found himself in front of a beautiful garden, in which were roses of all colours, and he said to himself, This is the garden in which the Laughing Flower grows; but how shall I pass the lion with the mane of snakes? And well might he ask himself that question, for he had barely reached the garden gate when he was met by a great lion with all his snakes hissing furiously. But courtesy, said Peronnik, is never lost, even upon a lion; and doffing his helmet he addressed himself to the lion with fair words, asking the beast after himself and his family, and begging to be directed forthwith to the Grey Castle. Now what do you seek in the Grey Castle? growled the lion, and Peronnik answered, I am the bringer of a pasty of larks for my lady Redemonde. Larks! said the lion, licking his chops, I have not tasted larks for many hundred years. Have you any larks to spare? Plenty, said Peronnik, for this sack is full of larks; and he began to imitate the twittering of larks, which he did so well that the lion was deceived. Look in and see how many larks there are, the lad said, opening the sack. The lion thrust his head therein and Peronnik drew the cord tightly, just as he had done about the dwarf's neck.

After plucking the Laughing Flower Peronnik rode to the dragon-haunted lake rejoicing, and seeing no bridge whereby he might cross it, he drove his horse into the water, saying to himself, Horses swim very well and as good as a boat mine will be to me. Nor was he deceived in this, for his horse bore him as well as any boat. But half-way across the lake the dragons began to swarm about him with gaping jaws, unable, however, to swallow him, for when their jaws were about to snap him up Peronnik plucked a rose from his garland and threw it down the black gullet; and immediately after swallowing the rose the dragon turned over and sank to the bottom, just as Sir Gilles had told him, advising him, however, never to throw a rose vainly; every one he threw must find its mark, for the dragons were very plentiful in the lake.

After crossing the lake Peronnik came to a valley which was guarded by a Black Man armed with an iron ball, who was chained by his feet to a rock. A terrible monster he was, with eyes all round his head, six of them in number, so that it mattered little on which side Peronnik stood, for the Black Man could see him; and he remembered that if the man's eyes fell upon him he would fling the ball before Peronnik could say a word. So dismounting Peronnik crept up, and hiding himself carefully behind bushes and rocks till he was within a few yards of the Black Man, he began singing the Church Service. He had not reached the end of the Introit before one of the eyes fell asleep, a couple more closed at the Kyrie, another began to wink when he was half-way through the Credo, and by the time he had reached the *Nunc dimittis* all the eyes were shut.

And after assuring himself that the Black Man was sound asleep Peronnik led his horse through the Valley of Delights, in great perplexity, it is true, for along the pathways were tables, and the savoury smell of the meat and wine rose to his nostrils, tempting him. But Peronnik knew he could overcome these temptations, for Sir Gilles and himself had eaten well of the food purchased overnight. More than of gluttony he was afraid that the sense he lacked might be revealed to him suddenly, and that with increased knowledge he might become prone, like his predecessors, to the temptations of the maidens who beckoned and called to him from the stream in which they were bathing and from the trees under

which they danced. Come and join us, they cried; and their shapes
and voices were so soft and sweet that the thought came to Peronnik
to tether his horse and mix with them; but he invoked all the saints
of Brittany to his help, and the faint thought passed out of his
mind altogether when he made the sign of the Cross, which he did
again and again. But in spite of his invocations and his signs his
horse's hooves went slower and slower till he bethought himself of
dismounting and cutting a bough from a tree to belabour him with.
If he had done this he might have fallen a prey to the maidens, for
they continued their beguiling dances through the mazy ways of the
gardens and the orchards in front of him all the way to the castle. At
every step his horse took the voices seemed to grow sweeter, and to
escape from the temptation (which was not really upon him, but
which might fall upon him at any moment) he began to play on
his pipe of elderwood; and to save his eyes from looking at the
maidens' shapes he fixed them on his horse's ears steadfastly, and
was able to pursue his way in safety through the Valley, the most
dangerous of all trials except the sorceress herself.

On emerging from the Valley he came upon the Ford at which
the Black Lady, of whom he had heard from Sir Gilles, sat, and
though her face was dusky yellow, like that of a Moor, he offered
to carry her across the river. I thank you, good knight, for your
courtesy, she said. All your companions fled from me. I am sorry,
Peronnik answered, that my companions-in-arms should have been
lacking in courtesy. Then the lady mounted before him and they
went into the water together, and when they were midway in the
stream the lady asked Peronnik if he knew who she was. Not I,
said Peronnik, but by your mien and raiment you would seem to
be a noble and mighty lady. Noble I may be, for my race dates
from the fall of Adam, and mighty also, for all the world would
retreat from me, all except you, sir knight, in whose heart there is
still innocence. Know, sir knight, that I am the Plague. At which
words Peronnik sought to draw himself away from her, and was
about to throw himself from his saddle into the stream when the
lady said, Fear nothing, for the one I am seeking is not you, sir,
but the sorceress Redemonde, who, though immortal, will become
subject to death if she eats of the apple which you plucked from
her tree, grown from a seed of the Tree of Good in the Garden
of Eden. Let her taste of that apple and I have but to touch her
and she will die at once. But how shall I find the Bowl and the
Spear? asked Peronnik, for I hear she keeps them underground in
a vault to which there is no key. The Laughing Flower, said the

Plague, can open all doors and make bright the darkest corner in the world. Well, said Peronnik, I will do as I am bidden, and if I can get you the sorceress's life you shall have it.

III

Now whilst Peronnik was performing the aforesaid great deeds Sir Gilles lay in very direful plight beneath an oak tree in the forest, unable to move by reason of his broken or disjointed knee, which he had forgotten whilst giving last instructions to Peronnik, holding on as he talked by the stirrup leather. His last words to the new knight were that he must hold himself forbidden from any food or drink that might be offered to him in the Grey Castle. And these words had barely passed his lips when the horse began to plunge and to strike out with his forelegs, and to escape the dangerous hooves Sir Gilles loosened his hand on the bridle. A moment after the Wood of Deceits engulfed Peronnik, and Sir Gilles set out to walk to the castle, distant about half a league, he judged it to be; far too far for him to walk, as his knee soon began to warn him, till at last he could not do else than fling himself upon the ground, overpowered by the pain.

As the pain in his knee dwindled, thoughts began of Peronnik arriving at the castle before him, for the lad would not succumb to the singing of the maidens – he was sure of that; but his youth, while protecting him from some temptations, would leave him more susceptible than a man to those of the fruit and honey cakes that the sorceress would offer him; the cups of sweet wine, too, she would raise to his lips might tempt him after his long ride. And were he to yield a search would be begun for the lost Sir Gilles at once, who, when he was found, would be brought back to the castle and laid by the heels in some dark dungeon amid damp and rats, for the sorceress was without mercy for those who sought to thwart her. Peronnik would be exalted in his place (a poor exaltation!), for when she was weary of him she would send him, just as he was sent, to beguile other knights to their doom.

All seemed lost to Sir Gilles till he remembered the plume from the tail of the cock that crew after Peter's third denial that he knew not Christ, a relic so powerful, the pardoner had told him, that it would protect his thoughts from Redemonde's knowledge, though he were in the sorceress's presence, and himself from any danger he might find himself in. But the forest would be searched and his relic taken from him if he did not reach the castle before Peronnik. Need brings a man courage, he said, and climbing to his feet Sir Gilles started on the journey, but had not gone far when the pain again brought him to the ground; and searching in his bosom for his relic he drew it forth and besought Jesus, reminding him that he had never doubted his power to be above that of Satan. Help me in this great extremity, he cried, and the words had barely passed his lips when his eyes were directed to a broken branch that he had not seen before, and out of which an excellent crutch could be made. It lay some little distance away, and while dragging himself slowly to it he prayed with such good effect that the branch lent itself to be trimmed into a crutch even easier than he thought for; and having a sharp knife in his girdle he made it into an excellent crutch, by the help of which he hobbled to the castle, reaching it, to his great joy, before Peronnik. For, said he to himself, if Peronnik were before me Redemonde would be sitting with him, whereas she is sitting by herself on the terrace muttering her spells, counting them over and taking great joy from them one by one, for all the world like a countess in front of her jewel-box.

But I must fortify myself, he said, and stopping behind a lilac bush he addressed himself to St Peter, whom he had almost forgotten till now. By virtue of the relic in my bosom, he muttered, the plume from the tail of the cock that warned thee of thy sin, I beg thee to go to Him with whom thy lot was cast on earth, and with whom thy lot is cast in Heaven, and bid Him strengthen me in adversity; bid Him give me courage and foresight to overcome the sorceress, the ally of Satan; tell Him that her belief is that while God rules in Heaven Satan rules the earth, gaining in power daily, that very soon the demons will be under the battlements of Heaven again, at war with the Cherubim and Seraphim. The saints, male and female, are all on my side, said Gilles to himself; it is a match between Heaven and earth, between God and Satan. And may all the saints and the Holy Virgin herself protect me from her if she should guess that I gave my horse to Sir Peronnik, unless indeed I invent a tale that will seem to her truthful. A better story I shall not find than that Sir Peronnik's horse reared and fell backwards and escaped before the knight could recover his feet, being unused to and hampered by his armour. His youth will awaken pity in her, he said; she will ask for news of him.

And being now out of the shelter of the lilac bush, Sir Gilles was mindful to whistle a tune to start Redemonde out of her brooding of wicked spells; and he continued to whistle till she raised her eyes, but the sun was in her eyes and she put up her hand to shade them. Sir Gilles continued for a few more bars till Redemonde rose to her feet and started to meet him, saying to herself, The minstrel can be none other than my own cripple! How is it, said Redemonde, that thou comest to me on a crutch instead of a horse, and in such great pain that to-morrow will be spent in thy bed? But how did she know that I was in pain? Sir Gilles asked himself, for he was always suspicious when with her. It is written in my face, maybe, he added; and to discover if his thoughts were known to her he kept his eyes upon her face and, reading no knowledge of them upon it, he said, My relic holds good. And with greater courage than he believed himself to be possessed of he began to prattle the story already arranged in his mind for telling. My relic, he said to himself, is more powerful than her spells; and he prattled on, lengthening his story out till she, wearying of it, picked up her magic mirror and looked into it for news of Peronnik.

He must have passed the dwarf and the lion and the dragon-haunted lake and the river, too, she said, rising from her seat, for hark, the sirens are singing. He will not listen to them and will arrive safely, be not afraid, Sir Gilles answered. We must prepare to welcome him, she said; come with me and bind up my hair, for none but thee can do it beautifully. I would wait here to meet him, Gilles answered, at which Redemonde's face flushed, and she bade him follow her, saying that she would change her raiment. None knows like thee which is most becoming to me. See, my hair is coming down. Come, Gilles, I need thee to bind up my hair; come at once. It is the last time I shall perform these servile duties for her, Sir Gilles muttered, for though I have pandered to her pleasures wickedly, my love of her shall not turn me into her maid-servant.

On the threshold of the portal they stayed their steps for a moment, and at the same moment the Black Lady asked Peronnik's leave to descend from his horse, saying that she would follow him to the castle.

So Sir Peronnik rode alone up the lawns that encircled the castle, where, after blowing the first fanfare, he waited, thinking that it would show little courtesy to the sorceress for him to blow a second. As if I wished to hurry her, he said to himself. But after waiting some minutes he bethought himself that she might not have heard the first, so he blew a second; and it was as he raised his horn to blow a third that Redemonde came from the castle to meet him, saying, In my mirror I have watched your triumphs, Sir Peronnik, over the dwarf and the lion. It was by the help of God and the Holy Virgin that I did these things, Peronnik replied, doffing his helmet, and I am glad to be of service to you, lady. But the ride round the ramparts, the greatest task of all, is still undone, and I would undertake it without delay, for the day is waning. But you would not, sir knight, attempt so hard a task on the day of your arrival without eating and drinking? And heedless of his denials she called to her maidens, who, bowing to signify their acceptance of her orders, entered the castle, to return soon after with jewelled dishes piled high with delicious cakes and wine in golden goblets. I thank you, lady of the castle, many times, Peronnik said, but the day is waning and I should be bringing back the Diamond Spear and the Golden Bowl to my village, where they are badly wanted. But a goblet of wine and a slice of cake will be welcome after your ride. The day is hot, Lady Redemonde, answered Peronnik, and he was about to partake of the refreshment, but the lightning flash of expectant triumph in the sorceress's eyes reminded that he must not partake of meat or drink in the castle. Forgive me, lady, but I have not a moment to lose for a bite or a sup, he said, not even for the eating of this Apple, which I hope you will not refuse to accept; and he doffed his helmet while handing it to her. Redemonde put the Apple in her bosom and Peronnik's face wore an abashment. Which becomes him not ill, said Redemonde, covering herself with her cloak coyly. Satan must look after his own, Peronnik said to himself, and if he doesn't the world will be none the worse without a wicked sorceress who has laid my country waste by her spells; and then aloud said, You will forgive me, lady, if I ask Sir Gilles, whom I see coming from the castle, the way to the ramparts. The way to the ramparts, Sir Gilles said, will be found by riding round the castle to the right; not very far, a little way round after passing the second tower, you will come upon a staircase of a hundred steps, which your horse will have to climb, and should he miss his footing he will not stop falling till he reaches the bottom. You hear what Sir Gilles says, Redemonde cried; but Sir Peronnik pricked on, and when he was out of sight Redemonde turned to Sir Gilles.

Now why did'st thou tell him the way to the staircase? she asked. But he could not have failed to find it, and it would be no gain to thee that he should delay his ride, Sir Gilles answered, till to-morrow or the day after, for he has, as thou must have seen, little else in his mind except the quest of the Spear and the

Bowl, and thy best chance that he shall get neither is that he rides to-night in the dusk.

Thinkest that he'll come to his death in the chasm? Redemonde asked. Sir Gilles did not answer, and heedless of his silence, as if she had not noticed it, she began to ask him how it was that in passing through the Wood of Deceits and the Valley of Delights other knights, all but thou, were turned from their quests by some enticing vision, the spells of my brother Rogéar; but this one rode on unmoved, plucking an Apple from my apple tree, despite my faithful dwarf, dead, alas, maybe! It is not by my will that he rides safely. How was it that this last adventurer overcame the lion and the dragons in the lake, and that his eyes did not kindle when we exchanged glances and no huskiness came into his voice when he spoke to me? Gilles, I fear impending doom. But thou'lt not desert me now? Thine eyes cloud and the wavering spirit finds an echo in me. Thou hast not faith in Satan and thine unfaith undoes my faith. My spells will be cast unavailingly.

And, leaving her whilom lover, Redemonde crossed the tessellated pavement towards a chamber that Gilles judged to be one of purifications, for on either side of the doorway were vases. Containing, no doubt, lustral water from the sacred river, he said, and to assure himself he moved towards them, but stopped, bewildered. Lost to me, he said, for ever in this world and the next. Did she speak of two worlds? And to which God am I to pray? Which is the stronger? Which do I love the better, my flesh or my soul? My flesh I know always, my soul only in rare whisperings. But the minutes are going by and I must ally myself to one God or the other. The thought of a prayer to Satan frightened him, and finding that he could not repent his sins with Redemonde his eyes wandered round the temple, and he began incontinently to count the arcades that led hither. There are five, he said, and to his astonishment he remembered that the ceilings were of chalk ribbed with hard stone. But why do I think of chalk and hard stone, things of interest only to builders? Satan puts these thoughts into my mind, for he would accomplish my ruin. Whereupon he began to beseech God to give him strength to resist Satan. But Gilles' heart was dry and his God mute, and in great perplexity he began to consider the style of architecture in which the temple was built. In Ionian or Doric, one or the other, he said; and his thoughts went back to the ten Doric columns that supported the pediment. There are four more, he said, on either side, and the sanctuary is square and vaulted, and the roof is of tiles; and he began to examine the statues in the niches, recognizing those of whom Redemonde had spoken to him.

From the statues his eyes wandered to the pictures with which the walls were decorated, each one representing men and women engaged in agriculture; wreathing vines from tree to tree, wains laden with corn, girls dancing in the vats, crushing the grapes under their feet. And seeing two palm trees carved in marble Sir Gilles asked himself why they were there, but remembered suddenly that the palm puts forth a branch every month and is therefore sculptured in Nature's temple. But Redemonde will be here in a few moments and all hope of escape for me will be lost. My soul will burn for ever, he cried; and his thoughts began to wander from the burning of souls to the lamps, the goblets, the cruets, the vases, the sprinklers, the mitres, the censers, the jewelled ornaments worn by the priests and priestesses of Satan, the timbrels, the trumpets, and the cymbals.

Along the walls were seats of silver and ivory, and in a great perplexity he strove to read the strange inscriptions interwoven through the pavement under his feet; and then forgetful of them he gave ear to the music with which the temple was slowly filling, voices coming from the arcades and the galleries! Devil music, he cried, for as his ears became accustomed to the rhythms he began to recognize them as litanies sung to an accompaniment of timbrels and flutes. And, walking to the measure of the music, Redemonde came, her long, thick hair falling into ringlets, floating over her shoulders; a many-shapen and many-coloured crown decked her head, and a silver moon shone upon her forehead, on either side of which serpents writhed amid ripe ears of wheat; her gown of shifting colours changed with every movement of the folds from the purest white to saffron-yellow, or seemed to catch the redness of flame; her cloak of deepest black was sown with stars and bordered with a luminous fringe; her right hand held a timbrel, which gave forth a clear sound, and in her left she carried a waxen image.

As she approached the brazier the singers seemed to Sir Gilles to have drawn nearer, or it may have been that his ears had grown accustomed to the music and could now distinguish individual voices and instruments; and the shapes too, of those in the processions passing through the different arcades and aisles and grouped in the galleries grew precise and then melted into shadow shapes and were lost in the great fume of incense rising from the brazier.

O great nature, Redemonde said, worshipped by man under

different names till his eyes were turned from the kingdom of
earth to the kingdom of Heaven and sin was born unto man, we,
thy worshippers, implore thee to come once again to the grapple
with thy rival, Sabaoth, at the edge of the chasm, for a knight
who knows thee not is riding thither. O Great Nature – Cybele
in Phrygia, Minerva in Athens, Ceres in Eleusis, Isis in Egypt,
Satan throughout Christendom – help us or see thy kingdom
pass away. I bring to the brazier a waxen image, and as the
wax melts, as the image begins to droop out of human shape, the
Christian knight loses strength. The spell works well. Hold up the
mirror, Gilles, that I may see whither he rides. He rides, Sir Gilles
answered, towards the chasm wherein I fell. Before he reaches it,
Redemonde replied, the image must pass into uncouth wax again.
But the embers in the brazier are dying, Gilles; heap some more
charcoal upon them quickly, for live embers are wanted to melt
the wax. Two handfuls of charcoal will revive the dying embers;
quickly, Gilles, quickly. Is thy faith still with the Christian God?
Art betraying me? she cried, and seeing that the brazier was not
giving enough heat to melt the wax she threw the image upon the
dying embers.

   He has crossed the chasm, Sir Gilles cried, rising from the mirror,
and I have lost thee, Redemonde, and for centuries the world is
delivered over to Satan's wrath. Redemonde passed from the
brazier and sank upon a seat, waiting for the doom that she knew
was imminent. The kingdom of Satan passes, and the kingdom of
the Lord God is at hand, she muttered, and Sir Gilles saw her take
the Apple that Peronnik had given her from her bosom and eat.
Will she not speak again? Have I lost her, have I lost her? he cried,
never to see her again? And the triumph that God had won over
Satan passed out of his mind, and he was about to throw himself
at her feet and confess his betrayal when Sir Peronnik came into
the temple and took the keys from the sorceress's girdle. Whither
is the way? asked Sir Peronnik, and the words awoke a fierce
exaltation in Sir Gilles' heart. I will point out the way, he said,
through the labyrinths of the castle to the dungeon in which the
Spear and the Bowl are hidden. But we shall need a lantern. We
have one here, said Peronnik, displaying the Laughing Flower, and
holding the Flower high like a lantern he followed Gilles out of the
temple.

   And their feet were barely on the steps leading to the vault when
the Black Lady moved from out of the shadows of the pillars and,
advancing towards Redemonde, touched her upon the shoulder. At

the touch of the Plague Redemonde fell dead, and the Plague, now no more than a mote in the air, floated out of the high windows. And when Peronnik and Sir Gilles returned with the Spear and the Bowl, Gilles, said Peronnik, touch her not. Why are you weeping for her? Why askest thou me this? Sir Gilles answered. I am wondering, Peronnik replied, why men set such store on women, and of all on wicked women. Life will reveal that secret to thee sooner or later, Peronnik; mayhap never. I have no head for thinking things out, said Peronnik, but now I must return to my village and redeem my country from a cruel drought.

IV

The many rooks were settling themselves in the branches of the beeches when the knights came from the castle, and the rooks continued for a long while to flop home through the evening sky. Hast thou no ears for what I am saying to thee, Peronnik, and no eyes to watch for a path that might lead us to a village? I thought, answered Peronnik, that I knew all the forest, but nobody knows all the trees and dells and hill-tops in it. To which Sir Gilles made no answer, it seeming to him that it was in the power of Peronnik to lead him out of or or to lose him in the forest. But, Peronnik, for what art thou loitering? Wouldst thou return to the Grey Castle and give back the Spear and the Bowl to Redemonde? The Plague has gotten her, Peronnik answered; and your lameness has departed from you, Sir Gilles. My lameness, Sir Gilles replied, was part of her and has gone with her. And her spells, he added, so thoughtfully that Peronnik began to wonder if he rued his swinging gait and wished himself back in the old pain. But of what art thou thinking, Peronnik? Of what they are saying about me in the village, of the herd of cows I left behind before watering them at the well. There was barely half a bucket to give them, poor animals, after much winding. Would indeed that I may live to see them supping the cool stream again.

The conqueror of Redemonde's spells thinking of cows, forgetful that he is no longer Peronnik the Fool but a knight of whom all the world will soon be talking, Sir Gilles said. One can't forget oneself all in a day and a night, Peronnik answered; nor am I thinking altogether of the cows, nor of the farmer at the head of a search party, but of the way we have lost, for the forest we're in seems more unlike my forest at every step we take. But we are in a path, said Sir Gilles, and have but to follow it. We are in a path, it is true, replied Peronnik, but who made the path? I am asking myself; not the feet of men nor of cows, but the hooves of deer. Or goats, maybe, Sir Gilles answered him. Deer, replied Peronnik. A little farther on Peronnik stopped again, and spying some new tracks he said, A bear has been paddling about here. But as long as the Spear is with us no man or beast can harm us. That is so, Sir Gilles replied. All the same, said Peronnik, it would be well for us to seek a comfortable tree, with large thick branches, where we might snooze. And fall out of, mayhap, Sir Gilles interrupted, and the Spear being up in the branches we should be eaten like common folk. And Peronnik having no reply to make, they wandered on and on in the hope of coming upon a path that would lead them to a village, till at last weariness overcame them, and, sitting down to rest, they fell asleep, forgetful of the wolves that might be about. Out of this sleep Peronnik was the first to awake, and he cried to Sir Gilles that he must come to his feet at once.

And through the dusk and through the day they fared, finding themselves sometimes in roads that seemed to lead direct to a village, but which stopped short or were lost in dense undergrowths. Sometimes it seemed to them that they were by the Grey Castle; about them was the rookery, but no castle. Yet it was not carried away as a rook's nest is by a storm, said Peronnik, a great big castle built with stones half as big as an ox cart. No, it cannot have been here, he continued, that the castle stood, and I'm thinking that the sorceress's spells are upon this wood. Speak not so, Sir Gilles replied, else my courage fails me altogether. Yet here, returned Peronnik, is the rookery that we passed yester-evening; and a dispute arose between the twain whether it was the same rookery or another one.

And for two days more they wandered, living on berries, slaking their thirst with such water as collects in hollows, till in a quiet sundown, overworn, weary, and hopeless, they lay in the belief that the wood they were in was spellbound. We are lost beyond hope of this world or the next, said Sir Gilles, and it might be well to lie down and die without further fatigue or dread of the phantoms that have their ghostly habitation here. Let us walk into yon morass and smother in it. Do you think, said Peronnik, his soul catching fear, that a dead sorceress is a greater peril to knights than a living one? The power of the dead over the living is great, Sir Gilles replied. But your relic, Sir Gilles. My relic! I had forgotten it, Sir Gilles muttered; and forgetfulness of a relic robs it of its power. But as it is our last hope let us both put our trust in it. And together they spoke of the stars above the Sea of Galilee until the forest was black about them. After each sleep they prayed, and at dawn Peronnik said, Let us put all our faith in the relic; and since I am a knight and wandering with thee in the forest, let it be "thou" and "thee". "Thou" and "thee" let it be then, Sir Gilles answered, till the time, not far away, when we shall bid each other goodbye for ever. Speak not so lest the relic fail us, Peronnik replied. And they wandered on till Sir Gilles fell lame, not with the old lameness which Redemonde's spells cast upon him to retain him in her service, a lameness which was that of Satan or Vulcan when they were cast out of Heaven, but a natural lameness that comes upon a man after wandering three days in a forest without rest or food. I can go no farther, Peronnik, he said, laying himself upon the ground; let death come. Take away thy berries; I cannot eat. If thou canst not eat thou canst still open thine eyes, said Peronnik; look, we've wandered to within half a league of the village. Thou speakest to hearten me, said Sir Gilles. Not so, answered Peronnik; courage, Gilles, for my promise to thee is that within an hour we shall be in my village. Go thou to the village, said Sir Gilles, and I will lie here and await thy coming. And be eaten by a wolf or a bear, perhaps, replied Peronnik. No, no; we fare on to the end together.

A weary faring this last half-league was to Sir Gilles, barely able to bear the pain of his feet and the sickness of hunger. Look round thee, Gilles, said Peronnik, and tell me if we are not hard by the village. And looking round Sir Gilles answered, It seems to me that I have seen yon fields shining between these trees before. In very truth we are on the verge of the forest. At the sight of the corn Sir Gilles was again heartened, and walked steadfastly till Peronnik stopped suddenly and said, Yonder! What seest thou yonder, Peronnik? Farmer Leroux, Peronnik whispered; and his knighthood fallen from him he was again Farmer Leroux's neat-herd, with no thought in his mind but how to escape from him into the forest. It was now the turn of Sir Gilles to grasp him by the arm and remind him again that he was no longer Peronnik the Fool, but the valiant knight who overcame Redemonde in her enchanted castle. And, leading him to Farmer Leroux, Sir Gilles asked him for news of a lad named Peronnik. Would indeed that I had news of him, said the farmer, for if I had I'd be quickly about my own business, which is to thrash the rascal for his desertion of the herd he was given in charge of four or five days ago. I have

chosen my stoutest stick to lay across his back, and not an inch
of unblackened skin will I leave on it, and if I kill him not his luck
will never desert him.

The farmer might have continued in this way for a long time
if Sir Gilles had not interrupted him with these words, But thine
eyes are upon him now, farmer. My eyes upon him! How am I
to understand your words, sir knight? What covert meaning – I
am bringing back to thee, said Sir Gilles, a knight of valiant deeds
in and about the Grey Castle, the conqueror of the sorceress who
cursed the land with a great drought. How bringing back to me?
enquired Leroux. The knight who stands before thee, Sir Gilles
answered, was once thy neat-herd. My Peronnik, the farmer
stuttered, my Peronnik in a suit of mail! And who may you
be, sir knight? I am Sir Gilles de Lacenaire, who admitted Sir
Peronnik into the Order of Knighthood that he might overcome
the sorceress's spells. My Peronnik, the farmer began again – No
longer thy Peronnik, Sir Gilles interrupted, but a knight of whom
all the world will be talking before many weeks are over, for he
brings the Spear and the Bowl. But will the Spear bring down the
rain that will save the rest of my herd, asked Leroux, or is it a mere
spear of chivalry that concerns me not? Soon after the hurling of
the Spear into the air, said Sir Gilles, the desert about us will be a
green country again, fresh as in May-time. Then let the Spear be
hurled at once, answered the farmer, and my poor cows put out
of the pain of thirst. We have neither eaten nor drunken for three
days, Sir Gilles replied; we are starving men; but as soon as we
are rested – In my house yonder, cried Farmer Leroux, you will
find bread and wine and cheese and butter and other things the
goodwife may have in her larder. So you have gotten the Spear,
the holy Spear that will bring us rain, and the story thereof will be
glad in the villagers' ears. But here we are at my house, Sir Gilles;
and now, wife, make ready the house to receive the knights who
have come back with the Spear that brings the rain.

And who may they be? the wife asked. First pile the table with
bread and wine and cheese and butter, and strike off from the
carcass above thee as much bacon as will end the hunger of men who
have not eaten for three days. But this is Peronnik, our Peronnik!
Thine eyes are quicker than mine, Leroux replied, and while the
knights eat a tale of many marvels thou shalt hear from me. Before
you, sir knights, is all my house has of meat and drink; and fall to
your food, Sir Peronnik, for you will need all your strength for
the hurling of the Spear. Sir Peronnik! the wife stuttered. Life is

a miracle, wife, full to the brim of wonders. But take thine eyes off him and listen to his story. So Peronnik got the Spear from her, said the goodwife, which doesn't surprise me overmuch now I come to get my mind to it, for we all knew there was something wonderful in him. Begin thy story, husband. When they have eaten they will tell it, answered the farmer. We will, we will, cried the famished knights. And while they eat I'll be up the street telling the folk that Peronnik has returned with the Spear. Nor was she long away when voices began to be heard about the doorway. In a little while calls for Peronnik broke forth, and when he appeared in all his mail the villagers could not show joy enough; and before Peronnik had told his story the folk were telling new stories among themselves, how the sorceress's castle had been scaled and how she had come by her death. It was said, too, that Sir Gilles had overcome the magical arts of Redemonde's brother, Rogéar, and that Rogéar had put a great curse upon the Spear before it was captured which would bring ill luck to whosoever possessed it.

But as long as it brings down the rain, what matter? cried a woman. The Spear may lose its virtue, cried another. What matter? cried a third, for God has conquered Satan in a last battle and he will see that we do not want for rain any more nor sunshine when we need it. At these word a great hymn of thanksgiving came upon the folk suddenly, words and music together, and till the hill-top was reached no word was spoken. If the Spear bringeth rain from yon sky, said a man, then it is God's own Spear, and the reign of Satan is over, as Marguerite Lebrun said on our way hither. And then a peasant, Pierre le Gros, spoke of the great fire that would break out in the forest if the Spear were not hurled quickly. The Spear has not come too soon, for after this drought the country would burn for months, covering the country with ashes. Hush, woman, hush, for Sir Peronnik is about to hurl the Spear.

The hurling of the Spear was the signal for the renewal of the hymn of thanksgiving, and the crowd sang it all through the afternoon and evening; and men, women and children were out of their beds singing to each other from window to window across the streetway till rain began to fall so heavily that they were driven back to their beds. After the first shower it seemed as if the storm were about to pass over, but after a pause the thunder crashed so loudly that in the village of Saint-Jean-de-Braie the world seemed to be overturning. The rain has come at last in right earnest, the villagers cried, returning to their beds, their ears open to the sound of water gurgling down the gutters. The folk listened, and fell asleep at last, happy in the knowledge that the Spear had saved their country from famine.

All next day it rained and all through the week. The ruts filled with water and the fields were green again with new grass. A second springtime, the villagers said; and then the rain came down fiercely and beat in the windows, and then it fell straight like a sheet. At the end of each day there were bright intervals of a few hours, but next day rain fell again and the farmers spoke of the great stock of wheat still uncarried. Our wheat will be spoilt if this rain does not cease, they said. Maybe it would have been as well for us if some of our cows had died for want of water and for us to have had our wheat. And July passed over and August was well begun before the rain ceased. We have rested long enough, Gilles said to Peronnik, in Saint-Jean-de-Braie. Our business is to the rescuing of honest men from thieves and maidens from lustful rogues.

When the news that the knights were leaving them was about many villagers came to Sir Peronnik to offer him in return for his services the beginning of a herd. Three young heifers are all I would ask, said Peronnik. Beware, replied Gilles, for no man returns whence he came. Thou hast entered the Order of Knighthood, and whosoever enters it never leaves it till he dies, if he leave it then. So we must on, Peronnik, taking from the village only a horse, for thou must be horsed according to thy quality. But shall we never see you again? Will you not return to us? the villagers cried as the twain rode forth. That may hap and it may not hap; all is in the hand of God, said Sir Gilles as he waved farewell to the folk who ran alongside and between the horses; and at last to escape them he pricked on. Though we never see Saint-Jean-de-Braie again, he said, we have done deeds that will bear fruit that the folk will find sweet under the tooth for many a day.

And it was as Sir Gilles foresaw, for during the winter of the same year the folk of Saint-Jean-de-Braie were telling the story of a beleaguered city in which Sir Peronnik fed the starving and with his lance routed the French. And the next year further exploits were related – that Sir Peronnik had conquered Anjou, Poitou, and Normandy, and was away now on the Crusades winning great triumphs over the Saracens, obliging Saladin to accept baptism and to give him his daughter in marriage. The years went by, and it became common gossip in Saint-Jean-de-Braie that the Saracen lady had borne him a hundred sons and that he had given to each a kingdom to rule over. And as the years passed over and generations came and went it came to be believed in Saint-Jean-de-Braie that by virtue of the Golden Bowl Sir Peronnik and many of his sons were still living. And then heresies, or shadows of heresies came over. Whence they came none knew, but it was whispered certainly by a sceptical generation that the enchanter Rogéar at last won the Spear and the Bowl back from the Christians, that he has them now, and that anybody who wants them may go and search for them like Peronnik the Fool.

THE LAST RAINBOW

Parke Godwin

Parke Godwin (b. 1929) is an American novelist, playwright and actor, who has shown a particular fascination for British heroic legends. His own Arthurian novel, Firelord *(1980), was followed by the story of Guinevere,* Beloved Exile *(1984), and the story of St Patrick,* The Last Rainbow *(1985). A further Arthurian novel is planned,* Sunburst, *which will explore Sir Gareth's adult years. Godwin has also written two novels about Robin Hood,* Sherwood *(1991) and* Robin and the King *(1993), with a third in the works, plus a novel about Beowulf,* The Tower of Beowulf *(1995). He also edited an anthology of Arthurian stories,* Invitation to Camelot *(1988). The following story (which is unrelated to the author's book of the same name) shows how the Grail legend continued to inspire quests even into the Middle Ages.*

The legend goes something like this:

Once upon a time a princess caught a faerie, one of the little folk, and demanded his treasure, since it was well known that all faeries had fabulous wealth hidden under some hill and were legend-bound to render it on request. The faerie reluctantly waved his hand, the hill opened up, and there was the treasure, its dazzle rivalling the sunlight. But, according to tradition, the little folk always ask something in return . . .

Thus the legend. The truth is more fun.

Once upon a time there was a girl named Brangaene ... but "once" is vague; we can be more specific. It was rather well on in the Middle Ages, late enough for dragons and quests to be quite *passé*, late enough for Brangaene to be literate and even over-read in that narrow, romantic field. She was the daughter of a harried baron who held a very small castle in a very small and agriculturally uninspired corner of England. His liege lord was both an earl and a bishop, which meant the earl could demand his secular rights and, if not forthcoming, the bishop could close the gates of heaven.

Such was the case one spring when Brangaene was fifteen. The earl had declared war on a neighbouring tenant and ordered Brangaene's father to send help or money. Since the baron depended heavily on his neighbour's grain mill, had no money and not enough men to populate a decent garden party, he declined with apologies.

The earl-bishop thundered and threatened excommunication. The poor baron was in up to his neck, and since his life had gone much this way for a long time, his temper was understandably short.

Brangaene longed to be of help, but the bishop was only peripheral to her enchanted world. She hunted for unicorns in the forest beyond their moat, nosed for faeries on moonlit nights, and though she never found either, her faith was undented by failure. As pure and good a man as Lancelot hunted the Grail, and Percival even saw it. More than one historical knight had slain a dragon or a giant; it said so in her books. Unicorns might be scarce and shy, but scarce was not non-existent. Faeries might be elusive –

"But so are foxes," she reasoned, turning to canonical precedent. If bushes could burn, seas part, tombstones roll aside and the dead rise, this fortuitous by-pass of natural law could not logically be confined to the Middle East. So her catechism and belief. The unicorns would come, white and willing, the little folk would be caught, their treasure demanded. Faith would be rewarded.

"I mean, Father, we only have to look for them."

"Ye gods." The baron brooded over his soup, the bishop's tyranny, and his daughter's mind. "What have I done to deserve this?"

Brangaene looked like her mother. This did not endear her to him. That pious woman had departed the world leaving behind an unfinished tapestry on the life of St Paul and, as his enduring penance for marrying a Celt, this unworldly, star-eyed, faerie-chasing wisp of a girl. Her marriage value declined with his own fortunes. Once he might have bargained for a prince or duke-ling, later a baron's son or even a plain knight. Now as he watched Brangaene running through the garden and tripping over her own dainty feet, he longed for a decent kidnapping.

She was forever racing up the steps with the news of (maybe) unicorns sighted across the moat, or (they looked like) faerie-folk peeping from behind trees in the forest. He had tolerated this until her twelfth birthday and then announced his incredulity by kicking her down the stairs. As Brangaene persisted in her optimism, his placekick and her nimbleness improved with time. She was even able to gauge her father's temper by the manner and sound of the kick. Mild irritation: side of the foot, a flat *bup*! Genuine wrath: point of the toe and swung from the hip with a resounding *poonk*! And as she became airborne, floating down towards the scullery, Brangaene meditated on the treasures and principles of her own, private, shining and utterly undeniable world. She was an unusual child.

Though her latest idea was truly inspired, Brangaene couldn't have chosen a worse day to break it to the baron. They were at dinner in the hall, the dogs rooting in the rushes for scraps and the baron dipping his bread in the soup and wishing it was the bishop's innards. That worthy had made good his threat. The baron was now excommunicate. The clerk in his soul quailed at the red tape involved: audiences with the archbishop, letters to the king and even to Rome, all for reconciliation with the earl bishop, might he strangle in his own *pallium*. Heaven aside, the re-elevation from goat to lamb would cost a bundle.

"But, Father." Brangaene pushed her bowl away and went on earnestly, "That's my plan. We'll give the bishop and the Church the greatest treasure they could wish. No, not the bishop, he's too small. We'll *allow* him to take it to Rome, and the Pope himself will reward you, and the king will make you an earl."

"And what had you in mind to present to His Holiness?" asked the baron with deceptive patience.

"Such a treasure," she bubbled. "I thought of it as I was reading in the garden. The Holy Grail, Father."

The baron sighed. "Oh yes, the Holy Grail." He dropped his bread in the soup where it sank like the rest of his luck. "You've seen it lately?"

"No one has seen it since Sir Percival."

"Some centuries back, I gather, and somehow mislaid since then."

"All we have to do is find it," she asserted. "The faerie have it without doubt – they steal everything. And today I found little footprints smaller than my own in the woods across the moat. I'll take the dogs and trap them, and say 'caught caught caught' three times for the charm, and –"

Thoughtfully the baron laid aside his spoon. Pensively he rose, tenderly he guided his only begotten child to the head of the stairs. Brangaene knew what was coming, but she was finished eating anyway.

Poonk! went the baron's full-inspired toe.

But Brangaene dreamed as she flew, and her dreams were not to be denied.

From the forest, the two small men in worn green tunics contemplated the unimpressive castle. Wary, dark and sharp-featured, they were accomplished thieves, and their present disagreement over method was conducted in a dialect ancient when the first Druids came to wild Britain.

Malgon, slightly the elder, held that the small keep was poor pickings: best steal two horses and be gone. Young Drust thought it shrewder to ask for a meal at the scullery door, tell a fortune or two, and filch from within. They strolled back into the copse that had sheltered them since yesterday and considered it.

"Yon's a starveling lord," Malgon guessed. "If a's got a horse, steal it now before a has to eat it himself."

Drust stretched out on the soft, marshy turf, grinning up at him. "Thee's so fond of sleeping on rock, will pass up soft straw?"

"I want my own bed," Malgon wished disconsolately.

"And I. How many days to home, Malgon?"

"Four, five, an thy mother's not moved our tents."

"Hast counted the time since we left her? A full year."

"The leaving was thy madness, not mine."

Arms behind his head, Drust squinted up at the sunlight filtering through the treetops. "But hast not travelled? Hast not seen armies and great battles and the lords of the tallfolk and learned their speech? Hast not thieved in glorious and honourable fashion for a year?"

Malgon snorted. "Hast not *worked* as well?"

"Aye, true," Drust admitted with a tinge of shame. "Too often hast been reduced to that. We'll not tell my mother."

Their kind did not mingle much with the tallfolk of the valleys and towns. They were upland dwellers, following their cattle and goats where the grazing led them, as their folk had done since the first of them tracked the reindeer when the land was half ice. Then the tallfolk had come with their bronze swords and their planted fields, taking the best lands, forcing the faerie ever further into the hills and heaths. They never planted grain like the bigger folk; if they had, how could they follow the herds? In hard times – and times were very hard now – they hung about the edges of the towns or hovered like Drust and Malgon about the twopenny barons' wars, and over the ages an unspoken contract grew up between faerie and tallfolk based on mutual distrust and fear. The tallfolk came to Drust's people for their magic and their gaiety, and even married them sometimes, though this was rare.

It was taken for granted that they stole as a way of life, but worked well when necessity drove them to it. Drust and Malgon could mend anything from harness to boots and clothing with a lasting skill denied bigger hands. Knowing their shyness, the work was left outside at night with a few coins or a little food carelessly placed about so that the bit of paid work could seem the whim of the little folk and the coins honourably filched. It paid to be on good terms with the faerie. The cattle blight that they could cure, they could bring again. They had the magic.

And they *were* small. They lacked the crossbreeding and the grain diet that lengthened the lowlanders' bones, but already legend and fireside tale were shrinking them further into Lilliputian creatures with shining wings, and faerie no longer meant what it had. They were men, but few and fading out, fading into the hills and fanciful stories. There was little left of their magic but the tallfolk's dread of it. If Drust had learned anything in the year away from his mother's tents, it was this.

He turned to face his friend, "Malgon, I think –"

A dry stick cracked nearby; his head swivelled round, and then down into the copse poured a conquering avalanche of three men-at-arms, four huge dogs, and a blonde girl yipping with delight.

"Caught!" she bounded at them. "Caught –" She tripped over a root and went down spectacularly as a fallen empire in a puddle. Undismayed, she leaped up, muddy but victorious.

"Caught! Three times is the charm, and you must yield to me or my men will chop you up and the dogs will eat you."

Drust and Malgon considered there seemed no future in the

vagaries of courage. The guards were shabby but armed, and the lean dogs of most uncertain benevolence.

"Yours, lady," Drust acceded in English.

She held onto him, not sure he wouldn't vanish if she let go. "You're faerie folk?"

"Aye, but –"

"And have the magic and yield it to my service?"

Drust glanced at the undernourished dogs. "My God, yes."

"Including all hidden treasures –"

"Well, there's sixpence in my –"

"And the whereabouts of dragons to be slain?"

"What's a dragon?"

"Be large and scaly, I think," Malgon ventured, "and dost fly."

Brangaene's free hand clamped on his arm. "Then you have seen them?"

"Not this far north," Malgon hedged.

"*Aargh*," snarled the largest dog, and Malgon shut up.

"No," said Brangaene, "you must uncover every lair, every trove of treasure, and grant me three wishes, or one at least, and if I just get one, it's going to be a crusher, and then," she paused for breath, "you must recommend my good fortune to the Queen of Faerie and bring me the Holy Grail.

She released them and waited, as it were, for wonders.

"A's mad," Malgon trembled. "Speak gently, Drust. Thee has the better English."

"Lady," Drust began, "it's true we're faerie and do a bit of trading, but –"

"But you will do magic?" Brangaene prompted.

Some of his composure regained, Drust managed a feeble smile. Even if Brangaene were an inch taller than he, her eyes were not difficult to look into, and he had seen very few blonde women.

"Not before dinner, lady."

"Of course, of course." She turned, gesturing to the guards. "To the hall. Our plans are perilous and there's not much time. Away!"

"Truly a sweet lass," Drust whispered as they were trundled towards the bailey bridge over the moat. "Such golden hair. None of our girls have golden hair."

"Dost cleverly hide the shape of her skull," Malgon hissed. "And but for that, would swear a was dropped on her soft little head at birth. Oh, if thy mother could see thee now: taken by a mad girl –"

"And three men."

"It retches me!"

"And four dogs, very large."

"Aye, and four dogs," Malgon glanced apprehensively at the drooling of the nearest hound, "and unreasonable at that."

They were hustled over the bridge, across the bailey and up the steps to the hall, Brangaene urging them on. "Hurry! Hurry!"

If prudence were Brangaene's long suit, she would not have disturbed her father just then. The baron had few good days, but this one was a negative gem. The earl bishop had descended on his delinquent neighbour, seized his lands, including the all-important mill, and now perched only two hours away to chastise the baron for his breach of fealty. Thus, his beleaguered lordship was not only excommunicate, he was technically under siege. Prices were going up.

"I can promise God," the baron moaned to Rainier, his steward, "but the bishop wants cash. Bishop, hell; he's a broker! I've got to buy him off when I couldn't afford his horse."

Rainier tried to be helpful. "Is there a crusade forming?"

"We lost the last two."

"Perhaps a pilgrimage to the Holy Land."

"Full of sandflies and Arabs selling pieces of the Cross. Rainier, we're sunk."

Voices, thumping feet, a skittering of hounds and then the stairwell erupted with Brangaene and her guards, four baying hounds and two rather stunted strangers. Caught up in the excitement, the dogs careered about, slipping on the rushes, *owoo*-ing in a frantic quartet until Rainier booted them into silence. The baron fixed his daughter with a dangerous eye.

"What is this?"

Brangaene's eyes shone. "Father! Guess what I have!"

"Bad manners and mud in your hair."

"I fell down."

"Again? I ought to put you on wheels."

"But I found them!" She tugged Drust and Malgon forward by their wrists, presenting them with a flourish. "They're ours."

Her father studied the two prisoners. "Indeed?"

Drust essayed a tentative smile. "How do you, sir?"

"Miserably, and shut up. Brangaene, your eye for value seems keener than my own. Found what?"

"The little folk."

"Their lack of height is apparent."

"But they're faerie!"

The baron looked again. They did not improve with definition. "These two . . . rabbit-droppings?"

Brangaene nodded, jubilant. "And they've been charged to give up their treasures and three wishes and find the Grail as I told you."

Her father turned away, suffering. "Ye gods."

"They look like thieves," Rainier judged. "What are they doing so close to the keep?"

Drust spoke up. "Just trying to get home, sir. We stole nothing from you."

"Which I take not as innocence but oversight," said the baron. "I ought to hang you – "

"That would be nice," said Rainier.

"But I'm at war and very busy. Brangaene, you and your treasures will accompany me to the head of the stairs."

She winced. "The *side* of the foot, father. They're really quite nice."

"Of course." He prodded Drust forward. "Come along now – no, wait. What's this?"

He fingered at the neck of Drust's tunic, opened it and extracted a heavy gold chain. From it, winking in the light, dangled a fair-sized emerald. Drust's hand caught his.

"That's mine. My mother gave it me."

"Where would your mother get a chain like that? Look, Rainier. Worth a warhorse at least."

Brangaene clapped her hands. "I knew it. I knew it."

Drust held on. "My mother gave it me."

"And who's she?" the baron demanded.

"Why, Queen Olwen," said Malgon.

The baron's eyebrows rose. "Who?"

"Queen of Faerie." Malgon struggled imperfectly with English. "Hast not stolen them; did give me one, too." He opened his tunic. "See?"

Rainier examined the rich chains and the undeniably precious stones. "This is not English work, my lord. Nor French or German, nor any I can recognize. Extremely antique."

The baron was a practical man, not given to unexamined belief;

practical, but in deep trouble. And he had eyes. He turned to Drust. "I've heard those treasure stories from every passing witch and gypsy all my life. Are they true, then?"

"Remember my wishes," Brangaene jiggled urgently. "Oh, please, please, we need them so much."

The two little men looked at the floor and were silent. Then Drust spoke quietly. "Take the chains, but let us go."

"Oh, no," the baron decided. "No, that was hasty. Rainier, deposit my guests in the tower room, it has a workable lock. Golden geese, you're laying in *my* barnyard now."

Standing tiptoe on a stool, Drust viewed the bustling bailey fifty feet below. The bars were meant to constrain larger men; they might wriggle through, but the drop would be terminal. No way out.

"There must be," said Drust.

Malgon hugged his knees on the straw pallet. "Thee's the fleet mind among us. Tell me how."

"By wit and wile. Am I Olwen's son for nothing?"

"Hast not heart? Thee's the property of that great, scowling man, the golden goose to drop eggs like breadcrumbs. And must not forget the mad lass with a's caught-caught-caught and the wishes and the grails." Malgon threw up his hands. "A thinks we're a mill for magic."

Drust studied him with a slow, thoughtful smile. "Then we will be one. The great baron wants treasure –"

Malgon's eyes flashed a stern warning. "Impossible."

"Just so," Drust nodded, "and therefore . . ."

They heard footsteps on the stone steps beyond their cell. A key groaned in the lock, then the door swung back and Brangaene hurried in with a tray. Two guards waited at the door. She placed the tray on a stool and closed the heavy door. The faerie men inspected their dinner: two apples, two slices of black bread, but only one bowl of leek and barley soup.

"There were two," Brangaene explained, "but I dropped one."

"Did guess." Malgon fell hungrily to the bread and apples. Brangaene noticed how he offered the soup first to Drust. Clearly this was Queen Olwen's son, a genuine faerie prince, and her luck was almost as great as her imminent need. The bishop would not be put off.

"You must give me my wishes very soon."

Drust spooned the soup, careful to leave half for Malgon. "Oh yes, the treasure."

"And the Grail."

"That's two."

Brangaene blinked. "Don't I get three?"

"Magic's hard, lady, and treasure's rare. There's the bargaining yet." Drust laid down the spoon and offered the bowl to Malgon without taking his eyes from Brangaene. "For a treasure, I'll ask value in return."

Brangaene gazed back at him, and suddenly found it a little hard to breathe. She ascribed it to his magic aura – and let that suffice for an answer. Inexperienced as she was, her glands worked very well, thank you, and Drust was something new. She had never seen hair so sleekly black or eyes so dark, or a male figure, though diminutive, so perfectly formed. He was her gleaming opposite, and the attractive force of that juxtaposition is magic of a very palpable cast. No man had ever looked at her quite like that before, especially one who came so close and took both of her hands.

"It won't be easy, Brangaene. It will take time."

"We don't have time!" she wailed. "The earl bishop is coming, and he'll want just buckets of money."

"The road itself is hard to find, the road of the gods."

"We're in trouble with God, too. Father's excommunicated." Brangaene fluttered to the door. "There's no time for roads. You must wave your hand and make the hill open. Forget the dragons; father doesn't hunt much anyway. Just one treasure, just a small one, and the Holy Grail. You're bound to do it. The books said."

"What books?" Malgon wondered.

"All of them," she said. "The tales of faerie."

Malgon bit into his apple. "Was't *writ* by faerie?"

"Well, no, but –"

"Did think not. Lies."

Drust frowned. "Peace, Malgon."

"It . . . *can't* be a lie," Brangaene said in a small voice.

Malgon chewed placidly. "Why not?"

"Because – because I need it so much. Because I've searched for you all my life."

"Yes," said Drust. "I see that."

"It *is* true . . . isn't it, Drust?"

Drust glanced once at Malgon. "Tell your father we will bargain."

The colour came back to her cheeks. "Oh, yes!"

"And bargain has two sides."

"Yes, yes," Brangaene flung open the door and plunged out. "And quickly, because the bishop –" She tripped over a guard's pike and went flying. Malgon winced.

The footsteps died away, the apparently unbreakable Brangaene in the van. "Hurry! Hurry!"

Malgon sighed. "Now thee's done it. Nay, don't cock thy brow or frown at me who swore to look after the queen's only son. A will whip me from her tent! And thee's no better than tallfolk with the mooning at yellow hair and watery blue eyes. 'May leave out the dragons. Just a small treasure and the Grail,' a says. Ha! What'll thee give little Sure-Foot and her greedy da but the lone, lorn sixpence between us?"

But Drust grinned from ear to ear. He threw himself down on the straw, glowing with satisfaction. "An impossible bargain, Mal: what I can't give for what the baron won't give up."

His mother's guess at the high birthrate of fools – one a minute – was rather informed, Drust realized. There were not one but two keys to their freedom, the baron's greed and the girl's belief.

Malgon was sceptical. "What won't a give up?"

"Brangaene."

With Adam's innocence, he bit lustily into his apple. As with Adam, it was only the prelude to his enlightenment.

The political axiom of the times was "every man must have a lord" – which is to say that no matter how big you were, someone had your number. Someone very definitely had the bishop's.

"Lord, hear Thy servant in his hour of need!"

By the altar of a small, roadside chapel, the earl bishop prayed very earnestly. He had attached the goods of one baron, his men waited outside amid the snorting of horses and the clank of mail to do the same thing to Brangaene's father, and all out of necessity. The earl bishop was in the same trouble as the baron, but larger.

By chance he was related to the king; by misfortune he was ambitious, since it led him to accept his bishopric from his royal cousin. The king thought it sound policy, in view of Rome's persuasive power, to have a bishop or two he could count on. Unfortunately, the bishop accepted his *pallium* of office from the crown and didn't wait, as was customary, to have one blessed and sent from Rome. This political oversight has filled volumes; suffice to say His Holiness took umbrage and a flurry of letters coursed between the crown, the bishop and the Vatican. When the diplomatic smoke cleared away, the bishop was regarded as unreliable in London, quite temporary in Rome, and had to decide which to placate first.

He prayed now for guidance with honest intensity. Truly conscientious, even dogmatic, in his holy office, he was less intelligent than shrewd and above all less fervent than superstitious. He could always feel the heat of hell and was not about to fan the flames. The king was a mere relative; he could wait. To pay Peter, Paul would be cheerfully robbed. The gift must be large and of noble intent, one grand gesture of faith.

He and Brangaene had more in common than either realized.

The earl bishop crossed himself, rose and strode out to take his horse from the groom. He mounted in a rattling of mail and an aura of sanctity.

"Quickly on. We'll raise his keep before vespers."

It was late afternoon and rather warm for April when the baron came into the hall carrying the two gold chains. Drust waited by the trestle table guarded by one man, all the baron could spare from the gates and watch towers. The baron dropped the chains on the table, sat and poured wine into a silver cup.

"Brangaene says you're willing to bargain for your freedom."

Drust sat and indicated the wine. "May I?"

"Please do. Tell me, how much are you prepared to pay?"

Drust sampled the wine pleasurably. "How much will you ask?"

"A heap, little man. The lot, the bundle. Where is it?"

"Oh, now, now, sir. That's not how it's done. The cup of wine begins the bargaining. Aye, there's treasure, but the way to it is a matter of when, not where."

The baron picked up the gold chains; the emeralds flashed in the light. "Did these come from that hoard?"

Drust sipped his wine dreamily. "Mother always liked those. The stones are like the green of wild Britain when we first found it. And the gold – is there any colour goes so well with green as gold? Like sunlight it is. But when you talk money to us, you talk of wives and cattle and goats. These we value, these bring children and make food. We love gold only because it's so pretty."

"And yet you steal it."

"A hard word, sir. Very hard. We were the first men in Britain, and the land belongs to us. We only charge you rent."

The baron choked on his wine. "You what?"

"My lord taxes his own tenants, doesn't he, for the use of the land? The earl bishop charges you, the great king takes from him. A clear logic."

Drily, the baron asked, "What do you charge the king?"

"Mother's rates go up for him. For you, we will be reasonable."

"That's gracious for a man who has no choice. Now, this treasure. How much is there?"

"Your wine is lovely." Drust settled back in the chair, helping himself to more. "How much? That's hard to say. And the road of the gods ... not where it is, but when. This is April, a fortnight yet to Beltane-fire – aye, could be soon, could be. But your king strikes his coin in silver, and we don't deal in that."

The baron frowned. "You don't?"

"Oh, a wee bit." Drust shrugged. "The larger pieces. It's not pretty as gold. Must think in silver weight; let me see. Fifty ... sixty ... aye, the chest of pearls, large ones only ... perhaps eighty –"

His host blinked. "Pearls?"

Drust's brow furrowed in concentration. "Eighty-five ..."

"Eighty-five *what*, damn it!"

"No, there's the rubies. I always forget them."

"You forget –"

"We don't like red. It's the colour of rage. That makes ninety ... and some trifles, cups, ewers and jewelled plate that Mother holds dear for the charm of them. Yes," Drust set down his cup. "Near a hundred thousand marks of silver."

Luckily, the baron's cup was empty, because he dropped it. He gasped. "A – hundred – thousand –"

"Oh, and the Grail." Drust snapped his fingers. "Lady Brangaene asked for it."

The baron was still stunned. "Part of the ... rent, I take it."

"Collected from Glastonbury church by Mother's own ancestor these thousand years gone. The Grail, the Cup of the Last Supper. Mother calls it her Jerusalem Cup. She may not wish to part with that."

The baron found his aplomb. "Quite, quite. Now, as to delivery –"

"But my lord, there's my bargain."

"Well, what is it? What do you want?" A good question. If the gold chains were only appetizer to a hundred thousand marks of silver, what could he toss in to humour this improbable pixie?

Drust picked up a candlestick, admiring the workmanship. When he spoke, his voice was gentle with an old sorrow. "Bronze: we learned from the first tallfolk how to make it, and that gave us swords to match theirs. Then others came with the iron we couldn't make or match. We don't like iron. But gold is beautiful, and beauty is what we love. Will you give me one thing with gold in it, even a little, for trade?"

"Done," said the baron.

"And if you fail me, your fields will blight and your cattle perish."

"Done. And if you cheat me – well, *media vita in morte sumus*. In the midst of life, eh? You're rather young to die."

Drust rose and gravely placed his small hand in the baron's. "Done for the third time and the charm. I want your daughter Brangaene for my wife."

The baron dropped his cup again – full, this time. "What?"

"Just that, sir. Not a jot more, not a hair less."

The baron began to chuckle, then to roar with it. Even the guard laughed. "My daughter marry *you*? I'll die laughing."

"Laughing and poor, alas." Drust rose. "Since there's no bargain –"

"Wait a minute!" The baron pushed him down again. "In the midst of life, remember? Ever see a man hanged, drawn and quartered?"

Drust regarded him imperturbably. "That will leave you with two gold chains and my mother's very long memory for injustice. Thy cattle will be Britain's wonder for their mortality." He tried to rise again; this time the guard quashed him back into the chair.

The baron thought: the earl bishop was imminent. Two dead faeries and two gold chains would benefit no one. He was still thinking furiously when Brangaene pattered up the stairs into the hall.

"Men, Father, a whole line of them on the west road. Good day, Drust, are you working on my wishes? At least five hundred men, Father, all in iron. When can I have the Grail, Drust?"

He shook his head. "There's no bargain made, lass. 'Done' my lord says and takes my hand on it, then 'undone' says he when he learns what I want. Alas – no Grail, Brangaene."

She flew at her father, stricken. "Why not? It has to be a bargain. The book said. Give him something."

"Don't tempt me." Her father drew her close with an acerbic

smile. "He's asked for the single rose among my weeds, the hope of my declining years."

She hopped up and down with the urgency. "So *give* it to him!"

"He wants you."

It caught Brangaene on the upswing of a hop. She came down with a thud. "Huh?"

Drust favoured her with what he hoped was a winning smile. "You'll be the only golden-haired girl among my people, a bright star in a midnight sky. No longer dreaming of faerie folk, but a princess among them, sharing their lives, learning to herd and milk goats –"

Rainier panted up the stairs and rushed across the hall. "My lord! The earl-bishop is at the gate with five hundred men, five times what we have on the walls. What defence can we make?"

"Against five hundred? What would you do, Rainier?"

"I'd bloody well let him in, sir."

"Precisely," the baron sighed. "Surrender politely, invite his grace to dinner and hope he chokes on it."

Rainier hurried away, his orders trailing behind him through the air like a ragged banner. "Open the gates. Open the gates . . ."

"Goats?" Brangaene said. "Smelly goats?"

Drust smiled. "The most fragrant in Britain. Will learn to skin cattle and scrape hides –"

Brangaene swallowed. "Scrape hides?"

"And wear them as our women do, and pitch and strike our tents when we follow the herds to graze. But look at you! So pale and startled." Drust held out his arms. "What do I offer you but your own dreams?"

"I never dreamed goats. Father –"

"Peace, child. Would I marry you to this?"

"I thought not." Drust rose with confident regret. "So, of course . . ."

Footsteps again. Rainier burst out of the stairwell, even more breathless. "Ruin, my lord! Poverty, destruction and the end of all! His grace is taking the cattle and swine and all that's not nailed or mortared down –"

There was a growing uproar in Rainier's wake, voices, dogs, dozens of feet tramping up the stairs into the hall. The earl bishop appeared out of breath, out of sorts, and perfunctory. Hardly an imposing figure, either as noble or man of God, he looked like a tax collector whose books were not yet balanced. Behind him came his entourage—soldiers, the almoner, the clerks already listing on vellum the valuables attached, one of them with a voice like deep-knelling doom reciting aloud as he scribbled: "Four ivory chests . . . one oaken *prie-dieu*."

Brangaene wailed to heaven "*I hate goats!*"

The bishop nodded to her. "Then you won't mind that I've removed yours."

"Eight goats," verified the clerk. "Seventeen hens . . ."

"I can't stay for supper, baron. I'm dispossessing you. Look to that table, you men. And the chairs, all of them."

Drust was picked up by two brawny soldiers and the chair swept out from under him.

"Five chairs . . ."

"Sorry about this, baron, but you wouldn't help when I needed, so I must foreclose."

The baron mopped his brow. "Your grace is known to be just. Can't we negotiate?"

"Your troubles are minuscule to mine." The bishop swept up the candlesticks. "That's it, men, all of it. Everything."

The hall was growing quite crowded with soldiers lugging out furniture and chests, and since it was near suppertime, the quartet of dogs elected to charge musically through the procession, eddying about the fringes of the activity. "Four . . . dogs," noted the clerk, but the bishop kicked him.

"Not them, you idiot!"

"Blot . . . four dogs."

"Not my goldware," moaned the baron. "It belonged to the baroness."

"One chest goldware."

"I'm ruined; I'm a poor man."

"*I hate tents!*" Brangaene screamed.

"Tent?" The clerk paused, looking up. "Did I miss a tent?"

"*Keep your Grail!*"

The baron muttered brokenly, "At a time like this . . . grails." Instantly the bishop was at his side. "What is this? What Grail?"

"Grail," the baron echoed in feeble despair. Then, slowly, he said it again. "Grail!" A dawning purpose lit his eye, already tinged with the madness to match a desperate hour. "Grail! Yes, look!" He thrust the two gold chains with their emerald pendants before the bishop. "Treasure, your grace. Gold, silver, pearls, a hundred thousand marks of it. Look at these!"

The earl-bishop looked, but he had heard something that

faded the emeralds to green clay. "The Holy Grail, did you say?"

It was to the baron's credit that he could think on his feet, and he knew how to play a trump. "*The* Holy Grail." His arm swept out to point triumphantly at the bewildered Drust. "He has it all and promised it to me."

"The Grail," whispered the bishop, sepulchral as his subject.

"But my *own* goods," the baron reminded him delicately.

The earl bishop looked, but he had moment. "Bring it all back! Everything!" And far down the stairs the order coursed and echoed. *Bring it bach. Bring it bach* . . . The trudging feet paused, turned and started back up the stairs, the dogs dodging around and among them, baying for supper. One of them nibbled at the clerk.

"Brangaene," said her father tenderly, "I'm a man of my word. Prepare yourself."

"Wait!" Drust looked hopelessly from father to weeping child. "You mean –"

"*I hate cows!*"

"So don't drink milk." The baron took her hand and placed it in Drust's, the world once again in place and revolving nicely. "I mean you made a bargain, you demented elf. You're getting married."

Malgon understood none of it as he waited by the saddled horse watching the approach of Drust and the great bishop. The world had turned turvy. The bishop's men peered from every casement and cranny of the small keep while their lord loped about muttering feverishly of grails. The baron looked doubtful. Drust and Brangaene were betrothed and miserable.

But Queen Olwen – he shuddered to think of *her* when he broke the news. Her merest irritation could blister paint, but her rage was lethal as it was silent and patient. Malgon shivered a little with the memory.

Drust seemed different, too. His open good nature was now masked with sober purpose and a kind of sorrow. It wasn't right for faerie to be so serious.

Drust halted by him, the earl-bishop hovering over them both like a thundercloud.

"Malgon, hast the message clear, what to ask the queen?"

"Clear, Drust."

"Her leave to follow the road of the gods."

"And the Grail," said the earl-bishop. "That above all. Her son's life in exchange."

Drust favoured him with an inscrutable look. "And the Jerusalem Cup," he verified. "Tell Olwen I would drink from it."

The bishop's mouth dropped open. "*Drink* from it? You would profane – are you serious?"

"Most gravely so," Drust assured him. "It is old custom. The queen would demand it if I didn't. Faerie are innocent – as the world goes – and when we travel out among tallfolk, we drink from the Grail on our return to show we are still God's first children. There are dangers ... your grace is a man of learning. Surely you know the legend of this holy vessel?"

The troubled bishop knew only too well. The most sacred relic in Christendom could not be touched or even approached by the impure without instant death. To drink from it as this vagrant pixie proposed was not only sacrilege but madness that beggared adjectives.

And yet the thought came unbidden – he would make confession of the pride – if he himself could be allowed ...

He shelved the thought. Devout he was, but the product of a suspicious world. Faerie were notorious deceivers. He knew not only the legends but the factual history of the relic. A few subtle questions would show the truth of it.

"Where was this stolen?" he demanded.

"Acquired," Drust amended tactfully. "At Glastonbury."

"The abbey, of course?"

"No, the old wattle church. No more than a mud hut it was then."

The bishop felt himself begin to sweat. "Where hidden? Behind the altar? Under the floor?"

"In a well, my mother said."

The earl-bishop swallowed hard. His heart skipped a beat. "Wh-why should it be brought to Britain at all?"

Drust answered easily. "The merchant had friends here."

"What friends? What friends would a poor Jew have in Britain?"

Drust smiled at Malgon. "Mark how dost try to catch me out. Your grace knows Joseph was a friend of the governor of Judea and a merchant in tin. Who needs hearsay when common knowledge will do? Every port in the Middle Sea, from Rome to Thebes on the Nile, shipped its tin from Cornwall. Is not Joseph still remembered and sung about there? Belike he made the journey more than once."

The earl-bishop hid his trembling hands in the folds of his robe.
"You have seen the Grail?"

"Olwen told me of it. 'Tis kept masked."

"Describe the jewels set in the vessel."

"There be no jewels," Drust shook his head. "No, *those* stories
were writ in French, and not even your grace would trust a Frank.
The Christ-man wasn't rich. Bronze it is and plain as truth. Mother
wouldn't prize it else." His glance flicked over the bishop's rich
mantle filigreed in cloth-of-gold. "Gaudy's not to her taste."

The bishop turned away to hide his excitement. He looked up
at his men perched like predatory birds on the walls, the baron and
his daughter waiting at the hall entrance. Most of the Grail stories
were maundering, allegorical romance, and over the centuries a
thousand liars claimed to have seen it. They all described a cup or
bowl too rich for most kings let alone the simple dwelling that
housed the yet-obscure band of the Nazarene on the night of the
Last Supper.

Now, the bishop was a religious man – as those things went –
though he could not believe the Grail had been withdrawn into
heaven or simply disappeared from mortal sight. Lost, stolen or
strayed, it had to be somewhere.

"Bring it." He turned and bustled away towards the chapel.

Drust embraced Malgon. "Haste thee back. The tower will be
lonely."

Malgon studied him closely. "Thee looks sad as death."

"No matter. Go."

But Malgon caught his arm. "Nay, tell. Hast been thy servant;
hast not been thy friend as well?"

Drust's eye twinkled with the ghost of his old merriment – and
an elusive something else behind it. "And will be when bishop
and baron be long forgot. Faerie's dealt with greedy men before,
else why our saying that one thing worse than wanting . . ."

"Is getting," Malgon finished it. "True, they be all stupid and
mad. Help me to shorten this stirrup, Drust; 'twas set for a giant."

Drust watched him across the bridge and onto the north road,
then turned back toward the keep. Brangaene left her father and
hurried across the bailey toward him. Drust's mouth curved ironically; this wishing business was quite beyond her now. She looked
like someone who'd conjured a rose and received a thorn.

"Drust, what happened to the bishop? Runs past us without a
word, talking to himself. Not even vespers yet, and he's in chapel
praying for all he's worth."

"That won't take long."

"What did he ask of you?"

His expression was strange, but the words were gentle when they came, as if he were teaching a child.

"What you all want of faerie: wishes granted, dreams come true, death put off till some far time when the world's lost all of its sweet. He wants magic in a bronze bowl. And what's your pleasure today?"

Brangaene saw the thing he had tried to conceal from Malgon, the pain. She might have missed it a week before, but even unicorn hunters, when they grow up, have to start somewhere.

"Poor Drust. I didn't mean to . . ."

"Ladybug, don't be sad. I was like you once. Because I couldn't see any further than a frog, I thought my lily pad was the world. Then I saw how big the world really was, and how little and how few we are. Olwen has less folk to call her queen than the great bishop brought here with him. Our cattle are scrawny, our children starve, and we have no land. What little graze is left the tallfolk's sheep tear away bit by bit, year by year. We move from poor to worse and must keep on moving until there's nothing left. Gold, jewels –" he spread his hands helplessly "– these buy *things*, Brangaene. They can't – there's a word in my tongue that means *what was then*, but more than that. It means the good, green time, all the good things that were. My mother will never understand. Malgon will never understand. And it's not in my poor pudding of a heart to tell them." After a moment, Drust took her hand and kissed it. "And *you* want magic?"

"Not any more," she confessed. "Not that you're not *very* nice, Drust, just . . ."

"Not entirely what you wished."

"I guess it's the goats."

Drust surveyed her, his manner changing abruptly. "Look, lass, when you make a gown, you don't just cut and stitch away with no thought to it. You measure what's needed. Well, it's the same with wishes: they have to fit *you*. I'll guess you've never done it right. Would you like to try?"

Brangaene hesitated; the whole phenomenon had proved hazardous. "Should I?"

"You have one left. Close your eyes and think of something you want so deep you never even whispered it."

Eyelids squeezed tight around the effort, Brangaene concentrated.

"Oh dear." She giggled. "Oh, my goodness!"

"You see?"

"I didn't even wish. It was just – there."

"No dragons or grails?"

"No," Brangaene blushed – rather more with anticipation than embarassment. "No, indeed."

Two men-at-arms marched out from the hall, halted, flanking Drust like falcons bracketing a sparrow. "The baron wants a word with you. Quick *march*! One-two-one-two – step *out*, you horrible little man! One-two . . ."

Drust tried to keep up with them.

The baron met them, rubbing his hands together nervously. "No problems? Your servant will return, of course?"

Drust nodded. "Until then, back to jail, I suppose."

"Just to keep things regular. The *cuisine* will not stint. There'll be a good supper."

"And wine," Brangaene prompted from behind the soldiers.

"Of course, he's our guest." The baron stepped close to Drust, lowering his voice. "My abbreviated friend, I don't know how you take to metaphor, but you and I are ripe wheat." He inclined his head significantly toward the chapel. "And *he* has a very large scythe."

"Just so, my lord," Drust said expressionlessly. "And what price wishes now?"

"Eh?"

"The Grail and treasure make two. 'Twas not in the bargain, mind, but if I *could* eke out a third . . ."

In the elogent silence of understanding, they listened to the interminable Latin braying forth from the chapel where the bishop was, as it were, covering his bet.

The baron sighed. "If indeed."

"Just a thought." Drust let it hang in the air between them. The guards in his wake, he started up the tower stairs.

A week passed, eight days, nine. Then a morning came when the sun climbed only half-heartedly into the sky, sulked and then hid its face in thick cloud. On the tenth day, the small world of the keep was wrapped in fog, and out of it came Malgon on the same manor horse, leading two of Olwen's ponies. Drust watched him cross the bailey bridge. Within minutes, he heard the heavy tread of the soldiers counterpointed with the light patter of Brangaene's feet.

"Drust! To the hall and quickly. Malgon's come with a letter from your mother, and the bishop's angry because no one can read it, and – oh, hurry!"

The guards hustled him away in the backwash of her haste. In the hall were the earl bishop, the baron and Rainier, and in the centre of their regard, like a spaniel pup among irritable greyhouds, the weary Malgon.

"This fool of yours can barely speak English," the bishop growled.

"Here, read." The baron thrust a rolled parchment at Drust. "I didn't think anyone still wrote on sheepskin."

"And a palimpsest at that." Rainier peered at it. "Ancient as those chains they wore. This queen doesn't write very often."

The heavy parchment was tied with a strip of worn linen. Drust undid it, speaking to Malgon in faerie, "How did the queen at this?"

"Cold," Malgon murmured. "So cold and quiet, would swear 'twas winter and not spring in a's tent. Then a smiles like death and sits down to write this."

Drust glanced at the rounded Gaelic script and the scrawled, looping signature. His mother styled herself, as her ancestors did, with a title that had not appeared on any map for a thousand years, if at all. He felt a pang; for Olwen and her people, nothing would ever change.

> To the English who hold Drust:
> I marvel that so many tallfolk can prize cold metal over the real treasures of this world and yet call themselves wise.
> Natheless, my son is precious to me. For his safety, you have my leave to travel the road of the gods and take such fortune as you find there, to the which is added my chiefest possession known as the Jerusalem Cup, excepting only our custom that Drust may prove the innocence of his soul by drinking therefrom.
> I wish only to see my son safe home.
> Olwen, Queen of Prydn

Rainer squinted quizzically. "Queen of what?"

Drust handed him the letter. "It means 'the very old people'."

The bishop's eyes were fevered. "But the Grail, where is it?"

"Olwen's word is good," said Drust. "Will be with the treasure. And I will drink from it." He went to the casement and scrutinized the air beyond it. "After this fog will come rain," he told them. "And we need the rain to find the road. We must leave now."

The bishop needed no urging. "To horse!" He whirled and hurried to the stairs, his officers in his wake. *To horse!* The relayed orders echoed after him.

"Well, Brangaene." Her father took her arm. "Will you come? It seems only right. This was your inspiration to begin with."

The guards had taken up their parenthetical position around Drust and Malgon. "Yes, ride with us, Brangaene," Drust laughed. "To the end of the road, the end of wishing. Who could miss that?" He shrugged philosophically to the guards. "Come, sirs."

They travelled north all day through a blanketing fog, Drust and Malgon in the lead, the bishop and two guards just behind, then the baron and Brangaene. Behind them, in a train stretching over a quarter-mile, came the bishop's entourage.

The road gave way to forest, the great trees looming up and fading again like ghosts behind them. When the last of the gaunt shapes disappeared in the fog, Brangaene missed them, nothing now but wild gorse, rolling moor and dampness that chilled through her heavy cloak. They pitched their tents in the middle of it before nightfall. The next day was drearier still. Though the fog was gone, heavy clouds loured over the barren hill tops. Before midday, the rain began, gentle at first, then harder, in a steady downpour through which they plodded all afternoon across the monotonous moor in the wake of the faerie men. Before they pitched camp for the night, Brangaene was sneezing with her worst cold in years.

Swathed in blankets, she huddled over a brazier in her small tent, hating quite beyond demure limits the weather, the moor, her father, the bishop and the whole blighted notion of wishes and magic.

"Dab!" she cursed. "Dabdab*dab*!"

"Odd; your da just said that."

Drust stood in the entrance of the tent with a steaming cup. "Magic's hard work, isn't it? Here." He handed her the cup. "Olwen's own tea. Made from honeycomb and flowers."

She sipped at it. "Oh, it's good."

"Some say it's the rose does the trick, some the pimpernel, but we never have colds."

"Where are we bound, Drust? Will this moor ever end?"

He nodded. "Soon enough. Tomorrow we must be in a certain place."

"Why?"

"Not why, lass. When. When the sun comes out."

Like much of what Drust said, Brangaene understood it not at all. She listened to the rain drumming against the tent sides. "What if it doesn't?"

"Then we wait till it does. Nothing is perfect."

An interesting aside: this logical question and answer just might have been the end of the Age of Faith and the beginning of the Renaissance. Everything starts somewhere, and Brangaene was no longer a child of pure belief.

The rain let up towards mid-morning of the next day. Their way ran through uplands now, wave after wave of bare, steepening hills and rocky outcroppings. Drust dropped back to ride at the baron's knee and found him red-eyed as his daughter and definitely out of sorts.

"If you know this treasure to the last pound, why must we look for some damned silly road-of-the-gods?"

"Only Olwen knows the way. I've seen it only once." Drust pointed to the hills, alike as wrinkles in a blanket. "Without the road, I couldn't find it again."

The baron exploded. "There's no bloody road! Nothing but heath and no end to that."

"Will be soon," Drust soothed him. "We must have passed the treasure an hour ago."

"An *hour* –?"

"Or thereabouts. Must go beyond to see back, like a lifetime. Brangaene, lass, how's your cold?"

She snuffled. "Bedder, thag you."

Up ahead, the earl bishop and his guards were paused over something on the ground. The bishop wheeled his horse and cantered back to Drust.

"There are tracks. They might be your people."

Drust urged his pony forward to the indicated spot. A hundred yards beyond, Malgon was halted, observing the lightening sky.

The prints were those of a single, small horse. Most were obliterated by rain, but they pointed south.

"Faerie horse," Drust confirmed.

The bishop pondered the print. "Should we follow?"

"You'd never find her. That mark in the print there? Olwen's horse. She's brought the Grail for me to drink."

The bishop regarded him solemnly. "You still persist in that madness?"

"The old custom, almost law. My mother expects it of me."
Drust smiled quickly as if to dispel any personal doubts. "Will
be no danger to your grace, of course, though it might be wise to
stand well back and perhaps not stare it straight on."

The earl bishop could no longer choke back the question. "How
many . . . men have drunk from the grail?"

"In a thousand years? Many."

"And died?"

"Only a few," said Drust offhandedly. "It may be the Christ-
man's more merciful than one thinks."

"Drust!"

It was Malgon ahead, pointing not to the sky now, but the
ground. "Be shadow! The sun!"

Abruptly, Malgon kicked the pony into a flat run up a rocky
defile. Drust beckoned the others forward in a sweeping wave
and galloped after him. The whole column rippled forward in
the rush up the narrow pass, the bordering rocks now showing in
sharp relief the shadows that raced across them as the last clouds
parted and the sun burned through. Up and up they clattered until
Brangaene felt the ground level out under her horse. She rounded
a sharp bend in the trail; there on the rocky ledge before her stood
Drust and Malgon looking away to the south, while the bishop
sat his horse with a foolish expression on his face, saying over
and over to himself, "I don't believe it. No, I don't believe it. We
could have – we should have known . . ."

And Brangaene's heart leaped with the last flicker of an old
dream. Sad, because it would never come again. The old tales
were not magic, no part of magic, only truth – and a kind of
map worn faint with time.

"There, Brangaene!" Drust's voice rang out over the bishop's.
"The road of the gods. *Where it goes down*!"

Across the moist prism of the morning sky, the rainbow bent
its glory to earth.

The long mound looked like any other low rise in the rolling hills.
Only when Brangaene knew what it was could she see that it rose
too smoothly, the length of its hundred-foot ridge too even. It had
been built of stone like the great circle on Salisbury Plain, Drust
told her, and sodded over so long it was truly part of the hills
around it.

Now she knew why Drust had stressed *when*. The rainbow lasted
no more than a quarter-hour, fading as the sun clouded over again.

Before it went, Drust carefully estimated the exact point at which it would touch the earth, selected a series of references, leading to that spot, then led them back along the trail.

Two more hours and the hardest riding of the whole journey, straight up hills, jolting down the other side. The mist rose rapidly, seeping like pale white snakes into the valleys and copses, rising toward the low hill tops. Just after they attained Drust's last reference point, Brangaene spied the figure that might have been a stunted tree or a large bush in the thickening fog, but she thought it moved slightly. Later, she saw it again: off to her left, slipping away into a wall of whiteness like a ghost-wolf padding their flank. But for a moment Brangaene had seen clearly, if only in silhouette, the pony and its small, hooded rider.

She could hardly see the others now in the mist. Drust must be moving on pure instinct. At last the wraith-figures of the two faerie men dipped into one last defile and disappeared briefly. When she and her father drew up on them, they were sitting their horses amid the bishop and his guards, and beyond loomed the long, regular shape of the cairn.

Drust slipped out of the saddle and knelt to examine something in the earth. The bishop followed him.

"What is it?"

Drust pointed to the small hoofprint. "Olwen."

If no one else believed, Brangaene did.

The baron studied the dimensions of the cairn. "This thing goes back for at least thirty yards. Is it all hollow?"

"And goes far down," Drust told him.

The bishop was all business now; "Set my tent here at the entrance . . . this *is* the entrance?"

"Hard by." Drust took several steps to the foot of the mound where a tumbled outcropping of stones rose some six feet above him. He leaned almost casually against one of the stones; with a grinding rumble, the largest boulder in the pile rolled back to reveal an aperture large enough for a man to wiggle through.

"Will need a torch," he said.

"Bring a resin torch, bring them all," the bishop commanded. "A fire here quickly. Set my tent."

Brushwood was collected, rubbed with tallow and lighted in a large brazier. With a great deal of bustle, the bishop's tent was pitched. Drust dipped his torch into the fire, slipped into the black opening and disappeared. Malgon waited by the rocks. Suddenly he knelt close to the opening. Brangaene heard him mumble something, then he rose and shouted to all of them.

"The Jerusalem Cup be here. All may look. Be covered with a cloth."

Drust's arm jutted out of the hole bearing an object swathed in a long dark cloth. "Take it, Mal, so I can climb out."

Malgon shrank back and fell on his knees, turning his face away. "Nay, cannot. Do not ask it of me. Be not shriven or heard mass this fortnight."

Still the arm protruded from the opening. Like that which caught Arthur's sword in the lake, Brangaene thought. All around her, the men were dismounting, sinking to their knees, the sound of their armour eerie and distorted in the mist. Only the bishop remained upright, rooted in front of his tent, gazing at the masked object.

"I need both hands to climb out," the voice came again. "Let him who is without fear of his soul take the Grail from me."

Head bowed over her hands in reverence, Brangaene felt the awed silence. Then a rustle of movement. Her eyes opened. Slowly, deliberately, the bishop moved towards the Grail. Brangaene swallowed hard. There must be fear in him, but the bishop kept going till he stood within reach of the upthrust arm.

He stretched out both hands and took the covered Grail. An exhalation of fright and wonder sighed through the company of his men. When Drust clambered out of the hole, he regarded the earl bishop with a grave respect.

"Your grace is the holiest of men – and the bravest. They may go in now. The treasure is there." He raised his hand for the watching men and opened it to reveal the rubies lying on his palm. He let them fall like so many pebbles. The men watched carefully where they rolled, their eyes wide, tongues licking out over dry lips.

"The treasure is there!" Drust raised his voice. "Olwen's word is kept."

"Yes . . ." The bishop's voice cracked slightly. He stared at his men and hardly saw them. "Yes, go in. Take the sacks. Get . . . get it all."

A dozen, twenty torches were dipped into the fire. A line of fireflies in the mist, the men squeezed through the opening and vanished into the cairn. The bishop appeared oblivious to it all. With stiff movements, he carried the covered prize to his tent.

Passing Malgon, Drust whispered something, received the other's silent affirmation, then joined Brangaene at the fire, listening with them to the growing clamour of discovery within the cairn.

"Now they're finding it, hear them? Finding out how much there is, how it shines in the light, thinking there's nothing lovelier, not even a fair woman. Feeling it in their hands. Wondering will it all disappear as they've heard tell. You can smell their greed. Don't go in, baron." Drust smiled up at him. "There *is* that third wish."

In his tent, the earl bishop placed his precious burden on a low chest. He prayed briefly, then contemplated on his – no, his soul's desire.

The first test was past. He was allowed to approach, to touch it, perceive its solidity. The shape under the woollen cloth was a foot and a half across by perhaps six inches deep. He fingered the edge of the cloth, took hold of it –

"Your grace."

Drust moved forward to face the bishop across the chest. "I came to drink, and so grave with the thought of it, I forgot to bring wine. May a frightened man beg that favour?"

"You will still do this?"

"I must," Drust said tonelessly. He indicated a wine skin. "May I?"

The bishop's throat tightened.

"God with us." With a quick motion, Drust jerked the cover from the bowl. As he did, the bishop shut his eyes and crossed himself. Nothing happened; the world churned on. When he looked again, the bowl sat quite mundanely on the chest, feeble light from the one candle darting with unusual brightness over the polished surfaces. He watched in horrified fascination as Drust unstoppered the wineskin and poured a good measure into the vessel. The red wine swashed and sparkled over the polished bottom.

"Your grace will send this to the Pope?"

"What? Yes . . . yes, I will."

"Don't tell him of this act. Would not bring on him the sin of envy." Drust laid hands on the bowl.

"*Faerie, are you mad*?"

The answer, when it came, was faint and weary. "No . . . no. Only a man from a small, weak people whose green time is gone, who will not walk Britain much longer. Olwen and I be their strength and their conscience, perhaps their soul. The Christ-man could not escape Gethsemane, neither can I."

Yet he hesitated, hovering over the vessel. The tent rustled back, and a beefy sergeant lumbered into view. "Pardon, your grace, but –" He saw the bowl and stopped. "God a mercy!"

"What is it?"

The man tried not to look at the vessel, but his agitation had to do with more immediate problems. "Sir, the treasure –"

"It is there?"

The sergeant's eyes seemed slightly glazed. "Th-there?" he stammered. "God, yes. And there and *there*! *Yards* of it, levels and stairs of it. Ringlets, plate, torques, jewels. We haven't sacks enough for all there is, and not to the bottom yet. The coins spill out of the chests like pebbles." He thrust out a handful. "See!"

The bishop examined the bronze and silver coins, all very ancient but legible. He turned them over, reading the inscriptions. "'Agricola', 'Trajanus'. These are Roman."

"For sure," said Drust blandly. "All Roman and writ of in the Saxon books. Some they took away, some they buried should they return. Faerie watched where they dug." He shrugged. "They were here four hundred years; did owe much rent."

The sergeant glanced nervously out of the tent. "Sir, the men outside. They hear those in the cave. They saw the rubies this madman tossed on the ground. I can't hold them back much longer."

The earl bishop bristled. "If one of them steals so much as one coin –"

"A wise man would let them," Drust observed. "How much can magpies steal from a granary? Let every man fill his pocket before he fills your sacks."

"That bunch?" The sergeant snorted. "They'll steal my lord blind, little man."

"Would do that anyway," Drust countered smoothly. "Your grace, when generosity comes cheap, buy a reputation. Will need them all to carry. Singing your praises will make light work of it. Let them go in."

It took only a moment for the bishop to see the wisdom. How much gold could one man tuck away in a tunic? "Give that order, sergeant."

"Yes, sir. God bless you, sir!" The sergeant hurried out. They heard his muffled, staccato orders, the answering shout and the rush of feet.

But Drust's attention had returned to the bronze bowl. "Was glad your man came in. It forestalled –" He broke off suddenly. "Pity a poor man. I must drink, but I cannot, not before shriving. You are a man of God and most blessed. Will you guard – It – while I pray?"

"It will be here." The bishop looked down at the bowl; the wine shone dark and red as rubies. He barely heard Drust leave the tent.

He looked at the bowl. After a long time, he bent and picked it up.

Drust joined the baron and Brangaene by the fire, a small island of light in the fog. For some minutes they watched the last of the bishop's men struggle through the small opening to the cairn. Brangaene wondered if there was room inside for all of them.

"And more," Drust told her.

Then the last man vanished into the black mouth. They heard his shout of discovery added to the others that faded as the men ran and stumbled from level to level, finding, filling their pockets. Then quiet. The grey-ghost horses stamped and snuffled. Only Drust noted the slight sound that might have come from the earl bishop's tent, as if something had fallen.

"This is a strange place." Brangaene shivered. "The eyes on those men when they went in . . ."

"Like their master," the baron growled. "And what's that holy hypocrite up to?"

"At war with conscience and need." Drust warmed his hands over the fire. "Will not be long."

"A moment's too long with such as these." The baron spat. "Greedy pigs, let 'em choke on the damned gold."

Drust favoured him with that odd smile – amusement, sadness, more wisdom than the cairn held treasure. "Yes. Your third wish."

He took several quick strides to the rocky outcrop of the cairn entrance. "Mark how faerie keeps his word. Three wishes. One, the gold. Two, the Cup. And three to choke them on it. One stone to open, another to close." Drust pressed against one of the stones. With a grating sound, the cairn was sealed tight again. His dark head snapped up. "And the third – now, Malgon!"

Brangaene looked up with him. On the roof of the cairn, dim with mist, she saw the little figure bend close to to the ground, move something, then run nimbly down one side. Before the booming began, before the earth trembled, she saw another, mounted figure race away behind Malgon. Then the shocks came, and the muffled roar that grew as the ground quaked beneath her feet.

Brangaene gasped, clutched her father's arm. Before their eyes, the long roof of the cairn buckled, went swaybacked and sank as five-ton stones toppled from the first interior level, ruptured the second, and the combined dead weight fell on the third . . . the fourth. The sickening concussions rumbled through Brangaene's feet again and again. At length they weakened, the distant roar faded, the shrieking echoes died. From the entrance stone, a small dust-wraith emerged.

"Good Jesus," the baron managed weakly. "What happened?"

"The end of wishing," said Drust.

Brangaene trembled under her father's arm. "All of them. All the b-bishop's men." The thought struck her like ice water. "The bishop!"

"Let him be," Drust held up his hand. "The thing's done; the queen will be calling me home. Baron, Brangaene, share a cup of wine with me before I go."

The baron stared at him. "But the bishop –?"

"Please," Drust protested mildly. "It is so peaceful now." He cocked an ear. "Aye, they're coming."

"But where is he?" the baron persisted, nervously eyeing the tent. "Is he deaf?"

"Quite."

The soft *clop* of hooves came out of the mist. One horse stopped, the other grew louder until Malgon materialized, leading Drust's pony up to the guttering fire.

"Thy mother wants thee home, Drust."

"Will come." Drust dug in his saddle bag, extracted a plain wooden bowl and gave it to Malgon. "Fetch me wine, Mal. Some of the bishop's best."

Malgon vanished into the tent. Some yards up the defile, barely limned in the fog, the cloaked and hooded rider waited, motionless.

Brangaene wondered. "Drust, is that –?"

"Olwen. Will not come close. Has been hurt too often by tallfolk."

Malgon reappeared with the filled bowl which he placed in his master's hand.

"His grace?" Drust asked delicately.

Malgon shook his head.

"Did drink, then?"

"Did."

The baron put his question very carefully; not that it troubled him overmuch. "The earl bishop is . . . dead?"

"Dead as pork," Malgon contemplated. "Not even Caesar be so well deceased."

"He was reaching for this from the first day," Drust mused. "Did only help him along." He chuckled softly. "Olwen burnished the bowl to make it shine, and in the burnish was rubbed foxglove and hemlock. Would kill six bishops."

Brangaene caught her breath. "You – poisoned – the Holy Grail?"

"We tempted him with a custom that never was, Brangaene. If that's a sin – well, I think your father will pray for me."

Malgon laughed. Out of the mist came another laugh like a silvery, musical echo. Drust drank from the bowl and passed it to the baron. "Especially when he has five hundred horses and their saddles to sell."

"Faerie," the baron judged, "I never realized, but you command a sterling quartet of talents: philosopher, diplomat, liar and thief. Have you thought of a career at Court?"

"Perhaps some day. If must take up a trade." Drust passed the bowl to Brangaene but she struck it out of his hand.

"*You poisoned the Holy –*"

"Nay, nay, nay, lass." Drust patiently retrieved the battered bowl. "Not the Grail. Olwen never promised the Grail. Did write of the Jerusalem Cup –"

"B-but – but wasn't that –?"

"Which belonged to Joseph's friend, the governor of Judea."

"The gov –" Suddenly the baron saw light. He could believe anything now. "You mean Pilate? *Pontius Pilate?*"

Drust nodded: "Does sound right, yes. 'Twas his wash-bowl."

Monstrously sacrilegious, but the baron had an irrepressible and quite secular urge to laugh. "Ye bloody gods."

"Brangaene," Drust offered her the old bowl again. "This is no great Jerusalem Cup; this was made for common folk like us. But it holds pease porridge well and doesn't leak, old as it is." He pressed it into her hands. "Take it as a favour to Drust. When you eat or drink from it, remember me." He kissed her lightly, gave her a wink. "And leave a supper at your gate for tired faerie men."

He nodded gravely to the baron, then mounted his pony. "Let's go home, Mal."

They rode away. Once, after the fog had swallowed them up, Brangaene heard Drust's joyful shout and again that other voice, low, melodious – welcoming.

That was all. She and her father were alone.

The baron spent some time stringing stallions into a train the mares would follow. He also inspected the tent. Malgon's assessment had been precise; his grace rivalled Caesar, even the pharaohs, for the finality of his past tense. When the baron returned to his daughter, she was pensively turning the ancient bowl in her hands.

"Father . . ."

When you eat or drink from it, remember me.

She recalled the text, almost the same words, written so long ago.

So worn it was. So *very* old . . .

Her voice was tiny, a whisper. "Father – what kind of wood is this?"

"Hm?" He examined it. "Not oak or ash . . . not English at all, I'd say. It's – well, I don't know."

"I do," Brangaene murmured. "Like my chests from Lebanon. This is cedarwood."

So ancient, dark-stained, the rim warped with time. Brangane held it to her heart, and her laugh was tremulous. "That man, that fine, beautiful man. He brought it after all. He brought it." Her eyes glistened with purpose. "Father, do you think the *arch*bishop –"

Her father understood then. "Oh, not again, Brangaene. That? You heard him; it's his porridge bowl."

"Father." There was something rising in Brangaene's voice that the baron should have heeded. "Listen to me. I think we should ask the archbishop –"

But he turned away and spread his arms to the fog. "She's hopeless. Hopeless! Will she never be done wishing?"

He did not see the subtle change of expression levelled at his back. *Just one more*, Branaene thought. Just the one Drust had taught her to realize, the never-even-whispered wish. It was a good day for miracles, and why not one of her own? She sighted coolly on the baron's posterior, wound up with a dainty hop-step and fired from the toe. "One to grow on!"

Poonk!

The baron flew.

As he lacked his daughter's practice his flight was brief and graceless. When he sat up, thoroughly stunned, he faced a new Brangaene – confident, serene and sure. She held up the bowl.

"On second thoughts," Brangaene said crisply. "Tell the archbishop *I* want to see *him*."

*   *   *

As it turned out, the baron's judgement was suspect on several counts. He thought his arse would never stop aching, but it did. He thought he might come back and dig up the gold, but he never found it. Though after a while, as they rode home, the sun came out and Brangaene sang sweetly.

The archbishop sent the bowl to Rome, where it was studied by ecclesiastic scholars imbued with the new spirit of rationalism. They are studying it yet, as cautious scholars will, though the history-minded may note how suddenly Grail stories went out of vogue. They might have asked Brangaene, but who in the wise new world would credit a girl who told fairy tales and still left a supper by the gate for no one in particular?

THE LOST ROMANCE

Brian Stableford

Brian Stableford (b. 1948) is a multi-talented British writer, editor and critic who has been writing professionally for over thirty years and has had over fifty books published since his first, Cradle of the Sun, *in 1969. Although his early novels were almost entirely science fiction, some with a tinge of fantasy, his latest offerings have been mostly horror and fantasy, some with a tinge of science! They include* The Empire of Fear *(1988),* The Werewolves of London *(1990),* The Angel of Pain *(1991),* Young Blood *(1992) and* Serpent's Blood *(1995). In the following story he brings together the Grail legend with another legend of our past.*

> *An anonymous tale recorded in Welsh by an unknown hand, circa 1380, here translated into English for the first time by Dafydd V. Evans, PhD, edited by Brian Stableford.*

I had this tale from a cousin in Chepstow, who had it in his turn from a Cistercian monk who had formerly been the confessor of Brother Simon, the scribe whose adventure it was. Given that it is little more than thirty years old, and that the tellers entrusted with it were undoubtedly honest, you may be sure that every word of it is true.

At the time of his journey, which took place in the Year of Our Lord 1348, Brother Simon was a young man of some twenty-one years. He had been given to the Cistercians at Valle Crucis nine years before and was highly valued by them on two counts. The first was his voice, which retained its melodic loveliness even after it had broken; the second was his intellect, which made him very quick with languages and letters.

By virtue of the latter quality he was trained by the Order as a scribe, whose principal duty it was to copy the manuscripts held in trust by the Abbey. These manuscripts included, in addition to the Holy Scriptures, a number of parchment scrolls which had been lodged there by the Abbey's founder, Madoc of Griffith Maellor, who was Lord of Bromfield and was acknowledged by some as Prince of Powis.

The texts comprising Madoc's bequest were written in French and Welsh rather than the Latin of the Church, but it so happened that Simon's father was descended from one of the captains who fought with William the Bastard at Hastings and his mother hailed from Carmarthen. By virtue of this mixed parentage he was fluent in both tongues, and could read as well in either as in Latin.

Although many an Abbot would not have considered manuscripts written in Vulgar tongues fit for copying, the Superior of Valle Crucis – who was nobly born, and knew French far better than English – had Simon read the French scripts aloud to him, so that he might discover whether there was anything therein worth preserving.

As it happened, the French texts included a prose version of Robert de Boron's poem *Joseph d'Arimathie*, which told the tale of how the Cup used by Christ at the Last Supper was employed to catch the blood of his wounds as he hung upon the Cross, how that Cup was then brought to Britain and how it subsequently came to be the concern of King Arthur's knights. This the Superior commanded Simon to copy, as a valuable lesson for the education of Christian Britain.

When Simon told the Superior that one of the Welsh scripts also concerned the Holy Grail, the Abbot – who had a low opinion of his immediate neighbours – was at first uninterested. When Simon persisted, telling the Abbot that the text told of the actual fate of the Grail and of its eventual hiding-place at Cockayne in the county of York, the grizzled Norman dismissed the tale as a crude Welsh lie, but he seemed interested in spite of himself.

"You doubtless have good reasons for your estimation of the Welsh, my lord Abbot," Simon said judiciously, although he had no sympathy at all for the Abbot's prejudice against his mother's people, "but while there is the slightest possibility that the tale might harbour a grain of truth, it must warrant preservation.

"Even if there is no truth in it at all, it might still do the Lord's work in teasing its hearers with the notion that the Grail still exists, though hidden, and might yet be found by a man sufficiently pure in heart. If I am not set to copy it, it will surely be lost for ever, for the ink in which it was inscribed was very poorly concocted, and the ill-cured parchment is rotting away even as we speak."

The Abbot eventually agreed to have the text copied.

At that time neither the Abbot nor Simon knew whether there actually was a place called Cockayne in the county of York, but, having agreed to the copying, the Abbot of Valle Crucis wrote to the Abbot of Rievaulx to make enquiries.

The Abbot of Rievaulx confirmed that there was indeed a village called Cockayne in the North York Moors, and expressed a strong interest in seeing the text, insisting furthermore that it must not be the copied version.

Because Rievaulx was the mother church of the mission established by Saint Bernard, and because the Abbot of Rievaulx was a cousin of the Harding family, he held a higher position in the Order than the Abbot of Valle Crucis. Simon's Superior had no alternative but to keep the copy Simon had made and send the original to Yorkshire – and he had also to send Simon along with it, so that he might translate its contents for the Abbot of Rievaulx.

We live in happier times nowadays, but in our grandfathers' day there were three times as many people living in England as there are now, and the land was less productive because the *carruca* was by no means as widely used for tillage as it is today. As your grandfathers will tell you, if any survive, the whole nation was awash with brigands and bandits in those days, and it would have been a very fortunate man who could travel all the way from Valle Crucis to York without encountering at least a few.

Simon was not a fortunate man – although he might have counted himself lucky to get as far as he did without running into trouble, and luckier still to escape with his life.

By the time he came within two days' ride of Selby, Simon had travelled nearly three hundred miles, but the journey had taken him a mere fifty-seven days because there had always been fellow-travellers willing to let him ride on their carts. He had shared space with cabbages and turnips, pigs and fowl, fodder and bones, but on the day he encountered the outlaw band he had been so privileged as to be given a place in a carriage which was taking a gentleman named Richard Shreve from Nottingham to York.

Master Shreve was, of course, accompanied by four servants on horseback, as well as the driver of the carriage, but the servants very prudently ran off when the twelve-strong band of brigands made their appearance and stopped the carriage. A charitable man might assume that their guiding impulse was to save their master's coursers from being looted along with his carriage-horses.

Master Shreve, on the other hand, drew his sword as soon as the carriage was stopped and leapt boldly down. He offered to meet any one of the marauders in a fair fight, but while he was blustering away at the green-clad man of dark complexion who was evidently the leader of the robber band one of the brigands slipped around behind him and bludgeoned him to the ground.

While the man with the cudgel was relieving Master Shreve of his pouch the outlaw chief addressed himself to the driver and the monk. "I beg you to note," he said, in English, "that I could easily have killed this reckless fool, but had him knocked on the noggin instead. He'll wake within the hour, none the worse. I wish you to note, also, that I did not instruct my men to fire arrows after his servants, even though I might have enriched myself to the tune of four more horses had my cunning marksmen contrived to bring the riders down. Nor shall I harm a hair on the head of either one of you, provided only that you play fair with me and surrender your possessions peacefully. All I ask in return is that you should tell anyone who asks that Reuben the Jew is the gentlest of all the brigands in England, and a man of honour after his own unorthodox fashion."

The coach-driver grudgingly gave up his own purse, which contained but a few copper coins, and a ring from his finger – and then, after some further persuasion, took off his coat and boots.

"I fear that I have nothing to surrender," Brother Simon said. "Neither coin nor ornament." It was, of course, plain to see that he had no coat to cover his habit, and nothing on his feet but sandals.

"What's that in the satchel?" the outlaw chief demanded.

"Merely a manuscript," the monk replied, "which I am commissioned to carry to the Abbot of Rievaulx."

"Give it to me," the brigand demanded, dismounting from his horse.

Brother Simon handed the satchel over to him.

"What language is this?" asked the brigand, as soon as he had unrolled the parchment. "Not Latin or Hebrew, that's for sure."

"Welsh," said Brother Simon.

"What use is a manuscript writ in Welsh?" said the robber sneeringly.

"As much use as any writ in Latin," Simon retorted, although it was far from clear that his opinion would coincide with the judgement of the Church, "to those who can read it."

The brigand laughed. "I've met the Abbot of Rievaulx," he said. "I once had the pleasure of robbing him, and a very tidy haul he provided. He could barely speak English, let alone Welsh – and although my French is as good as any man's, I never use it. That's for the sake of my loyal followers, who are English through and through."

"Nevertheless," Simon replied stubbornly, "the Abbot of Rievaulx has asked to see the manuscript and it is my duty to convey it to him. I shall translate the tale for him, if God will see me safely to my destination."

"A *tale*, is it?" said the outlaw. "What kind of tale, pray tell?"

"It tells of the Cup that caught Christ's blood on Calvary," Simon said, "and how it was brought to England by Joseph of Arimathea."

"Oh, *that* tale," said the outlaw, in a tone of frank disgust. "Flowery French rubbish glorifying the exploits of petty barons and their hired thugs, pretending that they were honest and chaste and engaged in God's good work rather than the brutal oppression of common folk for the sake of their own enrichment. Chrétien de Troyes and his lying kin have much to answer for. Such stuff would be hateful to every honest British man, if only he could look beyond the studied piety to see the vile truth."

"That is not so," said Simon, boldly. "Arthur was a British king, and the knights he sent in search of the Grail were British too. Arthur was neither Norman nor Saxon and had not a drop of Viking blood within him – he was a Welshman by blood and by instinct, and his knights were probably Welsh too, no matter how the Norman poets have chosen to rename them. This tale – and others I have seen, similarly written in Welsh – make it abundantly clear that Britain is the true home of chivalry."

There was some restlessness among the outlaws now, and for a moment Simon thought that his brave words had either disturbed or enthused them – but then he realized that they were simply impatient to be on their way, lest Master Shreve's servants should have summoned help. They did not approve of their leader pausing to argue about the substance of romances with a monk who had nothing worth stealing.

"Yes, lads," said the robber chief, "you're right. But I haven't quite finished with this lad and I want him brought along. John, you must ride bareback on one of those horses taken from the carriage, for I doubt that a monk has the skill to ride without a saddle."

The man addressed as John protested at this, not relishing the idea of being put up on a carthorse, but his legs were uncommonly long and the animal's great girth posed no real problem to him. When he walked past the fallen body of Richard Shreve, however, the fallen gentleman grabbed his ankle and tripped him up. Shreve was conscious but very befuddled, and his sword had been taken away, so he posed no real danger to anyone, but when John got up again he hauled the man unceremoniously to his feet and made as if to smash a meaty fist into the the neatly shaven face.

"No!" said the outlaw chief. "I said that I wouldn't harm the man and I meant it. Set him up before you on the carthorse and bring him along – he and his bookish friend shall both be our guests for supper."

John scowled more fiercely than before, but he obeyed. He and Richard Shreve set themselves on the bare back of the carthorse, with the bigger man's arms enfolding the torso of the smaller as they grasped an improvised rein. Simon was given a saddled horse and allowed to ride freely – but the outlaw chief still had his satchel and his manuscript, so he had no alternative but to follow meekly where the outlaws led.

The bootless coachman was left to his own devices, to make his way to Selby in his own good time.

The outlaw band rode through forest and field for some three miles before arriving at an isolated cottage on the edge of a wood. It had no stable, but the horses were put away in a barn a hundred yards away and half the outlaws stayed with them. The chief and his remaining half-dozen men took Richard Shreve and Brother Simon indoors, where there was a good fire burning with a huge cooking pot set on top of it.

Simon had noticed a vegetable garden behind the cottage, and he did not doubt that the outlaws were accomplished poachers, so he was not surprised to find that the odour of the stew was very pleasing – rather more so than that of many of the stews which bubbled away before the kitchen fire at Valle Crucis.

The outlaws, pleased with their afternoon's work, passed stone jars of ale back and forth between them while their prisoners sat on the floor in a corner of the room. Simon and Master Shreve were virtually ignored for the best part of an hour, but the gentleman was in no mood for conversation. He heaped muttered curses upon the head of the outlaw chief and repeatedly threatened vengeance, but it was half bluster and half delirium, and Simon continually urged him to be quiet lest he arouse the wrath of their captors.

"Well," said the outlaw chief, when he finally turned his attention back to his prisoners. "Master Shreve has paid for his supper with good silver coin. How will you pay for yours, Brother Welshman?"

"I thought I had been brought here to read you the tale contained in the manuscript," Simon replied. "Is that not price enough?"

"It would be price enough for me," the chief admitted, "but I'm an educated man. To my lads it would seem rather more like penance – especially now they're merry with the ale. Can you do aught else that might please them more?"

"I can sing," said Simon frankly.

The outlaws laughed at that, as if they did not believe him, but their chief put on a show of exaggerated delight.

"Then you must sing for your supper, in the grand old tradition," he said. "But I warn you – we want none of your accursed cantos, none of your troubadour French and none of your gibberish Welsh. The only thing that we'll accept in fee is a good English ballad. Can you give us that?"

Simon's repertoire of English ballads was not extensive, but there was never a man in the world, be he Churchman or Welshman, who did not know at least a few of the most popular songs of his day. He immediately began to sing a ballad about a shepherd boy lamenting the death of the girl who was to have been his bride. Although it was mournful, and had not a single hint of impropriety about it, the outlaws fell silent and listened respectfully to the end.

"Well, boy," said the outlaw chief, "you're uncommon honest for a Churchman. You *can* sing, and no mistake about it. You've earned your supper. If you'll give us another when we've eaten, we'll be in *your* debt, and we'll see you safely back to the road in the morning."

The stew tasted as good as its aroma had promised, and Simon sipped it gratefully from a wooden bowl, gladly fishing for fugitive pieces of meat with his fingers. The robber chief came to sit beside him on the floor, bringing his own bowl, and broke a loaf of bread which was only a little stale, offering a quarter of it to the monk.

"Now," said the outlaw, "Tell me what else is in this tale of yours – not the whole of it, but the gist."

Simon gave a brief account of the tale, explaining that it told how the Holy Grail had been given into the charge of a company of Welsh Benedictine monks who – fearing that it might fall into pagan hands in a time when the island was torn apart by the strife of war – had conveyed it secretly to Yorkshire, where they had hidden it away beneath an altarstone in a little church in the village of Cockayne. He went on to explain how he had found the manuscript among those left to the Abbey by Prince Madoc, where it must have lain unread for more than a hundred years, and how the Abbot of Valle Crucis had written to Rievaulx to ask whether there actually was such a place as Cockayne.

The outlaw's brow furrowed when he heard that. "Is *that* why the Abbot of Rievaulx wants your script? Does he think it might be the key to buried treasure?"

"He is a man of God!" protested Simon. "If he thinks there is the slightest possibility that the Grail still rests in Cockayne, his one desire must be to restore it to the Church that it might delight the hearts of good Christians. Only an outlaw could think of it as *buried treasure*."

Even as he spoke these words, however, he wondered if he might have been foolish in telling the tale to the outlaw. What if the brigand band rode north in the morning, directly to Cockayne? There was little doubt that they could get to the village long before he could arrive at Rievaulx. Suppose the Grail *had* been buried at Cockayne, and was resting still where the monks had laid it? What a calamity it would be if the Cup were to fall into the hands of such a man as this!

Simon realized, perhaps with a pang of conscience, that he had been thinking of the manuscript as a romance, like that of Chrétien de Troyes or Robert de Boron, and had given no thought at all to the possibility that it might be a true account. Now, as he watched the outlaw chief unwind the scroll again, he wondered whether he had been blind to the truth.

"The ink is poor," the outlaw said, staring at the script, "and the handwriting is poorer. Even the parchment is badly made. This is not the work of a careful copyist working patiently in a monkish cell. When was it inscribed, do you think?"

"Not much more than a hundred years ago," Simon said, wishing that he were not so confident of the estimate. "During Madoc's lifetime, for sure."

"Then it's certainly a romance," said the outlaw. "It can be nothing else. And as soon as the Abbot of Rievaulx finds out that there's nothing buried beneath the altarstone at Cockayne, it'll be cast aside and forgotten – gone for ever. Good riddance to it."

"It will *not* be lost," Simon assured him, having been stung to annoyance by the outlaw's dismissiveness. "The fresh copy which I made at Valle Crucis will last a good deal longer than a hundred years, and will certainly be copied again if I have aught to do with it. What has been written down and committed to the care of the Church can never be lost – that is the whole virtue of writing."

"Nonsense," said the outlaw. "Writing relieves men from the responsibility of keeping what they know within their heads. What is copied and recopied a hundred times might survive, but that which is not thought worth copying is bound to be utterly lost. I say again: as soon as it is proven that nothing is buried beneath the altarstone at Cockayne, this silly tale will be condemned to oblivion. That ballad you sang will outlast this script by a thousand years, let alone a hundred, because there's reason in its sweetness for ordinary men to remember it and preserve it in their heads."

Simon was by now half convinced that the outlaw meant to establish for himself whether anything was buried in the church at Cockayne, and to do so before the Abbot of Rievaulx could mount an expedition on the Church's behalf. He reassured himself, however, that if the tale *were* true – which he could not quite believe, as it seemed so obviously a romance – then God would certainly prevent the outlaw from finding the Grail. After all, if the adulterous knight the French had misnamed Lancelot had only been able to see the Grail in visions, by virtue of his sinfulness, a Jewish thief would most certainly not be allowed to lay a finger on it, no matter how loudly he proclaimed that he was a man of honour.

That last thought reminded Simon of a question he had wanted to ask before – and he thought it wise, in any case, to change the subject.

"Why are you so loud in proclaiming your refusal to hurt anyone?" the monk asked the outlaw. "If they catch you, they'll hang you as a common thief, whether you've hurt anyone or not.

You can't expect the slightest mercy from the law – especially given that you're a Jew."

The robber chief laughed at that. "Dolt," he said, not altogether unkindly. "It's not for the law's benefit that I take care to spread the news that I'm a gentle thief who will not hurt anyone unless he has to – it's to reassure my future victims. If they know that they'll not be injured, they're far more likely to hand over their belongings meekly. If they feared for their lives, they'd be more disposed to put up a fight. There's always the odd fool, like that man beside you, who'll fight regardless, but his servants had far more sense. They'd heard my name before, you see. In these parts, I'm as famous as any Frenchified knight who ever went hunting the Holy Grail."

Master Shreve, who had been sullenly listening to the conversation, reacted to this with his usual bullishness, pouring more curses upon the outlaw's head and swearing that he would have his revenge very soon.

"An outlaw is merely an outlaw," said Master Shreve as he concluded his tirade, "no matter how many men have heard his name. Once hanged, you'll be forgotten in a day – and I'll see to it that you're hanged. Make no mistake about it."

"You're an uncommonly tedious dinner guest," the outlaw said, "and a silly one to boot. I could be remembered long after you're forgotten, and the Abbot of Rievaulx too, simply for having my name set into a ballad like the one which my young friend sang before we settled down to eat. One ballad, if it had tune enough, would outlast a thousand tattered parchments like the one he is carrying to Rievaulx."

Master Shreve's sole response to this was a curse, but Brother Simon found himself rather intrigued by the possibility. He had always had a secret hankering to compose a ballad or two – while regretfully recognizing, of course, that any such activity was quite incompatible with his religious duties.

"I fear that you are wrong, sir," he said teasingly. "There are plenty of ballads which tell of bold knights and plenty which tell of lovesick shepherds, but there are no ballads about outlaw Jews. In order to be sung and sung again, a ballad must have the sympathy of its audience – just as a text, if it is to be copied and copied again, requires the sympathy of scribes."

"Then we must do with the ballad what scribes do with the substance of their texts at the behest of their Norman overlords," the outlaw retorted. "If Welsh bully-boys no better than outlaws themselves can be disguised as French knights of unbearable piety for the sake of making their stories palatable to the patient scriveners of Christian England, then a Jewish brigand may be disguised as a heroic Englishman fighting for a cause. Transform me, if you will, Brother Balladeer, into an Englishman through and through.

"Give me worthy enemies to oppose – shift me back in time if you need to, for there's a certain respectability in antiquity. Change my name, if you like – but only a little, for we must not dabble in the purest fantasy. Reuben the Jew won't do, but there are Englishmen a-plenty named Robin, and my father's name was Hud, which will pass for English readily enough, although folk like Master Richard Shreve of Nottingham would have reckoned him a dirty foreigner. Only make a ballad of me, Brother Songbird, and repeat it in that glorious voice of thine, and I'll wager that my name will be on the lips of men far longer than any hired thug who ever laid false claim to knighthood."

"Perhaps I will," said Brother Simon. "Perhaps I will. In fact, I'll give you a solemn promise to do exactly that if you'll give me your word in exchange that you'll not set foot in the church at Cockayne for at least a year and a day."

The robber chief laughed uproariously at that, and offered Simon his hand to clasp. "Gladly, lad," he said. "Gladly indeed – and you know full well that you can trust me, for Reuben the Jew is famed from York to Sherwood as the most honourable outlaw who ever stalked these roads."

In the morning, after a tolerable night's sleep beneath a solid roof, Brother Simon and Master Shreve were guided back to the Selby road, while the outlaws rode away to the east – conspicuously taking the direction opposite to that in which the cottage lay.

"We'll meet again, Sir Brigand, I promise you," the gentleman said – but he waited until there was only Brother Simon to hear him.

"It might be wiser to avoid that meeting," Simon advised him, "unless you want your body pierced by a dozen arrows. You left him with no reason to think charitably of you."

"Unlike you, I suppose?" Shreve retorted hotly. "I never thought to hear a man of the cloth speak so softly and so cravenly to a thief and murderer. Everything they say about the Welsh is evidently true."

Brother Simon prudently made no reply to this insult, preserving a dignified silence while the two of them walked to Selby, where they found Master Shreve's servants – including the coachman – waiting dutifully at a very pleasant inn.

Brother Simon reached Rievaulx five days later and was received with moderate hospitality, although he was required to sleep in an outhouse, without even a mattress of straw, because the Abbey was so crowded

The Abbot of Rievaulx did indeed send a deputation to Cockayne to dig beneath the altarstone. His men found nothing. If the Holy Grail had ever been there, it was there no longer.

If Brother Simon ever made the ballad he had promised, he certainly would not have mentioned it to his confessor – and my tale must therefore leave the matter unresolved. But I am reckoned to be one of the best storytellers west of Neath – and I assume that the Church agrees with me, or your Abbot would not have granted you permission to write this down – and I can testify to this: I, at least, have never heard the name of Reuben the Jew, or Robin Hud, spoken or sung in any inn-yard in Wales. I think we may be perfectly confident that the name of an outlaw braggart cannot possibly be long remembered in a Christian land whose wisdom is in the charge of faithful clerics like yourself.

Editor's note: Having no competence of my own in the Welsh language, I must take it on trust that Dr Evans has rendered an accurate translation of this remarkable document – or, at least, as accurate a translation as is compatible with the avoidance of too many inconvenient archaisms. Given that Dr Evans holds a post at a good university and still attends chapel at least twice a year, I think we can be confident of the story's substance, even if he has permitted himself the occasional embroidery in its dialogue. My own role has been restricted to the preparation of Dr Evans's handiwork for the printer.

It is, of course, well-established that the earliest ballads featuring Robin Hood date from the late fourteenth century and that their setting does indeed seem to be South Yorkshire rather than Sherwood Forest; the present manuscript, if it is to be reckoned anything more than a romance, may help to explain that confusion. It is, of course, extremely unlikely that any further evidence will ever turn up, and it is not at all surprising that the earlier manuscript to which this one refers has been utterly lost; Brother Simon's northward course to Rievaulx was followed only a year later by another traveller, whose devastating effects are noted *en passant* by the storyteller: the Black Death.

THE GREAT RETURN

Arthur Machen

It was impossible to complete this anthology without one story featuring the Holy Grail in the modern world. The Grail holds considerable symbolism for students of the occult. One of the most complete studies of the Grail is The Holy Grail: Its Legends and Symbolism *(1933) by A.E. Waite (1857–1942), a leading figure in the Hermetic Order of the Golden Dawn. A close friend of Waite's was Arthur Machen (1863–1947), who was also a member of the Golden Dawn, and one of Britain's leading writers of supernatural fiction at the turn of the last century. Machen was born at Caerleon in Wales, the site of Arthur's Court, according to Geoffrey of Monmouth. He was fascinated with the Holy Grail. In addition to the following story, he developed the rather more esoteric novel* The Secret Glory *(1922). Some of his other writings about the Grail were collected as* The Glorious Mystery *(1924).*

Although Machen's fiction was highly influential, it is less well remembered today than that of some of his contemporaries, especially M.R. James, although Machen did help to create one story that has now become a legend in its own right, that of the Angel of Mons. His tale "The Bowmen" told of how Henry V's archers from the battle of Agincourt appeared as ghosts at the battle of Mons to protect the troops from harm during their terribly arduous and dangerous retreat. Although written as a story, it appeared just like a news item in the London Evening News *for 29 September 1914, and confirmations of the sighting poured in from readers. There is something of that same reportage in this story, which was serialized in the London* Evening News *in the following year.*

I The Rumour of the Marvellous

There are strange things lost and forgotten in obscure corners of
the newspaper. I often think that the most extraordinary item of
intelligence that I have read in print appeared a few years ago in the
London press. It came from a well-known and most respected news
agency; I imagine it was in all the papers. It was astounding.

The circumstances necessary – not to the understanding of this
paragraph, for that is out of the question – but, we will say, to
the understanding of the events which made it possible, are these.
We had invaded Tibet, and there had been trouble in the hierarchy
of that country, and a personage known as the Tashi Lama had
taken refuge with us in India. He went on pilgrimage from one
Buddhist shrine to another, and came at last to a holy mountain
of Buddhism, the name of which I have forgotten. And thus the
morning paper:

> His Holiness the Tashi Lama then ascended the Mountain
> and was transfigured – Reuter.

That was all. And from that day to this I have never heard a
word of explanation or comment on this amazing statement.

There was no more, it seemed, to be said. "Reuter", apparently,
thought he had made his simple statement of the facts of the case,
had thereby done his duty, and so it all ended. Nobody, so far
as I know, ever wrote to any paper asking what Reuter meant
by it, or what the Tashi Lama meant by it. I suppose the fact
was that nobody cared twopence about the matter; and so this
strange event – if there were any such event – was exhibited
to us for a moment, and the lantern show revolved to other
spectacles.

This is an extreme instance of the manner in which the
marvellous is flashed out to us and then withdrawn behind
its black veils and concealments; but I have known of other
cases. Now and again, at intervals of a few years, there appear
in the newspapers strange stories of the strange doings of what
are technically called "poltergeists". Some house, often a lonely
farm, is suddenly subjected to an infernal bombardment. Great
stones crash through the windows, thunder down the chimneys,
impelled by no visible hand. The plates and cups and saucers are
whirled from the dresser into the middle of the kitchen, no one
can say how or by what agency. Upstairs the big bedstead and
an old chest or two are heard bounding on the floor as if in a

mad ballet. Now and then such doings as these excite a whole neighbourhood; sometimes a London paper sends a man down to make an investigation. He writes half a column of description on the Monday, a couple of paragraphs on the Tuesday, and then returns to town. Nothing has been explained, the matter vanishes away; and nobody cares. The tale trickles for a day or two through the press, and then instantly disappears, like an Australian stream, into the bowels of darkness. It is possible, I suppose, that this singular incuriousness as to marvellous events and reports is not wholly unaccountable. It may be that the events in question are, as it were, psychic accidents and misadventures. They are not meant to happen, or, rather, to be manifested. They belong to the world on the other side of the dark curtain; and it is only by some queer mischance that a corner of that curtain is twitched aside for an instant. Then – for an instant – we see; but the personages whom Mr Kipling calls the Lords of Life and Death take care that we do not see too much. Our business is with things higher and things lower, with things different, anyhow; and on the whole we are not suffered to distract ourselves with that which does not really concern us. The transfiguration of the Lama and the tricks of the poltergeist are evidently no affairs of ours; we raise an uninterested eyebrow and pass on – to poetry or to statistics.

Be it noted; I am not professing any fervent personal belief in the reports to which I have alluded. For all I know, the Lama, in spite of Reuter, was not transfigured, and the poltergeist, in spite of the late Mr Andrew Lang, may in reality be only mischievous Polly, the servant girl at the farm. And to go farther: I do not know that I should be justified in putting either of these cases of the marvellous in line with a chance paragraph that caught my eye last summer; for this had not, on the face of it at all events, anything wildly out of the common. Indeed, I dare say that I should not have read it, should not have seen it, if it had not contained the name of a place which I had once visited, which had then moved me in an odd manner that I could not understand. Indeed, I am sure that this particular paragraph deserves to stand alone, for even if the poltergeist be a real poltergeist, it merely reveals the psychic whimsicality of some region that is not our region. There were better things and more relevant things behind the few lines dealing with Llantrisant, the little town by the sea in Arfonshire.

Not on the surface, I must say, for the cutting – I have preserved it – reads as follows:

> *Llantrisant. – The season promises very favourably: temperature of the sea yesterday at noon, 65 deg. Remarkable occurrences are supposed to have taken place during the recent Revival. The lights have not been observed lately. The Crown. The Fisherman's Rest.*

The style was odd certainly; knowing a little of newspapers, I could see that the figure called, I think, "tmesis," or "cutting," had been generously employed; the exuberances of the local correspondent had been pruned by a Fleet Street expert. And these poor men are often hurried; but what did those "lights" mean? What strange matters had the vehement blue pencil blotted out and brought to naught?

That was my first thought, and then, thinking still of Llantrisant and how I had first discovered it and found it strange, I read the paragraph again, and was saddened almost to see, as I thought, the obvious explanation. I had forgotten for the moment that it was war-time, that scares and rumours and terrors about traitorous signals and flashing lights were current everywhere by land and sea; someone, no doubt, had been watching innocent farmhouse windows and thoughtless fanlights of lodging-houses; these were the "lights" that had not been observed lately.

I found out afterwards that the Llantrisant correspondent had no such treasonous lights in his mind, but something very different. Still; what do we know? He may have been mistaken, "the great rose of fire" that came over the deep may have been the port light of a coasting-ship. Did it shine at last from the old chapel on the headland? Possibly; or possibly it was the doctor's lamp at Sarnau, some miles away. I have had wonderful opportunities lately of analysing the marvels of lying, conscious and unconscious; and indeed almost incredible feats in this way can be performed. If I incline to the less likely explanation of the "lights" at Llantrisant, it is merely because this explanation seems to me to be altogether congruous with the "remarkable occurrences" of the newspaper paragraph.

After all, if rumour and gossip and hearsay are crazy things to be utterly neglected and laid aside; on the other hand, evidence is evidence, and when a couple of reputable surgeons assert, as they do assert in the case of Olwen Phillips, Croeswen, Llantrisant, that there has been a "kind of resurrection of the body", it is merely foolish to say that these things don't happen. The girl was a mass of tuberculosis, she was within a few hours of death; she is now full of life. And so, I do not believe that the rose of fire was merely a ship's light, magnified and transformed by dreaming Welsh sailors.

But now I am going forward too fast. I have not dated the paragraph, so I cannot give the exact day of its appearance, but I think it was somewhere between the second and third week of June. I cut it out partly because it was about Llantrisant, partly because of the "remarkable occurrences". I have an appetite for these matters, though I also have this misfortune, that I require evidence before I am ready to credit them, and I have a sort of lingering hope that some day I shall be able to elaborate some scheme or theory of such things.

But in the meantime, as a temporary measure, I hold what I call the doctrine of the jigsaw puzzle. That is: this remarkable occurrence, and that, and the other may be, and usually are, of no significance. Coincidence and chance and unsearchable causes will now and again make clouds that are undeniable fiery dragons, and potatoes that resemble eminent statesmen exactly and minutely in every feature, and rocks that are like eagles and lions. All this is nothing; it is when you get your set of odd shapes and find that they fit into one another, and at last that they are but parts of a large design; it is then that research grows interesting and indeed amazing, it is then that one queer form confirms the other, that the whole plan displayed justifies, corroborates, explains each separate piece.

So; it was within a week or ten days after I had read the paragraph about Llantrisant and had cut it out that I got a letter from a friend who was taking an early holiday in those regions.

"You will be interested," he wrote, "to hear that they have taken to ritualistic practices at Llantrisant. I went into the church the other day, and instead of smelling like a damp vault as usual, it was positively reeking with incense."

I knew better than that. The old parson was a firm Evangelical; he would rather have burnt sulphur in his church than incense any day. So I could not make out this report at all; and went down to Arfon a few weeks later determined to investigate this and any other remarkable occurrence at Llantrisant.

II Odours of Paradise

I went down to Arfon in the very heat and bloom and fragrance of the wonderful summer that they were enjoying there. In London there was no such weather; it rather seemed as if the horror and fury of the war had mounted to the very skies and were there reigning. In the mornings the sun burnt down upon the city with a heat that scorched and consumed; but then clouds heavy and horrible would roll together from all quarters of the heavens, and early in the afternoon the air would darken, and a storm of thunder and lightning, and furious, hissing rain would fall upon the streets. Indeed, the torment of the world was in the London weather. The city wore a terrible vesture; within our hearts was dread; without we were clothed in black clouds and angry fire.

It is certain that I cannot show in any words the utter peace of that Welsh coast to which I came; one sees, I think, in such a change a figure of the passage from the disquiets and the fears of earth to the peace of paradise. A land that seemed to be in a holy, happy dream, a sea that changed all the while from olivine to emerald, from emerald to sapphire, from sapphire to amethyst, that washed in white foam at the bases of the firm, grey rocks, and about the huge crimson bastions that hid the western bays and inlets of the waters; to this land I came, and to hollows that were purple and odorous with wild thyme, wonderful with many tiny, exquisite flowers. There was benediction in centaury, pardon in eyebright, joy in lady's slipper; and so the weary eyes were refreshed, looking now at the little flowers and the happy bees about them, now on the magic mirror of the deep, changing from marvel to marvel with the passing of the great white clouds, with the brightening of the sun. And the ears, torn with jangle and racket and idle, empty noise, were soothed and comforted by the ineffable, unutterable, unceasing murmur, as the tides swarm to and fro, uttering mighty, hollow voices in the caverns of the rocks.

For three or four days I rested in the sun and smelt the savour of the blossoms and of the salt water, and then, refreshed, I remembered that there was something queer about Llantrisant that I might as well investigate. It was no great thing that I thought to find, for, it will be remembered, I had ruled out the apparent oddity of the reporter's – or commissioner's? – reference to lights, on the ground that he must have been referring to some local panic about signalling to the enemy; who had certainly torpedoed a ship or two off Lundy in the Bristol Channel. All that I had to go upon was the reference to the "remarkable occurrences" at some revival, and then that letter of Jackson's which spoke of Llantrisant church as "reeking" with incense, a wholly incredible and impossible state of things. Why, old Mr Evans, the rector, looked upon coloured stoles as the very robe of Satan and his angels, as things dear to the heart of the Pope of Rome. But as to incense! As I have already familiarly observed, I knew better.

But as a hard matter of fact, this may be worth noting: when I went over to Llantrisant on Monday, August 9th, I visited the church, and it was still fragrant and exquisite with the odour of rare gums that had fumed there.

Now I happened to have a slight acquaintance with the rector. He was a most courteous and delightful old man, and on my last visit he had come across me in the churchyard, as I was admiring the very fine Celtic cross that stands there. Besides the beauty of the interlaced ornament there is an inscription in Ogham on one of the edges, concerning which the learned dispute; it is altogether one of the more famous crosses of Celtdom. Mr Evans, I say, seeing me looking at the cross, came up and began to give me, the stranger, a résumé – somewhat of a shaky and uncertain résumé, I found afterwards – of the various debates and questions that had arisen as to the exact meaning of the inscription, and I was amused to detect an evident but underlying belief of his own: that the supposed Ogham characters were, in fact, due to boys' mischief and weather and the passing of the ages. But then I happened to put a question as to the sort of stone of which the cross was made, and the rector brightened amazingly. He began to talk geology, and, I think, demonstrated that the cross or the material for it must have been brought to Llantrisant from the south-west coast of Ireland. This struck me as interesting, because it was curious evidence of the migrations of the Celtic saints, whom the rector, I was delighted to find, looked upon as good Protestants, though shaky on the subject of crosses; and so, with concessions on my part, we got on very well. Thus, with all this to the good, I was emboldened to call upon him.

I found him altered. Not that he was aged; indeed, he was rather made young, with a singular brightening upon his face, and something of joy upon it that I had not seen before, that I have seen on very few faces of men. We talked of the war, of course, since that is not to be avoided; of the farming prospects of the country; of general things, till I ventured to remark that I had been in the church, and had been surprised to find it perfumed with incense.

"You have made some alterations in the service since I was here last? You use incense now?"

The old man looked at me strangely, and hesitated.

"No," he said, "there has been no change. I use no incense in the church. I should not venture to do so."

"But," I was beginning, "the whole church is as if High Mass had just been sung there, and –"

He cut me short, and there was a certain grave solemnity in his manner that struck me almost with awe.

"I know you are a railer," he said, and the phrase coming from this mild old gentleman astonished me unutterably. "You are a railer and a bitter railer; I have read articles that you have written, and I know your contempt and your hatred for those you call Protestants in your derision; though your grandfather, the vicar of Caerleon-on-Usk, called himself Protestant and was proud of it, and your great-grand-uncle Hezekiah, *ffeiriad coch yr Castletown* – the Red Priest of Castletown – was a great man with the Methodists in his day, and the people flocked by their thousands when he administered the Sacrament. I was born and brought up in Glamorganshire, and old men have wept as they told me of the weeping and contrition that there was when the Red Priest broke the Bread and raised the Cup. But you are a railer, and see nothing but the outside and the show. You are not worthy of this mystery that has been done here."

I went out from his presence rebuked indeed, and justly rebuked; but rather amazed. It is curiously true that the Welsh are still one people, one family almost, in a manner that the English cannot understand, but I had never thought that this old clergyman would have known anything of my ancestry or their doings. And as for my articles and suchlike, I knew that the country clergy sometimes read, but I had fancied my pronouncements sufficiently obscure, even in London, much more in Arfon.

But so it happened, and so I had no explanation from the rector of Llantrisant of the strange circumstance, that his church was full of incense and odours of paradise.

I went up and down the ways of Llantrisant wondering, and came to the harbour, which is a little place, with little quays where some small coasting trade still lingers. A brigantine was at anchor here, and very lazily in the sunshine they were loading it with anthracite; for it is one of the oddities of Llantrisant that there is a small colliery in the heart of the wood on the hillside. I crossed a causeway which parts the outer harbour from the inner harbour, and settled down on a rock beach hidden under a leafy hill. The tide was going out, and some children were playing on the wet sand, while two ladies – their mothers, I suppose – talked together as they sat comfortably on their rugs at a little distance from me.

At first they talked of the war, and I made myself deaf, for of that talk one gets enough, and more than enough, in London. Then there was a period of silence, and the conversation had passed to quite a different topic when I caught the thread of it again. I was sitting on the further side of a big rock, and I do not think that the two ladies had noticed my approach. However, though they spoke of strange things, they spoke of nothing which made it necessary for me to announce my presence.

"And, after all," one of them was saying, "what is it all about? I can't make out what is come to the people."

This speaker was a Welshwoman; I recognized the clear, over-emphasized consonants, and a faint suggestion of an accent. Her friend came from the Midlands, and it turned out that they had only known each other for a few days. Theirs was a friendship of the beach and of bathing; such friendships are common at small seaside places.

"There is certainly something odd about the people here. I have never been to Llantrisant before, you know; indeed, this is the first time we've been in Wales for our holidays, and knowing nothing about the ways of the people and not being accustomed to hear Welsh spoken, I thought, perhaps, it must be my imagination. But you think there really is something a little queer?"

"I can tell you this: that I have been in two minds whether I should not write to my husband and ask him to take me and the children away. You know where I am at Mrs Morgan's, and the Morgans' sitting-room is just the other side of the passage, and sometimes they leave the door open, so that I can hear what they say quite plainly. And you see I understand the Welsh, though they don't know it. And I hear them saying the most alarming things!"

"What sort of things?"

"Well, indeed, it sounds like some kind of a religious service, but it's not Church of England, I know that. Old Morgan begins it, and the wife and children answer. Something like: 'Blessed be

God for the messengers of Paradise.' 'Blessed be His Name for Paradise in the meat and in the drink.' 'Thanksgiving for the old offering.' 'Thanksgiving for the appearance of the old altar.' 'Praise for the joy of the ancient garden.' 'Praise for the return of those that have been long absent.' And all that sort of thing. It is nothing but madness."

"Depend upon it," said the lady from the Midlands, "there's no real harm in it. They're Dissenters; some new sect, I dare say. You know some Dissenters are very queer in their ways."

"All that is like no Dissenters that I have ever known in all my life whatever," replied the Welsh lady somewhat vehemently, with a very distinct intonation of the land. "And have you heard them speak of the bright light that shone at midnight from the church?"

III A Secret in a Secret Place

Now here was I altogether at a loss and quite bewildered. The children broke into the conversation of the two ladies and cut it short, just as the midnight lights from the church came on the field, and when the little girls and boys went back again to the sands whooping, the tide of talk had turned, and Mrs Harland and Mrs Williams were quite safe and at home with Janey's measles, and a wonderful treatment for infantile earache, as exemplified in the case of Trevor. There was no more to be got out of them, evidently, so I left the beach, crossed the harbour causeway, and drank beer at the Fisherman's Rest till it was time to climb up two miles of deep lane and catch the train for Penvro, where I was staying. And I went up the lane, as I say, in a kind of amazement; and not so much, I think, because of evidences and hints of things strange to the senses, such as the savour of incense where no incense had smoked for three hundred and fifty years and more, or the story of bright light shining from the dark, closed church at dead of night, as because of that sentence of thanksgiving "for paradise in meat and in drink".

For the sun went down and the evening fell as I climbed the long hill through the deep woods and the high meadows, and the scent of all the green things rose from the earth and from the heart of the wood, and at a turn of the lane far below was the misty glimmer of the still sea, and from far below its deep murmur sounded as it washed on the little hidden, enclosed bay where Llantrisant stands. And I thought, if there be paradise in meat and in drink, so much the more is there paradise in the scent of the green leaves at evening and in the appearance of the sea and in the redness of the sky; and there came to me a certain vision of a real world about us all the while, of a language that was only secret because we would not take the trouble to listen to it and discern it.

It was almost dark when I got to the station, and here were the few feeble oil lamps lit, glimmering in that lonely land, where the way is long from farm to farm. The train came on its way, and I got into it; and just as we moved from the station I noticed a group under one of those dim lamps. A woman and her child had got out, and they were being welcomed by a man who had been waiting for them. I had not noticed his face as I stood on the platform, but now I saw it as he pointed down the hill towards Llantrisant, and I think I was almost frightened.

He was a young man, a farmer's son, I would say, dressed in rough brown clothes, and as different from old Mr Evans, the rector, as one man might be from another. But on his face, as I saw it in the lamp-light, there was the like brightening that I had seen on the face of the rector. It was an illuminated face, glowing with an ineffable joy, and I thought it rather gave light to the platform lamp than received light from it. The woman and her child, I inferred, were strangers to the place, and had come to pay a visit to the young man's family. They had looked about them in bewilderment, half alarmed, before they saw him; and then his face was radiant in their sight, and it was easy to see that all their troubles were ended and over. A wayside station and a darkening country; and it was as if they were welcomed by shining, immortal gladness – even into paradise.

But though there seemed in a sense light all about my ways, I was myself still quite bewildered. I could see, indeed, that something strange had happened or was happening in the little town hidden under the hill, but there was so far no clue to the mystery, or rather, the clue had been offered to me, and I had not taken it, I had not even known that it was there; since we do not so much as see what we have determined, without judging, to be incredible, even though it be held up before our eyes. The dialogue that the Welsh Mrs Williams had reported to her English friend might have set me on the right way; but the right way was outside all my limits of possibility, outside the circle of my thought. The palaeontologist might see monstrous, significant marks in the slime of a riverbank, but he would never draw the conclusions that his own peculiar science would seem to suggest to him; he would choose any explanation rather than the obvious, since the obvious would also be the outrageous – according to our established habit of thought, which we deem final.

The next day I took all these strange things with me for consideration to a certain place that I knew of not far from Penvro. I was now in the early stages of the jigsaw process, or rather I had only a few pieces before me, and – to continue the figure – my difficulty was this: that though the markings on each piece seemed to have design and significance, yet I could not make the wildest guess as to the nature of the whole picture, of which these were the parts. I had clearly seen that there was a great secret; I had seen that on the face of the young farmer on the platform of Llantrisant station; and in my mind there was all the while the picture of him going down the dark, steep, winding lane that led to the town and the sea, going down through the heart of the wood, with light about him.

But there was bewilderment in the thought of this, and in the endeavour to match it with the perfumed church and the scraps of talk that I had heard and the rumour of midnight brightness; and though Penvro is by no means populous, I thought I would go to a certain solitary place called the Old Camp Head, which looks towards Cornwall and to the great deeps that roll beyond Cornwall to the far ends of the world; a place where fragments of dreams – they seemed such then – might, perhaps, be gathered into the clearness of vision.

It was some years since I had been to the Head, and I had gone on that last time and on a former visit by the cliffs, a rough and difficult path. Now I chose a landward way, which the county map seemed to justify, though doubtfully, as regarded the last part of the journey. So, I went inland and climbed the hot summer by-roads, till I came at last to a lane which gradually turned turfy and grass-grown, and then on high ground, ceased to be. It left me at a gate in a hedge of old thorns; and across the field beyond there seemed to be some faint indications of a track. One would judge that sometimes men did pass by that way, but not often.

It was high ground but not within sight of the sea. But the breath of the sea blew about the hedge of thorns, and came with a keen savour to the nostrils. The ground sloped gently from the gate and then rose again to a ridge, where a white farmhouse stood all alone. I passed by this farmhouse, threading an uncertain way, followed a hedgerow doubtfully; and saw suddenly before me the Old Camp, and beyond it the sapphire plain of waters and the mist where sea and sky met. Steep from my feet the hill fell away, a land of gorse-blossom, red-gold and mellow, of glorious purple heather. It fell into a hollow that went down, shining with rich green bracken, to the glimmering sea; and before me and beyond the hollow rose a height of turf, bastioned at the summit with the awful, age-old walls of the Old Camp; green, rounded circumvallations, wall within wall, tremendous, with their myriad years upon them.

Within these smoothed, green mounds, looking across the shining and changing of the waters in the happy sunlight, I took out the bread and cheese and beer that I had carried in a bag, and ate and drank, and lit my pipe, and set myself to think over the enigmas of Llantrisant. And I had scarcely done so when, a good deal to my annoyance, a man came climbing up over the green ridges, and took up his stand close by, and stared out to sea. He nodded to me, and began with "Fine weather for the harvest" in the approved manner, and so sat down and engaged me in a net of talk. He was of Wales, it seemed, but from a different part of the country, and was staying for a few days with relations – at the white farmhouse which I had passed on my way. His tale of nothing flowed on to his pleasure and my pain, till he fell suddenly on Llantrisant and its doings. I listened then with wonder, and here is his tale condensed. Though it must be clearly understood that the man's evidence was only second-hand; he had heard it from his cousin, the farmer.

So, to be brief, it appeared that there had been a long feud at Llantrisant between a local solicitor, Lewis Prothero (we will say), and a farmer named James. There had been a quarrel about some trifle, which had grown more and more bitter as the two parties forgot the merits of the original dispute, and by some means or other, which I could not well understand, the lawyer had got the small freeholder "under his thumb". James, I think, had given a bill of sale in a bad season, and Prothero had bought it up; and the end was that the farmer was turned out of the old house, and was lodging in a cottage. People said he would have to take a place on his own farm as a labourer; he went about in dreadful misery, piteous to see. It was thought by some that he might very well murder the lawyer, if he met him.

They did meet, in the middle of the market-place at Llantrisant one Saturday in June. The farmer was a little black man, and he gave a shout of rage, and the people were rushing at him to keep him off Prothero.

"And then," said my informant, "I will tell you what happened. This lawyer, as they tell me, he is a great big brawny fellow, with a big jaw and a wide mouth, and a red face and red whiskers. And there he was in his black coat and his high hard hat, and all his money at his back, as you may say. And, indeed, he did fall down on his knees in the dust there in the street in front of Philip James, and every one could see that terror was upon him. And he did beg Philip James's pardon, and beg of him to have mercy, and he did implore him by God and man and the saints of paradise. And my cousin, John Jenkins, Penmawr, he do tell me that the tears were falling from Lewis Prothero's eyes like the rain. And he put his hand into his pocket and drew out the deed of Pantyreos, Philip James's old farm that was, and did give him the farm back and a hundred pounds for the stock that was on it, and two hundred pounds, all in notes of the bank, for amendment and consolation.

"And then, from what they do tell me, all the people did go mad, crying and weeping and calling out all manner of things at the top of their voices. And at last nothing would do but they must all go up to the churchyard, and there Philip James and Lewis Prothero they swear friendship to one another for a long age before the old cross, and everyone sings praises. And my cousin he do declare to me that there were men standing in that crowd that he did never see before in Llantrisant in all his life, and his heart was shaken within him as if it had been in a whirlwind."

I had listened to all this in silence. I said then:

"What does your cousin mean by that? Men that he had never seen in Llantrisant? What men?"

"The people," he said very slowly, "call them the Fishermen."

And suddenly there came into my mind the Rich Fisherman who in the old legend guards the holy mystery of the Graal.

IV The Ringing of the Bell

So far I have not told the story of the things of Llantrisant, but rather the story of how I stumbled upon them and among them, perplexed and wholly astray, seeking, but yet not knowing at all what I sought; bewildered now and again by circumstances which seemed to me wholly inexplicable; devoid, not so much of the key to the enigma, but of the key to the nature of the enigma. You cannot begin to solve a puzzle till you know what the puzzle is about. "Yards divided by minutes," said the mathematical master to me long ago, "will give neither pigs, sheep, nor oxen." He was right; though his manner on this and on all other occasions was highly offensive. This is enough of the personal process, as I may call it; and here follows the story of what happened at Llantrisant last summer, the story as I pieced it together at last.

It all began, it appears, on a hot day, early in last June; so far as I can make out, on the first Saturday in the month. There was a deaf old woman, a Mrs Parry, who lived by herself in a lonely cottage a mile or so from the town. She came into the marketplace early on the Saturday morning in a state of some excitement, and as soon as she had taken up her usual place on the pavement by the churchyard, with her ducks and eggs and a few very early potatoes, she began to tell her neighbours about her having heard the sound of a great bell. The good women on each side smiled at one another behind Mrs Parry's back, for one had to bawl into her ear before she could make out what one meant; and Mrs Williams, Penycoed, bent over and yelled: "What bell should that be, Mrs Parry? There's no church near you up at Penrhiw. Do you hear what nonsense she talks?" said Mrs Williams in a low voice to Mrs Morgan. "As if she could hear any bell, whatever."

"What makes you talk nonsense yourself?" said Mrs Parry, to the amazement of the two women. "I can hear a bell as well as you, Mrs Williams, and as well as your whispers either."

And there is the fact, which is not to be disputed; though the deductions from it may be open to endless disputations; this old woman who had been all but stone deaf for twenty years – the defect had always been in her family – could suddenly hear on this June morning as well as anybody else. And her two old friends stared at her, and it was some time before they had appeased her indignation, and induced her to talk about the bell.

It had happened in the early morning, which was very misty. She had been gathering sage in her garden, high on a round hill looking over the sea. And there came in her ears a sort of throbbing and singing and trembling, "as if there were music coming out of the earth", and then something seemed to break in her head, and all the birds began to sing and make melody together, and the leaves of the poplars round the garden fluttered in the breeze that rose from the sea, and the cock crowed far off at Twyn, and the dog barked down in Kemeys Valley. But above all these sounds, unheard for so many years, there thrilled the deep and chanting note of the bell, "like the bell and a man's voice singing at once".

They stared again at her and at one another. "Where did it sound from?" asked one. "It came sailing across the sea," answered Mrs Parry quite composedly, "and I did hear it coming nearer and nearer to the land."

"Well, indeed," said Mrs Morgan, "it was a ship's bell, then, though I can't make out why they would be ringing like that."

"It was not ringing on any ship, Mrs Morgan," said Mrs Parry.

"Then where do you think it was ringing?"

"*Ym mharadwys*," replied Mrs Parry. Now that means "in paradise", and the two others changed the conversation quickly. They thought that Mrs Parry had got back her hearing suddenly – such things did happen now and then – and that the shock had made her "a bit queer". And this explanation would no doubt have stood its ground, if it had not been for other experiences. Indeed, the local doctor (who had treated Mrs Parry for a dozen years, not for her deafness, which he took to be hopeless and beyond cure, but for a tiresome and recurrent winter cough), sent an account of the case to a colleague at Bristol, suppressing, naturally enough, the reference to paradise. The Bristol physician gave it as his opinion that the symptoms were absolutely what might have been expected. "You have here, in all probability," he wrote, "the sudden breaking down of an old obstruction in the aural passage, and I should quite expect this process to be accompanied by tinnitus of a pronounced and even violent character."

But for the other experiences? As the morning wore on and drew to noon, high market, and to the utmost brightness of that summer day, all the stalls and the streets were full of rumours and of awed faces. Now from one lonely farm, now from another, men and women came and told the story of how they had listened in the early morning with thrilling hearts to the thrilling music of a bell that was like no bell ever heard before. And it seemed that many people in the town had been roused, they knew not how, from sleep; waking up, as one of them said, as if bells were ringing and the organ playing, and a choir of sweet voices singing all together: "There were such melodies and songs that my heart was full of joy."

And a little past noon some fishermen who had been out all night returned, and brought a wonderful story into the town of what they had heard in the mist; and one of them said he had seen something go by at a little distance from his boat. "It was all golden and bright," he said, "and there was glory about it." Another fisherman declared: "There was a song upon the water that was like heaven."

And here I would say in parenthesis that on returning to town I sought out a very old friend of mine, a man who has devoted a lifetime to strange and esoteric studies. I thought that I had a tale that would interest him profoundly, but I found that he heard me with a good deal of indifference. And at this very point of the sailors' stories I remember saying. "Now what do you make of that? Don't you think it's extremely curious?" He replied: "I hardly think so. Possibly the sailors were lying; possibly it happened as they say. Well; that sort of thing has always been happening." I give my friend's opinion; I make no comment on it.

Let it be noted that there was something remarkable as to the manner in which the sound of the bell was heard – or supposed to be heard. There are, no doubt, mysteries in sounds as in all else; indeed, I am informed that during one of the horrible outrages that have been perpetrated on London during this autumn there was an instance of a great block of workmen's dwellings in which the only person who heard the crash of a particular bomb falling was an old deaf woman, who had been fast asleep till the moment of the explosion. This is strange enough of a sound that was entirely in the natural (and horrible) order; and so it was at Llantrisant, where the sound was either a collective auditory hallucination or a manifestation of what is conveniently, if inaccurately, called the supernatural order.

For the thrill of the bell did not reach to all ears – or hearts. Deaf Mrs Parry heard it in her lonely cottage garden, high above the misty sea; but then, in a farm on the other or western side of Llantrisant, a little child, scarcely three years old, was the only one out of a household of ten people who heard anything. He called out in stammering baby Welsh something that sounded like "*Clychau fawr, clychau fawr*" – the great bells, the great bells – and his mother wondered what he was talking about. Of the crews of half a dozen trawlers that were swinging from side to side in the mist, not more than four men had any tale to tell. And so it was that for an hour or two the men who had heard nothing suspected his neighbour, who had heard marvels, of lying; and it was some time before the mass of evidence coming from all manners of diverse and remote quarters convinced the people that there was a true story here. A might suspect B, his neighbour, of making up a tale; but when C, from some place on the hills five miles away, and D, the fisherman on the waters, each had a like report, then it was clear that something had happened.

And even then, as they told me, the signs to be seen upon the people were stranger than the tales told by them and among them. It has struck me that many people in reading some of the phrases that I have reported will dismiss them with laughter as very poor and fantastic inventions; fishermen, they will say, do not speak of "a song like heaven" or of "a glory about it". And I dare say this would be a just enough criticism if I were reporting English fishermen; but, odd though it may be, Wales has not yet lost the last shreds of the grand manner. And let it be remembered also that in most cases such phrases are translated from another language, that is, from the Welsh.

So, they come trailing, let us say, fragments of the cloud of glory in their common speech; and so, on this Saturday, they began to display, uneasily enough in many cases, their consciousness that the things that were reported were of their ancient right and former custom. The comparison is not quite fair; but conceive Hardy's old Durbeyfield suddenly waking from long slumber to find himself in a noble thirteenth-century hall, waited on by kneeling pages, smiled on by sweet ladies in silken cotehardies.

So by evening time there had come to the old people the recollection of stories that their fathers had told them as they sat round the hearth of winter nights, fifty, sixty, seventy years ago; stories of the wonderful bell of Teilo Sant, that had sailed across the glassy seas from Syon, that was called a portion of paradise, "and the sound of its ringing was like the perpetual choir of the angels".

Such things were remembered by the old and told to the young that evening, in the streets of the town and in the deep lanes that climbed far hills. The sun went down to the mountain red with fire like a burnt offering, the sky turned violet, the sea was purple, as one told another of the wonder that had returned to the land after long ages.

V The Rose of Fire

It was during the next nine days, counting from that Saturday early in June – the first Saturday in June, as I believe – that Llantrisant and all the regions about became possessed either by an extraordinary set of hallucinations or by a visitation of great marvels.

This is not the place to strike the balance between the two possibilities. The evidence is, no doubt, readily available; the matter is open to systematic investigation.

But this may be said: The ordinary man, in the ordinary passages of his life, accepts in the main the evidence of his senses, and is entirely right in doing so. He says that he sees a cow, that he sees a stone wall, and that the cow and the stone wall are "there". This is very well for all the practical purposes of life, but I believe that the metaphysicians are by no means so easily satisfied as to the reality of the stone wall and the cow. Perhaps they might allow that both objects are "there" in the sense that one's reflection is in a glass; there is an actuality, but is there a reality external to oneself? In any event, it is solidly agreed that, supposing a real existence, this much is certain – it is not in the least like our conception of it. The ant and the microscope will quickly convince us that we do not see things as they really are, even supposing that we see them at all. If we could "see" the real cow she would appear utterly incredible, as incredible as the things I am to relate.

Now, there is nothing that I know much more unconvincing than the stories of the red light on the sea. Several sailors, men on small coasting ships, who were working up or down the Channel on the Saturday night, spoke of "seeing" the red light, and it must be said that there is a very tolerable agreement in their tales. All make the time as between midnight of the Saturday and one o'clock on the Sunday morning. Two of those sailormen are precise as to the time of the apparition; they fix it by elaborate calculations of their own as occurring at 12.20 a.m. And the story?

A red light, a burning spark seen far away in the darkness, taken at the first moment of seeing for a signal, and probably an enemy signal. Then it approached at a tremendous speed, and one man said he took it be the port light of some new kind of navy motor boat which was developing a rate hitherto unheard of, a hundred or a hundred and fifty knots an hour. And then, in the third instant of the sight, it was clear that this was no earthly speed. At first a red spark in the farthest distance; then a rushing lamp; and then, as if in an incredible point of time, it swelled into a vast rose of fire that filled all the sea and all the sky and hid the stars and possessed the land. "I thought the end of the world had come," one of the sailors said.

And then, an instant more, and it was gone from them, and four of them say that there was a red spark on Chapel Head, where the old grey chapel of St Teilo stands, high above the water, in a cleft of the limestone rocks.

And thus the sailors; and thus their tales are incredible; but *they* are not incredible. I believe that men of the highest eminence in physical science have testified to the occurrence of phenomena every whit as marvellous, to things as absolutely opposed to all natural order, as we conceive it; and it may be said that nobody minds them. "That sort of thing has always been happening," as my friend remarked to me. But the men, whether or no the fire had ever been without them, there was no doubt that it was now within them, for it burned in their eyes. They were purged as if they had passed through the Furnace of the Sages governed with Wisdom that the alchemists know. They spoke without much difficulty of what they had seen, or had seemed to see, with their eyes, but hardly at all of what their hearts had known when for a moment the glory of the fiery rose had been about them.

For some weeks, afterwards, they were still, as it were, amazed; almost, I would say, incredulous. If there had been nothing more than the splendid and fiery appearance, showing and vanishing, I do believe that they themselves would have discredited their own senses and denied the truth of their own tales. And one does not dare to say whether they would not have been right. Men like Sir William Crookes and Sir Oliver Lodge are certainly to be heard with respect, and they bear witness to all manner of apparent eversions of laws which we, or most of us, consider far more deeply founded than the ancient hills. They may be justified; but in our hearts we doubt. We cannot wholly believe in inner sincerity that the solid table did rise, without mechanical reason or cause, into the air, and so defy that which we name the "law of gravitation". I know what may be said on the other side, I know that there is not true question of "law" in the case; that the law of gravitation really means just this: that I have never seen a table rising without mechanical aid, or an apple, detached from the bough, soaring to the skies instead of falling to the ground. The so-called law is just the sum of common observation and nothing more; yet I say, in our hearts we do not believe that the tables rise; much less do we believe in the rose of fire that for a moment swallowed up the skies and seas and shores of the Welsh coast last June.

And the men who saw it would have invented fairy tales to account for it, I say again, if it had not been for that which was within them.

They said, all of them and it was certain now that they spoke the truth, that in the moment of the vision, every pain and ache and malady in their bodies had passed away. One man had been vilely drunk on venomous spirit, procured at Jobson's Hole down by the Cardiff Docks. He was horribly ill; he had crawled up from his bunk for a little fresh air; and in an instant his horrors and his deadly nausea had left him. Another man was almost desperate with the raging hammering pain of an abscess on a tooth; he says that when the red flame came near he felt as if a dull, heavy blow had fallen on his jaw, and then the pain was quite gone; he could scarcely believe that there had been any pain there.

And they all bear witness to an extraordinary exaltation of the senses. It is indescribable, this; for they cannot describe it. They are amazed, again; they do not in the least profess to know what happened; but there is no more possibility of shaking their evidence than there is a possibility of shaking the evidence of a man who says that water is wet and fire hot.

"I felt a bit queer afterwards," said one of them, "and I steadied myself by the mast, and I can't tell how I felt as I touched it. I didn't know that touching a thing like a mast could be better than a big drink when you're thirsty, or a soft pillow when you're sleepy."

I heard other instances of this state of things, as I must vaguely call it, since I do not know what else to call it. But I suppose we can all agree that to the man in average health, the average impact of the external world on his senses is a matter of indifference. The average impact; a harsh scream, the bursting of a motor tyre, any violent assault on the aural nerves will annoy him, and he may say "damn". Then, on the other hand, the man who is not "fit" will easily be annoyed and irritated by someone pushing past him in a crowd, by the ringing of a bell, by the sharp closing of a book.

But so far as I could judge from the talk of these sailors, the average impact of the external world had become to them a fountain of pleasure. Their nerves were on edge, but an edge to receive exquisite sensuous impressions. The touch of the rough mast, for example; that was a joy far greater than is the joy of fine silk to some luxurious skins; they drank water and stared as if they had been *fins gourmets* tasting an amazing wine; the creak and whine of their ship on its slow way were as exquisite as the rhythm and song of a Bach fugue to an amateur of music.

And then, within; these rough fellows have their quarrels and strifes and variances and envyings like the rest of us; but that was all over between them that had seen the rosy light; old enemies shook hands heartily, and roared with laughter as they confessed one to another what fools they had been.

"I can't say how it has happened or what has happened at all," said one, "but if you have all the world and the glory of it, how can you fight for fivepence?"

The church of Llantrisant is a typical example of a Welsh parish church, before the evil and horrible period of "restoration".

This lower world is a palace of lies, and of all foolish lies there is none more insane than a certain vague fable about the mediaeval freemasons, a fable which somehow imposed itself upon the cold intellect of Hallam the historian. The story is, in brief, that throughout the Gothic period, at any rate, the art and craft of church building were executed by wandering guilds of "freemasons", possessed of various secrets of building and adornment, which they employed wherever they went. If this nonsense were true, the Gothic of Cologne would be as the Gothic of Colne, and the Gothic of Arles like to the Gothic of Abingdon. It is so grotesquely untrue that almost every county, let alone every country, has its distinctive style in Gothic architecture. Arfon is in the west of Wales; its churches have marks and features which distinguish them from the churches in the east of Wales.

The Llantrisant church has that primitive division between nave and chancel which only very foolish people decline to recognize as equivalent to the Oriental iconostasis and as the origin of the Western rood-screen. A solid wall divided the church into two portions; in the centre was a narrow opening with a rounded arch, through which those who sat towards the middle of the church could see the small, red-carpeted altar and the three roughly shaped lancet windows above it.

The "reading pew" was on the outer side of this wall of partition, and here the rector did his service, the choir being grouped in seats about him. On the inner side were the pews of certain privileged houses of the town and district.

On the Sunday morning the people were all in their accustomed places, not without a certain exultation in their eyes, not without a certain expectation of they knew not what. The bells stopped ringing, the rector, in his old-fashioned, ample surplice, entered the reading-desk, and gave out the hymn: "My God, and is Thy table spread."

And, as the singing began, all the people who were in the pews within the wall came out of them and streamed through the archway into the nave. They took what places they could find up and down the church, and the rest of the congregation looked at them in amazement.

Nobody knew what had happened. Those whose seats were next to the aisle tried to peer into the chancel, to see what had happened or what was going on there. But somehow the light flamed so brightly from the windows above the altar, those being the only windows in the chancel, one small lancet in the south wall excepted, that no one could see anything at all.

"It was as if a veil of gold adorned with jewels was hanging there," one man said; and indeed there are a few odds and scraps of old painted glass left in the eastern lancets.

But there were few in the church who did not hear now and again voices speaking beyond the veil.

VI Olwen's Dream

The well-to-do and dignifed personages who left their pews in the chancel of Llantrisant church and came hurrying into the nave could give no explanation of what they had done. They felt, they said, that they "had to go", and to go quickly; they were driven out, as it were, by a secret, irresistible command. But all who were present in the church that morning were amazed, though all exulted in their hearts; for they, like the sailors who saw the rose of fire on the waters, were filled with a joy that was literally ineffable, since they could not utter it or interpret it to themselves.

And they too, like the sailors, were transmuted, or the world was transmuted for them. They experienced what the doctors call à sense of *bien être*, but a *bien être* raised to the highest power. Old men felt young again, eyes that had been growing dim now saw clearly, and saw a world that was like paradise, the same world, it is true, but a world rectified and glowing, as if an inner flame shone in all things, and behind all things.

And the difficulty in recording this state is this, that it is so rare an experience that no set language to express it is in existence. A shadow of its raptures and ecstasies is found in the highest poetry; there are phrases in ancient books telling of the Celtic saints that dimly hint at it; some of the old Italian masters of painting had known it, for the light of it shines in their skies and about the battlements of their cities that are founded on magic hills. But these are but broken hints.

It is not poetic to go to Apothcaries' Hall for similes. But for many years I kept by me an article from the *Lancet* or the *British Medical Journal* – I forget which – in which a doctor gave an account of certain experiments he had conducted with a drug called the Mescal Button, or Anhelonium Lewinii. He said that while under the influence of the drug he had but to shut his eyes, and immediately before him there would rise incredible Gothic cathedrals, of such majesty and splendour and glory that no heart had ever conceived. They seemed to surge from the depths to the very heights of heaven, their spires swayed amongst the clouds and the stars, they were fretted with admirable imagery. And as he gazed, he would presently become aware that all the stones were living stones, that they were quickening and palpitating, and then that they were glowing jewels, say, emeralds, sapphires, rubies, opals, but of hues that the mortal eye had never seen.

That description gives, I think, some faint notion of the nature of the transmuted world into which these people by the sea had entered, a world quickened and glorified and full of pleasures. Joy and wonder were on all faces; but the deepest joy and the greatest wonder were on the face of the rector. For he had heard through the veil the Greek word for "holy", three times repeated. And he, who had once been a horrified assistant at High Mass in a foreign church, recognized the perfume of incense that filled the place from end to end.

It was on that Sunday night that Olwen Phillips of Croeswen dreamed her wonderful dream. She was a girl of sixteen, the daughter of small farming people, and for many months she had been doomed to certain death. Consumption, which flourishes in that damp, warm climate, had laid hold of her; not only her lungs but her whole system was a mass of tuberculosis. As is common enough, she had enjoyed many fallacious brief recoveries in the early stages of the disease, but all hope had long been over, and now for the last few weeks she had seemed to rush vehemently to death. The doctor had come on the Saturday morning, bringing with him a colleague. They had both agreed that the girl's case was in its last stages. "She cannot possibly last more than a day or two," said the local doctor to her mother. He came again on the Sunday morning and found his patient perceptibly worse, and soon afterwards she sank into a heavy sleep, and her mother thought that she would never wake from it.

The girl slept in an inner room communicating with the room

occupied by her father and mother. The door between was kept open, so that Mrs Phillips could hear her daughter if she called to her in the night. And Olwen called to her mother that night, just as the dawn was breaking. It was no faint summons from a dying bed that came to the mother's ears, but a loud cry that rang through the house, a cry of great gladness. Mrs Phillips started up from sleep in wild amazement, wondering what could have happened. And then she saw Olwen, who had not been able to rise from her bed for many weeks past, standing in the doorway in the faint light of the growing day. The girl called to her mother: "Mam! Mam! It is all over. I am quite well again."

Mrs Phillips roused her husband, and they sat up in bed staring, not knowing on earth, as they said afterwards, what had been done with the world. Here was their poor girl wasted to a shadow, lying on her death-bed, and the life sighing from her with every breath, and her voice, when she last uttered it, so weak that one had to put one's ear to her mouth. And here in a few hours she stood up before them; and even in that faint light they could see that she was changed almost beyond knowing. And, indeed, Mrs Phillips said that for a moment or two she fancied that the Germans must have come and killed them in their sleep, and so they were all dead together. But Olwen called out again, so the mother lit a candle and got up and went tottering across the room, and there was Olwen all gay and plump again, smiling with shining eyes. Her mother led her into her own room, and set down the candle there, and felt her daughter's flesh, and burst into prayers, and tears of wonder and delight, and thanksgivings, and held the girl again to be sure that she was not deceived. And then Olwen told her dream, though she thought it was not a dream.

She said she woke up in the deep darkness, and she knew the life was fast going from her. She could not move so much as a finger, she tried to cry out, but no sound came from her lips. She felt that in another instant the whole world would fall from her – her heart was full of agony. And as the last breath was passing her lips, she heard a very faint, sweet sound, like the tinkling of a silver bell. It came from far away, from over by Ty-newydd. She forgot her agony and listened, and even then, she says, she felt the swirl of the world as it came back to her. And the sound of the bell swelled and grew louder, and it thrilled all through her body, and the life was in it. And as the bell rang and trembled in her ears, a faint light touched the wall of her room and reddened, till the whole room was full of rosy fire. And then she saw standing before her bed three men in blood-coloured robes with shining faces. And one man held a golden bell in his hand. And the second man held up something shaped like the top of a table. It was like a great jewel, and it was of a blue colour, and there were rivers of silver and of gold running through it and flowing as quick streams flow, and there were pools in it as if violets had been poured out into water, and then it was green as the sea near the shore, and then it was the sky at night with all the stars shining, and then the sun and the moon came down and washed in it. And the third man held up high above this a cup that was like a rose on fire; "There was a great burning in it, and a dropping of blood in it, and a red cloud above it, and I saw a great secret. And I heard a voice that sang nine times: 'Glory and praise to the Conqueror of Death, to the Fountain of Life immortal.' Then the red light went from the wall, and it was all darkness, and the bell rang faint again by Capel Teilo, and then I got up and called to you."

The doctor came on the Monday morning with the death certificate in his pocket-book, and Olwen ran out to meet him. I have quoted his phrase in the first chapter of this record: "A kind of resurrection of the body." He made a most careful examination of the girl; he has stated that he found that every trace of disease had disappeared. He left on the Sunday morning a patient entering into the coma that precedes death, a body condemned utterly and ready for the grave. He met at the garden gate on the Monday morning a young woman in whom life sprang up like a fountain, in whose body life laughed and rejoiced as if it had been a river flowing from an unending well.

Now this is the place to ask one of those questions – there are many such – which cannot be answered. The question is as to the continuance of tradition; more especially as to the continuance of tradition among the Welsh Celts of today. On the one hand, such waves and storms have gone over them. The wave of the heathen Saxons went over them, then the wave of Latin mediaevalism, then the waters of Anglicanism; last of all the flood of their queer Calvinistic Methodism, half-Puritan, half-pagan. It may well be asked whether any memory can possibly have survived such a series of deluges. I have said that the old people of Llantrisant had their tales of the bell of Teilo Sant; but these were but vague and broken recollections. And then there is the name by which the "strangers" who were seen in the marketplace were known; that is more precise. Students of the Graal legend know that the keeper of the Graal in the romances is the King Fisherman, or the Rich Fisherman; students of Celtic hagiology know that it was prophesied before the birth of Dewi (or David) that he should be "a man of acquatic life", that another legend tells how a little child, destined to be a saint, was discovered on a stone in the river, how through his childhood a fish for his nourishment was found on that stone every day, while another saint, Ilar, if I remember, was expressly known as the Fisherman. But has the memory of all this persisted in the church-going and chapel-going people of Wales at the present day? It is difficult to say. There is the affair of the Healing Cup of Nant Eos, or Tregaron Healing Cup, as it is also called. It is only a few years ago since it was shown to a wandering harper, who treated it lightly, and then spent a wretched night, as he said, and came back penitently and was left alone with the sacred vessel to pray over it, till "his mind was at rest". That was in 1887.

Then for my part – I only know modern Wales on the surface, I am sorry to say – I remember three or four years ago speaking to my temporary landlord of certain relics of Saint Teilo, which are supposed to be in the keeping of a particular family in that country. The landlord is a very jovial merry fellow, and I observed with some astonishment that his ordinary, easy manner was completely altered as he said, gravely, "That will be over there, up by the mountain," pointing vaguely to the north. And he changed the subject, as a freemason changes the subject.

There the matter lies, and its appositeness to the story of Llantrisant is this: that the dream of Olwen Phillips was, in fact, the vision of the Holy Graal.

VII The Mass of the Sangraal

"*Ffeiriadwyr Melcisidec! Ffeiriadwyr Melcisidec!*" shouted the old Calvinistic Methodist deacon with the grey beard, "Priesthood of Melchizedek! Priesthood of Melchizedek!"

And he went on:

"The Bell that is like *y glwys yr angel ym mharadwys* – the joy of the angels in paradise – is returned; the Altar that is of a colour that no men can discern is returned, the Cup that came from Syon is returned, the ancient Offering is restored, the Three Saints have come back to the church of the *tri sant*, the Three Holy Fishermen are amongst us, and their net is full. *Gogoniant, gogoniant* – glory, glory!"

Then another Methodist began to recite in Welsh a verse from Wesley's hymn.

> God still respects Thy sacrifice,
> Its savour sweet doth always please;
> The Offering smokes through earth and skies,
> Diffusing life and joy and peace;
> To these Thy lower courts it comes
> And fills them with Divine perfumes.

The whole church was full, as the old books tell, of the odour of the rarest spiceries. There were lights shining within the sanctuary, through the narrow archway.

This was the beginning of the end of what befell at Llantrisant. For it was the Sunday after that night on which Olwen Phillips had been restored from death to life. There was not a single chapel of the Dissenters open in the town that day. The Methodists with their minister and their deacons and all the Nonconformists had returned on this Sunday morning to "the old hive". One would have said, a church of the Middle Ages, a church in Ireland today. Every seat – save those in the chancel – was full, all the aisles were full, the churchyard was full; everyone on his knees, and the old rector kneeling before the door into the holy place.

Yet they can say but very little of what was done beyond the veil. There was no attempt to perform the usual service; when the bells had stopped the old deacon raised his cry, and priest and people fell down on their knees as they thought they heard a choir within singing "Alleluya, alleluya, alleluya." And as the bells in the tower ceased ringing, there sounded the thrill of the bell from Syon, and the golden veil of sunlight fell across the door into the altar, and the heavenly voices began their melodies.

A voice like a trumpet cried from within the brightness:

Agyos, Agyos, Agyos

And the people, as if an age-old memory stirred in them, replied:

Agyos yr Tâd, agyos yr Mab, agyos yr Yspryd Glan. Sant, sant, sant, Drindod sant vendigeid. Sanctus Arglwydd Dduw Sabaoth, Dominus Deus.

There was a voice that cried and sang from within the altar; most of the people had heard some faint echo of it in the chapels; a voice rising and falling and soaring in awful modulations that rang like the trumpet of the Last Angel. The people beat upon their breasts, the tears were like rain of the mountains on their cheeks; those that were able fell down on their faces before the glory of the veil. They said afterwards that men of the hills, twenty miles away, heard that cry and that singing, rushing upon them on the wind, and they fell down on their faces, and cried: "The offering is accomplished," knowing nothing of what they said.

There were a few who saw three come out of the door of the sanctuary, and stand for a moment on the pace before the door. These three were in dyed vesture, red as blood. One stood before two, looking to the west, and he rang the bell. And they say that all the birds of the wood, and all the waters of the sea, and all the leaves of the trees, and all the winds of the high rocks uttered their voices with the ringing of the bell. And the second and the third; they turned their faces one to another. The second held up the lost altar that they once called "Sapphirus", which was like the changing of the sea and of the sky, and like the immixture of gold and silver. And the third heaved up high over the altar a cup that was red with burning and the blood of the offering.

And the old rector cried aloud then before the entrance:

Bendigeid yr Offeren yn oes oesoedd – blessed be the Offering unto the ages of ages.

And then the Mass of the Sangraal was ended, and then began the passing out of that land of the holy persons and holy things that had returned to it after the long years. It seemed, indeed, to many that the thrilling sound of the bell was in their ears for days, even for weeks after that Sunday morning. But thenceforth neither bell nor altar nor cup was seen by anyone; not openly, that is, but only in dreams by day and by night. Nor did the people see strangers again in the market of Llantrisant, nor in the lonely places where certain persons oppressed by great affliction and sorrow had once or twice encountered them.

But that time of visitation will never be forgotten by the people. Many things happened in the nine days that have not been set down in this record – or legend. Some of them were trifling matters, though strange enough in other times. Thus a man in the town who had a fierce dog that was always kept chained up found one day that the beast had become mild and gentle.

And this is stranger: Edward Davies, of Lanofon, a farmer, was roused from sleep one night by a queer yelping and barking in his yard. He looked out of the window and saw his sheep-dog playing with a big fox: they were chasing each other by turns, rolling over and over one another, "Cutting such capers as I did never see the like," as the astonished farmer put it. And some of the people said that during this season of wonder the corn shot up, and the grass thickened, and the fruit was multiplied on the trees in a very marvellous manner.

More important, it seemed, was the case of Williams, the grocer; though this may have been a purely natural deliverance. Mr Williams was to marry his daughter Mary to a smart young fellow from Carmarthen, and he was in great distress over it. Not over the marriage itself, but because things had been going very badly with him for some time, and he could not see his way to giving anything like the wedding entertainment that would be expected of him. The wedding was to be on the Saturday – that was the day on which the lawyer, Lewis Prothero, and the farmer, Philip James, were reconciled – and this John Williams, without money or credit, could not think how shame would not be on him for the meagreness and poverty of the wedding feast. And then on the Tuesday came a letter from his brother, David Williams, Australia, from whom he had not heard for fifteen years. And David it seemed, had been making a great deal of money, and was a bachelor, and here was with his letter a paper good for a thousand pounds: "You may as well enjoy it now as wait till I am dead." This was enough, indeed, one might say; but hardly an hour after the letter had come the lady from the big house (Plas Mawr) drove up in all her grandeur, and went into the shop and said: "Mr Williams, your daughter Mary has always been a very good girl, and my husband and I feel that we must give her some little thing on her wedding, and we hope she'll be very happy." It was a gold watch worth fifteen pounds. And after Lady Watcyn, advances the old doctor with a dozen of port, forty years upon it, and a long sermon on how to decant it. And the old rector's old wife brings to the beautiful dark girl two yards of creamy lace, like an enchantment, for her wedding veil, and tells Mary how she wore it for her own wedding fifty years ago; and the squire, Sir Watcyn, as if his wife had not been already with a fine gift, calls from his horse, and brings out Williams and barks like a dog at him: "Goin' to have a weddin', eh, Williams? Can't have a weddin' without champagne, y' know; wouldn't be legal, don't y' know. So look out for a couple of cases." So Williams tells the story of the gifts; and certainly there was never so famous a wedding in Llantrisant before.

All this, of course, may have been altogether in the natural order; the "glow", as they call it, seems more difficult to explain. For they say that all through the nine days, and indeed after the time had ended, there never was a man weary or sick at heart in Llantrisant, or in the country round it. For a man felt that his work of the body or the mind was going to be too much for his strength, then there would come to him of a sudden a warm glow and a thrilling all over him, and he felt as strong as a giant, and happier than he had ever been in his life before, so that lawyer and hedger each rejoiced in the task that was before him, as if it were sport and play.

And much more wonderful than this or any other wonders was forgiveness, with love to follow it. There were meetings of old enemies in the marketplace and in the street that made the people lift up their hands and declare that it was as if one walked the miraculous streets of Syon.

But as to the "phenomena", the occurrences for which, in ordinary talk, we should reserve the word "miraculous"? Well, what do we know? The question that I have already stated comes up again, as to the possible survival of old tradition in a kind of dormant, or torpid, semi-conscious state. In other words, did the people "see" and "hear" what they expected to see and hear? This point, or one similar to it, occurred in a debate between Andrew Lang and Anatole France as to the visions of Joan of Arc. M. France stated that when Joan saw St Michael, she saw the traditional archangel of the religious art of her day, but to the best of my belief Andrew Lang proved that the visionary figure Joan described was not in the least like the fifteenth-century conception of St Michael. So, in the case of Llantrisant, I have stated that there was a sort of tradition about the holy bell of Teilo Sant; and it is, of course, barely possible that some vague notion of the Graal cup may have reached even Welsh country folks through Tennyson's *Idylls*. But so far I see no reason to suppose that these people had ever heard of the portable altar (called "Sapphirus" in William of Malmesbury) or of its changing colours "that no man could discern".

And then there are the other questions of the distinction between hallucination and the vision, of the average duration of one and the other, and of the possibility of collective hallucination. If a number of people all see (or think they see) the same appearances, can this be merely hallucination? I believe there is a leading case on the matter, which concerns a number of people seeing the same appearance on a church wall in

Ireland; but there is, of course, this difficulty, that one may be hallucinated and communicate his impression to the others, telepathically.

But, at the last, what do we know?

BIBLIOGRAPHY

If you want to know more about the Holy Grail there is a vast wealth of literature. The following lists some of the books which you will find of interest, most of which were consulted in the preparation of this anthology.

Bogdanow, Fanni, *The Romance of the Grail*, Manchester University Press, 1966.

Briggs, Katharine, *A Dictionary of Fairies*, Allen Lane, 1976.

Cavendish, Richard, *King Arthur & the Grail*, Weidenfeld & Nicolson, 1978.

Coghlan, Ronan, *The Encyclopedia of Arthurian Legends*, Element Books, 1991.

Dixon-Kennedy, Mike, *Arthurian Myth & Legend: An A–Z of People and Places*, Blandford, 1995.

Goodrich, Norma Lorre, *King Arthur*, Franklin Watts, 1986.

Guest, Lady Charlotte, *The Mabinogion*, in the Everyman's Library edition, J.M. Dent, 1906.

Jung, E. and von Franz, M.L., *The Grail Legend*, trans. A. Dykes, Hodder & Stoughton, 1971.

Lacy, Norris J. (editor), *The Arthurian Encyclopedia*, Boydell Press, 1986.

Loomis, Roger Sherman, *The Grail: From Celtic Myth to Christian Symbol*, Columbia University Press, 1963; reissued by Constable & Co., London, 1963.

Matthews, John, *The Elements of the Grail Tradition*, Element Books, 1989.

Matthews, John, *The Grail*, Thames & Hudson, 1981.

Matthews, John and Green, Michael, *The Grail Seeker's Companion*, Aquarian Press, 1986.

Owen, D.D.R., *The Evolution of the Grail Legend*, Oliver & Boyd, 1968.

Owen, D.D.R. (editor), Chrétien de Troyes, *Arthurian Romances*, Everyman's Library, J.M. Dent, 1987.

Phillips, Graham, *The Search for the Grail*, Random House, 1995.

Sinclair, Andrew, *The Sword and the Grail*, Century, 1993.

Waite, A.E., *The Holy Grail: Its Legends and Symbolism*, Rider & Co., 1933.

Robinson Publishing, PO Box 11, Falmouth,
Cornwall TR10 9EN
Tel: +44(0) 1326 317200 Fax: +44(0) 1326 317444
Email: books@Barni.avel.co.uk

UK/B.F.P.O customers please allow £1.00 for p&p for the first book, plus 50p for the second, plus 30p for each additional book up to a maximum charge of £3.

Overseas customers (inc Ireland), please allow £2.00 for the first book plus £1.00 for the second, plus 50p for each additional book.

Please send me:

_____ The Camelot Chronicles £7.99

_____ The Merlin Chronicles £5.99

_____ The Mammoth Book of Historical Detectives £5.99

_____ The Mammoth Book of Historical Whodunnits £5.99

NAME (Block Letters) ....

ADDRESS ....

....POSTCODE ....

I enclose a cheque/PO (payable to Robinson Publishing Ltd) for _____

I wish to pay by Switch / Credit card

Number _____Card Expiry Date_____